BROWNSTEIN

D0860999

PLAYS AND PLAYWRIGHTS

2003

edited and with an introduction by

Martin Denton

This collection copyright © 2003 by The New York Theatre Experience, Inc.

Introduction and Editor's Notes copyright © 2003 by Martin Denton

All rights reserved. Except for brief passages quoted in newspaper, magazine, radio or television reviews, no part of this book may be reproduced in any form or by any means, electronic or mechanical, including photocopying or recording, or by an information storage and retrieval system, without permission in writing from the publisher.

CAUTION: These plays are fully protected, in whole, in part, or in any form, under the copyright laws of the United States of America and of all countries covered by the International Copyright Union (including the Dominion of Canada and the rest of the British Commonwealth), and of all countries covered by the Pan-American Copyright Convention and the Universal Copyright Convention, and of all countries with which the United States has reciprocal copyright relations, and are subject to royalty. All performance rights, including professional, amateur, stock, motion picture, radio, television, recitation, and public reading are strictly reserved. Please refer to Permissions, beginning on page iii, for information concerning such inquiries.

Published by The New York Theatre Experience, Inc.
P.O. Box 744
Bowling Green Station
New York, NY 10274-0744

Visit The New York Theatre Experience on the World Wide Web at:
http://www.nytheatre.com
email: info@botz.com

ISBN 0-9670234-4-0
Library of Congress Card Number: 2002117662

Plays and Playwrights 2003 is made possible in part with public funds from the New York State Council on the Arts, a state agency.

Plays and Playwrights 2003 is also made possible in part with funds from the Peg Santvoord Foundation.

Book designed by Nita Congress
Cover designed by Steven Waxman

PERMISSIONS

A Queer Carol copyright © 1999 by Joe Godfrey. All rights reserved. All inquiries regarding rights to perform this play or the use of this script should be directed to the author at 127 Cross Brook Road, Woodbury, CT 06798; 203-263-0949 (voice); 203-263-6231 (fax); josephfgodfrey@aol.com (email).

Pumpkins for Smallpox copyright © 2002 by Catherine Gillet. All rights reserved. For all inquiries regarding rights and permissions for the use of this script, please email CGLCSW@aol.com.

Looking for the Pony copyright © 2002 by Andrea Lepcio. All rights reserved. For all inquiries regarding rights and permissions for the use of this script, please contact the author in care of The New York Theatre Experience, Inc., P.O. Box 744, Bowling Green Station, New York, NY 10274-0744.

Black Thang copyright © 2002 by Ato Essandoh.

CAUTION: Amateurs and professionals are hereby warned that *Black Thang* is fully protected by the laws of copyright and is subject to royalty. All rights in all media are strictly reserved. No part of this work may be used for any purpose without the written consent of the copyright holder. All inquiries concerning production or publication rights or requests to reprint any portion of the work should be directed to the author in care of The New York Theatre Experience, Inc., P.O. Box 744, Bowling Green Station, New York, NY 10274-0744; 212-375-9991 (voice).

The Ninth Circle copyright © 2001 by Edward Musto. All rights reserved. For all inquiries regarding rights and permissions for the use of this script, please contact the author through the Dramatists Guild of America, 1501 Broadway, Suite 701, New York, NY 10036; 212- 398-9366.

The Doctor of Rome copyright © 2002 by Nat Colley.

CAUTION: Amateurs and professionals are hereby warned that *The Doctor of Rome* is fully protected by the laws of copyright and is subject to royalty. All rights in all media are strictly reserved. No part of this work may be used for any purpose without the written consent of the copyright holder. For all inquiries regarding rights and permissions for the use of this script, please contact the author at P.O. Box 741825, Los Angeles, CA 90004; 323-769-5753 (voice); 323-417-4776 (fax); natcolley@earthlink.net (email).

Galaxy Video copyright © 2002 by Marc Morales. All rights reserved. For all inquiries regarding rights and permissions for the use of this script, please contact the author via email at Alphaville2@hotmail.com.

The Last Carburetor copyright © 2002 by Leon Chase. All rights reserved. All inquiries regarding rights and permissions for the use of this script should be directed to the author in care of The New York Theatre Experience, Inc., P.O. Box 744, Bowling Green Station, New York, NY 10274-0744; or via email at leonchase@yahoo.com.

Out to Lunch copyright © 2002 by Joseph Langham. All rights reserved. For all inquiries regarding rights and permissions for the use of this script, please contact the author in care of The New York Theatre Experience, Inc., P.O. Box 744, Bowling Green Station, New York, NY 10274-0744; or via email at brokearm@earthlink.net; http://home.earthlink.net/~brokearm (Web).

Ascending Bodily copyright © 2002 by Maggie Cino. All rights reserved. For inquiries regarding rights and permissions for the use of this script, please contact the author in care of The New York Theatre Experience, Inc., P.O. Box 744, Bowling Green Station, New York, NY 10274-0744.

Last Call copyright © 2002 by Kelly McAllister. All rights reserved. For all inquiries regarding production and/or publication, contact the author at 533 Metropolitan Avenue, 2nd Floor, Brooklyn, NY 11211; 212-388-7124 (voice); kelberto@hotmail.com (email).

TABLE OF CONTENTS

ACKNOWLEDGMENTS

Plays and Playwrights 2003 is in your hands only because many, many people have given selflessly of their time to put it there. First and foremost, I thank the eleven playwrights who have entrusted their plays to me: Leon Chase, Maggie Cino, Nat Colley, Ato Essandoh, Catherine Gillet, Joe Godfrey, Joseph Langham, Andrea Lepcio, Kelly McAllister, Marc Morales, and Edward Musto. Without them, obviously, there would be no book at all.

Second, I need to mention the people who helped me find these terrific plays. They are: Mark Cannistraro, artistic director of SourceWorks Theatre Company and director of *A Queer Carol*; Stephen Sunderlin, artistic director of Vital Theatre Company, where both *Pumpkins for Smallpox* and *Looking for the Pony* premiered in the Vital Signs festival; Carrie Keranen and Karina Miller, each of whom urged me to see their work in *Black Thang* at Manhattan Theatre Source; Tim Haskell of Publicity Outfitters, who got me into *The Ninth Circle*; Ralph Carhart, artistic director of Revolving Shakespeare Company, which produced *The Doctor of Rome*; Scott Stiffler, the publicist who introduced me to Edge of Insanity and *Galaxy Video*; Susan O'Connor, Paul Witte, Tania Kirkman, and Susanna Harris, each of whom made me want to see *The Last Carburetor*; and Monica Sirignano, whose company Screaming Venus sponsors the annual festival of new one-woman shows called "Eve's Apple" where *Ascending Bodily* debuted. *Out to Lunch* and *Last Call* were both part of the 2002 New York International Fringe Festival, whose producing artistic director Elena K. Holy needs to be acknowledged here as well. I also thank publicists Brett Singer and Ron Lasko for their help in getting me in touch with some of the authors.

Third, I am immensely grateful to the people who helped make *Plays and Playwrights 2002*, the predecessor to this volume, into a successful endeavor: Nicoye Banks, Ebbe Bassey, Andy Breving, Tezra Bryant, Steve Caporaletti, Joel Carino, Lu Chekowsky, Kate Chell, Marc Chun, Ronald Cohen, Julie Congress, Sarah Congress,

Curtiss I'Cook, Sarah Dandridge, Gerry Downey, Zeke Farrow, Susan Ferrara, Matt Freeman, Anderson Gabrych, Tara Gibson, Steven Gridley, Capathia Jenkins, Portia Johnson, Michael Colby Jones, Jaymes Jorsling, Sonoko Kawahara, Carrie Keranen, Jennifer Larkin, Stacy Leigh, D.L. Lepidus, Jonathan Lisecki, Laura Marks, Kristin Marting, Erin McGuire, James Mack, Chiori Miyagawi, Andres Munar, Jeannine Myers, Jayne Napier, Brian Nishii, Sandra Nordgren, Barrett Ogden, Edith O'Hara, Adenrele Ojo, Jeff Pagliano, Peter S. Petralia, Thomas Pilutik, Shawn Randall, Robin Reed, J. Scott Reynolds, Stephanie Sanditz, Camille Shandor, Ellen Shanman, Maggie Sharp, Sophia Skiles, David Sochet, Marc Spitz, Brian Thorstenson, Keith Tisdale, Erin Treadway, Ken Urban, Edward Washington, Ben Wilson, Paul Witte, Steve Wood, and Jason Zinoman. Also, Rozanne Seelen, Sasha Domnitz, Allen Hubby, and everyone at Drama Book Shop; and Danielle Bobker and Carrie Preston of the English Department at Rutgers University.

Fourth, gigantic thank yous to the people behind the scenes who make the *Plays and Playwrights* books happen: Nita Congress, editor/book designer/advisor, who makes the plays look terrific; Steven Waxman, who designs our covers with unerring instinct and good taste; and Rochelle Denton, who does everything else.

Fifth, my appreciation to Mario Fratti, the playwright and theatre critic, who has become a great friend to *Plays and Playwrights* and contributed the lovely foreword to this volume.

Sixth, all of us at The New York Theatre Experience, Inc., are indebted to the organizations whose funding, in part, makes this book possible: The Peg Santvoord Foundation and the New York State Council on the Arts.

Finally, I am deeply grateful to John Clancy, who as director, producer, Advisory Council Member, colleague, and friend has been instrumental in helping us get the *Plays and Playwrights* books off the ground. From the launch of our first volume in 2000, which he hosted at the Present Company Theatorium, John has been an ardent supporter of this project; if he hadn't believed in what we were doing then, it's likely that the book you're reading now wouldn't exist. This book is dedicated to John and his wife, Nancy Walsh.

Martin Denton
New York City
December 2002

FOREWORD

I keep going to the theatre every night and I see most of the time the critics Rochelle and Martin Denton. We smile at each other before the play starts. We do hope—all critics hope—to spend a pleasant evening with good, solid drama.

We also hope to discover new voices.

At the end of the play we sometimes smile at each other because we are pleased by what we saw; sometimes we do not look at each other. We hate to read disappointment in the eyes of our friends.

We review these plays and I keep a list of the ones I really like. Just a list.

Rochelle and Martin do much more. They publish the best (The New York Theatre Experience, Inc.).

They have now prepared this fourth volume of new plays, *Plays and Playwrights 2003*. I have seen and read most of the plays they have chosen and I recommend them. It is always a joy discovering new playwrights.

And I am sure Rochelle and Martin are proud of their noble effort: putting new young playwrights on the map of the American Theatre. I remember when my first play was published. I felt an indescribable feeling of achievement.

I am sure that Joe Godfrey, Catherine Gillet, Andrea Lepcio, Ato Essandoh, Edward Musto, Nat Colley, Marc Morales, Leon Chase, Joseph Langham, Maggie Cino, and Kelly McAllister will feel what I felt.

Mario Fratti
Playwright and Drama Critic
November 2002

INTRODUCTION

Martin Denton

Plays and Playwrights 2003 is a book of journeys. On the pages that follow you will meet some remarkable, memorable characters and accompany them as they discover and experience life's potentialities. There's Sadie, a delightful "old woman who happens to still be young," whose collection of handbags ensures that she's always prepared for any emergency. There's Keith, a thirty-something man who one day forgets all his PIN numbers and takes that as a sign to throw his laptop computer into San Francisco Bay and hitchhike back home; and there's David, about the same age, who realizes, in the aftermath of the World Trade Center attacks, that he's turning into an "asshole" and hits the road in search of his truer, better self. There's Sam and Mattie, a black man and a white woman who embark on a romance their friends can't quite fathom; and there's Lucy and Laura, two teenage girls who are coping with, among many other things, the prospect of a field trip to New York City post 9/11. There's Tom, whose life, on the fateful election night of 1980, careers into a scary descent toward degradation and hell; and there's B, an anonymous woman whose older sister is stricken with breast cancer and consequently finds herself heading toward the scary places where that disease takes her. There's a pair of clueless clowns camping out at a restaurant's Sunday brunch who seem unable to fathom the apocalyptic events going on around them; and there's a pair of contrasting clerks at a humongous video store who are adopting very different strategies for handling the less-than-challenging work with which they're confronted. Finally, there's Daniel, grandson of Shylock (from Shakespeare's *Merchant of Venice*) on a mission to uncover the truth about himself and his heritage; and there's Ben, an updated version of Ebenezer Scrooge, now a sour and repressed middle-aged gay interior decorator, who takes the familiar trips backward and forward in time with a trio of ghosts to learn how to become a better man.

They've all got something cogent to teach us, these people who inhabit the eleven extraordinary plays in this collection. As for the plays and their authors, well, they're a wonderfully diverse lot, as has become the habit of the *Plays and Playwrights* series. This year's collection comes from theatres of every size and description, from vibrant new works festivals such as the New York International Fringe Festival, Vital Theatre Company's semi-annual *Vital Signs*, and Screaming Venus Productions' one-woman-show showcase *Eve's Apple*; to established off-off-Broadway spaces like the 45th Street Theatre in Midtown and the Greenwich Street Theatre in Soho; to up-and-coming venues such as manhattantheatresource near Washington Square and Horse Trade Theater Group's Red Room in the East Village; to a venerable cabaret space—The Duplex on Christopher Street, right down the street from Stonewall Inn.

The playwrights themselves are perhaps unfamiliar to you now, but it is the editor's fond hope—and indeed, one of the principal objectives of the publication of this book—that that will change, rapidly. They are: Joe Godfrey (*A Queer Carol*), Catherine Gillet (*Pumpkins for Smallpox*), Andrea Lepcio (*Looking for the Pony*), Ato Essandoh (*Black Thang*), Edward Musto (*The Ninth Circle*), Nat Colley (*The Doctor of Rome*), Marc Morales (*Galaxy Video*), Leon Chase (*The Last Carburetor*), Joseph Langham (*Out to Lunch*), Maggie Cino (*Ascending Bodily*), and Kelly McAllister (*Last Call*).

These eleven authors place themselves, with these works, among the front rank of America's newest playwrights; the plays they have written and will write are going to help shape the way we think about ourselves as a nation and a culture. They're part of an exciting renaissance in serious drama that's been happening in what's loosely referred to as "downtown theatre" in New York—brave and smart and imaginative artists who, with hundreds of producers, directors, actors, and designers, are collaborating to create a theatre that is relevant and challenging. Their work, as you will see, bursts with energy and invention; it's the kind of work that—quietly or explosively—can change people's lives.

The idea behind this book is to give these plays and playwrights the permanence and long life that they deserve. On page iii you will find contact information for each of the authors represented herein. Put their plays on—these or others that they have written or will write; spread the word about the important and necessary work they are doing by keeping the flame of American drama hot and glowing.

❋

Every December in New York, a dozen or more different productions of Charles Dickens's *A Christmas Carol* turn up on our stages. So why care about, let alone publish, another one? Two reasons. First, Joe Godfrey's *A Queer Carol* is refreshingly original: in transplanting the familiar story to a contemporary gay milieu, Godfrey has added a new layer to Ebenezer (here Ben) Scrooge's character, fueling his retreat from the world not just with a broken heart but also with a lifetime of repression and pain at the receiving end of homophobic bigotry. This *Carol* mines a whole spectrum of pop gay iconography to translate Dickens, with Marilyn Monroe as its Ghost of Christmas Past and an exuberant drag queen as its Ghost of Christmas Present. Marley's Ghost appears not just in chains, but also in leather; Fezziwig, now a lovable old queen, gives a roomful of young gay decorators a different sort of Christmas goose at his party; and there's even an inevitable naughty joke about "Tiny" Tim (here Bob Cratchit's HIV+ lover).

But underneath all the fun and campiness is a spirit that's quite genuine; the second reason that *A Queer Carol* is in this book is that it, more than any recent adaptation I know of (and I've seen quite a few), captures the true meaning of the Dickens novel with the warm, simple felicity it deserves. Godfrey comes right to the point in the play's first scene, when Scrooge is visited in his elegant Chelsea townhouse by a fellow named Nick, who is fundraising for Broadway Cares/Equity Fights AIDS:

> NICK: You know, Bob, that's what I love about Christmas. It's a unique time. A time when people—even New Yorkers—forget about themselves for a while and want to help other people. It's the only time I know of when everyone—
>
> *(SCROOGE reenters.)*
>
> NICK: —well, almost everyone—takes pleasure in being helpful and charitable, realizing—if only briefly—that we are all fellow passengers on the same big roller coaster.

Nick's words felt particularly resonant right after the World Trade Center attacks; now, just a little more than a year later, they're sadly wistful. Which is why, I guess, we need to be reminded—not just in December, but all the time—of *A Christmas Carol*'s message of fellowship and responsibility.

A Queer Carol isn't afraid to be sentimental, by the way; its heart is on its sleeve much of the time. But when Tim makes a Christmas Eve toast at a humble gathering of his makeshift "family"—his lover Bob Cratchit and a lesbian couple who are their closest friends—he says (what else?) "God bless us, everyone." And for once, we entirely believe.

❋

It was always clear that at least one "9/11 play" needed to be part of this anthology. In a way, of course, every one of the eleven plays in *Plays and Playwrights 2003* deals with 9/11 (see my remarks about *A Queer Carol*, for example, above). But only one confronts the subject head-on, and indeed Catherine Gillet's *Pumpkins for Smallpox* is still, more than a year after it was written, practically the only play I know of that concerns itself directly with what the events of that day mean for the future of our country.

Gillet zooms in here on our children. In *Pumpkins for Smallpox*, two teenagers who live in a town not far from New York City are raising money for a good cause outside their neighborhood church on a Sunday morning. Nothing unusual about that—except that the money is to go to providing smallpox vaccine to protect the residents of this community; and all of the talk shared by these two girls has to do with what they call the Thing, the never-named catastrophe that has, quite obviously and irrevocably, changed these youngsters' lives.

Gillet gets under her two protagonists' skins so precisely it hurts.

> LAURA: Ever heard of Post-traumatic Stress Syndrome?
>
> LUCY: Duh. Like every day. My mom keeps askin' if I have it like she used to ask if I had my period. Really pisses me off.
>
> LAURA: Ditto.
>
> LUCY: It's like we're not allowed to be like regular, you know?, normal. Before the Thing I got mad at stuff. I freaked out like when she wouldn't drive me somewhere. Now I've got Post—
>
> LUCY: I don't sleep at night.

Pumpkins for Smallpox is very short, just ten minutes long, but it is by no means slight. It is, I fear, already a little bit dated: what seemed to be far-fetched when Gillet thought it up—mass inoculations against smallpox—is, alas, already very real. Nevertheless, the raw potency of Gillet's work makes it valuable; *Pumpkins for Smallpox* is a testament to a moment in our history that must be remembered.

❋

A more personal kind of catastrophe is the setting for Andrea Lepcio's *Looking for the Pony*, another brief play of shattering intensity. Taking its title from the old saw about a barn full of manure ("there has to be a pony in here somewhere"), this drama concerns a pair of sisters, known only as A and B, who are forced to travel, as Lepcio puts it, to "the places cancer takes you." The brilliant leap the playwright makes in this piece is to keep it entirely impressionistic: A, the sister with breast cancer, is kept at a slight remove, while B, the other sister, tells the story—not exactly as it happened, but as she experienced it. We hear what B heard, as opposed to what the legion of doctors, nurses, insurance company personnel, and other health care industry professionals actually said, and, as a result, *Looking for the Pony* has an immediacy and intimacy that's rare in the theatre:

> B: Her gynecologist sits down.
>
> A: We sit.
>
> B: She says,
>
> C [the gynecologist]: It's cancer.... Here's the name of a doctor. Immediately you are beyond what this office can do. This is the name of the first doctor you need a surgeon and then an oncologist or an oncologist and then a surgeon. There needs to be a surgeon but there will be an oncologist and a surgeon both and a radiologist although from the way the tissue looks on film there is no doubt you have cancer.

Lepcio takes our breath away as she deconstructs the state of contemporary health care and the myriad feelings of fear, powerlessness, anxiety, anger, victimhood, frustration, and disbelief that are experienced by anyone in real trouble up against it. *Looking for the Pony* has moments of not-so-gentle satire that raise smiles, juxtaposed with instances of profound humanity as her characters come face to face with issues of mortality and grief.

Lepcio mines the most essential stuff of life with enormous compassion and intelligence in this play. *Looking for the Pony* has already been performed by several New York City theatres since its premiere; I expect many, many others around the world will want to follow suit, to bring its potent wisdom to as large an audience as possible.

❖

Black Thang is written with such wit and assurance it's hard to believe that it's the very first full-length play its author, Ato Essandoh, has written. This charming and insightful one-act is a romantic comedy about Sam, a young black man, and Mattie, the white woman with whom he falls in love. Trouble is, Mattie is obsessively afraid of commitment. Complicating matters are Sam's best friend Jerome and Mattie's roommate Keisha, both of whom are convinced that the interracial relationship is doomed—and, worse, are only too happy to say so, every chance they get.

Essandoh lets these splendidly authentic characters say whatever is on their minds; as a result, *Black Thang* turns out to be a richly observed comedy of contemporary manners. The playwright interweaves scenes of Sam and Mattie going through the expected stages of courtship with morning-after "debriefings," allowing us to watch the evolution of this coupling from every possible perspective. Sam and Mattie's interplay feels as natural as walking; Essandoh has given us a couple to really root for in this attractive pair.

He's also come up with some of the funniest dialogue in recent memory for a play of this type. The love scenes between Sam and Mattie are surprisingly frank and intimate, but they never feel gratuitous or sensational; they work precisely because they have such a sweet ring of truth about them. Similarly, Jerome and Keisha's various diatribes on all sorts of outlandish subjects, from the lack of what Jerome calls "Ass Content" in white women to a hilariously tragic account of Keisha's grandmother-in-law-to-be's lifelong fear of horses, are all the funnier because they sound so much like something you heard yesterday at work or in a bar.

Actors are going to be clamoring to perform these roles. Consider this first meeting between Jerome and Mattie. Jerome's had too much to drink already and has been on Sam's back for some time because Mattie is vegan:

> JEROME: Okay, let's say perchance that you were stuck on a deserted island and there was nothing there but a cow. Nothing but sand and a fucking cow. Would you then?
>
> MATTIE: Nope.
>
> JEROME: You would die?
>
> MATTIE: Yup.
>
> JEROME: And if the cow ate you?
>
> MATTIE: The cow wouldn't eat me.
>
> JEROME: How do you know? How do you know this cow?
>
> MATTIE: Cows don't eat meat. They're herbivores.
>
> JEROME: Yeah, when it suits them. When it's convenient for them. When they're living the plush pansy cow life chewing cud and getting milked all day. Maybe. But I'm telling you. Put a cow in an extreme situation where it's got to choose between its beliefs and living another day and I'll show you one fucking scary cow—

Essandoh nails us in all our imperfect glory. *Black Thang* is a propitious debut of a writer to watch.

❖

The anxious state of the world has made many of us try to pinpoint the moment when things started to go wrong for America. Playwright Edward Musto has fixed the date as November 4, 1980, which was the night when Ronald Reagan won his landslide victory over President Jimmy Carter, ushering in a political regime that remains largely intact at this writing. That same night is the setting for Musto's dark play *The Ninth Circle*, which depicts the most harrowing of this book's journeys, that of a thirty-five-year-old middle manager trapped in a corporate America he no longer likes or understands.

In ten riveting scenes, Musto charts Tom's journey through an increasingly dark and murky night. The play begins in a seedy hotel room, where Tom has just had quick, meaningless sex with a teacher he picked up at the school where he was supposed to vote. It progresses through encounters at a bar, an art gallery, a late business dinner at an exclusive restaurant, a porno movie house, a hospital emergency room, Tom's office, the steam room in a health club, Tom's apartment, and, finally (inevitably) in a club called the Inferno: the dead end. Each stop pits Tom against something of value in his life—his secretary, his job, his wife; eventually the very core of his moral fiber—and each confrontation drives him further away from life and closer to a cathartic but bitterly nihilistic revelation.

The Ninth Circle is bleak and despairing and, in its final resolution, hopeless. But Musto's writing is sharp and incisive and potent: the people Tom meets, especially the strangers, at once compel and repel, both drawing us toward and pulling us away from the damaging drift of humanity that they represent. These characters—Alley, the promiscuous elementary school teacher; Score, the stoned drug dealer; Jo-Jo, the scarily accommodating porno house manager; Julio, the arrogant mailroom clerk; and Ian, the exhausted gay businessman with whom Tom connects in a sauna—are unexpectedly unforgettable. We don't want them to, we resist—but these folks get under our skin:

> IAN: Took out a membership here strictly for working out. Already know where to go for sex.
>
> TOM: Anywhere.
>
> IAN: Right.
>
> *(Pause.)*
>
> TOM: Anytime you want to start.
>
> IAN: You start.
>
> TOM: I can't.
>
> IAN: Neither can I.

The Ninth Circle is raw and it is epic. Musto isn't afraid to push the envelope here, depicting the corrosion of Tom's soul in brutally uncompromising terms. At the same time, the play is sharp and literate (liberally sprinkled with symbols and allusions to the classics); much of its power to disturb and unsettle comes from the contrast between the elegance and order of its surface and the anguished moral turpitude beneath.

❖

The Doctor of Rome by Nat Colley is a sequel to *The Merchant of Venice*, and like that work it is not easily pegged as being about simply this thing or that. What first attracted me to it is its clear-eyed examination of what really matters to people in power, i.e., maintenance of the economic order and the status quo. The Duke of Venice, the official who ordered Shylock to convert to Christianity at the end of Shakespeare's play, explains why he did what he did early on in *The Doctor of Rome*:

> DUKE: Shylock's conversion was part of a case settled before this court long ago. The laws of Venice must always be constant. Much trade depends upon the reliability and consistency of those laws. Shylock understood that.

Later, after Shylock's grandson Daniel causes another suit to be brought before the Duke, come these frighteningly pragmatic words:

> DUKE: I am not the Duke of mercy, young man, but of Venice. And it is Venice I must protect, and its markets I must defend. All the world must know that in Venice they may trade freely and safely. The economy of the entire city depends upon it... All those who would corrupt the course of capitalism, or fail to turn them in once known, must be penalized, quickly, publicly, and severely...

How much or how little have things changed since Shakespeare's day? Colley considers that question and many others in this impressive sequel, which brashly borrows form as well as characters from the original and manages, quite gratifyingly, to live up to its famous predecessor.

The doctor of the title is of course Portia, or rather her alter ego, Balthazar, that learned young man of law who spoke so eloquently of mercy at Shylock's trial. It is now fifteen years later, and Portia and Bassanio, childless, are merrily vying for control over the future of Daniel, the son of Jessica and Lorenzo and grandson of Shylock. Portia is still not above playing tricks on her beloved to get her way; and neither is Colley above toying with that infernal ring that Portia made Bassanio swear to hold onto at all costs to make a point of his own about the nature of loyalty.

Colley shows us in his play what happens to most of the familiar characters from *The Merchant of Venice*, and introduces several compelling new ones: Daniel, of course, whose Jewish heritage has been hidden from him by his mother until Tubal visits Belmont with the news of Shylock's death; Daniel's love interest, Rachel, the half-Moorish daughter of Shylock's servant Launcelot Gobbo; and Largo, a merchant of Rome who sets in motion the machinery of Colley's canny plot.

The Doctor of Rome finally turns deadly serious on a number of thorny subjects, such as self-identity, religious bigotry, and the tenuous balance between justice and truth. As the Duke says—and as Shakespeare's own work ultimately proved—mercy unfortunately has little place in any of it.

※

All of the plays discussed so far have been largely traditional in their structure. But it wouldn't be a *Plays and Playwrights* book without at least a few representative experiments in form, and *Galaxy Video* is perhaps the most innovative piece included here. What *Galaxy Video* most resembles is a long music video, but this is no mere appropriation of quick-cuts and short-attention-span snippets for their own sake. Playwright/director Marc Morales has something weightier in mind, though he'd probably be loathe to say so himself: *Galaxy Video*, and the plays he has written since (*The Lounge* and, most recently, *The Show*) are all attempts to explain Generation X in the context of the art form they invented. Like Sondheim and Lapine's *Follies*, *Galaxy Video* uses popular culture to explore our dreams and ideals.

Okay, maybe that's a little too lofty. *Galaxy Video* feels, mostly, like an antic, turbo-charged farce, set in the biggest video store imaginable, through which traipse a motley assortment of customers and employees. What they have in common, apart from their location, is a desire for control: over what video gets rented tonight, in particular; but more broadly over their destinies. Their adventures, as they try to locate a copy of *Midnight Cowboy* among the endless maze of video shelves or try to figure out what they want to be when they grow up, are depicted in short, sharp, swift scenes that sometimes last no longer than a few seconds. There are more than a dozen leading characters in this play, and every one of them gets to be the star of his or her own "video," at least for a brief moment.

Galaxy Video makes liberal use of pop culture references and running gags, linking it both to MTV and vaudeville; and it stops over and over again to interpolate a musical number or break dance that has nothing and everything to do with what's happening in the story. It's breathless, shameless, and boundary-less. It's also enormously funny and enormous fun:

JERRY: Welcome to Galaxy Video. *(Strikes the pose.)* How may we assist you?

MAN: Yeah, buddy. You got a bathroom here I can use?

JERRY: Yes, I do have a bathroom, and no, you can't use it. Customers only sir. Sorry.

MAN: You don't understand. I really got to go.

JERRY: I am sorry. Store rule, not mine. Customers only.

MAN: Man. Okay. How do I become a customer?

JERRY: Well, just rent one of our fine films. We have an infinite number of movies here at Galaxy Video.

MAN: I ain't a member.

JERRY: Well then, you can purchase one of our fine snacks from our concession area.

MAN: Okay. Give me these. *(Grabs a packet of M&Ms with peanuts.)*

JERRY: Fine selection, sir. That will be nine dollars and ninety-nine cents.

❋

The American family, or what's left of it anyway, comes under scrutiny in Leon Chase's play, *The Last Carburetor*. Following in the footsteps of Eugene O'Neill, Arthur Miller, and—most emphatically—Sam Shepard, Chase has fashioned here a taut drama of dysfunctionality centered around tension between a father and his sons. The patriarch here is Doug, very much a broken-down shadow of a man, not unlike the rotting 1970 Plymouth Hemi Barracuda that has awaited repair in his suburban Detroit garage for more than two decades. Doug's elder son, Keith, left home for college and never looked back, becoming a success in the computer biz on the West Coast. Younger son Josh, who idolized dad and car, got neither affection nor respect, and went off to fight in Desert Storm (to the consternation of his Vietnam vet father) and then took a job as a bounty hunter.

Now it's 2000. Mom has left, though Doug seems unable to say for sure whether she's on vacation or gone for good. The youngest child, Ayla, is in college at Ann Arbor looking eagerly forward to escape from her family. Josh and Doug maintain an uneasy truce. And then Keith turns up, unannounced, in a ditch near Doug's house.

KEITH: This one morning I was outside the door to go into work. I was late, too… I was trying to remember this number to get into the door, but I kept getting it mixed up with all the other numbers. The office code. My network password. My e-mail password. The PIN number for my ATM card. The code for my voicemail. My home phone number. My cell phone number. Social Security.

> My credit card number. My account number at the bank... They'd never been a problem before. Then, there I was, just standing there, all of it mixed up... so bad it made my head hurt.
>
> JOSH: So how'd you get in?
>
> KEITH: I didn't... I just left.

And thus begins, in earnest, Chase's drama, in which all the stuff Doug thought he knew, and all the stuff Ayla and Josh thought they understood, and all the stuff Keith thinks he's going to rediscover—all these things blow up in everybody's face, in a cathartic, life-changing weekend. Chase's debt to Shepard is clear throughout, and indeed acknowledged with a wonderful homage in the form of a box of melting popsicles on the kitchen counter. But he has his own heartfelt, distinctive voice, and *The Last Carburetor* eventually winds up covering quite different ground than we initially expect, especially in the stories of Keith and Ayla.

❖

I was personally very heartened by the resurgence of politically minded theatre in the off-off-Broadway community during the past year; explosive national and international events seem to have triggered activist reaction among at least some of our playwrights. Joseph Langham's *Out to Lunch* is certainly the most polemical play in this collection. Drawing from a variety of dramatic and cultural reference points, Langham has crafted a dada allegorical farce about, among other things, the dangers of apathy. *Out to Lunch* is deliberately off-the-wall and deliberately provoking; a frenzied parade of calculated, wanton shock effects, it manages to jolt its audience out of complacency, even though leaving them laughing all the way.

At the center of the *Hellzapoppin'*-ish shenanigans are Numba Won and Numba Too, a pair of clueless geeks who spend their entire Sunday camped out at a table at a neighborhood restaurant. Here they conduct an inane and endless conversation about Internet chat partners and scanning their "booties," all the while blissfully unaware of (a) the increasing consternation of the restaurant staff and (b) the intermittent interruptions of a crazed gunman looking for an excuse to open fire. These guys are *Godot*'s Vladimir and Estragon without anything to wait for; virtually nothing happens to them during *Out to Lunch*, and yet we understand that they are vitally central to it.

A lot happens, on the other hand, to the other characters, who include a temperamental Waitress who at one point takes off all her clothes as a token protest against her immovable customers; her boss, the Manager, a (very) frustrated ballet dancer; his boss, the Owner, who wears a crown and is attended by two sexy "Goils"; *his* boss, the

Owner's Wife, who is so vile that she tells her nanny to shoot her children if they won't behave; and the aptly named JesterDishwasherFrenchChef, a hard-working soul who speaks, in his way, for the oppressed everywhere. Each of these, from his or her rung on the food chain, tries to make at least a ripple, if not a wave, as when the Manager explodes with this tirade:

> MAN: yeah, yeah, well i'm sick of it. i'm sick of all these rules, everywhere you go. no smoking, no parking, stop, go, the customer is always right, don't take candy from strangers, do this, do that, blah blah blah. well, i'm sick of it!! i want to be a ballerino, a ballet guy, what's the term for that? balleretta? balleronio? heck i dunno. but i'm for once in my short pathetic life going to follow my dream. and i'm going to break the rules. all of them. look mister mayor, i'm smoking in a restaurant, you nonsmoking republican nazi motherfrigger!

Langham uses stylized language and punctuation to make sure that we're constantly on our guard, paying attention to the apocalyptic events of *Out to Lunch*, lest we fall into the trap of his two clueless "heroes." Rowdy and risky and entirely pertinent, *Out to Lunch* reminds us that theatre can be on the front line of social and political protest.

❖

Langham's shock tactics wouldn't be necessary if we were all as resilient and resourceful as Sadie, the heroine of Maggie Cino's solo work *Ascending Bodily*. More a performance text than a conventional drama, this monologue originated as a character study intended to be developed into a movement-based piece by its author. Cino tells us in her author's note that Sadie soon took on a life of her own, and she emerges here full-blown as the unlikely subject of her own very unusual little one-act play.

Her tale, which she narrates herself, is one of great adventure, in places like the Siberian Desert and the Serengeti Jungle, and involving extraordinary creatures such as the enormous gentleman with a bald head like the moon, not to mention the teeny tiny llamas of the Himalayan Andes. Armed only with her handbags, Sadie exults in the joys of every new acquaintance. In the end, she teaches us a great deal about life, love, and loss.

Cino has endowed Sadie not only with great spirit and wisdom, but with a fantastical, inimitable voice:

> SADIE: The second time I met my enormous gentleman I was walking among the ancient stones when I saw his great knees and his bald head like the moon. And I ran to them and looked up and up and up—and there was nothing above his knees, and

> his bald head was the moon. Then I heard laughter behind me and there was my gentleman friend! He reached across and broke off bits of the moon. They rained around me and he said,
>
> "For you you you..."

Ascending Bodily is a magical piece, full of wonder and nuance. Cino says she will continue to perform it, and I'm sure she will continue to learn more about her remarkable creation as she does so. But she's eager for others to bring Sadie to life, and I am hopeful that once people meet her within these pages, they'll want to put Sadie on stage in places she's never even dreamed of.

❖

I've given the final word, so to speak, to Kelly McAllister, and his immensely moving play *Last Call.* It is, at first glance, a *Big Chill*-ish piece about a reunion of old friends in a small California town, all of them stuck in early-middle-age ruts and some of them eager to get out of them. McAllister populates his play with vividly recognizable figures: Vinnie, a barfly who spouts movie quotes and obscenities and little else; Jerry, his buddy who still lives in his parents' garage and harbors unrequited desires for a high school sweetheart; Molly, Vinnie's smart, sharp-tongued wife; Kristen, the still-glamorous object of Jerry's desire, now married to a successful but nerdy businessman named Karl whom everybody else calls Fievel, the village idiot; Carlos, the avuncular Vietnam vet who runs the local watering hole; and Jack, a sweet-natured frump who has never recovered—emotionally or physically—from a long-ago car crash.

Into this mix arrives David, the local boy made good, the one who got away, moving to New York City after college. It's a few months after the World Trade Center attacks, and David is heeding—and attempting to deliver—the last call of the play's title:

> DAVID: It was about three months after 9/11. After everyone started acting like their normal, boring, creepy selves.
>
> VINCE: Including you?
>
> DAVID: Oh yeah. Especially me. Thousands of people dead. A war on terrorism that just gets curiouser and curiouser. Anthrax, some kid putting pipe bombs in mailboxes—things are totally fucked up. And there I am, buying this and selling that, closing deals like nothing ever happened. Keep going on like before. That's what everyone said to do to fight the terrorists. Keep going on like before. Even if you're an asshole, keep going on like before. It's all so fucked and weird.

I will leave it to you discover what happens to David and his friends in *Last Call.* I will tell you that McAllister respects the awful complexity of real life; in my review of the original production at the New York International Fringe Festival, I said that the play is messy and poetic, like life; I still can't think of a better way to describe it.

❖

We need our Kelly McAllisters to encapsulate, so deftly and truthfully, what's in our heads and hearts. He and each of the other contributors to this volume—Joe Godfrey, Catherine Gillet, Andrea Lepcio, Ato Essandoh, Edward Musto, Nat Colley, Marc Morales, Leon Chase, Joseph Langham, and Maggie Cino—have used their extraordinary talents to show us, in wonderfully different ways, what it means to be human at this particular moment in time. The journeys they have brought to the stage this past year and have now set down for us in this volume are signposts on our way to whatever's next. They await you as soon as you turn this page. I wish for you a trip as rewarding as mine.

A QUEER CAROL

Joe Godfrey

JOE GODFREY was born in Boston and raised in Westchester County, New York. His play *Bed & Breakfast* was produced in the 2000 Key West Theatre Festival and has also been seen in Provincetown, Massachusetts, and Lexington, Kentucky. His award-winning play *The Call Back*, first produced by Manhattan Punch Line Theatre, was seen last June at the Repertory Theatre of New Britain, Connecticut, after productions by the Henrico Theatre in Richmond, Virginia, and the Gallery Players in Brooklyn, New York. His new play, *Massage Therapy,* received a runner-up award in the 2002 Eric Bentley New Play Competition. Additionally, Godfrey's one-act plays *Communications, Flight, Swan Song, Take Two, Beep, Rabbit Ears,* and *Wild Spots,* among others, have been featured in festivals by Native Aliens, Theatre Three, and numerous others around the country. Godfrey has written for the *Westchester County Monthly, Washingtonian*, the *New York Times, Harper's*, and the *Litchfield County Times.* He has also acted in dozens of shows in New York and around the country, most recently playing FDR in *Annie* at the Helen Hayes Performing Arts Center in Nyack, New York. He graduated cum laude from Lehigh University and taught English at the Peddie School in New Jersey. He studied comedy writing with Mark O'Donnell and acting with Austin Pendleton and Uta Hagen. He is a member of the Dramatists Guild, the Playwrights Group of TOSOSII, AEA, AFTRA, and SAG.

The New York City premiere of *A Queer Carol* was presented by SourceWorks Theatre (Mark Cannistraro, Artistic Director) on December 6, 2001, at the Duplex Cabaret Theatre with the following cast and credits:

Bob Cratchit .... J.D. Lynch
Ebenezer Scrooge .... John Marino
Fred/Fezziwig/Pytor .... Yaakov Sullivan
Nick/Father/Employee/Noel/Fence .... Nathan Johnson
Svetlana/Ghost of Christmas Past/Carol .... Cynthia Pierce
Jacob Marley .... Henry David Clarke
Young Scrooge/Tim .... Dan Pintauro
Mother/Employee/Nurse/Maria/Jean .... Virginia Baeta
Ghost of Christmas Present .... Michael Lynch

Director: Mark Cannistraro
Costumes: Michael Piatkowski
Set: Jeffrey Tuballes

A Queer Carol was previously presented in a workshop production by the New Phoenix Theatre (Richard Lambert, Artistic Director) in December 1998 in Buffalo, New York.

ACKNOWLEDGMENTS

Just as three spirits guided Scrooge through his transformation, three wonderful directors, who each had an invaluable hand in making *A Queer Carol* happen, deserve my gratitude. My thanks first to Richard Lambert, Artistic Director of the New Phoenix Theatre in Buffalo, New York, who plunged in and gave *Carol* its first and very effective production at his theatre. A big hug to Richard Sabellico in Manhattan, who subsequently directed two excellent staged readings in New York City, and whose insight and suggestions greatly strengthened the play. Finally, I'm indebted to Mark Cannistraro, Artistic Director of SourceWorks Theatre in New York City, who produced and directed the New York City premiere at the Duplex Cabaret Theatre. Mark worked tirelessly and diligently to make *A Queer Carol* a production to be proud of.

CHARACTERS

EBENEZER SCROOGE: Mid-50s. Interior designer. Intelligent, smartly dressed, stern. A contemporary version of the classic character.

BOY SCROOGE: 10.

YOUNG SCROOGE (BEN): Late 20s. Attractive, smart, at first shy, in reality repressed.

ROBERT CRATCHIT: 30s. A good soul. Scrooge's assistant.

TIM: 30s. Cute, Sweet and kind. Cratchit's lover.

JACOB MARLEY: 30ish. Handsome and aggressive.

GHOST OF CHRISTMAS PAST: Marilyn Monroe.

GHOST OF CHRISTMAS PRESENT: Ideally, an over-the-top drag queen; could also be a woman.

SVETLANA: Scrooge's maid.

PYTOR: Svetlana's husband.

FEZZIWIG: Scrooge's first boss, older, fun-loving, and campy.

SCROOGE'S MOTHER (MOM).

SCROOGE'S FATHER (DAD).

CAROL: Bob and Tim's close friend.

MARIA: Carol's lover, a Dominican woman.

NICK: A fundraiser.

JEAN: Nick's girlfriend.

FRED: Scrooge's age, a fabric salesman.

NOEL: A friend of Fred's.

BLAKE: Fred's cousin.

NURSE.

FENCE.

The play works well with nine actors, seven men and two women. BOY SCROOGE, BEN, and TIM should be played by the same actor. MARLEY and BLAKE should be played by the same actor. Two men and two women may take the following roles:

MAN 1: SCROOGE'S FATHER, NICK, NOEL, FENCE
MAN 2: FRED, FEZZIWIG, PYTOR
WOMAN 1: SVETLANA, GHOST OF CHRISTMAS PAST, CAROL
WOMAN 2: SCROOGE'S MOTHER, MARIA, JEAN, NURSE

The GHOST OF CHRISTMAS FUTURE should be an ominous sound and light effect, surrounding SCROOGE and the stage.

TIME

Christmas Eve, 2000.

NOTES ON STAGING

The play may be performed in two acts or without intermission.

Though the play takes place in Manhattan, theatre companies should feel free to change the site-specific locations and businesses to names more familiar to their own locale.

Believe it or not, less can be more here. A unit set with little more than a table or desk, a comfortable easy chair, and extra chair, perhaps a stool, etc., will suffice. A great deal can be done with creative sound effects, as was shown in the New York City production. Unlike most traditional and grandiose productions of Dickens's *A Christmas Carol*, this play is intimate.

ACT I
SCENE 1

The office of Scrooge & Marley, Interior Design. Manhattan. The room is tasteful and elegant. There is a grand desk where SCROOGE works and a smaller desk at one side for CRATCHIT. It is chilly in the office. At rise: Christmas Eve. About five o'clock. As house lights go to half, we hear "Hark the Herald Angels Sing." The song continues in the darkness, as we realize it comes from a radio on CRATCHIT's desk.

CRATCHIT: *(Entering and singing as he goes to phone and dials.)* "Peace on earth and mercy mild, God and sinners reconciled…" *(Speaks into phone.)* Hi, babe. How are you feeling? Yup. I'm still here. Till the bitter end, I'm sure.

SCROOGE: *(From offstage.)* Robert, have those samples arrived yet?

CRATCHIT: Not yet, Mr. Scrooge. *(Back to phone call.)* No, I haven't asked him about that yet, but I will. You know how he is. I have to find the right moment.

SCROOGE: *(Entering.)* Robert! Call up Clarence House and tell them if they value my business, they will get those fabrics here immediately.

CRATCHIT: *(On phone.)* Got to go, hon. See you tonight. Love you. *(Hangs up.)*

SCROOGE: And turn off that radio!

CRATCHIT: *(Turns off radio.)* I just called them ten minutes ago. Sounded like quite a party. They said they're having a problem getting a messenger, what with Christmas deliveries and all, but that someone should be here soon.

SCROOGE: I've called them myself twice in the last hour. Inept clerks. Intolerable inefficiency. Perhaps we should order from a company that takes its work more seriously.

CRATCHIT: I'm afraid we won't have much luck at this hour on this day, sir.

SCROOGE: Since when is Wednesday a particularly difficult business day?

CRATCHIT: When it's the night before…

SCROOGE: Yes. I know. I know.

"'Twas the night before Christmas, and
all through the town
People partied and played as their profits went down."

CRATCHIT: *(Chuckling.)* That's something you'll never have to worry about.

SCROOGE: The reason this firm thrives, Robert, is that I *do* worry about it. As you have learned by now, I devote myself completely to my work. I think of nothing else.

CRATCHIT: You know what they say about all work and no play.

SCROOGE: Yes, it creates a very dull and very rich boy—or middle-aged man—as the case may be.

(A knock is heard.)

SCROOGE: Finally!

(FRED, a business associate, enters with package.)

FRED: *(To CRATCHIT.)* Merry Christmas, Bob!

CRATCHIT: Merry Christmas, Fred.

FRED: *(Going toward SCROOGE.)* And for what it's worth, a Merry Christmas to you, Ben. I'm sure you're planning all sorts of wonderful surprises for everyone this Christmas.

SCROOGE: Do you have the fabrics?

FRED: *(Tossing fabric samples down.)* Voilà. Delivered personally, because I am not sadistic enough to coerce any of my valued employees to face you on Christmas Eve.

SCROOGE: Spare me the melodrama.

FRED: I don't care how you speak to me, Ben, but do not ever call and talk like that to one of my staff, no matter what their position. It's no wonder you can't keep an employee. *(Turns to CRATCHIT.)* Sorry, Bob.

SCROOGE: *(Looking at fabrics.)* I'm amazed that you're still in business, with all the revelry that goes on over there.

FRED: It's called a party. And yes, we celebrate events like Christmas because we enjoy life and each other.

SCROOGE: I'm touched.

FRED: And you are invited, as always, to ruin your health with my famous artery-clogging eggnog at our annual Christmas Eve bash tonight.

SCROOGE: I'm afraid not.

FRED: *(Trying to encourage him.)* Oh, come join us for once, Ben. You might enjoy it. Parlor games. Business associates. Fruitcake and friends? Of course, most of the friends *are* fruitcakes! *(He laughs.)*

SCROOGE: I cannot conceive of anything more loathsome than to feign jocularity at a party with people I can't stand.

FRED: Well, can't blame me for trying. Just thought you might surprise me this year.

SCROOGE: Did you, really? Now, if you'll excuse me, Fred, I have things to do.

FRED: *(Looking around.)* Yes, you haven't put your tree up yet! *(He laughs.)*

(SCROOGE moves away.)

CRATCHIT: It's nice to see you again, Fred.

FRED: *(Preparing to leave.)* You, too, Bob. How is Tim?

CRATCHIT: He has his ups and downs. But he's fine.

FRED: That's great. Listen, I didn't expect Simon Legree over there to come to my party tonight, but I'd love it if you and Tim would stop by.

CRATCHIT: Thanks, but we're having some friends over ourselves. But, hey, drop in on us tomorrow, will you?

FRED: *(Starts to leave.)* I'd love to, Bob. Merry Christmas. *(To SCROOGE.)* You, too, Ben. I'm sure you'll be very merry, indeed! *(Exits.)*

SCROOGE: Why is the design world full of lunatics?

CRATCHIT: He seems to be a fairly successful lunatic.

SCROOGE: God knows why. Time is money. And he's squandered both.

(NICK, a fundraiser, enters, dressed festively.)

NICK: Merry Christmas!

CRATCHIT: Merry Christmas.

SCROOGE: *(To NICK.)* The fabrics are already here.

NICK: I beg your pardon?

SCROOGE: You're not from Clarence House?

NICK: *(Laughing.)* No. But they're on my list, too...

(SCROOGE turns away.)

CRATCHIT: You don't look like a messenger.

NICK: Well, I am, in a way. *(Trying to warm himself.)* Frosty night! Feels like snow.

CRATCHIT: That would be nice for the kids, wouldn't it?

NICK: *(Reacting to SCROOGE.)* A bit cold in here too, isn't it?

CRATCHIT: *(Heading toward thermostat.)* Yes, I'm afraid it is.

SCROOGE: Don't touch that thermostat, Robert.

NICK: *(To SCROOGE.)* Mr. Scrooge—or Mr. Marley?

SCROOGE: Mr. Marley is dead. He died twelve years ago this very night.

NICK: *(Going to SCROOGE.)* Oh, I'm sorry. But the name of the firm...

SCROOGE: ...is a solid one and has not changed. I am Ebenezer Scrooge.

NICK: It's a pleasure to meet you.

(He attempts to shake hands. SCROOGE refrains.)

SCROOGE: What do you want? *(To CRATCHIT.)* Robert, take care of this.

(CRATCHIT takes the fabrics.)

NICK: What a wonderful townhouse. Colonial?

SCROOGE: It dates from the Federal period.

NICK: And so beautifully appointed.

SCROOGE: That is my work—to provide beauty and good taste to those who have little.

NICK: Well, speaking of those who have little, I represent a group of charities, Mr. Scrooge—may I call you Ebenezer?

SCROOGE: You may not.

NICK: Curious name—"Ebenezer."

SCROOGE: It's biblical. And you are wasting my valuable time.

NICK: Time *is* valuable, Mr. Scrooge, more so to others less fortunate than the three of us.

(CRATCHIT turns away.)

SCROOGE: I'm a busy man. What is your point?

NICK: Every Christmas, a group of us volunteers pick a charity and make personal visits to our neighbors, hoping that the holiday spirit will prompt them to dust off their checkbooks and boost the spirits of those in need. This year it's Broadway Cares/Equity Fights AIDS.

SCROOGE: *(Disgusted.)* Actors? Please!

NICK: *(Trying to lighten things up.)* Perhaps you've attended one of their fund-raising events? "Broadway Bares?"

SCROOGE: Certainly not!

NICK: *(Opens small notebook or computer.)* Well, anyway, what may I put you down for?

SCROOGE: Nothing.

NICK: You wish to be anonymous?

SCROOGE: I wish to be left alone.

NICK: With all due respect, if those of us who are blessed or just plain lucky don't open our hearts a bit more, who will?

SCROOGE: I understand there are hospices.

NICK: Yes, there are but…

SCROOGE: And the city shelters? Have they all closed down?

NICK: No, but perhaps some of them should.

SCROOGE: The city taxes me more than enough for social services.

NICK: But honestly, there are those who would rather die than spend Christmas in a city shelter.

SCROOGE: If they would rather die, let them do it and decrease the surplus population.

NICK: I beg your pardon?

SCROOGE: Good evening!

NICK: *(Starting to go.)* I see I am talking to a man with no feelings.

SCROOGE: I have feelings. And my feeling is that those who infect themselves with the virus have only themselves to blame.

NICK: I'm sure that will be a great comfort to them all tonight.

SCROOGE: Please leave. *(Gets up to go into other room.)*

NICK: Merry Christmas.

SCROOGE: Humbug! *(Exits.)*

NICK: *(To CRATCHIT.)* Humbug?

CRATCHIT: It's an archaic word he picked up somewhere.

NICK: Archaic, all right. He's like something out of the Middle Ages. Must be a barrel of laughs working for him!

CRATCHIT: He's a very talented designer.

NICK: Sorry. None of my business.

CRATCHIT: *(Taking a bill from his pocket.)* This isn't very much, but I'd like to help a bit.

NICK: *(Taking the bill.)* That's very kind of you, Mr.…?

CRATCHIT: Cratchit. Bob Cratchit.

NICK: You know, Bob, that's what I love about Christmas. It's a unique time. A time when people—even New Yorkers—forget about themselves for a while and want to help other people. It's the only time I know of when everyone—

(SCROOGE reenters.)

NICK: —well, almost everyone—takes pleasure in being helpful and charitable, realizing—if only briefly—that we are all fellow passengers on the same big roller coaster.

(NICK embraces CRATCHIT.)

SCROOGE: *(Interrupting.)* Robert, if you wish to keep your job...

NICK: *(To SCROOGE.)* And since I came here in the proper spirit of Christmas, I'll be damned if I'm going to leave without wishing you *both* a very Merry Christmas!

SCROOGE: Humbug!

NICK: And a Happy New Year!

CRATCHIT: And the same to you.

(NICK exits.)

SCROOGE: Christmas—open season for all sorts of bloodsuckers to implore you with their sob stories, as if we didn't receive enough solicitations every day in the mail! Everybody's got a hand outstretched.

CRATCHIT: It's only once a year.

SCROOGE: *(Preparing to leave the office.)* A poor excuse for picking a man's pocket. If I had my way, every idiot running around wishing "Merry Christmas" to people they don't even know should be drowned in eggnog and whipped with branches of holly!

CRATCHIT: *(Laughing.)* Sounds pretty kinky.

SCROOGE: I'm quite serious, Robert. What has Christmas become other than one massive marketing opportunity?

CRATCHIT: I suppose that's true to a degree, but...

SCROOGE: *(Interrupting.)* Before you go home, Robert, get these proposals to FedEx, these invoices to the post office, and take this deposit to the bank. And don't forget to close up properly down here and set the alarms.

CRATCHIT: Mr. Scrooge?

SCROOGE: Yes.

CRATCHIT: Well, sir, I was wondering...

SCROOGE: Wondering what?

CRATCHIT: I just thought...

SCROOGE: I haven't got all afternoon, Robert. What is it?

CRATCHIT: Christmas is on a Thursday this year...

SCROOGE: I am aware of that.

CRATCHIT: Well, I was just thinking that since Tim has Friday off, and since he could use some help with a doctor's appointment and a few other things, I thought maybe I could have an extra day off, too—if it's convenient, that is?

SCROOGE: It's not convenient. And I am not Santa Claus.

(CRATCHIT laughs at the thought.)

SCROOGE: What are you laughing at?

CRATCHIT: Nothing. What you said. It's a—a funny joke.

SCROOGE: As you should know by now, Robert, I never joke. *(He starts to exit.)*

CRATCHIT: Do you have any plans for tomorrow?

SCROOGE: Since those fabrics—wonder of wonders—finally arrived, I shall work on the Kitty Carlisle job.

CRATCHIT: Perhaps you would like to

join Tim and me and a few friends for a Christmas dinner.

SCROOGE: I don't think so.

CRATCHIT: Tim's a wonderful cook. He can create masterpieces out of the simplest things. Remember that rosemary bread he made for you. I know you liked it.

SCROOGE: Robert, you celebrate Christmas in your way, and I shall in mine.

CRATCHIT: But you don't celebrate it.

SCROOGE: Allow me to endure it then.

CRATCHIT: *(Handing him small gift.)* Anyway, these are for you. Tim baked them.

SCROOGE: What are they?

CRATCHIT: Butter cookies. Rich and sinful.

SCROOGE: Is that supposed to be funny?

CRATCHIT: No. I didn't mean it that way.

(SCROOGE heads out.)

CRATCHIT: Well, then, goodnight and Merry Christmas, sir.

SCROOGE: It's ludicrous. You, my assistant, living in God-knows-what in the East Village, without a pot to piss in, wishing me a Merry Christmas. *(Chuckling.)* I'll check into Bellevue. *(Exits, leaving cookies behind.)*

(CRATCHIT immediately turns on radio again. We hear "What Child Is This." He excitedly gathers his things and dials the phone.)

CRATCHIT: Me again. Yeah, finally closing up. Thought he'd never leave! Got to drop off some things on the way. Did Carol call? Are they coming? Great. You sure you want to cook tomorrow? And if you feel like shit, just sleep. They won't mind. Yes, I'm going to stop by the video place. Tim, babe, no, I cannot sit through *The Grinch* one more time. *(Laughs.)* I work for him, for God's sake! I'll find something. Hey, how about Bette Davis's Christmas movie? Sure, she made one—"All About Christmas Eve"! No, I didn't get the extra day off, but what the hell, I tried. Oh, yeah, he loved the cookies. No, he's not going to join us. Big surprise, huh? He just left and went upstairs. Another Christmas alone fingering fabrics, no doubt. Hey, enough about *Cruella deScrooge* okay? It's Christmas Eve, and I love you. Get ready to hang up a stocking—fishnet, preferably. *(He hangs up and continues singing carol as he leaves.)* "This, this is Christ the King, the babe, the son of Mary..."

SCENE 2

The bedroom of SCROOGE's townhouse. There is a large, comfortable bed, easy chair, table, etc. The room is rich and stylish. There is a portrait of Marley on the wall. A radio is on, and we hear the carol "What Child Is This" continue. SCROOGE's housekeeper, SVETLANA, is singing as she straightens things up.

SVETLANA: "What child is this, who laid to rest, on Mary's breast is sleeping..."

(SCROOGE enters, wearing a dressing gown, and turns off radio.)

SCROOGE: *(Annoyed.)* Please, Svetlana, I've had a long day, and I'm getting a mammoth headache.

SVETLANA: Oh, I'm sorry, Mr. Scrooge. But I love that carol. It's my favorite.

SCROOGE: *(He makes himself a cocktail from a decanter near the bed.)* How nice.

SVETLANA: You know why is my favorite?

SCROOGE: Quick—the suspense is killing me.

SVETLANA: Because is about Mary and birth of her beloved son. The coincidence! You know? I am poor like Mary and I love my little boy, too.

SCROOGE: Goodnight, Svetlana.

SVETLANA: Of course my Rudy was born in hospital, not like Jesus in stable—although hospital smell like stable.

SCROOGE: Goodnight, Svetlana.

SVETLANA: Rudy so excited about Christmas. And me, too. I always feel like little girl again this time of year.

SCROOGE: Svetlana! I'm dead tired.

SVETLANA: Remember how wonderful it was wondering what presents you'll find in the morning?

SCROOGE: No, I don't.

SVETLANA: Hoping Santa Claus not forget you?

SCROOGE: Have you finished?

SVETLANA: *(Haltingly.)* Well, I just thought… is Christmas… and presents cost lots of money… and maybe…

SCROOGE: Maybe what?

SVETLANA: *(Embarrassed.)* Nothing. Nothing. Is anything else you need, Mr. Scrooge?

SCROOGE: Nothing that you can provide.

SVETLANA: Well, then, I just say goodnight and Merry Christmas.

SCROOGE: Goodnight. Make sure you lock both locks when you leave.

(She starts to go.)

SVETLANA: *(Taking small gift out of her bag.)* Mr. Scrooge, I almost forget. Rudy make this for you. Merry Christmas. *(She hands him gift.)*

SCROOGE: What is it? *(He opens gift.)*

SVETLANA: Just something he sew together. To put on tree. Is an angel.

SCROOGE: *(Momentarily transfixed.)* He made this?

SVETLANA: Uh-huh.

SCROOGE: All by himself?

SVETLANA: Little artist, my Rudichka!

SCROOGE: I don't have a tree.

SVETLANA: Well, you can put it on the mantle or something. We all need some angels in our lives. Anyway, I'm leaving. *(She starts to go.)* Mr. Scrooge?

SCROOGE: Yes.

SVETLANA: Mr. Scrooge, I was wondering… I could use a bit more work from you if you could give me extra day or few more hours.

SCROOGE: One day a week is perfectly adequate for me. More than I need, actually. So I don't think I would try to push my luck.

SVETLANA: Maybe you know some friends who might want good help?

SCROOGE: I have no friends.

SVETLANA: Oh, that's true…

SCROOGE: Svetlana. One call to the immigration service, and you could be back scrounging for scraps near the Kremlin.

SVETLANA: Sorry. Good night, Mr. Scrooge. Merry Christmas. *(She leaves.)*

(SCROOGE looks at gift for a moment, then turns on TV via remote control. He settles into chair as we hear an excerpt from How the Grinch Stole Christmas.*)*

SCROOGE: I may vomit. *(He clicks remote, and we hear an excerpt from* It's a Wonderful Life.*)* Please! Just jump off the bridge and be done with it! *(He clicks again, and we hear a promo for a TV show.)*

TV VOICE: Tonight, celebrate Christmas inside some of the stately homes and castles of England...

SCROOGE: That sounds promising...

TV VOICE: Only on HBO at eight p.m.

SCROOGE: Goddamit, another fucking premium channel...

(The portrait of Marley glows dimly, and we hear the voice of MARLEY, low and faint.)

MARLEY: Scrooge!

SCROOGE: *(He does not see painting glow, but reacts to sound.)* What the hell is... *(Calling offstage.)* Svetlana, is that you? *(He shrugs, puts down remote, and turns on radio. He pours himself another drink.)* Cable TV! Either pay through the nose, or be subjected to shit!

(The portrait glows stronger, and the ghostly voice of MARLEY is heard.)

MARLEY: *(Sad and extended.)* Scrooooge.

SCROOGE: *(Looking at portrait.)* Jake Marley?

(The light fades.)

SCROOGE: Humbug. *(Gulps from drink.)* I must be more tired than I thought.

MARLEY: *(Much louder now, as portrait glows again.)* Scroooooooge!

SCROOGE: *(Looking at his glass.)* Maybe I shouldn't buy such cheap scotch. *(Fidgets with fabric swatches, nervously.)*

(Lights dim, the music from the radio grows much louder, and the radio itself lights up and smokes, as we hear the sound of shuffling and chains being dragged toward the room. The noise increases to a crescendo, and the ghost of JACOB MARLEY appears in the room. He is dressed in black leather, very S&M, bare chest with harness, chaps, dragging long chains with fabric swatches attached to them. He is buff and sexy, but also pale and mournful. A tragic soul.)

SCROOGE: *(Terrified.)* Who are you?

MARLEY: Ask me who I was.

SCROOGE: All right—who were you then?

MARLEY: In life, I was your partner, Jake Marley.

SCROOGE: Jake! My God! But you're dead!

MARLEY: Are you sure it's me who's dead?

SCROOGE: What the hell is this? Some kind of joke?

MARLEY: As you should know by now, Ben, I never joke.

SCROOGE: I just said that very same thing to Cratchit about an hour ago. How did you know?

MARLEY: I have been near you often, Ben, at your side without you knowing, for many years now.

SCROOGE: That's a cheery thought. Everywhere?

MARLEY: Everywhere. And only now do I have the power to appear to you. I don't know why.

SCROOGE: What do you want from me?

MARLEY: It is not what I want from you. It is what I wish to give to you. *(He sits.)*

(SCROOGE looks away.)

MARLEY: You don't believe in me, do you?

SCROOGE: No, I don't.

MARLEY: Why do you doubt your senses?

SCROOGE: Because sometimes things affect them. It could be fatigue. It could be something I ate. *(After a pause.)* It could be the Prozac.

MARLEY: You must believe in me, Ben. My time is limited.

SCROOGE: *(Getting up.)* Then by all means, leave! My time is important, too, and I am not going to spend it conversing with an apparition that is most likely a figment of my creative and overworked imagination!

MARLEY: *(Standing up and screaming an ungodly shriek while shaking his chains.)* Ebenezer Scrooge, do you believe in me, or not?!

SCROOGE: *(Trembling, on his knees.)* I do, I do. But tell me, Jake, why are you here?

MARLEY: It is required of every man that the spirit within him should walk among his fellow men. And if that spirit did not do so in life, it is condemned to do so after death—doomed to wander through the world and witness what it cannot share, but might have shared on earth.

SCROOGE: Are there many like you, Jake?

MARLEY: More than you can imagine. But I am here to offer you a chance, Ben—a chance to escape my fate.

SCROOGE: That's very kind of you, Jake.

MARLEY: Look closely at what I wear.

SCROOGE: Well, I knew you were into bondage, Jake, but my God...

MARLEY: I wear the chains I forged in life, lusting after money, wallowing in an orgy of pleasures, ignoring humanity.

SCROOGE: Well... nobody's perfect.

MARLEY: I was perfect. Perfectly involved in greed and self-indulgence.

SCROOGE: You were always a good businessman, Jake. You understood fabric.

MARLEY: *(Shaking his chains.)* The fabric of mankind was my business. Their common welfare was my business. Kindness, charity, and benevolence were all my business. Ben, you should see the length and weight of the chain you bear. It is huge.

SCROOGE: *(Examining himself and laughing nervously.)* Well, then, I'll just look like one of those bicycle messengers, won't I?

MARLEY: You are well known on the other side, Ben.

SCROOGE: Really? By reputation?

MARLEY: By your life. Do you know what they call you?

SCROOGE: I think I'll let you keep that little secret to yourself, Jake.

MARLEY: A squeezing, wrenching, grasping, scraping, clutching, covetous old sinner!

SCROOGE: I'm not old.

MARLEY: I am deadly serious.

SCROOGE: Please, no puns.

MARLEY: But I am here to offer you some hope.

SCROOGE: Thank you, Jake.

MARLEY: You will be visited by three spirits.

SCROOGE: Three spirits?

MARLEY: Tonight.

SCROOGE: Jake, this is Christmas Eve, not Halloween.

MARLEY: Expect the first at one a.m.

SCROOGE: Is that the chance of hope?

MARLEY: It is.

SCROOGE: Well, you know, I am really a little busy tonight, Jake, and I'd planned to work on a job for Kitty Carlisle...

MARLEY: Fuck Kitty Carlisle!

SCROOGE: You know, Jake, that's the kind of attitude that never really helped us...

MARLEY: *(Leaving.)* Without their visits, you cannot possibly escape my fate. Goodbye, Ben. *(He walks away.)* Look to see me—no more. *(He exits.)*

SCROOGE: *(Locking the door.)* This is insane. I must be hallucinating. I wonder. Svetlana? She could have put something in the scotch. No, that's ridiculous. *(He heads to bed.)* Jacob Marley, indeed! The night of the living dead! Hah! Probably something I ate. Of course—that leftover meatloaf. A little too green around the edges. Ghosts! There's more gravy than grave to all this. Humbug. *(He takes something from bedside table.)* Nothing a little Maalox can't remedy. And maybe a Valium. *(He turns out light.)*

SCENE 3

Same setting. We hear a clock strike one as the radio starts to glow, and we hear a recording of Marilyn Monroe singing, "Diamonds Are a Girl's Best Friend." SCROOGE tries to shut it off, but the music continues as the GHOST OF CHRISTMAS PAST appears—an impersonation of Marilyn Monroe. She is dressed in the white dress that she wore in The Seven Year Itch *or the pink dress from* Gentlemen Prefer Blondes.

VOCAL MUSIC: *(On radio.)* "A kiss on the hand may be quite continental, but diamonds are a girl's best friend..."

PAST: Isn't that right, Ben? There's nothing like diamonds and cash.

SCROOGE: This isn't happening.

PAST: Cartier! Tiffany's! Talk to me, Harry Winston! *(She points at SCROOGE.)* Talk to me, Ebby, honey!

SCROOGE: Don't tell me you're the first spirit?

PAST: That's me. The ghost of Christmas Past.

SCROOGE: Whose past?

PAST: Your past...

SCROOGE: But I never liked Marilyn Monroe.

PAST: There's a lot of things you never liked, Ebby honey.

SCROOGE: Nicknames like that, for instance.

PAST: I mean about the fifties.

SCROOGE: I'll admit there's a certain retro appeal to some of the furnishings, but those dreadful colors—aqua, orange—and those god-awful cars with all that chrome and huge tail fins.

PAST: Hey, don't knock my wheels, Ben, 'cause we're about to cruise off in my high-flying El Dorado.

SCROOGE: Are you really who I think you are?

PAST: I am tonight. Every seven years I get this itch! *(Laughs.)* Don't you think I'm fabulous?

SCROOGE: That's not the word that comes to mind.

PAST: I need you to love me Ben.

SCROOGE: I don't even know you.

PAST: They say gentlemen prefer blondes.

SCROOGE: Well, I preferred Stanwyck.

PAST: Ooh, so butch!

SCROOGE: What are you here for?

PAST: Your welfare.

SCROOGE: A good night's sleep would do me wonders.

PAST: It's time for your rebirth.

SCROOGE: Please, tell me you're not a Baptist!

PAST: *(Laughing.)* No way! Now come with me.

SCROOGE: Where are we going?

PAST: We're going to Niagara! *(Laughing.)* Just kidding. Ebby, honey. You're in for a nostalgia trip! Take my hand.

(He grabs her hand.)

PAST: We're going to do something really cool. *(Laughs.)* Of course, some like it hot!

("Marilyn" music grows much louder as scene changes to SCROOGE's childhood home. Music transforms into "Silent Night"—Bing Crosby, Ella Fitzgerald, or another fifties artist singing—and emanates from the room's radio.)

SCENE 4

SCROOGE and GHOST OF CHRISTMAS PAST watch as scene changes to a simple living room where a boy of about ten is seated on the floor. His mother is nearby. It is 1959.

BOY (BEN): I wish Christmas could be every day. Don't you, Mom?

MOM: Then it wouldn't be so special, would it, Ben?

BOY: Can we open a present now? Please.

MOM: Daddy's not home yet. Just another half hour or so. Then we'll each open one and save the rest for Christmas Day.

BOY: I made Daddy something he'll really love.

MOM: That's the nicest kind of gift—something you make yourself.

BOY: Why is Daddy so late?

MOM: Honey, they have Christmas parties at offices like Daddy's, and sometimes they go on a little later than normal.

BOY: But Santa won't come till Daddy's here.

MOM: *(Sighs.)* You're right. Let's open one gift and save Daddy's for later. *(She gets present.)*

BOY: Cool!

MOM: Here, honey. This is for you, my little artist, to help you create masterpieces.

BOY: *(Opens present.)* I hope it's what I think it is! *(He finds a pastel set and sketch pad.)*

MOM: All the colors of the rainbow.

BOY: Pastels, wow! Thank you, Mom.

(He hugs her.)

BOY: I love you.

MOM: I love you, too, Ben. Merry Christmas.

(DAD enters. He is an executive and a bit drunk.)

BOY: Daddy!

DAD: What a charming Christmas scene—Mary and her little saint.

BOY: *(Races toward DAD and is brushed away.)* Now we can open some more presents!

PAST: *(To SCROOGE.)* Ringing any bells, honey?

SCROOGE: My dear, ineffectual mother.

PAST: And the man?

SCROOGE: I never knew him.

PAST: Nor he you.

SCROOGE: *(To the vision.)* I love you, Mother…

PAST: Save your breath, Ebby. They can't hear you.

BOY: Merry Christmas, Daddy! *(He picks up gift.)* This is for you.

DAD: Wait a minute. Daddy needs a drink if we're going to rush through Christmas. *(He pours a drink.)*

MOM: Do you really think you need another right now, Ron?

DAD: Need, no. Want, yes.

MOM: You might have left the party a little earlier.

DAD: I was having fun.

BOY: We saved you dinner, Dad.

DAD: I'm not hungry.

MOM: Better food at the party?

BOY: *(Excited.)* Here, Daddy, open this. I made it myself.

DAD: Jesus Christ, give me a minute, will you?

MOM: Don't take that tone with Ben.

DAD: *(To MOM.)* I'll take whatever tone I want… *(He unwraps gift—a sweater, preferably purple or lavender.)*

MOM: Please, Ron, this is supposed to be a night for children…

BOY: Do you like it?

DAD: What is it?

BOY: It's a sweater.

MOM: Oh, it's beautiful, Ben.

DAD: You made this?

BOY: I went to the yarn store, picked out the color, and taught myself how to do it.

DAD: *(Tosses sweater down.)* What a lucky man I am! I've got a son and daughter in the same person.

MOM: *(Sensing trouble.)* Ben, darling, why don't you take the pastels to your room for a bit.

DAD: See if you can paint yourself a dress.

MOM: Really, Ron!

DAD: Knitting? Pastels? For Christ's sake, Kay…

MOM: How much have you had to drink?

DAD: Enough to see what's happening here!

BOY: Please don't fight. It's Christmas.

MOM: Give him some encouragement for a change.

DAD: Don't start lecturing me.

MOM: He makes beautiful things. That's his talent. He needs your support, and all you can do is berate him.

DAD: You're turning him into a goddamn fairy!

MOM: For God's sake, Ron!

BOY: *(Crying.)* Daddy, Mommy, stop it!

DAD: Shut up! *(He raises his hand.)*

MOM: Don't you dare hit your son!

DAD: Son? I don't see any son here!

MOM: I don't see any father here. Just a drunk!

DAD: *(He raises fist at her.)* You'd better watch yourself!

BOY: *(Crying.)* Don't hit Mom!

DAD: I told you to shut up!

(He hits BOY.)

MOM: You son of a bitch. A ten-year-old boy.

DAD: A ten-year-old pansy.

BOY: *(Crying.)* Please stop it. Please stop it.

(They disappear.)

SCROOGE: Please stop it. Please stop it.

PAST: *(Laughs.)* Reminds me of a movie I made, *The Misfits*. Your dad shipped you off to boarding school, didn't he?

SCROOGE: The less he had to see me, the better.

PAST: And school?

SCROOGE: A thrill a minute.

(BOY SCROOGE runs across stage, reacting to recorded voices.)

BOY 1: Hey, Ebenezer, suck my weezer.

BOY 2: I like you, Scrooge—you're fairy nice!

BOY SCROOGE: Shut up, both of you.

BOY 1: Ooh, such language, Ben. Bend over, Ben, and I'll give you what you want.

BOY SCROOGE: *(Crying and running out.)* Just leave me alone, please!

BOY 2: Oh-oh, the little girl's crying now.

BOY SCROOGE: I hate you both.

(BOY SCROOGE runs off.)

SCROOGE: *(To PAST.)* Why are you showing me this?

PAST: You fit in a little more in college, didn't you?

SCROOGE: I had grown wiser.

PAST: About yourself?

SCROOGE: About the world.

PAST: You joined a fraternity.

SCROOGE: No one knew I was gay.

PAST: I beg your pardon?

SCROOGE: Believe me, I would have fooled you, too.

(BEN appears and reacts to voices.)

GUY 1: Hey, guys, get a move on. It's keg night at the house.

GUY 2: Got a date coming, Ben?

BEN: Nah, not this weekend.

GUY 1: Tomorrow! Road trip time. We are all gonna get laid!

BEN: *(Laughing.)* Don't you ever think of anything else?

GUY 1: What else is there!

BEN: Baseball. I'm in training.

GUY 2: Screw training. Let's get blasted!

(BEN exits.)

PAST: Baseball?

SCROOGE: Yes, I butched it up. I even went out for a sport.

PAST: Well, that's one way to get into the locker rooms. But, Ben, honey, you're making me miss my own sweet Joe DiMaggio.

SCROOGE: I'll bet you didn't haunt *him*!

PAST: Yes, I did. All his life, I think... By the way, Ben, which were you—a pitcher or a catcher? *(She laughs.)*

SCROOGE: I never did anything with any guy while I was in college.

PAST: And were you happy?

SCROOGE: I was popular.

PAST: Well, that fine arts degree got you to New York.

SCROOGE: It sure did.

PAST: And an entry position with one of the leading interior designers in town. What was his name?

SCENE 5

Music, "We Need a Little Christmas," is heard from a tape deck in the offices of Fezziwig Fabrics, as FEZZIWIG and others including MARLEY, a ruggedly handsome young thirty-year-old, assemble. It is Christmas Eve, 1971.

SCROOGE: *(Seeing figure.)* My God, there he is—Old Fezziwig—what a wonderful, fun-loving old queen he was.

FEZZIWIG: Jake, Ben, all of you—stop all that boring work immediately, my little elves, and fill yourself up with spiced rum and cookies.

BEN: But Mr. Fezziwig, sir, it's only two o'clock.

FEZZIWIG: Never mind the clock, boys. This is Fezziwig Fabrics—not a sweatshop. It's Christmas Eve, and I believe the operative mood should be merry—very merry indeed. So grab an ass—I mean a glass—jingle your bells and make merry... or anyone else for that matter. *(He laughs loudly.)*

SCROOGE: He was outrageous... a great soul. It was so...

PAST: Liberating?

SCROOGE: Yes! Exactly. My God, he didn't care what people thought.

FEZZIWIG: *(Attaching two Christmas ornaments to his ears and singing.)* "Don we now our gay apparel!" What do you think, boys? Not too much, is it? I'll bet Diana Vreeland would love it! Now if I only had the proper gown...

MARLEY: Will this do?

(MARLEY hands him a throw. FEZZIWIG drapes it around himself.)

FEZZIWIG: Fantabulous! Just call me Christine Kringle! Now, boys, if you want to receive something from Miss Kringle, you've got to 'fess up—have you been naughty or nice? It would be awfully nice if you've been naughty! Uh, oh. Dangerously close to the mistletoe!

(He grabs MARLEY and kisses him.)

FEZZIWIG: Oh, you are beyond naughty. You are lascivious. And that's why you've done so well here, Jake. *(Laughs.)* All right. Who's next?

(He spots a boy and kisses him.)

FEZZIWIG: There's no escaping Miss Kringle! *(He laughs.)*

PAST: She's too much!

SCROOGE: Yes, wasn't it wonderful?

("We Need a Little Christmas" has been playing under, and now the instrumental dance part begins, and FEZZIWIG reaches toward BEN.)

FEZZIWIG: Come on, Ben, come dance with your Auntie Mame!

(He grabs BEN.)

FEZZIWIG: Or maimed old Auntie, as the case may be! *(He laughs.)*

BEN: *(Embarrassed and hesitant.)* Oh, Mr. Fezziwig, I don't think I…

FEZZIWIG: Angela Lansbury, eat your heart out!

(They dance a bit, FEZZIWIG exuberant, BEN awkward. MARLEY laughs.)

BEN: Mr. Fezziwig, I'm afraid I'm not much of a…

FEZZIWIG: *(Broadly.)* "On Dancer, on Prancer…"

(BEN looks at MARLEY as if to say, "Rescue me!" MARLEY cuts in on the couple. FEZZIWIG laughs.)

FEZZIWIG: Well, you're more of a prancer than a dancer, Ben, but then again, around here… who isn't?

(He laughs and exits with the others. BEN and MARLEY stop dancing as music diminishes in volume.)

BEN: I think Mr. Fezziwig's already had a few glasses of punch.

MARLEY: It only takes one glass to get him drunk.

BEN: One glass?

MARLEY: I'm not sure if it's the ninth or tenth one that does it!

(They laugh.)

BEN: I've never had this much fun at Christmas. It's all so…

MARLEY: Gay!

(They laugh.)

BEN: "New" is what I was going to say. It's all so new and wonderful.

MARLEY: This is the first chance I've had to really talk to you. And believe me, I've wanted to.

BEN: Me too.

MARLEY: I've seen you looking at me. Right?

BEN: Well, yes. I've wanted to get to know you better, too. I mean, I'm just starting out and all.

MARLEY: It's called cruising.

BEN: You're embarrassing me.

MARLEY: Hey, I've been cruising you, too. And I always get what I go after.

BEN: I'll bet you do. You're very attractive.

MARLEY: Now we're getting somewhere. So tell me—have you got a lover?

BEN: Oh, no!

MARLEY: Hey, I didn't ask you if you were an embezzler or anything. You're in New York, you're bright, you're gay, you're what—twenty-one?

BEN: Twenty-two.

MARLEY: And you're very hot.

BEN: Jake, stop it.

MARLEY: Hey, man, you should be flattered.

BEN: I am, I guess... but I'm not comfortable with this kind of talk.

MARLEY: Oh, I see. Sorry. The world doesn't know you're gay.

BEN: I don't think I should broadcast my sexuality to everyone.

MARLEY: Honey, they know.

BEN: That's not true. Why would anyone know I was gay?

MARLEY: Because they're alive!

BEN: What?

MARLEY: Ben, loosen up a little bit. It's not healthy to be repressed.

BEN: It's funny. My father used to think it unhealthy that I was so nelly, and now you think it's unhealthy for me to be butch.

MARLEY: Hey, be butch, but don't try to be straight. You'll only cause yourself pain. For Christ's sake, you're an "interior desecrator." You are guilty by association! *(He laughs.)*

BEN: I guess so.

MARLEY: Sorry if I riled you. But believe me, this town's a gold mine for a good-looking gay guy, if you learn how to work it. It's gotten me where I want to be so far.

BEN: I can see why.

MARLEY: So, you going home to your family tonight?

BEN: Nope.

MARLEY: Too far away?

BEN: My mother died last year. And my father is... gone.

MARLEY: Oh, I'm sorry.

BEN: That's all right. It's just that I don't have a lot of great Christmas memories.

MARLEY: That's funny. Somehow I pictured you in a Norman Rockwell painting.

BEN: More like George Bellows. You know those paintings of boxers? I felt like the referee.

MARLEY: Well, we had a different way of dealing with Christmas at my house.

BEN: Oh?

MARLEY: We ignored it.

BEN: Sometimes I wish we'd done that.

MARLEY: You should have been Jewish like me.

BEN: Oh, I see.

MARLEY: Then you could feel really guilty about being gay!

(They laugh.)

MARLEY: Hey, you are the lucky winner of Christmas dinner for two at a little place in the Village called Shun Lee Jake! You do accept, don't you?

BEN: I've never heard of it.

MARLEY: Okay, so it's Chinese takeout at my place! You got anything better to do?

BEN: No. Thanks Jake. It sounds great.

MARLEY: And who knows what our fortune cookies will say? Something salacious, I hope.

BEN: Do they make cookies like that?

MARLEY: Sure. They have them at that gay Chinese place—Hung So Lo!

BEN: *(Laughing.)* That's very funny.

MARLEY: My God, you do have a sense of humor! Ben, this is fate. I've got no family either. Two lost souls on Christmas Eve. We were meant to be together.

BEN: Do you believe in fate?

MARLEY: Only when it works in my favor… like tonight.

(They embrace.)

MARLEY: Hey, what do you say we go back to my place now? I've got a bottle of cheap champagne in the fridge—and poppers in the freezer!

BEN: You've got what?

MARLEY: What cave have you been living in? Well, don't worry. I'll teach you how to have fun.

BEN: You know what, Jake? I'm already having fun.

MARLEY: And it's just beginning, Ben!

(MARLEY hugs BEN. FEZZIWIG returns with the others, holding mistletoe. He runs to the couple and dangles the mistletoe over them.)

FEZZIWIG: Mary Mistletoe strikes again! *(He laughs.)*

(MARLEY quickly kisses BEN, relishing the opportunity.)

FEZZIWIG: *(To BEN.)* Oooh, watch out for that one, Ben. She's the naughtiest one of the bunch. Lucky you! *(To the crowd.)* Now, everyone, the moment you all—or at least I—have been waiting for. It's time for me to give you each a Christmas goose!

(He laughs and chases them.)

SCROOGE: And he did, too! Everyone of us, God bless him.

PAST: But what did all this partying cost him? More than a few bucks, I'll bet.

SCROOGE: Oh, he was never a good businessman, but that's not the point. What did it matter? He made everyone happy. He cared about us. He was like a father to us… *(SCROOGE stops.)*

PAST: A dollar for your thoughts, daddy!

SCROOGE: Nothing. Nothing.

SCENE 6

BEN and MARLEY appear. They are in their underwear, pajama bottoms, or robes. They have just made love. Music from radio plays "Have Yourself a Merry Little Christmas." Christmas, 1972.

PAST: Take a look over there, Ebby honey, and see yourself a year later. Cupid seems to have aimed well.

MARLEY: *(Lovingly.)* Thank you for my Christmas present.

BEN: What present? I didn't give you any present.

MARLEY: Oh yes you did. Just now.

BEN: *(Dawning on him.)* Oh. That present. A very personal one.

MARLEY: *(Laughing.)* And it didn't cost you anything either!

BEN: Careful. I might want to take it back.

MARLEY: No refunds. Only exchanges.

(They kiss.)

BEN: You know, when I was a kid, my mother once told me that the best Christmas gifts are the ones you make yourself. I guess she was right.

MARLEY: No, I think what she meant was that the best gifts are *guys* you make yourself.

(They laugh.)

BEN: Oh, Jake, I really do love you.

MARLEY: I'm glad we met, Ben.

BEN: Why do you find it so hard to say?

MARLEY: What?

BEN: Don't you love me?

MARLEY: Of course I do.

BEN: I like to hear it sometimes.

MARLEY: I'm sorry, Ben. It's just the way I am, I guess. My family wasn't very emotional… at least not that way.

BEN: Neither was mine. That's why I'm going to say once more—just to be redundant—I love you.

MARLEY: Me, too.

BEN: *(Laughing.)* You humpy son of a bitch.

(He grabs MARLEY's arm, teasingly, and tries to restrain him.)

BEN: Now, repeat after me. I love you!

MARLEY: *(Laughing, quickly escaping from BEN's grip and easily pinning him on the bed in a wrestling hold.)* Oh, you want to play rough, huh?

BEN: Ow! Stop it.

MARLEY: Yeah. You like it, don't you!

BEN: No, I don't!

(Escaping from grip as MARLEY lets go.)

BEN: Boy, you got a little carried away there, Jake.

MARLEY: *(Laughing.)* Well, you'll get a lot more of that sort of thing once we build the dungeon.

BEN: Are you on something?

MARLEY: So what do you think, do you want to have dinner out and see a film or something?

BEN: I don't know.

MARLEY: Come on, it's Christmas Eve. Let's have dinner in the Village and then go to Flamingo later and dance our tits off.

BEN: I'd rather stay here tonight. Just the two of us.

MARLEY: I wish you liked to dance more.

BEN: I do… it's just…

MARLEY: Just what?

BEN: It's the whole scene. It's too intense. It's too…

MARLEY: Too gay?

BEN: Yeah, I guess so.

MARLEY: Jeez, you're still hung up on that shit. Come on out and live, for Christ's sake.

BEN: I just don't want to.

MARLEY: Then what do you want?

BEN: I want to be with you. I want you to move in with me.

MARLEY: I'm not sure it's the right thing, Ben.

BEN: Of course it's the right thing. You said it yourself. We were made for each other.

MARLEY: It's a big move for me.

BEN: *(Laughs.)* It's not that big a move. You're only twelve blocks away.

MARLEY: You know what I mean.

BEN: We'll pack your things this weekend.

MARLEY: I do miss it when I'm not with you.

BEN: *(Teasing.)* You'll save money.

MARLEY: That's true.

BEN: So is it a done deal?

MARLEY: Done deal!

(They embrace.)

MARLEY: But don't get the idea that I'm going to sit home at night and knit with you, okay?

BEN: We'll see. We'll see. Thank you, Jake. I love you.

MARLEY: I'm not taking any wedding vows!

BEN: *(Handing MARLEY a box.)* Merry Christmas, Jake.

MARLEY: *(Looking at box.)* My God, Tiffany?

BEN: Open it.

MARLEY: *(Taking out watch and looking at it.)* Oh, baby… it's gorgeous.

BEN: Just like you.

MARLEY: But you shouldn't have, Ben. It's too extravagant.

BEN: You're worth it.

MARLEY: No, I'm not.

BEN: Hey. It looks great on you. It'll let everyone know we're moving up. And every time you look at it, it will remind you how much I love you.

MARLEY: Thank you, Ben.

BEN: *(Embracing MARLEY.)* I said, "I love you."

MARLEY: *(Laughing.)* Okay. Okay. I love you, too.

(He kisses BEN.)

MARLEY: Satisfied?

BEN: Very.

(Music, "Have Yourself a Merry Little Christmas," comes back up on the radio. BEN sings it to MARLEY, as scene blacks out. They disappear.)

PAST: *(Singing.)* "I want to be loved by you, just you, and nobody else but you…" So you moved in together, worked your fannies off, and did become an unbeatable team, at least in business. And dear old Fezziwig. What happened to him?

SCROOGE: He ran into some financial difficulties.

SCENE 7

FEZZIWIG and BEN alone in office.

BEN: You wanted to see me, Mr. Fezziwig?

FEZZIWIG: *(Troubled.)* Ben, you are the smartest and sharpest one in this company. I wonder if you would look over my books for me. I'm afraid I'm in a bit of a mess.

BEN: Of course, if you like, sir…

FEZZIWIG: I'm only showing this to you, Ben.

BEN: *(Looking at books.)* Thank you. I understand, sir. How long have these people owed you money, Mr. Fezziwig?

FEZZIWIG: A few years. They've been down on their luck recently, and I wanted to give them more time…

BEN: Why did you ever agree to a loan like this? And, my God, you owe this bank a fortune…

FEZZIWIG: Can you help me, Ben?

BEN: Well, yes, I think so, but you've got to start by refinancing this and… *(He stops and looks away.)*

FEZZIWIG: What's the matter?

BEN: Nothing. Let me take the books home tonight, Mr. Fezziwig. I'm sure I can handle this.

FEZZIWIG: Thank you, Ben. Thank you.

(Scene fades.)

SCENE 8

BEN stays. MARLEY enters.

MARLEY: We've got him by the balls now, Ben. *(Looking at papers.)* These books were a gift from heaven.

BEN: He's got no way out, unless we help him to…

MARLEY: Fuck him. Now's the time to pounce. *(Into telephone.)* Hello. Jake Markowitz calling for Mr. Cohn. Yes, I'll hold. *(To BEN.)* His problems are our opportunities, buddy. Survival of the fittest.

BEN: I think I've worked out all the details.

MARLEY: You sure have. It's brilliant. *(Back into phone.)* Hello, Roy. Jake here. Great party last night. I'm still recovering. Where do you find those guys? Roy, about the Fezziwig thing— Let's go ahead and make the offer. I know it's lowball—so low it's almost hellish. But he'll accept. He's up shit's creek. Right. Thanks, Roy. *(He hangs up.)*

BEN: Well, Jake, tomorrow we'll own the company.

MARLEY: You and me, babe. We're going to rule New York.

BEN: Kindred spirits.

MARLEY: *(High-fiving or embracing BEN.)* Kindred spirits.

(They exit.)

PAST: Talk like that gives us good spirits a bad name, honey. I wanted to marry a millionaire once in a movie, but I would have drawn the line at you two, Ebby! How did you feel when dear old Fezziwig lost everything to you two pit vipers?

SCROOGE: Marley and I were men of business.

PAST: At the risk of sounding repetitious, baby, mankind was also your business. Their common welfare was your business. But, I got to agree, you two were damn good at making money. Yet something was happening to both of you.

SCENE 9

BEN and MARLEY in office. January, 1974.

MARLEY: We're in the big time now, Ben. All of Fezziwig's clients. Fag hag matrons with no taste. We'll take their money and give them class—or a reasonable facsimile.

BEN: *(Sternly.)* Two things: Do not ever use the phrase "fag hag" again. I don't like the implication. And speaking of class, the first thing to go is the name of this firm.

MARLEY: I'm way ahead of you. *(Proudly.)* "We are proud to announce that Fezziwig Fabrics is now Markowitz & Scrooge!"

BEN: Uh-uh.

MARLEY: What? Scrooge & Markowitz? That's okay, I guess. You deserve the honor.

You're the one who had the idea and did all the work to make it happen.

BEN: No.

MARLEY: Just the initials? S&M Fabrics! Fabulous. Love it.

BEN: Yes, you would. Jake, it's your name. It has to go.

MARLEY: What? Scrooge & Co.? No way.

BEN: My point eludes you. It's "Markowitz." It just doesn't sound right.

MARLEY: Change my name?

BEN: Markham? Marston?

MARLEY: Do you really think it's that important?

BEN: Do you trust my marketing instincts?

MARLEY: Absolutely. You are one shrewd son of a bitch.

BEN: Arnold Isaacs or Arnold Scaasi—which has the better ring?

MARLEY: Are you joking?

BEN: As you should know by now, Jake, I never joke.

MARLEY: Yeah, well, maybe you should a little more. I used to think I was ruthless, but you're beating me at my own game, Ben. You're getting a little scary.

BEN: "You gotta make things happen for yourself." Your words, Jake. And very true. And they are much more likely to happen if we change your name.

MARLEY: You are too much. But, hey, fuck it... If you think it will mean higher fees to become a WASP, just call me... uh... Mr. Marley.

PAST: *(Laughs.)* Well, honey, the former Norma Jean Baker can relate to that sort of thing... And your fees did go up, as you became grossly overpaid to offer design to the upper crust.

SCROOGE: I learned quickly how to please them, and they had lots of money.

PAST: I guess they kind of liked your stern demeanor and rigid opinions. Talk about S&M! But what about Jake? Was he still pleased with you?

SCROOGE: He started spending much more time out of the house.

PAST: So as you two grew richer, your relationship took a turn for the worse. Well, eventually, something's got to give, honey... *(Sings from* Some Like It Hot.*)* "Running wild, lost control..." etc.

SCENE 10

Music up: some disco version of a Christmas song. MARLEY is singing and moving to the music as he prepares a line of cocaine. He is a bit high. Christmas Eve, 1979.

BEN: *(Entering with fabric swatches or workbooks.)* Please turn that shit off. I'm trying to work.

MARLEY: It's Christmas Eve, for Christ's sake.

BEN: That is a redundancy. *(Turns off radio.)*

MARLEY: Very funny. I'm trying to get into the Christmas spirit. *(He staggers a bit.)*

BEN: You've gotten into the spirits all right.

MARLEY: Right you are. Chivas Regal. A regal scotch, indeed. Fit for a queen.

BEN: You're getting a little too fond of your scotch, Jake. It's unbecoming.

MARLEY: Unbecoming to whom? I find it perfectly becoming. And fitting. I must have been Scottish in an earlier life.

BEN: Yes, I can see you now, cruising the Highlands in a leather kilt.

MARLEY: Well, I'm no longer a Jew. You took care of that for me. Maybe I'll come back as Rob Roy after I'm gone and haunt you. Boo! *(He laughs.)*

BEN: *(Looking at cocaine.)* What are you doing?

MARLEY: *(Snorts the line.)* What do you think?

BEN: I told you to keep that out of the house.

MARLEY: All gone! Come on, give me a kiss.

(He tries to embrace BEN, who pushes him away.)

BEN: Jake, your breath is beyond belief.

(MARLEY gets his coat.)

BEN: Where are you going?

MARLEY: Out. Remember that, Ben? Going out? *(After a beat.)* Come with me. Let's have some fun.

BEN: Fun? Some smoke-filled bar downtown, followed by chemically induced euphoria on the dance floor? No, thank you.

MARLEY: Don't be that way, Ben. We used to like doing things together. *(He picks up newspaper.)* Hey, how about the opera! You like the opera. We could do that tonight. *(Excited as he sees listing.) La Traviata*! Fabulous. One of your favorites.

BEN: Do you know what the Met charges for tickets these days?

MARLEY: I hope you're joking.

BEN: As you know, Jake…

(MARLEY joins in.)

BOTH: I never joke!

MARLEY: What's the point of making all this money if you don't spend some of it?

BEN: You'd have a lot more if it didn't keep vanishing up your nostrils.

MARLEY: Fuck you, Ben. At least I have a life.

BEN: I thought our business was our life.

MARLEY: That's not enough. Call it selfish or sleazy or whatever you want, but I like pleasure, and I've got the money to do anything I want. This is my life, and I'm going to enjoy the ride. When it's over, it's over. If I need a lecture on morality, I'll go to a church. I'll be damned if I'm going to stay here and rot with you. I've got better things to do.

BEN: Sex with strangers, for instance?

MARLEY: They don't lay guilt trips on me all the time.

BEN: We used to have sex here.

MARLEY: Ben, you can have sex any time you want it.

BEN: Really? How?

MARLEY: Pay! *(He laughs.)*

BEN: Very funny.

MARLEY: Not me, of course. I mean, I know I'm a slut, but I have to draw the line somewhere. But I do know a couple of working boys who will do a lot for a couple of hundred bucks.

BEN: You disgust me.

MARLEY: No, you might like these two guys, Ben. They're like a younger version of you and me. They'll screw anything—and anyone—for the right price. Hey, think of it as a charity. You're just helping a couple of boys to afford life in New York. Yeah, I like that. Scrooge and Marley finally support their favorite charity!

BEN: *(Starting to exit.)* There's no point in continuing this conversation.

MARLEY: Ben, I'm sorry. Maybe it's me. Maybe I need things I don't get from you anymore. But if you ever really loved me, please try to understand…

BEN: How can I love what you've become?

MARLEY: What? What have I become, Ben?

BEN: A self-indulgent faggot!

MARLEY: *(Laughs.)* And your point is?

BEN: I've had enough of it.

MARLEY: Excuse me?

BEN: I'm not going to take it any more. It's going to stop!

MARLEY: What's going to stop?

BEN: Your lifestyle. I don't like it.

MARLEY: Deal with it, Ben.

BEN: *(Angrier.)* I won't deal with it!

MARLEY: You are my lover, not my father!

BEN: I hate that word.

MARLEY: Which one?

BEN: You're not my lover. You're a pathetic victim of your own indulgence. Out all night, sleeping half the day. You're a vampire.

MARLEY: No, Ben, a vampire needs blood to feed on. And you've got none. You're a corpse.

BEN: It's you who's killing me!

MARLEY: That's it. I'm out of here. *(He starts to leave.)*

BEN: Off to the Club Baths? Or is it the St. Marks tonight?

MARLEY: Both, probably!

BEN: Then go. Get out! I'm tired of your escapades and what it's doing to our business.

MARLEY: Our business? You know how many of our clients I'm going to run into tonight? You know how many jobs we've gotten because I've slept with them? Wake up, Ben. You screw them at the office, and I screw them at the baths! *(He laughs.)*

BEN: And what about our firm's reputation?

MARLEY: What are you afraid of? That they'll find out you're queer too? They know, Ben. They all know. You are probably the only one in New York who doesn't know that you're a big fucking fairy!

BEN: *(Raising his hand.)* Shut up right now!

MARLEY: Please! Hit me, for Christ's sake. At least it'll be some physical contact!

BEN: Go on, go out and get drunk, get high, and drop dead, for all I care.

MARLEY: *(Leaving.)* If I do, at least I'll know I lived. Merry fucking Christmas! *(Exits.)*

PAST: Gee, you *are* human, Ebby honey! I was starting to wonder. Well, you two continued to make more money, lots of it. Diamonds may be a girl's best friend, but I think you went overboard, honey.

SCROOGE: I committed myself entirely to my work. I had lost the only other thing I loved.

PAST: Or had Jake lost you?

SCROOGE: I don't know.

PAST: Whatever happened, Ben, you got even richer.

SCROOGE: I became more focused.

PAST: "Cutthroat" is the word I would have picked.

SCROOGE: Ours is a very competitive area.

PAST: And what about Jake? Seems like he went off the deep end.

SCROOGE: He partied even harder than he worked. All night, every night.

PAST: And the drugs. The way he indulged, he should have been a pharmacist.

SCROOGE: Why? Why?

PAST: Perhaps to numb the pain? Some people call me a dumb blonde, but, Ebby honey, I think I understand.

SCROOGE: Perhaps.

PAST: You two hardly spoke to each other anymore, even after he got sick.

SCROOGE: There was nothing I could do.

PAST: Except be there.

SCROOGE: It happened so fast.

PAST: Come on, Ebby, we've got one more bus stop to make. Do you remember visiting him at St. Vincent's twelve years ago?

SCROOGE: I do. A bitterly cold night.

SCENE 11

"Silent Night" is playing, as we see MARLEY in bed or chair in a hospital room, IV attached. Christmas Eve, 1988. We hear the constant beep of a heart monitor.

LOUDSPEAKER VOICE: Attention, please. Visiting hours are now over.

MARLEY: *(Faintly.)* Ben...

BEN: *(Awkwardly.)* Well, Jake, I've got to leave. There's nothing else you need?

MARLEY: Wrong...

BEN: What? Don't talk, Jake.

MARLEY: Wrong. My life.

BEN: Who's to say you were wrong? It's too late now.

MARLEY: You.

BEN: Me? With all due respect, Jake, it's you who had the wild lifestyle and...

MARLEY: Save yourself.

BEN: What's that, Jake? Save myself?

MARLEY: Love...

BEN: You'd better try to rest now.

(NURSE enters, sensing trouble.)

NURSE: I'm sorry. Visiting hours are over.

(BEN starts to leave.)

BEN: Yes. Yes.

MARLEY: *(Pointing to his watch.)* Ben...

BEN: Don't talk, Jake.

MARLEY: For you... keep this...

(BEN takes watch.)

BEN: Yes, Jake. I will.

MARLEY: Believe me... believe me...

(NURSE escorts BEN out.)

NURSE: I'm sorry, sir. You really do have to go.

MARLEY: Believe me.

BEN: Yes, yes. I'm leaving now, Jake. Goodbye.

(NURSE and BEN exit. Lights stay on MARLEY.)

SCROOGE: *(To PAST.)* Why are you showing me this? This is too painful. Take me out of here.

PAST: Not yet, honey. Your timing leaves a bit to be desired…

(She gestures to MARLEY, and SCROOGE looks at him.)

MARLEY: Please, Ben, believe me. I always loved you. I always loved you. I always…

(The beep of the heart monitor changes to a steady tone; MARLEY dies. SCROOGE recoils.)

SCROOGE: Jake, Jake, I'm sorry. I loved you, too, Jake. I don't know what happened. I don't know why. Forgive me, Jake. I'm sorry. I'm so sorry…

PAST: Sometimes I think it would be easier to avoid old age, to die young, but then you'd never complete your life, would you? You'd never wholly know yourself…

SCROOGE: It sounded like he had just seen hell.

PAST: Maybe he did. Anyway, it didn't seem to affect you too badly at the time. Did you feel sorry when you took over his townhouse and moved your offices there? Did you feel any sense of gratitude to someone who once shared his life with you? Or did you feel he— *(She mimics SCROOGE's earlier comment.)* "had only himself to blame" and got what he deserved? *(Laughs and starts to go.)* Bye-bye, Ben, honey. Thank you ever so. "Money, that's what it's all about…"

(Music starts again as she sings.)

PAST: "'Cause we all lose our charm in the end. But square cut, or pear shaped, these rocks don't lose their shape, diamonds are a girl's best friend…"

(She laughs loudly and exits as music rises to a deafening crescendo.)

SCROOGE: *(Puts his hands to his ears and runs back to his bed.)* None of this is happening! I don't believe it! I won't believe it! It's all a figment… It's all a nightmare… It's all humbug… humbug… *humbug! (He throws the covers over his head and collapses.)*

(Blackout.)

ACT II
SCENE 1

After a short pause, a bell strikes two, and a bright light appears. Music comes up from radio (something outlandish), and SCROOGE tries to shut it off. It continues, louder. The GHOST OF CHRISTMAS PRESENT appears—a buoyant, radiant, woman dressed festively and flamboyantly with ornaments, holly, etc., as part of her wardrobe. She is dancing with the music. (Note: Ideally, this ghost should be a drag queen. In a small theater, she might enter from the audience, looking for SCROOGE.) Music continues under scene.

PRESENT: Get your ass out of bed, and look over here, Ben. That's right. You've never seen the likes of me before, have you? *(She laughs.)*

SCROOGE: I rarely get to Cherry Grove.

PRESENT: No, you don't get anywhere. That's why I am here.

SCROOGE: Who are you?

PRESENT: I am the Spirit of Christmas Present.

SCROOGE: Are you a man or a woman?

PRESENT: What would you like me to be?

SCROOGE: Gone!

PRESENT: Not until I've dragged you out of here for a bit.

SCROOGE: Where did you get that outfit?

PRESENT: I made it myself! Well, I did have a little help from Carmen Miranda. What do you think? *(She turns around, showing off costume.)*

SCROOGE: Stunning.

PRESENT: Not refined enough for you, I'm sure, but bright and festive and gay—if I may use that word in its old-fashioned way. All the things that you disdain. But let's sashay out of here, Ben, because we are about to share Christmas with some folks you may recognize.

SCROOGE: You know, I'm a little tired from the last ghost. Couldn't I just sit this one out?

PRESENT: Time's a wasting. Walk this way.

(She sashays a bit to the side. SCROOGE follows.)

PRESENT: I was speaking figuratively, honey! Now, touch my robe.

(SCROOGE grabs firmly.)

PRESENT: Hey, not that tight. And not that close. You don't know me that well! *(À la Bette Davis.)* Fasten your seat belt. It's going to be a bumpy night! *(She laughs.)*

SCENE 2

Music changes to a Christmas rock song from a radio/tape deck in CRATCHIT's apartment. It is an East Village studio simply but smartly furnished. CRATCHIT and his lover TIM are there.

CRATCHIT: Yup, another Christmas all alone. I don't know why I even bother to invite him every year. He looks at me like I'm crazy to have suggested it.

TIM: But you do suggest it, and that's why I love you, Bob.

CRATCHIT: Anyway, what's he missing? Just a potluck meal, and, if our friends come through for us, some undrinkable wine. *(He laughs.)*

TIM: *(Holding up box of chocolates.)* At least we'll have a fabulous dessert, thanks to Sotheby's!

CRATCHIT: You got them at an auction?

TIM: No, I temped there this week, remember? One of the executives gave it to me yesterday. He said I looked thin.

CRATCHIT: Maybe you shouldn't work too much. I don't want you to wear yourself down again.

TIM: I'm fine. And good news. They can use me for a few weeks after the new year. Who knows—maybe they'll hire me full time… with benefits!

CRATCHIT: Okay, New Year's resolution: I will demand that Scrooge give us health insurance, or I quit. Simple as that.

TIM: I don't want you to quit. And if you do that, he'll fire you.

(He embraces CRATCHIT.)

TIM: We're doing okay.

CRATCHIT: I could always find another job somewhere. Maybe.

TIM: Don't be silly. He's one of the top designers in New York. And let's face it, if you weren't valuable to him, he would have fired you already.

CRATCHIT: I'm only valuable to him 'cause he could get me cheap! I started at the bottom, and I stayed there.

TIM: That's not true, and you know it.

CRATCHIT: But I'd like to be appreciated, at least.

TIM: I appreciate you. I love you very much, and I don't want to see you quit something that could be great for you in the future. You've learned so much already.

CRATCHIT: Yeah, I guess so. I do think he values my opinions, on the rare occasions that he actually asks for them.

TIM: Of course he does. How could he not. He's got to have *some* redeeming qualities.

CRATCHIT: Yeah, well, Hitler loved his dogs, too.

(Buzzer sounds.)

TIM: The family's here. *(He gets up and presses button by the door.)*

CRATCHIT: I love you, Tim.

TIM: I love you, too. *(He pauses, then says broadly.)* Prediction for the new year! Scrooge recognizes your incredible talent, promotes you, and hires me as secretary and office manager!

CRATCHIT: And Jesse Helms leads the Gay Pride Parade this June!

TIM: Hey, you gotta believe…

CRATCHIT: Here's what I believe, with all my heart. That I love you, will always love you, and that no matter what, together we are unbeatable.

(Knock on door. CRATCHIT opens door. CAROL and MARIA enter. They are lovers. CAROL has a shopping bag, and MARIA has a tiny, sad-looking tree. MARIA speaks with an accent.)

CAROL: Merry Christmas, boys. Wait till you see what Father Christmas found for you!

MARIA: "Twas the night before Christmas, and all through the city,
I looked for a tree that you boys could make pretty." Feliz Navidad!

CRATCHIT: What the hell is that?

MARIA: What do you think it is? A Christmas tree!

CAROL: From Chernobyl!

MARIA: Hey, what do you want? This is New York. I had a lot of trouble finding it. These things don't grow on trees, you know.

CRATCHIT: That one certainly didn't.

CAROL: *(Laughs.)* You won't believe how much she paid for it!

CRATCHIT: You gave someone money for that?

MARIA: Nah, actually, if you want the truth, I found it on the street.

TIM: It's divine.

MARIA: That way, I could save my money to buy some ornaments to make it fabulous. And look at these! *(She takes two beautiful ball ornaments out of her knapsack.)*

TIM: I always knew you had balls, Maria!

(They laugh.)

SCROOGE: Their place is so small.

PRESENT: It's called a studio. Or more precisely, a chopped up railroad flat. But, hey, rents are high.

SCROOGE: And yet it looks quite comfortable. Like they've created something wonderful out of nothing.

PRESENT: Well, baby, look who Cratchit learned from—one of the crowned heads!

SCROOGE: He's really quite talented.

PRESENT: And even in this tiny apartment, with no money, they seem so happy. Strange, huh?

(TIM coughs a bit.)

SCROOGE: Is Tim all right?

(PRESENT gestures toward the others.)

TIM: I love the tree. It reminds me of Snoopy.

MARIA: *(Tries to say "Snoopy.")* What is "Es-Snoopy?"

CAROL: *(Noticing TIM and getting a gift.)* I can't wait any longer. I want you to have this now. Merry Christmas, Tim.

TIM: *(Opening present.)* What can it be? A Rolex watch? A Caribbean cruise? A year's supply of T-cells?

MARIA: Maybe it's an Es-Snoopy?

CRATCHIT: Snoopy is a dog.

MARIA: Oh, forget it, man. No dogs allowed near this tree!

(They laugh.)

TIM: *(Sees it's a knit sweater.)* Oh, Carol, it's gorgeous. Did you make it?

CAROL: *(Laughing.)* No, it came from Bergdorf's!

MARIA: She only shoplifts at the best places.

CAROL: Of course I made it. Try it on.

(He does. CRATCHIT helps.)

MARIA: Hey, everyone, get yourself a cup or glass, because I have another surprise for us. *(She takes bottle of wine from her bag.)* Vino! Good stuff, too. *(She twists off cap and pours wine into each glass.)*

CAROL: And if there's any left over, you can use it as a paint remover!

CRATCHIT: At least it's not a cardboard box.

TIM: Have some of this bread I baked.

CAROL: I don't know how you do it. I can't even bake a potato.

CRATCHIT: Who cares when you have style like yours! Look at you. You dress to kill.

MARIA: That's the way she cooks, too!

(They laugh.)

TIM: Baking bread is easy. You just have to start with a good dough.

MARIA: It smells fabulous. What is it?

TIM: Dill. It's dill bread.

CRATCHIT: And to make a good dill bread, you have to start with...

TIM: A good dill dough.

(They laugh.)

CAROL: Was that a setup?

CRATCHIT: I cannot tell a lie. Yes.

CAROL: *(Laughing.)* What is it with you guys? All you ever think about is sex.

CRATCHIT: And you don't?

CAROL: Of course not.

MARIA: *(To CAROL.)* Speak for yourself, babe!

TIM: So, Carol, when you see a beautiful woman on the street, you don't give her a second thought?

MARIA: *(Laughing.)* No, she's too busy with the first one!

CAROL: Excuse me. It's Christmas Eve. Could we please talk about something else?

MARIA: Good idea. Change of subject. Let's talk about you two. What do you two think about sex?

CAROL: Oh, please.

(They laugh.)

MARIA: No. What do you think? Does size really matter?

CRATCHIT: I don't know. Why don't you ask Tiny Tim?

TIM: *(Laughing.)* You bitch! No one's ever called me that and lived!

SCROOGE: They're having such fun.

PRESENT: Oh, I don't know. Squandering their valuable time and what little money they have?

SCROOGE: It's… it's perplexing.

PRESENT: It's my influence, Ben. They know me very well here. They invite me to join them every year.

CAROL: *(Taking a glass.)* Well, gang, let's get this party off the runway.

TIM: I'd like to make a toast.

MARIA: Go for it, chico.

TIM: To Mr. Scrooge!

(They recoil.)

CAROL: Scrooge! That son of a bitch? What in God's name would make you think of toasting a man like that?

TIM: Christmas.

CRATCHIT: Oh, Tim.

TIM: Hey, he's a miserable old fart and all, but we're celebrating the birth of someone who urged us to love our enemies, so I wish him well.

MARIA: Well, I don't, that fucking *maricon*! He makes Bob work like a dog and pays him crap, and he can't even provide health care, with you sick as shit… oh, sorry.

CAROL: No health care?

CRATCHIT: He doesn't believe in it—for me, that is. He says it's a bad investment. Of course, I know he has it for himself.

CAROL: It's inhuman. How can you work for a man like that?

CRATCHIT: What else am I going to do?

CAROL: Find a job where you're appreciated.

CRATCHIT: I don't have a degree. I'm still learning. Who's going to hire me?

CAROL: Lots of people. And I'm going to keep pushing you till you do.

TIM: We're getting by.

CRATCHIT: Barely. But there are organizations that help. It's sad about Scrooge. But he's his own worst enemy.

MARIA: Not while I'm alive!

CAROL: I'd rather work for the Marquis de Sade.

MARIA: *(To CAROL.)* I'll bet you would, you kinky thing.

TIM: Let's not talk about all this now. It's Christmas.

CRATCHIT: You're right, Tim. Let's not let the Grinch steal our Christmas.

CAROL: Well, there's one thing I have that Mr. Scrooge will never have.

MARIA: An overdrawn checking account.

(They lift their glasses.)

CAROL: A family! I would like to wish a very Merry Christmas to my best friends.

MARIA: But since they can't be here, us three will have to do...

(They laugh.)

CAROL: My family! You.

(She kisses MARIA.)

CAROL: You.

(She kisses CRATCHIT.)

CAROL: And you.

(She kisses TIM.)

MARIA: Salud!

TIM: God bless us, everyone!

SCROOGE: Is he very ill?

PRESENT: He's doing all right at the moment. New medications have helped.

SCROOGE: Yes, I hear they are very effective.

PRESENT: And very expensive.

SCROOGE: Will he be all right?

PRESENT: What business is it of yours?

SCROOGE: What will become of him?

PRESENT: Are there no hospices? Are there no shelters? *(She laughs.)*

(PRESENT gestures, and a new scene appears.)

SCENE 3

NICK, who was the fundraiser in the opening scene, talks to his girlfriend, JEAN, on a street. They are carrying gift baskets and presents.

NICK: He actually used the word "humbug!"

JEAN: *(Perplexed.)* Humbug?

NICK: *(Putting up his hands.)* Don't ask! Pathetic, really. Alone and miserable in a huge old house where he shuts out the world. *(Laughing.)* My God, he's Miss Havisham!

JEAN: *(Laughs.)* You should have asked if he might donate the wedding cake!

NICK: I thought for a moment he was joking. But believe me, there's nothing funny about him. And he makes tons of money as a decorator.

JEAN: Having good taste does not make you a nice person. Look at you, for instance. You've got the most awful shirt on I've ever seen, and you're the kindest man I know.

NICK: What's the matter with this shirt? It's a Christmas shirt.

JEAN: It is festive. And very much in keeping with the Christmas spirit.

NICK: Speaking of the Christmas spirit, do you believe it's better to give than receive?

JEAN: I do indeed.

NICK: Then give me a kiss, please.

(She kisses him.)

NICK: No, you're wrong. It's definitely better to receive.

JEAN: Are you sure?

NICK: Well, I'd better make sure.

(He kisses her.)

NICK: I take it back. It is definitely better to give.

JEAN: *(Laughs.)* We'd better get going. We've got a lot to do tonight.

NICK: Are you sure you don't mind spending Christmas Eve this way?

JEAN: *(Laughing.)* No, I'd rather be home listening to Handel's *Messiah* for the thousandth time.

NICK: At least you'd be warmer.

JEAN: Darling, I am doing exactly what I want to do tonight. And I am with you.

NICK: What made me lucky enough to have you in my life?

JEAN: *(Laughs.)* I've always wanted to meet a man secure enough to wear a shirt like that!

SCROOGE: What are they talking about?

PRESENT: You just don't get it, do you?

SCROOGE: Well, what are they doing?

PRESENT: They're bringing Christmas gifts to people like Tim. And then they'll stop by some hospitals and shelters.

SCROOGE: Some of the gifts look like toys.

PRESENT: What else would you bring children?

SCROOGE: Children? Are there many sick children?

PRESENT: What does that matter? If they're going to die, perhaps they should do so and decrease the surplus population?

SCROOGE: How can you be so…

PRESENT: So… what, honey?

SCENE 4

Festive music as scene switches to stylish East Side apartment living room, where FRED and a close friend, NOEL, are preparing for a Christmas party.

FRED: *(Arranging things while singing "Jingle Bells.")* "Bells on bobtail ring, making spirits bright…"

NOEL: *(Entering with a glass and saying to FRED, as if at an audition.)* Thank you, thank you. We'll be in touch with your agent.

FRED: What the hell is a bobtail, anyway?

NOEL: I don't know… a horse's ass?

FRED: Oh, that reminds me. Guess who made me come to his office today and service him?

NOEL: You trashy slut!

FRED: Scrooge.

NOEL: *(Spitting out drink.)* What are you, a necrophiliac?

FRED: He made me bring over some goddamn fabrics. At five o'clock! Just to bust my chops, I'm sure.

NOEL: To quote a former first lady, why didn't you just say no?

FRED: I wanted to make a point of telling him in person what I thought of him.

NOEL: And did you?

FRED: In a way. But I sort of chickened out. You know, I've known him since the Fezziwig days, and he wasn't always such an ogre.

NOEL: Yeah, well, that was then. This is now.

FRED: I don't know. I kind of feel sorry for him. He's not really all *that* bad.

(They groan.)

FRED: I mean, there's got to be some hope, right?

NOEL: The only hope you have is that he'll buy more fabrics from you.

FRED: *(Laughing.)* That's true. He is a very good client. How's the eggnog?

NOEL: Lethal. Who's coming?

FRED: The usual suspects.

NOEL: *(Taking a stack of cards from his pocket.)* I brought a great game. Gay trivia.

FRED: Fabulous.

NOEL: *(Taking a card.)* Here. Try one. "Name one gay British monarch."

FRED: Henry the Eighth!

NOEL: Henry the Eighth?

FRED: Big queen!

NOEL: What about those six wives?

FRED: All covers! Anyone who built Hampton Court had to be gay.

NOEL: Sorry, you lose. Edward the Second would have worked, among others.

FRED: *(Taking a card.)* My turn. "At what age did Oscar Wilde first have sex with a man?"

NOEL: Six!

FRED: Thirty-two.

SCROOGE: *(To GHOST.)* I knew that! I knew that!

FRED: Wilde was already married and thirty-two when he first did it with a guy. As opposed to you, darling, who first did it at six with thirty-two guys.

(They laugh.)

SCROOGE: *(Enjoying himself.)* I'd be very good at this game.

PRESENT: And yet why are they wasting their time with it? It's not making them money.

SCROOGE: That's not the point. It's fun.

FRED: *(Taking another card.)* "In *The Wizard of Oz*, what is the name of the character who later becomes the Wicked Witch of the West?"

SCROOGE: *(Excited.)* Oh, that's so easy. Everyone knows that!

NOEL: Margaret Hamilton!

FRED: Wrong! Not the actress. The name of the character. *(Giving a hint by mimicking the "bicycle music" of the character: "Da-Da Da-Da Da-Daaah Duh…" etc.)*

SCROOGE: *(Yelling out toward them.)* Elvira Gulch!

FRED: *(Giving another hint.)* I can see her now, all in black, that miserable, dried-up old crone…

NOEL: Ebenezer Scrooge!

FRED: *(Mimicking Billie Burke as Glinda.)* Oh, no, that's her sister, and she's even worse…

(SCROOGE turns away. They laugh.)

NOEL: *(Taking a drink.)* God! Can you imagine anyone even touching that repulsive reptile?

FRED: I suppose a hustler might, on a slow night, for triple the going rate.

NOEL: I hear Scrooge used to be in the phone book under "Old Maids," but now she's just an unlusted number!

(They laugh.)

SCROOGE: *(Moving in and addressing them.)* I had someone who loved me, dammit. Someone who loved me very much...

PRESENT: *(Singing in a mocking way.)* "I talk to the trees, but they don't listen to me..."

FRED: Well, what goes around, comes around. He'll get his some day.

NOEL: I hope so. It's not fair. All the wonderful people we've lost, and *she's* still alive!

FRED: God'll get her. *(Taking card.)* Okay, one more. "Name a famous anti-communist, right-wing American politician who was also a closeted homosexual."

NOEL: Ronald Reagan!

(They laugh as scene fades.)

PRESENT: Isn't it wonderful, Ben, to know you make people laugh so much? *(She laughs and gestures.)* Now, honey, let's go to the beach!

SCROOGE: What?

PRESENT: Brighton Beach!

SCENE 5

SVETLANA and her husband PYTOR in their home. We see SVETLANA, dressed simply, looking for a spot to place a small present. She sings a Christmas carol.

SVETLANA: *(Singing.)* "What child is this," etc.

PRESENT: Recognize this woman?

SCROOGE: Why, of course, it's my housekeeper, Svetlana.

(PYTOR enters. He is brusque and drunk.)

PRESENT: And the man?

SCROOGE: Her husband, I suppose.

PRESENT: You suppose? This woman changes your sheets and scrubs your floors, and you don't even know if she has a family? Quick—what's her last name?

SCROOGE: I don't know.

SVETLANA: *(She turns to him expectantly.)* You have tree?

PYTOR: *Nyet.*

SVETLANA: Why not?

PYTOR: No trees left. All gone.

SVETLANA: Where you been? Rudichka asleep now.

PYTOR: Looking for trees.

SVETLANA: In bar? *Da*... no trees in bar! *(Confronting him.)* Give me money back. I get tree.

PYTOR: I said, *no trees.*

SVETLANA: We must have tree for Rudichka. Is Christmas!

PYTOR: Rudichka! Rudichka! Everything for Rudichka.

SVETLANA: Everything? No! Something! We must have *something* for Rudichka.

PYTOR: *(Taking pint vodka bottle from pocket.)* All right! Here! Give him this. *(He laughs.)*

SVETLANA: You use money for this?

PYTOR: Why not? Is good use for money. More useful than tree.

SVETLANA: *(Trying to reach in his pocket.)* What you have left? Whatever, give me. I get something for Rudichka...

(PYTOR grabs her by the arm.)

PYTOR: Keep away from me, if you know what's good for you…

(He pushes her away brusquely.)

SVETLANA: What's good for me is out of here… Me and Rudichka. Out of here…

PYTOR: Where you go? What you do? *(He laughs.)*

SVETLANA: *(Breaking down.)* I don't know. I don't know…

(PYTOR and SVETLANA exit.)

PRESENT: No place like home for the holidays, eh Ben?

SCROOGE: Is her husband always like that?

PRESENT: You might say so, when he drinks. But hey, it's not your problem.

SCROOGE: But the child shouldn't grow up in a home where… *(SCROOGE stops.)*

PRESENT: What's the matter? Cat got your tongue?

SCROOGE: It's all so…

PRESENT: Humbug! Humbug! *Humbug! (She laughs as she disappears.)*

SCENE 6

Electronic music echoing the three "humbugs" builds to a climax and abruptly transforms to somber, ominous extended chords. SCROOGE is alone on stage as light and sound effect appears dramatically as GHOST OF CHRISTMAS FUTURE. (Note: Ideally, the ghost should be represented by abrasive, threatening chords and laser lights.) SCROOGE looks around.

SCROOGE: Who are you? *(Looks all around, terrified by the effect.)* I've seen the past and the present. I can only guess you are the Ghost of Christmas Yet-to-Come. Am I correct? I fear you more than the other two. But I know you are here to help me, like Jake Marley was. Is that what you're here for? To help me? Please! Speak to me.

(FUTURE effect of sound and light changes abruptly and new scene appears.)

SCENE 7

A FENCE and the housekeeper, SVETLANA.

FENCE: So what have you got there, lady?

SVETLANA: *(Nervously taking things out of a bag.)* One pair of cufflinks—gold, I think—a pen…

FENCE: *(Inspecting them.)*This is crap. Why didn't you grab something more valuable?

SVETLANA: And this watch.

(FENCE looks at watch.)

SVETLANA: I feel so awful taking these things. But I want my child to have something for Christmas, and since he was dead and all and just lying there all alone…

FENCE: You took it off his wrist?

SVETLANA: *(Breaks down.)* He never gave me anything while he was alive. At least he could when dead…

FENCE *(Recoiling.)* He didn't die of nothing catching, did he?

SVETLANA: *(Taking things back.)* I'm sorry. I'm so ashamed. I make a terrible mistake…

FENCE: Hey, hey, lady, chill out. I'm just saying there ain't much I can give you for this shit. Maybe fifty bucks tops.

SVETLANA: *(Controlling herself.)* But I know he have some good things. That watch. He love that watch. It must be very valuable. He never took it off.

FENCE: Okay. Fifty-five.

SVETLANA: I'm sure that watch is from someplace like Tiffany's.

FENCE: Take it or leave it.

SVETLANA: *(She takes money.)* I wish I never come here. *(She exits.)*

FENCE: Merry Christmas, lady! *(He looks at the watch gleefully.)* Gonna be a happy new year for me! *(FENCE goes off.)*

SCROOGE: My housekeeper. What is she doing? Who is she talking to? That looked like my watch.

(Sound and light appear forcefully again, as FUTURE effect transforms again to lead to new scene.)

SCENE 8

CRATCHIT's home again. Music is low key, subdued. CRATCHIT, CAROL, and MARIA are there, but not TIM.

CAROL: How did he die?

CRATCHIT: Just collapsed at home. Probably a stroke.

MARIA: So he croaked. No great loss. Miserable old bastard.

CRATCHIT: On Christmas Eve too, just like Marley.

CAROL: And all alone, too.

MARIA: At least he finally did something nice for Christmas!

CRATCHIT: Spooky, huh?

CAROL: Yeah, well, he was pretty spooky himself. I wonder what he did with all his money?

CRATCHIT: He didn't leave it to me, that's for sure.

CAROL: Oh, Bob, I'm so sorry. Not for him, God knows, but for you. What are you going to do?

CRATCHIT: I don't know. All I've heard from his lawyer is that the business will be sold, and I am not in the picture.

MARIA: You mean that son of a bitch didn't leave you anything—not even your job?

CRATCHIT: *(Holding back tears.)* Guess not. I don't know what to do. Tim used to always say to me, "Just stay with him—he'll come through some day."

CAROL: *(Embracing him.)* We're here for you, Robert.

CRATCHIT: I miss Tim so much.

SCROOGE: What happened to Tim? He was on those inhibitors, wasn't he? Please tell me he's all right. I've got to know. *(Pause.)* Please. What am I seeing? Are these glimpses of what will happen, or what might happen? I've got to know there's a chance! *(Pause.)* Why won't you say something? Please tell me there's hope! Please tell me there's hope!

SCENE 9

FUTURE effect builds to a fierce crescendo and then abruptly disappears as SCROOGE continues repeating the line about hope. Lights come up on SCROOGE in his room on the floor near his bed.

SCROOGE: Please tell me there's hope. Please tell me… *(He looks around.)* I'm back in my room. I'm alive! At least I think I am… *(He looks at watch.)* Jake's watch. She didn't sell it! *(He looks at picture.)* Oh, thank you, Jake, wherever you are. I'll make it up to you. I'll make it up to everyone. Oh, I hope I didn't miss it! *(He dials phone.)* Please let it still be... Hello! Operator! What day is it? *(Pause.)* Hello? *(He laughs.)* She hung up! Must think I'm a wacko! Well, I am! Or was, anyway! But I'm a happy wacko! I feel so... light. As light as a feather. Well, I've always been a bit light in the loafers! *(He laughs.)* Oh, I made a joke! It's wonderful. Exhilarating! *(He dials again.)* I feel so giddy, so daffy—that's me, the daffy decorator! Oh, I like it. Hello, operator! What day is it, please? *(Pause.)* Oh, thank God! And Merry Christmas to you... or Seasons Greetings—oh, I've never liked that phrase—and a Happy New Year! *(He hangs up.)* Then I didn't miss it! They did it all in one night. The spirits. Of course they did—they're spirits, for God's sake! *(Turning on radio.)* Music! Have to have music. It's Christmas!

(Radio glows and "The Twelve Days of Christmas" plays. We hear the lyrics: "...and a partridge in a pear tree," etc.)

SCROOGE: Cratchit! Oh, yes, I've got to surprise Cratchit for Christmas—Christmas for Cratchit—Cratchit for Christmas... *(He laughs again and dials phone.)* They'll get more than a partridge from me! Oh, somebody's got to be open today. Or I'll make them open. *(Pause.)* Yes, the number for Zabar's, please.

SCENE 10

Interior of CRATCHIT's home. They are examining a huge gift basket of food. Music continues from their radio/tape deck.

CAROL: There's no note with it.

MARIA: Man, look at all this stuff. Fantastic!

CRATCHIT: Maybe it's a mistake.

MARIA: Their loss is our gain.

CRATCHIT: *(To TIM.)* Maybe Fred sent it.

CAROL: Who?

CRATCHIT: Fred Fallon from Clarence House. I invited him to come by.

TIM: He would have enclosed a card.

MARIA: So, who sent this?

TIM: Scrooge.

MARIA: What drugs are you taking?

CRATCHIT: Tim, are you sure you're not tripping? Scrooge?

TIM: Miraculous things happen on Christmas.

CAROL: That's true. Let's just view it as a Christmas miracle and enjoy it.

MARIA: *(Singing.)* "Joy to the world, the food is come..."

(They laugh and hug.)

ALL: Merry Christmas.

(Buzzer sounds.)

CRATCHIT: Now what?

TIM: Maybe it's Santa Claus.

MARIA: Maybe it's another delivery—some wine to go with the food!

(CRATCHIT presses buzzer.)

CAROL: Maybe it's the delivery guy realizing he made a mistake.

MARIA: Quick, hide the basket!

TIM: It's certainly a great holiday so far.

CAROL: As long as it's not April Fool's Day!

(A knock at the door. CRATCHIT goes to open it.)

CRATCHIT: Hey, maybe it's Mayor Giuliani!

TIM: Maybe it's Kitty Carlisle!

MARIA: Maybe it's Ebenezer…

(CRATCHIT opens door. SCROOGE is there.)

MARIA: …Scrooge!

CRATCHIT: Mr. Scrooge!

SCROOGE: Robert, may I come in?

MARIA: You? Scrooge? What the hell do you think you're doing here?

CRATCHIT: *(To MARIA.)* It's all right, Maria. *(To SCROOGE.)* Of course you can. Please come in.

(SCROOGE enters.)

CRATCHIT: Uh, Mr. Scrooge, this is my lover, Tim.

SCROOGE: Yes, I know.

TIM: I've—uh—heard a lot about you.

SCROOGE: I'm sure you have. *(To CRATCHIT, sternly.)* Cratchit, I'll be brief and to the point. I feel very strongly that I no longer have need of you in your present capacity, and I have therefore decided that as of today you are no longer employed as my assistant…

CRATCHIT: *(Shocked.)* But Mr. Scrooge, on Christmas Day?

CAROL: How dare you!

SCROOGE: No, Robert, I'm sorry but I am firm about this. I have no alternative—but to make you my full partner! With a huge bonus for starters.

(SCROOGE laughs. CRATCHIT and others are stunned.)

SCROOGE: "Scrooge & Cratchit"—how does that sound? I know "Cratchit & Scrooge" is alphabetically correct, but let's not push it.

CRATCHIT: I don't know what to say.

SCROOGE: Oh, Robert, I should have done this ages ago. Can you forgive a foolish old bastard who shut himself out of your life—and life itself—for all these years?

CRATCHIT: I can't imagine a nicer Christmas present than the fact that you are here.

SCROOGE: Are you shocked?

TIM: You did send the gift basket.

SCROOGE: I hope it's good. It took a bit of doing to get it to you today—last minute and all. But money talks.

TIM: It's wonderful.

SCROOGE: *(To TIM.)* Don't ask me why, but I feel as if I've known you for some time now, and I hope to get to know you a lot better in the future.

TIM: I hope so, too.

CRATCHIT: I'm overwhelmed. Uh, Mr. Scrooge, these are our friends…

SCROOGE: Ben, please…

CRATCHIT: Ben, these are our dear friends, Carol and Maria.

SCROOGE: How do you do?

CAROL: I'm somewhat flabbergasted.

SCROOGE: I'm not surprised.

(He goes to shake MARIA's hand.)

MARIA: I'm not so sure I want to shake your hand. We Dominicans are proud people.

SCROOGE: I wouldn't want to shake the hand of the old Scrooge either. But please do shake the hand of the new Scrooge.

MARIA: Well, what the hell—as Tim said, miracles happen on Christmas!

(She shakes SCROOGE's hand.)

SCROOGE: You're from the Dominican Republic? Do you know Oscar de la Renta?

MARIA: *(Facetiously.)* Oh sure, I have lunch with him all the time.

SCROOGE: A man of some talent. Perhaps we should all go to Casa de Campo for New Year's! My treat, of course.

MARIA: Now I know why he's here and talking this way. He's loco!

TIM: Maria, *basta*!

SCROOGE: No, I haven't taken leave of my senses. I've come to them. And after all, what is money for, if not to make things nicer for people.

CRATCHIT: I'm in shock. I don't know what to do.

SCROOGE: *(Taking a check from his pocket.)* I'll tell you what to do, Robert. First thing tomorrow morning... No, make that first thing *Monday* morning, you take this check to that gentleman who came to the office yesterday.

CRATCHIT: *(Looking at check.)* Are you sure you meant that many zeros?

SCROOGE: I have a lot of years to make up for.

(Buzzer sounds.)

TIM: *(Going to intercom and buzzing.)* That must be Fred.

SCROOGE: Then you call my housekeeper and tell her I'm tripling what I pay her, and then engage an insurance agent to obtain health care for all of us. And tonight, allow me to take you all out to dinner at the restaurant of your choice—as long as it's not an establishment where the waiters are transvestites. I'm coming to life, but I'm not quite ready for that yet.

(Knock at door. TIM opens it. FRED, NOEL, and BLAKE enter. BLAKE is played by the same actor who played MARLEY.)

TIM: Hey, Fred! Merry Christmas.

FRED: Merry Christmas to you, Tim.

CRATCHIT: Fred. Welcome.

FRED: Bob, you know my friend, Noel, and this is my cousin who just moved here from Boston... *(He presents BLAKE.)*

SCROOGE: *(Transfixed.)* Jake!

BLAKE: No, Blake. Are you okay?

SCROOGE: Yes... I'm sorry... it's just that you remind me of somebody...

CRATCHIT: We're all kind of... overwhelmed today.

SCROOGE: Somebody... I loved very much.

BLAKE: Then I'm flattered.

SCROOGE: Forgive me. I'm Ben.

BLAKE: Nice to meet you.

FRED: Ben! I'm... uh... surprised to find you here.

SCROOGE: There are going to be a lot more surprises to come, Fred.

CRATCHIT: *(Introducing.)* Fred, Noel, Blake—these are our two dearest friends, Carol and Maria.

(They say hello.)

CAROL: So you're from Boston? I was born there.

BLAKE: Whereabouts?

CAROL: Dorchester.

BLAKE: *(To MARIA.)* You, too?

MARIA: No. I was born a little south of Boston!

TIM: Welcome to New York!

BLAKE: Thank you.

CRATCHIT: So, Blake, what do you do?

FRED: My handsome and talented cousin has moved here to write the great American musical!

MARIA: Oh, so you're a waiter.

(They laugh. MARIA shakes his hand.)

MARIA: Hey, good luck, man.

BLAKE: Thanks. I'll need it.

SCROOGE: Do you like the opera?

BLAKE: Love it, but I can't afford to go…

SCROOGE: We must talk.

CAROL: Hey, let's get this party hitting on something.

(She changes music to "We Wish You a Merry Christmas." They sing.)

SCROOGE: And let's open that gift basket!

(They go to basket. They all react happily and sing. The GHOST OF CHRISTMAS PRESENT appears and delivers the final lines, as the rest of the cast move downstage.)

PRESENT: Scrooge was better than his word. He did it all and infinitely more. He became as good a friend and as good a man as the good old city knew. And it was said of him that he knew how to keep Christmas well. May that be truly said of us all.

SCROOGE: *(To the group on stage.)* Merry Christmas!

ALL: God bless us, everyone.

(Christmas music comes up.)

(End of play.)

PUMPKINS FOR SMALLPOX

Catherine Gillet

CATHERINE GILLET attended the University of Florida and received a master's degree from Fordham University Graduate School. As a member of the Playwrights Project at Circle Repertory Theater, she studied with Milan Stitt; she is also currently a member of Circle East Theater. Gillet's plays have appeared at, among others, the Circle Repertory Company Lab, Circle in the Square, Naked Angels, Soho Repertory Company, and Vital Theatre. She is the author of thirty short plays and seven full-length plays including *Wyoming*, which was the recipient of a grant from The Jerome Foundation and was produced in New York at the 78th Street Theater Lab in fall 2000. Another full-length play, *Anomalies of the Heart*, was a finalist for the 2001 Princess Grace Award. In addition to being a playwright, Gillet is a clinical social worker with a private practice in Bedford, New York. She is also a painter and sculptor, and composes the music for her plays, which often have a strong musical presence.

Pumpkins for Smallpox was first produced by Vital Theatre Company (Stephen Sunderlin, Artistic Director; Sharon Fallon, Managing Director), as part of the Vital Signs New Works Festival, on May 9, 2002, at Vital Theatre, New York City, with the following cast and credits:

Lucy .... Robyn Simpson
Laura .... Kristen Mudge

Directed by: Annie Levy
General Manager: Michael Schloegl
Production Manager: Christian J. Pedone
Assistant Production Coordinator: Jorinde Keesmaat
Lighting: Gina Priano-Keyser
Stage Manager: Lisa Webb

TIME

Fall 2001.

PLACE

Somewhere in the suburbs of New York City.

Intro music: Simon and Garfunkel's "America." At rise: Two high school girls on the lawn in front of a church. They stand behind a makeshift stand full of pumpkins. LUCY, cheerleader type, and her best friend, LAURA, who wears black-rimmed glasses which only make her prettier.

LUCY: *(Yells.)* "Pumpkins for Smallpox! Pumpkins for Smallpox!" C'mon Laura, we promised we'd do this.

LAURA: I'm having trouble remembering why.

LUCY: It's our civic duty, K? *(She whispers.)* Customers.

LAURA: K. *(Feebly.)* "Pumpkins for..." Could you repeat your question?

(Hysterical whispers.)

LUCY: Laura...!

LAURA: Sorry, I wasn't payin' attention!

(Both listen to unseen customer.)

LUCY: The proceeds from the sale of these pumpkins will go to our local Lions Club chapter. Mr. Thompson, the president, has secured a source for the smallpox vaccine which will protect all the residents of Hopeboro Center in the event of a biological warfare attack.

LAURA: The large ones are twenty-five dollars. Medium, fifteen, small, ten—

LUCY: And the minis are five apiece. Or you could get five minis for twenty dollars.

LAURA: *(Takes "money" and puts it in cashbox.)* Thank you.

LUCY: You can pick 'em out yourself.

(They watch as "customers" walk away.)

LUCY: Thirty bucks. How much have we made so far?

LAURA: One hundred. Plus thirty.

LUCY: Wow. Wonder how much that stuff costs. A large pumpkin per person? How many people live in Hopeboro?

LAURA: Five thousand eight hundred seventeen.

LUCY: We should call Mr. Thompson. At this rate we need another truckload. We've only been here two hours! "Pumpkins for Smallpox!" We've sold like—

LAURA: Twenty-three.

LUCY: Wow.

LAURA: Lucy? That might be enough to vaccinate like, *your* family.

LUCY: No way. Really? That is so depressing. Are you sure?

LAURA: The *New York Times* said. Very expensive.

LUCY: Whatshisface has enough to kill like the entire population of the entire known universe. I wish my parents were that rich. *(Slight realization regarding what she just said.)*

LAURA: *(Referring to Osama bin Laden.)* Joey calls him "Son'a Ben Franklin."

LUCY: Joey's four years old.

LAURA: I think it's kinda perfect. It's like we made him. He's like our... legacy or something.

LUCY: "Pumpkins for Smallpox!"

LAURA: Put the price sign up here so we don't have to say it three thousand more times, K? We can just point to it.

LUCY: Not a good idea. You gotta think public relations in a time like this. People need some, you know, the human connection thing, very important, they need to know—

LAURA: You're tellin' every single one of them every single detail. Might as well tell 'm Mr. Thompson and your mother are having an affair.

LUCY: That was beyond way mean.

LAURA: Sorry.

LUCY: Forgiven. *(She gestures behind her.)* Mass started at ten fifteen. We'll be slow for a little while, then we've got the eleven forty-five rush.

LAURA: People who go to mass at eleven forty-five aren't in a rush.

LUCY: Yeah, probably aren't even thinkin' about smallpox. Calm people make me nervous lately.

LAURA: How come?

LUCY: *(Shrugs.)* Ever since the Thing. I've noticed. There's people who look like, real worried and people who look like zombies, like they're numb or something.

LAURA: They're depressed.

LUCY: Yeah well, maybe if they *did* something. Like *we* are, they'd feel, like you know, like... like they're *doin'* something.

LAURA: Making a difference?

LUCY: Yeah. "Pumpkins for Smallpox! Pumpkins for—"

LAURA: Just, stop, Luce. Look, there's no one here, K?

LUCY: They shoulda put us closer to the road. The firemen with the boot? They get to stop traffic even. That's what we should be... "Fill the Pumpkin." But guess we'd have to add "for Smallpox" after and it doesn't have the right ring; make sense, does it.

LAURA: No. It doesn't make any sense at all.

LUCY: What are you wearing Thursday?

LAURA: Nothing.

LUCY: Hope you've been workin' out...

LAURA: I'm not goin'. *(Beat.)* Ever heard of Post-traumatic Stress Syndrome?

LUCY: Duh. Like every day. My mom keeps askin' if I have it like she used to ask if I had my period. Really pisses me off.

LAURA: Ditto.

LUCY: It's like we're not allowed to be like regular, you know?, normal. Before the Thing I got mad at stuff. I freaked out like when she wouldn't drive me somewhere. Now I've got Post—

LAURA: I don't sleep at night.

LUCY: How come?

LAURA: Dreams.

LUCY: What kinda dreams?

LAURA: I don't know, you know, mostly rescuin' people. My family mostly. Last night? I dreamed I threw a stick into the lake for Molly and it went out pretty far and it was the wrong kinda wood, so it sunk and you know Molly. She wouldn't come back without a stick if you had an entire *box* of Beggin Strips for her, so she kept looking, kept swimmin' around, started coughin' and stuff and then her head started goin' under and she was tryin' real hard to get back to me—her eyes looked so scared, Luce. Me screamin' for her to come but she couldn't make it so I jumped in and by the time I got to her? She was dead.

LUCY: Bet you were glad when you woke up and it wasn't real.

LAURA: Yeah.

LUCY: Dylan treatin' you right?

LAURA: We broke up. Well, I broke up.

LUCY: When?!

LAURA: Yesterday.

LUCY: Why didn't you tell me?!

LAURA: I just did. God!

LUCY: Not on your own you didn't. Laura, we're best friends! I'm supposed to be the first one to know this stuff! God!

LAURA: You are. K?

LUCY: K. How come?

LAURA: I don't know. It's just hard, you know, with "other" people. I can't be around them too long.

LUCY: They're the only ones I wanna be around.

LAURA: Thanks a lot.

LUCY: 'Cept you. I'll call him tonight. Do some damage control for ya. You need him.

LAURA: I don't need anyone. Especially—

LUCY: Yeah, I know, but at least they're not talkin' about it all the time. Goin' to their houses feels normal, you know?

LAURA: That's the part I don't like.

LUCY: Hungry?

LAURA: Nah.

LUCY: I brought four Power bars. Two for each of us. Only other food around here is, as you know, 7-Eleven unedibles.

LAURA: Did you stop eating regular food before or after the Thing?

LUCY: *(Deflecting.) Everything* has sugar in it. They've determined high glucose intake causes premature aging. You want to look like your mother when you're thirty-five?

LAURA: My mother smokes.

LUCY: Thought she quit.

LAURA: Started again. Now she's buying Marlboros. Regulars. That's one of the signs.

LUCY: Puhleese...

LAURA: "People often revert to habitual forms of coping with stress including nicotine, drugs, and alcohol."

LUCY: Julia Roberts is old. She's like thirty and she still looks pretty good. Secret? No sugar.

LAURA: Lucy? Power bars have sugar in them.

LUCY: No. They have complex carbohydrates. Way different.

LAURA: I haven't had any appetite.

LUCY: I've been starving. *(She unwraps a bar and eats.)*

LAURA: Both, signs.

LUCY: So how come you don't wanna go to the city Thursday?

LAURA: I hate field trips.

LUCY: Yeah, right.

LAURA: Have you even *thought* about how weird it'll be?

LUCY: My mind only gets as far as being on the bus, with my friends.

LAURA: You know, the actual seeing of it?, the *nothing* of it?

LUCY: You're lettin' your mind go further. That's your whole problem.

LAURA: I know.

LUCY: So stop it.

LAURA: I can't. I keep seein' it, Luce. I'll be just walkin' around and I see it. The whole thing. I see fire. A lot.

LUCY: 'Cuz it's fall. The colors… looks like fire everywhere.

(Slight pause.)

LAURA: Did they give your mom the jar?

LUCY: She's got it on the nightstand next to her bed. Freaks me out. I wanna flush it down the toilet, if she'd ever leave the damn house. What did yours do with hers?

LAURA: We sprinkled it over that lake on Route One Seventeen he liked to fish in.

LUCY: Weird.

LAURA: It was windy. We got him all over us.

LUCY: *(Tenderly.)* It wasn't really him, Laur.

LAURA: No, it was everyone. All over us, on our hands, all of them. When we breathed in they came into our lungs, now they're in our blood, our hearts, every one of them… They live inside us now.

LUCY: Laura! Look! They're comin' out!

(LUCY begins, LAURA joins in, both experiencing a new intensity bordering on hysteria, possibly anger.)

LUCY and LAURA: "Pumpkins for Smallpox! Pumpkins for Smallpox, Pumpkins for Smallpox, Pumpkins for…"

(Lights fade as music from top resumes. End of play.)

LOOKING FOR THE PONY

Andrea Lepcio

ANDREA LEPCIO was born and raised in Boston. She received a BA in human ecology from the College of the Atlantic, an MBA from the University of California at Berkeley, and an MFA from the Carnegie Mellon University School of Drama. She has studied playwriting with Milan Stitt, Tina Howe, and Marie Irene Fornes. Lepcio's produced plays include *Whodunit*, *Night, Night*, and *Hook & Eye*; these have received productions at Vital Theatre, Culture Project, and Trustus Theatre. *Hook & Eye* was the winner of the 2001 Trustus Playwrights' Festival. *The Wife Seller* and *Average Family Business* had workshops at Hangar Theater in a 1999 Lab Company Playwright Residency. Lepcio received a Sloan Foundation Dramatic Writing Award in 1999 for her screenplay *A September Spring*. Recently, she was selected to be the Dramatist Guild Fellowship Alternate 2002, and her ten-minute play *Whodunit* was published in a Canadian literary journal. Her rock musical *The Bronx Casket Co.* (music/lyrics by D.D. Verni, direction/choreography by Hinton Battle), developed at HERE Arts Center and the Broadway Theater Institute, was the first presentation of Hinton Battle Theatre Laboratory. She is a member of the Dramatists Guild, Women's Project and Productions Playwrights Lab, and International Centre for Women Playwrights. She lives in New York City.

Looking for the Pony was first produced by Vital Theatre Company (Stephen Sunderlin, Artistic Director; Sharon Fallon, Managing Director), as part of the Vital Signs New Works Festival, on May 30, 2002, at Vital Theatre, New York City, with the following cast and credits:

A .... Emma Palzere-Rae
B .... Karen Eterovich
C .... Ginnine Cocuzza
D .... Anthony Scavone

Directed by: Brooke O' Harra
General Manager: Michael Schloegl
Production Manager: Christian J. Pedone
Assistant Production Coordinator: Jorinde Keesmaat
Lighting: Gina Priano-Keyser
Stage Manager: Lisa Webb
Dramaturg: Shawn Hirabayashi

The Vital Theatre production was also presented as part of the Samuel French Off-Off-Broadway Festival, August 10, 2002, with the same cast, except Dina Comolli played C.

Looking for the Pony was subsequently produced as part of the Riant Theater's Strawberry Festival (Van Dirk Fisher, Artistic Director), on July 22, 2002, with the same cast, except Mary Regan as C; and August 5–7, 2002, with Dina Comolli as C.

Looking for the Pony was produced as part of Estrogenius 2002 at Manhattan Theatre Source (Fiona Jones, Founder and Executive Producer), September 25–28, 2002, with the following cast and credits:

A .... Adrienne Hurd
B .... Michelle Hurd
C .... Catherine Zambri
D .... Kim Martin-Cotten

Directed by: Barbara Gulan
Set: Maruti Evans
Lights: Pamela Kupper
Sound: Giovanna Sgarlata
Costumes: Kristin Gedney
Stage Manager: Jill Heller

This play is dedicated in loving memory of Meryl Nakamura Gladstone.

CHARACTERS

A: A woman, 30s to 40s
B: Her younger sister
C: Female, 30s
D: Male or Female, 30s to 50s

B tells the audience the story. A and the other characters are in the story and never address the audience. C and D play miscellaneous doctors, nurses, and technicians. Their speeches are what A and B are able to hear, comprehend, or remember under the circumstances of cancer. Thus, we only hear what A and B hear, not what the doctors actually say.

TIME

The past three years.

SETTING

The places cancer takes you.

NOTE

Asterisks separate the action, indicating passage of time or shift of location.

B: *(To audience.)* There once were two children who could see the bright side of any situation. One day, they are put in a room filled with manure. Hours later they are discovered laughing, scooping up the manure, digging underneath. "What on earth are you doing," the children are asked. With beaming smiles they answer, "All this poop, there has to be a pony in here somewhere."

A: *(To B. In the moment.)* This morning,

B: *(B is telling us.)* My sister.

A: I woke up with my hand on my,

B: Right breast,

A: Last night I showered, clean, thorough.

B: No way she couldn't have felt it.

A: But I didn't.

B: And now, she does.

(Together, experiencing the discovery.)

A: It's a lump. A large lump.

B: Aren't they supposed to be small and stony?

A: This is huge.

B: Maybe that's good?

*

Examination room.

D: A mammogram,

C: Had been taken,

D: Six months ago.

C: Said mammogram,

D: Was reviewed.

C: Showed nothing.

D: New one taken.

C: We'll just place your breast on the plate and press down.

B: Smoooosh… smash!

A: I'm okay.

*

At home waiting for the results.

C: *(Calling.)* Phone call.

A: Glorious!

B: Thrilling!

A: They say it's nothing!

B: Unbelievable relief.

*

At home celebrating.

C: *(Calling.)* Second phone call.

B: Short.

A: Terrifying.

C: There's been a mistake.

D: We read… the old film.

C: Come in right away.

*

Fast car ride. They are there—that cliched moment when…

B: Her gynecologist sits down.

A: We sit.

B: She says,

C: It's cancer.

(Beat.)

C: *(Saying what A and B hear.)* Here's the name of a doctor. Immediately you are beyond what this office can do. This is the name of the first doctor you need a surgeon and then an oncologist or an oncologist and then a surgeon. There needs to be a surgeon but there will be an oncologist and a surgeon both and a radiologist although from the way the tissue looks on film there is no doubt you have cancer.

B: Six months ago there was nothing. I read the words that said come back next year, monthly self-exams. Six months ago, you had nothing…

A: And now, I do.

*

First thing in the morning.

B: *(To audience.)* We call for an appointment.

C: The doctor can see you at four forty-five p.m. on April fifth.

B: That's three weeks from now!

A: Isn't there anything sooner?

C: No.

B: Call the next guy.

C: All booked up.

B: There's one more name on the list.

C: The doctor is not seeing new patients at this time.

A: Cancer, apparently, my cancer, is no one else's emergency.

B: This doctor wrote a book, that one treated this celebrity. All busy. WHO WILL SEE MY SISTER?

A: I need this taken off.

B: *(To audience.)* A cousin, thank God, married an oncologist, thank God, lives close by, thank God, gets us in.

A: Thank God.

*

B: *(To audience.)* We buy books. Spend hours on the floor of the breast health section of Barnes & Noble.

A: *(To B, not the audience.)* People stop by the house, bring us more books and lots of pink ribbons.

B: *(To audience.)* By the end of the first day, we possess five copies of Dr. Susan Love's *Breast Book.*

A: Let's read them all.

B: Sprawled on her bed. *(To A.)* See this is the thing I don't get. This book says—look at the picture—it takes yeeaars to grow a tumor of the smallest size. Yeeaars like eight to ten before you can even feel it with your fingers. How did yours happen so fast?

C and D: We don't know.

*

Examination Room. C and D are all over A poking, prodding.

D: Fine needle aspiration comes first.

(Ultrasound illuminates the tumor on a monitor. The doctor injects a large needle into the breast to pull out cells.)

C: Comfortable?

A: I'm okay.

C: Full body x-rays next.

(Technician puts patient in multiple positions to view all body parts.)

D: Bone scans.

(Different machine, more positions.)

C: Magnetic resonance imaging.

(Tight, circular tube. The patient must be perfectly still.)

A: I'm okay.

B: Just make sure there isn't any more cancer.

(The doctors are looking for tumors. There is no method to detect microscopic cells.)

C: We can only see.

D: What we can see.

*

In waiting room at hospital.

B: *(To audience.)* We wait for the radiologist to read the film.

A: It's taking too long. She sees something.

B: Something... else?

(C approaches.)

C: T-10.

B: What's that?

C: Lower rib.

A: *(Pointing to her back.)* Here.

C: There's a spot.

B: A spot? What kind of spot? What are we going to do about the spot?

*

At doctor's office.

D: Results in.

B: *(To audience.)* Oncologist. Funny man.

A: We are grateful you can see us.

B: *(To audience.)* Spills diet coke all over his desk. Explains—

D: This is why I'm not a surgeon.

B: *(To audience.)* Rescues her pathology report. Dabs at the coke. Starts to talk.

D: Surgery first, twelve weeks of chemotherapy, followed by a likely course of additional chemotherapy if more than four nodes are positive, Herceptin if estrogen receptive, there are always new drugs to try, followed by radiation.

B: *(To audience.)* First you hear cancer and it is scary, then you read the books, optimist that you are, and you think maybe it's not so bad after all and then doctors start to talk.

D: It's bad.

B: *(To audience.)* Unspeakably bad.

*

In the car.

A: *(Meaning be sick, die.)* I don't want to do this to you.

B: I'm okay.

A: Let's stop by Costco.

B: What for?

A: Groceries.

B: Now?

A: I need to get food in the house before everything starts.

B: I'll do the shopping. I'll take care of everything. You don't have to—

A: I want to.

*

B: *(To audience.)* Costco has very large carts. We fill two. To the brim.

A: Grab a ketchup.

B: *(To audience.)* A ketchup is actually two thirty-two-ounce glass bottles linked by a plastic thing disguised as a handle but is really a trick. When I lift one of the bottles, the other smashes to the floor.

A: Leave it.

B: *(To audience.)* Ketchup glass everywhere I grab another with all hands.

A: We're home.

B: *(To audience.)* Lug in the bags, unload. I grab the ketchup.

A: You're going to make the same mistake—

C: Smash.

B: Ketchup glass all over the dining room floor.

A: It's okay.

B: Everything is far from okay.

*

Phone calls at home.

D: Surgery has been scheduled.

A: *(To B.)* Insurance says I have to wait.

B: For what?

C: *(On telephone.)* According to your policy, a mastectomy is considered elective surgery. For elective surgery, you have to wait ten days.

A: *(To C.)* Would you elect to have your boob cut off?

B: Let me talk to them.

(A hands her the phone.)

C: According to her policy—

B: My sister is scheduled for surgery Thursday—

C: If you'd let me finish—

A: *(Meaning the cancer.)* Get this off.

C: According to her policy—

B: There is a malignant tumor in her breast five centimeters—that's two inches. There already is a spot on T-10 and who the hell knows where else. Every minute you wait more cells sluff off and migrate to who knows where inside her body. Breast cancer goes to bone, liver, lungs. Save my sister not your money do not kill her with your rules and regulations save her life.

C: We require a letter explaining why this is an emergency.

B: The surgeon is writing faxing you right now she is having surgery on Thursday approve it Thursday approve it Thursday approve it.

*

Day of surgery.

B: *(To audience.)* They wheel her away. The surgeon removes the tumor, her right breast, and twelve lymph nodes.

D: I got it all.

B: Excuse me?

D: Clean margins. I got it all.

B: *(To audience.)* I'm thinking why is the oncologist scaring us with chemo and radiation if the big bad surgeon cured her.

*

At the hospital.

A: The next day.

B: *(To audience.)* True story.

A: The surgeon comes to check on me. He walks in, I notice, kind of sidewise with his hand held up covering his face.

D: Sorry, I had dental surgery yesterday and I look a little funny.

A: That's okay, I had a mastectomy yesterday and I look a little funny too.

*

At doctor's office.

D: Surgical pathology report.

B: *(To audience.)* Oncologist. This time, no diet coke.

D: Six out of twelve nodes are positive. We start the first twelve-week cycle of chemotherapy today. Then you will need more, there are several research hospitals you can investigate, I will give you names. Insurance won't like it, start early, you need this treatment, insurance won't approve, you will have to fight them, all the doctors will write, you may need a lawyer.

*

B: *(To audience.)* Don't think there's no hope. There is hope.

A: I just need time.

B: Treatment equals time.

*

A: Insurance says no.

C: This treatment is experimental. According to your policy, there is no experimental treatment allowed.

B: *(To audience.)* We get a lawyer.

*

D: The lawyer

C: And insurance company

(Arm wrestling.)

D and C: Negotiate.

*

B: *(To audience.)* We hang mezuzahs on all the doorposts.

A: Turns out there are kosher and non-kosher mezuzahs.

B: Let's get the kosher ones.

*

A and B watch C and D arm wrestle.

A: Still at it.

B: They are costing you valuable time.

A: I'm okay.

B: You were supposed to start this treatment weeks ago.

(D defeats C.)

C: Okay, little miss pain in the ass, make a fuss, break all the rules, cost us lots of money, your lawyer scared us so go ahead and get your experimental treatment if you want. But now you have to travel sixty miles on the truck-congested freeway instead of three miles from your house. You still can change your mind and save us money.

*

B: *(To audience.)* When people cut her off on the freeway,

A: I whip off my wig.

*

B: *(To audience.)* At the research hospital, we settle in. There's a special channel on the television with tips on tying scarves around your head, draping scarves down your chest, stuffing scarves in your bra. *(To A.)* It is amazing what they think you can fix with scarves.

C: Here are the papers you need to sign.

A: What does it say?

B: You don't have to worry about cancer any more because there's lots of ways they can kill you with the cure.

A: Give me the pen. I'll sign.

*

B: *(To audience.)* She lies still. She says a complete inability to move one minute and the next she's flipped on all fours retching then back and immobile again not knowing how she ever moved.

A: *(To B, not the audience.)* It ends. It does end. I come home. I feel lousy, but better. I'm okay. Grateful.

*

C: Time for radiation.

B: *(To audience.)* Since the morning she woke up with her hand on her breast, she hasn't had a break from treatment.

A: Bring it on.

B: *(To audience.)* Time. We are optimists not fools. We believe all this treatment will buy her time.

*

At radiation.

C: *(Bitchy.)* Take off your clothes. Sit there. Wait.

A: In this thin gown?

B: *(To audience.)* The door is open to the hall. People walk by, look in.

A: Isn't there someplace more private?

C: I SAID SIT!

A: Are you having a bad day?

C: My boyfriend dumped me, my car ran out of gas, I'm constipated, my hair won't stay straight, I have a zit…

B: *(To audience.)* Everyday life puts cancer in perspective.

*

At a restaurant.

B: *(To audience.)* Eating becomes life and death.

A: The experts don't agree.

C: Phytoestrogens found in soy stimulate breast cancer cell growth.

D: Soy has potent anti-angiogenesis properties.

(C becomes the waitress.)

A: You order first.

B: I'll have the stir-fry tofu.

C: Okay.

A: Can I have what she's having with some deletions?

C: I'll try.

A: No tofu.

*

B: *(To audience.)* Year Two begins. That was all Year One.

(At doctor's office.)

D: It's in your back.

B: T-10?

A: There's more, higher and lower. And in my pelvis.

B: Bone. Only bone. Tumors on your bones is much better than your organs.

A: I'm okay.

D: We're going to continue Taxol twice a week and add Arimidex to strengthen your bones. And you'll need to come in everyday for hydration.

B: What's that?

D: Calcium is a byproduct of bone cell division. We need to flush your system for four hours every single day.

A: That's okay.

C: Apparently a mistake was made. Your cancer is estrogen receptive. You should have started Herceptin twelve months ago.

B: What does all that wasted time mean?

A: At least I'm on it now.

*

B: *(To audience.)* It's now Year Three.

A: Time.

B: *(To audience.)* She is still here. There are new treatments. She is on them. She puts up with anything, everything, for more time.

A: Cancer keeps me very busy, but every day I also live my life. I love my life.

B: In the spring, she whelps puppies. In the summer, she kayaks. In the fall she renovates a house. In the winter…

D: It's in your liver.

B: Oh, God.

A: I stopped by the beach coming back from hydration on my way to work and I sat. It was so beautiful.

*

B: For three years, we've been in that roomful of manure.

A: Scooping up the poop, tossing it back, giggling.

B: Because we need to believe.

*

B: *(To audience.)* A Feng Shui expert combs the house for hours.

C: Your bed is in the death spot.

A: My bed now blocks the bedroom door but is in the direction of my nein yen.

*

B: *(To audience.)* She starts to use a walker.

A: This is so much better.

B: It's raining.

A: You go in.

B: I don't want you to slip.

A: I don't want you to get wet.

B: The leaves.

A: The rain. Go in.

*

B: *(To audience.)* Now she needs a wheelchair. *(To A.)* You okay?

A: I'm great.

*

D: There is no pony.

B: What did you say?

C: There are no more treatments.

A: None?

B: How can that be so suddenly after all this time?

A: Isn't there anything else? Please give me something.

C: For pain.

A: For time.

D: There is just possibly this one pill you could take. It is too late. You need to just go home, stay home.

*

A: *(Meaning everything she needs done for her family after she is gone.)* Will you?

B: Yes, I will.

*

B: *(To audience.)* I remember the good old days when she was on a walker. In a wheelchair. Lucid.

A: I think I'd like to work on some protein nutrition.

B: *(To audience.)* And with that last effort, she is gone. The faintest beat in her wrist and then nothing. I lie down beside her, my head on her arm. We bury her body. Time passes. Life goes on.

Sometimes a roomful of shit is just shit. Sometimes there isn't a pony to be found. But I had a sister, my sister... And I still find her everywhere.

(Curtain.)

BLACK THANG

Ato Essandoh

ATO ESSANDOH was born in Schenectady, New York, and grew up there and in Westchester County, New York. He received a BS in chemical engineering from Cornell University and studied theatre at the Acting Studio under James Price and acting under Bob Krakower. Essandoh has been acting in New York for the past three years and has appeared in *Tallboy Walking* by Joshua James and *Raisin in the Sun* by Lorraine Hansberry. He was featured in the independent movies *The Accident*, *The Experience Box*, and *Nadezdha*. Essandoh is co-founder of The Defiant Ones Production Company. He coauthored several plays produced in the festivals *Eat My Shorts* and *Close Encounters*. He has never studied playwriting but was mentored and encouraged by playwright, friend, and producing partner, Joshua James. He lives in the Bronx.

Black Thang was first presented by The Defiant Ones in association with Common Factor on August 21, 2002, at manhattantheatresource, New York City, with the following cast and credits:

Sam .... Ato Essandoh
Mattie .... Carrie Keranen
Keisha .... Jo Bennett
Jerome .... Brian Karim

Directed by: Karina Miller
Lighting: Justin Burleson
Dramaturg: Joshua James

I would like to dedicate this play to Carrie for the voice in my head and Joshua for the kick in the ass.

CHARACTERS

SAM: Black man. Attractive. Intelligent. Sensitive. Strong.

MATTIE: White woman. Attractive. Intelligent. Vivid. Vibrant.

JEROME: Black man. Sam's best friend. Says whatever he wants, whenever he wants.

KEISHA: Black woman. Mattie's best friend and roommate. Says whatever she wants, whenever she wants. She's rabidly planning for her wedding.

SETTING

New York City. Present day.

NOTES

The action of this play takes place over a three-month span in various locations in New York City. The set should be minimal, using understated suggestions of time and place. It is the author's preference that all set changes be executed by the actors in character, as part of the performance so as not to interrupt the flow of the piece.

SCENE 1

SAM's apartment. Morning. SAM's in bed. MATTIE is getting dressed.

MATTIE: Hello.

SAM: Hi.

MATTIE: How ya doing?

SAM: I'm cool.

MATTIE: You're cool?

SAM: I'm cool if you're cool.

MATTIE: I'm cool.

SAM: Cool.

MATTIE: My name is Mattie by the way. I mean just in case you forgot. I mean I'm not saying you forgot or would forget or anything like that, but just in case you did, which would be totally understandable given the circumstances, I just wanted to say that it's totally fine and that my name was Mattie.

SAM: Sam.

MATTIE: Yup. Hi Sam.

SAM: Hello Mattie.

(Slight pause.)

MATTIE: And I just wanted to let you know that last night was great. And I don't mean that in a stroke-your-prickly-male-ego-to-make-you-feel-better kind of way. I mean that in a yee-haw-you-should-go-on-the-road-with-that-show-cowboy kind of way. Excellent work.

SAM: Uh. Thanks—

MATTIE: Yup and I'm totally cool with this whole thing by the way. These things happen all the time and I'm certainly not going to get all sappy and emotional and key your car or call you at odd hours and hang up. I mean we are two adults here let's not get all crazy right?

SAM: Right—

MATTIE: It's not like I'm super religious or anything—I don't get the sense that you are either. Are you? You'd be a hypocrite if you were, unless of course you were involved in some freaky cult religion that actually condoned aggressive uninhibited sex with semi-complete strangers. And if that's the case then sign me up you know what I mean? Heh heh heh—

SAM: Yeah—

MATTIE: But I mean it's not like I'm married or seeing anyone and you according to your own testimony are not married or seeing anyone, so what happened happened and that's what happened any and all consequences are solely ours to bear.

SAM: Uh-huh—

MATTIE: And speaking of consequences, I feel safe, I hope you do too. I think we did the safe thing quite well just in case you were wondering. I don't think any of your little X-wing Fighters blew up the Deathstar if you know what I mean. I mean they couldn't have with the battery of contraceptives at my disposal—plus you had condoms—so I would say that we were safe all around. No babies. No scabies. That's my motto.

SAM: Thanks.

MATTIE: I just like things to be clear.

(Slight pause.)

MATTIE: So then great I think we're done here.

SAM: What?

MATTIE: Yup. I promise not to let the door hit my ass on the way out. See ya—

SAM: Hey!

MATTIE: Yes?

SAM: Where are you going?

MATTIE: Home.

SAM: Why?

MATTIE: I live there.

SAM: Yeah. Well, can I see you again?

MATTIE: No.

SAM: Why?

MATTIE: I'm leaving for Calcutta tonight. Peace Corps. I'm betrothed to an Indian sheep herder named Rajesh. It was an arranged marriage. Me in exchange for a set of golf clubs and a time-share in Orlando. That was my dream last night. Or maybe it was my dad's dream. I don't know. Why would you want to see me again?

SAM: I just do.

MATTIE: I don't want a boyfriend.

SAM: Neither do I.

MATTIE: Heh heh heh. Cute.

(Slight pause.)

MATTIE: Sam, me leaving right now not only guarantees you a fantastic writeup in my diary tonight, but you also get to brag to all your boys about the cute white girl you macked at a bar last night. Fantasy fulfilled. Not to be repeated. Because if you repeat it, then it's not a fantasy anymore is it? It's the roller coaster ride that you've been on one too many times, or the prom dress that makes you realize how much fatter you've become—

(SAM kisses her.)

SAM: Want some eggs?

MATTIE: Eggs?

SAM: Eggs.

MATTIE: I'm vegan.

SAM: Yeah?

MATTIE: Yeah. I can't eat anything with a face or that could, at one point, have had a face.

SAM: We could get tofu.

MATTIE: I hate tofu.

SAM: Major conflict of interest.

MATTIE: Tell me about it…

(They kiss.)

SCENE 2

A gym. SAM works out. JEROME "helps."

JEROME: Freak? Freak? Freak? She a freak?

SAM: She's cool.

JEROME: Freaky deaky?

SAM: Great fucking dancer. I like that—

JEROME: Freak nasty?

SAM: And she's nutty. In a good way. I think she wants to see me again.

JEROME: Come on. You broke it off didn't you?

SAM: Nah. We had a good time.

JEROME: Come on! You know you broke that shit off didn't ya? Didn't ya?

(Slight pause.)

SAM: Yeah I did.

JEROME: Yeah! Had her screaming like the slave master's daughter didn't ya? Didn't ya?

SAM: Jerome.

JEROME: See that's the great thing with white chicks. You ain't gotta have money, you ain't gotta have a job, education, you ain't gotta have shit. Just a big dick and a smile and if they like you, they'll fuck you. You know what I mean? All I gotta say is… Once you go white… You do it for spite! Fuck sisters man. Too much work. Too much drama. Baby daddys pounding on your door at three in the morning. *(Mimicking "Baby Daddy.")* "A yo! Shaneequa! I know you in there!" Fuck that shit. White girls? No muss, no fuss. Just handle your business in the dicking department and they'll buy you shit, cook for you, take care of you. Plus they can hail you a cab anytime you want man. What more do you need?

SAM: You have some serious issues man.

JEROME: You know what your problem is man?

SAM: What is my problem?

JEROME: Lack of ambition. You're not seeing the big picture my friend. This is not about you and one white chick. This is about you and all the white chicks. This is God saying, "Go forth my son and plunder the white man's natural resources." You owe it to yourself. You owe it to us. Power to the people! That's what I'm talking about. I mean look at you man. Ya fine-ass-Mandingo-looking-motherfucker. How are you not fucking every minute of the day? I mean you're so good-looking I'd fuck you. And I don't mean that in the gay way. I mean it in the prison way. If we were in lockdown, I'd be fucking the shit outta you right now. Shit I'd let you fuck me. That's how good-looking you are.

SAM: All right. I'm out.

JEROME: Good. You do that. Go home get some rest. Wake up, find another white girl and fuck her. You won't be sorry.

SAM: *(Exiting.)* Peace.

JEROME: And when you're done there, come back to me, and we'll talk about Asian chicks.

SCENE 3

MATTIE and KEISHA's apartment. KEISHA flips through a wedding magazine. MATTIE paints her toenails.

MATTIE: It was simple. Eye contact. A coy smile and a hair flip. "Hi what's your name?" "Nice to meet you Sam." A little "What do you do, what's your sign." He's a Pisces. Graphic arts. Moving into design. Pretty smart. Then a bit of "Do you want to dance?" Great fucking dancer by the way. Then some "Where are you from?" New York. "Buy you a drink?" Pinot Grigio. I had the Pinot Grigio. He drinks whiskey. And finally "My place or your place?" His place. Always his place. And then of course the obligatory "Nice apartment. Is this your room? Ooo love the pea soup bed sheets. Condoms? Yes." I wasn't going to tell him that I was on the pill.

KEISHA: And how was he?

MATTIE: Good. Very good I should say. Excellent. Very high on the sexual compatibility scale. He moves well. Kinky but not perverted. Inventive. Good staying power. Good on the repeat. Sweats, but not profusely. Patient. Listens. Takes direction. A tad bit concerned with his performance, which is probably just a general personality trait. He is a Pisces after all and he ran track in high school. But all in all, good marks all around.

KEISHA: Mm-hmm. So this is your first one isn't it?

MATTIE: First what?

KEISHA: You know.

MATTIE: Yeah? And?

KEISHA: I'm just surprised it took you this long.

MATTIE: What do you mean?

KEISHA: Well we've known each other since school. I thought you would have by now. Omar's friends are cute. Remember Terrell? I always wondered why you didn't hook up with him.

MATTIE: Keisha, Terrell was semi-retarded and smelled like broccoli. But that's not the point. The point is I'd like to think my taste ranges a little beyond generalized stereotypes.

KEISHA: Oh please. You were curious.

MATTIE: And you aren't?

KEISHA: Me? Hell no.

MATTIE: Oh come on—

KEISHA: Omar's the only man for me—

MATTIE: Oh fuck Omar.

KEISHA: We're getting married.

MATTIE: Oh fuck marriage.

KEISHA: Mattie—

MATTIE: Oh come on you're telling me you're not curious? Okay so tell me, how many black men are in *Top Gun*? I'll tell you. One! And he's an extra. He barely has a speaking role. Yet every time you return my *Top Gun* video it always just so happens to be stopped right after the Tom Cruise/Val Kilmer volleyball scene. Now why is that?

(Slight pause.)

KEISHA: *(Holding up the magazine.)* What do you think, Sweep or Castillion? Castillion. Yeah definitely the Castillion.

SCENE 4

SAM's apartment. During the monologue MATTIE walks backward playfully urging SAM on. He follows as they remove each other's clothes.

MATTIE: Okay. Here I am. I am the salmon swimming upstream. Look at me swim. Swim. Swim. Swimming along. Heedless of my own safety, sanity and good sense. Just mindlessly swimming along! Hello Mr. Darwin! Hello Mr. Freud! Yes. Here I am adhering to the irresistible forces of id and natural selection—

(SAM kisses her.)

MATTIE: Okay. Wait. Wait. Wait. Cool your jets there speed racer. I see that we've got this cool *Wild-Kingdom-Nine-and-a-Half-Weeks* thing going on here. I get that. I totally get that and I'm totally going with it. But here's the deal. I don't want a boyfriend.

SAM: Neither do I.

MATTIE: Heh heh heh. Cute. Do you have a pen?

SAM: A what?

MATTIE: A pen. You know. An instrument that writes with ink?

SAM: *(Finding one.)* Um… Yeah?

MATTIE: Great. Paper? *(Looking. Finds a notebook and opens it.)* Wow did you draw this?

SAM: Um yeah. It's my grandfather.

MATTIE: Oh. Where is he supposed to be?

SAM: Kenya. He always wanted to go to Kenya. Never made it. So I drew him that picture before he died last year… *(Rips out a slice of paper and gently places the notebook back where it was.)* You can use this.

MATTIE: Oh… Okay…

SAM: So what is this?

MATTIE: Oh! It's a contract. Exit clause, now that I'm thinking about it. Yes. A contractual exit clause. Something simple and direct. Hm. *(Writing.)* In regards to the nature of the relationship between Mattie Winifred Carlson and—

SAM: Whoa, whoa, whoa. What is this?

MATTIE: A contract.

SAM: A contract?

MATTIE: Yes, what's the problem?

SAM: I'm sorry. I thought we were going to be having sex here.

MATTIE: That's not funny… There's nothing funny about wanting clarity.

SAM: Okay so… What is this a pre-nup?

MATTIE: A pre-nup would mean that we were getting married. That's kinda what I'm trying to avoid.

SAM: Well who the hell said we were getting married?

MATTIE: Well if you would just let me finish—

SAM: Okay go ahead—

MATTIE: Look, I'm not forcing you to do anything here. If you don't agree, I'll call a cab, and we can forget we ever met.

SAM: Okay. Mattie. What were you going to say?

MATTIE: Are you going to listen?

SAM: I've been listening I— *(Off her look.)* Okay.

MATTIE: What's your full name?

SAM: Samuel Malik Williams.

MATTIE: Oh I like that name. That's cute. Malik.

SAM: It's my grandfather's name... My other grandfather. He's still alive.

MATTIE: Okay... In regards to the nature of the relationship between Mattie Winifred Carlson and *(Writing.)* Samuel Malik Williams—

SAM: Winifred huh?

MATTIE: What?

SAM: Nothing it's just kinda *Little House on the Prairie* sounding. No seriously it's cute. Look, we *are* going to be having sex here right?

MATTIE: *(Writing.)* Each said party does hereby solemnly swear not to become emotionally attached i.e. fall in love with the other said party.

SAM: What?

MATTIE: *(Writing.)* Should either said party violate said agreement, the violated party is free to nullify any and all ties with the violating party. Signed Mattie Winifred Carlson. Today's date. *(Holds out the pen to SAM.)* I just like things to be clear.

(Pause. SAM signs. They kiss.)

SCENE 5

A bar. SAM and JEROME are drinking beers.

JEROME: There is one thing that I have to warn you about my brother. One very important thing that, as you embark on this new frontier of dating, you will find lacking. One thing that cannot be duplicated, cannot be replicated, cannot be approximated, or facsimilated. That one thing my brother... is the Ass. White women don't have It. They may think they have It. They may act like they have It. But they don't have It. They just don't. It's the law of nature. The amount of Ass, or the Ass Content per se, is directly proportional to the concentration of pigmentation in the skin. Therefore Sisters have high Ass Content while White girls and other pigmentally challenged females have low Ass Content. It's just the way it is. Can't do nothing about it. As a result, you will experience what I like to call A.W.... Ass-Withdrawal. A.W. is a painful ordeal my brother, and you may have thoughts of going back, but you must work it through because in the end, remember, it's for the best. Your case is particularly critical because you're going straight from sisters to white girls. See I did me a couple of Puerto Ricans in order to ease the transition. You know what I'm saying?

SAM: You are a very sick man.

SCENE 6

MATTIE and KEISHA's apartment. MATTIE's getting ready to go out. She's late.

KEISHA: Boughie or ghetto?

(Note: Boughie, pronounced with a soft "g," is short for bourgeois and slang for a "yuppified" black person.)

MATTIE: What?

KEISHA: Is Sam boughie or ghetto?

MATTIE: Is Sam what?

KEISHA: Are we talking Bryant Gumbel or Ol' Dirty Bastard?

MATTIE: Old dirty what?

KEISHA: Châteaux Neuf de Pap or Colt 45? *Cosby Show* or *Good Times*?

MATTIE: Oh. Does it matter?

KEISHA: It absolutely matters. And trust me you don't want either. Too ghetto and you're spending most of your time reading his pathetic love letters from Upstate if you know what I mean. Too boughie and well… You may as well date a white guy cause there's really no difference. And it's a lot safer.

MATTIE: That's fascinating Keisha. I'll be sure to call you when I write my thesis on the Socio-Economic Stratification of African-American Men.

KEISHA: Scoff all you want but these are things you're going to have to start thinking about now that you've officially reached the point of no return, as they say. Mm-hmm. See now Omar, I will admit, is a little bit on the ghetto side. But I have been able to boughie him up over the years. Not so much that he listens to chamber music now, but enough so that he realizes that dinner at Red Lobster is definitely *not* an example of fine dining. And speaking of eating out, does he go down on you?

MATTIE: What?

KEISHA: I'm just asking because as a rule, black men don't respect the cooch. I mean, sure they'll plow into it any chance they get, but the delicate art of cunnilingus? Not on your life. They look at it as a sign of weakness. As if eating pussy makes them less of a man. So what I'm telling you is that if he is ready willing and eager to go down on you… he's probably gay.

MATTIE: *(Exiting.)* I'll keep that in mind.

KEISHA: Good. You do that. And let me know if he wants you to pee on him or something nasty like that because that's an entirely different thing all together… And don't let him borrow any money!

SCENE 7

SAM's apartment. MATTIE sits on the bed. SAM enters.

SAM: Okay before we get started with tonight's festivities, I have a request to make.

MATTIE: Yes?

SAM: We invite some of my friends.

MATTIE: Excuse me?

SAM: I've got a couple of friends I'd like you to meet.

MATTIE: Um this wasn't in the agreement.

SAM: Yeah but I think you'll like these guys.

MATTIE: Okay. You know what? I think I'm going to sit this one out—

SAM: *(Turning on CD player. Miles Davis's "So What" is heard.)* Too late they're already here. Mattie. I'd like to introduce you to Mr. Davis and Mr. Coltrane. Two of my very good friends. Fellas. This is Mattie.

MATTIE: Wait a minute… Are you macking me?

SAM: Shh…

MATTIE: You are? What for? The macking's done. I'm here. I'm macked. There's no reason to re-mack let's just—

SAM: Just listen for a second—

MATTIE: But—

SAM: *(Putting a finger to her lips.)* Shh. Close your eyes—

MATTIE: Oh come on what is this?

SAM: Mattie. Close your eyes.

MATTIE: You're not going to ask me to pee on you are you?

SAM: What?

MATTIE: Forget it. Forget I said that.

SAM: Will you just close your eyes?

MATTIE: Okay. Fine. Closing.

SAM: Okay. Relax. Listen. What do you hear?

MATTIE: Music.

SAM: What kind of music?

MATTIE: Okay look this better not be one of those "Show the poor ignorant white chick what real music is all about" lessons. Because I can't even tell you how over that I am—

SAM: Will you just shut up and listen for a second?

MATTIE: Okay. Fine. Listening.

SAM: What kind of music do you hear?

MATTIE: Jazz.

SAM: Good. What does it make you think of?

MATTIE: Vinyl, smoke and puke.

SAM: Excuse me?

MATTIE: Vinyl. Smoke. Puke. When I was little, my uncle Eddie would sometimes give us rides in his Cadillac. He smoked cigars and it would make me puke.

SAM: What does that have to do with Jazz?

MATTIE: That's what he listened to while he was driving. Duh.

(Slight pause. SAM laughs.)

MATTIE: What?

SAM: *(Laughing.)* Okay. You got me. I was trying to mack you.

MATTIE: I know. It was so adorable, and I was totally trying to go with it, but believe me, there's no way you're getting laid while I'm thinking about my uncle Eddie.

SAM: *(Smiling.)* I'll shut it off.

MATTIE: No wait don't... That is nice...

SAM: Yeah?

MATTIE: Yeah... I don't want to puke... Mr. Davis and Mr.?

SAM: Coltrane.

MATTIE: Coltrane... I like it.

(She kisses him. Music rises.)

SCENE 8

MATTIE and KEISHA's apartment. Miles Davis plays in the background.

KEISHA: Okay. So Adam. Why were you seeing Adam?

MATTIE: He had a motorcycle.

KEISHA: Why'd you stop seeing him?

MATTIE: I joined Greenpeace. Couldn't deal with the motorcycle anymore.

KEISHA: Mm-hmm. And how about Matt? Why were you seeing Matt?

MATTIE: His name was Matt. You know. Mattie. Matt. Get it?

KEISHA: Why'd you stop seeing him?

MATTIE: His name was Matt. You know. Mattie. Matt. Get it?

KEISHA: Thor?

MATTIE: Thor. Always wanted to date a Thor. So I did. One day I asked him if he had a magic hammer. He didn't get it. So I stopped seeing him.

KEISHA: Aha. Apollo?

MATTIE: Same idea as the Thor thing.

KEISHA: What about Dan?

MATTIE: Dan?

KEISHA: Dan… Dan… Forget it. Alex?

MATTIE: Alex! Loved his cat. Great cat. Love, love, loved that cat.

KEISHA: And why'd you stop seeing him?

MATTIE: The cat died.

KEISHA: Uh-huh. So then what about Sam?

MATTIE: Sam?

KEISHA: Yeah. Why are you seeing Sam?

MATTIE: Um… I don't know.

KEISHA: You don't know?

MATTIE: No… No… I don't know.

KEISHA: *(Makes a gesture indicating how "big" SAM is.)* You don't know?

MATTIE: Oh stop it Keisha. I hate when you do shit like that.

KEISHA: Oh please Mattie. It's not like this is anything new. You guys all want black men. And it's not like they don't want you. Mm-hmm. I mean look at all these famous athletes and actors and politicians all got some fake-tittied, fake-tanned, fake-collagen-lipped, chippy-cha white chick in the stands rooting for them—talking about how they love these women because they was there since the beginning—completely forgetting about the poor black woman who actually *was* with them back in the day when these tired-assed, shit-talking, forty-drinking, no-job-having niggas wasn't about shit.

(Slight pause.)

MATTIE: What are you talking about?

KEISHA: Huh? Nothing. Oh come on Mattie I was just playing. It's just that you always have some trifling reason to sleep with someone. So he's black. Whatever. I mean come on, you just admitted to sleeping with someone because you liked his cat.

MATTIE: You didn't know that cat. You never knew that cat!

KEISHA: Mattie. Why are you so afraid to dig deeper into the emotional core of your relationships—

MATTIE: Keisha. I am not doing the Oprah thing with you right now—

KEISHA: I mean look at Omar and I. Don't you want that?

MATTIE: What you and Omar have? I don't think so.

KEISHA: What's that supposed to mean?

MATTIE: Well it's just that Omar's never really around and you guys are engaged—

KEISHA: He's busy. He works hard. He has a job. He works hard okay?—

MATTIE: I know but—

KEISHA: He works very hard—

MATTIE: I know. I just… Look I didn't mean anything by it. Okay?

KEISHA: Mm-hmm.

MATTIE: Keisha.

KEISHA: What?

MATTIE: Nothing.

(Pause.)

KEISHA: *(Indicating music.)* This is nice.

MATTIE: Yeah. It's Miles Davis. Sam let me borrow it. It's like a really rare bootleg or something. It's really nice isn't it?

KEISHA: Yeah. Too bad you'll have to give it back when you dump him.

SCENE 9

A grocery store. SAM shops. JEROME tags along.

JEROME: You're going to fuck this thing up.

SAM: What thing?

JEROME: This thing. This fuck thing you have going with this Mattie chick. You're going to fuck it up.

SAM: What are you talking about?

JEROME: I know you man. You're going to fuck up a really good fuck thing.

SAM: Jerome, what the hell are you talking about?

JEROME: I've got two words for you: Tyiesha Turner.

SAM: Who?

JEROME: You know who. Tyiesha Turner.

SAM: Tyiesha Turner.

JEROME: Uh-huh.

SAM: What about her?

JEROME: You had a good thing going with her and you fucked it up.

SAM: That was the fourth grade. We peed in a bush together.

JEROME: Yes! Yes you did! And then what did you do? You got all sensitive and started carrying her books to school, picking dandelions and shit like that. Did you get to pee in the bushes after that? No! Why? Because you turned into mister respectable guy, mister want to get to know you guy, mister let's bake brownies with mommy guy. Guys like you don't get to pee in the bushes. Guys like you don't get the bush period— ...what the hell is that?

SAM: Seitan.

JEROME: Say what?

SAM: Faux meat.

JEROME: Fo' what?

SAM: It's a veggie product.

JEROME: Tofu?

SAM: Not exactly. Mattie hates tofu.

JEROME: Aw man! You see? You see what you're doing here brother? Why are you going to let her tell you what to eat man?

SAM: She's not telling me what to eat man—

JEROME: See you do this shit to yourself all the time man. Letting these women run you man—

SAM: Nobody's running me man I'm just trying some new stuff—

JEROME: Damn. I was so happy when you started dating this white chick man. I thought you'd finally start to assert yourself with a woman. Face it man, woman run you all the time.

SAM: Why does it have to be about all that? I'm just buying food.

JEROME: This ain't about food man! This is about dignity! Supremacy! This is about who's on top!

SAM: Can I just shop in peace?

JEROME: Don't you see? She's already telling you what to eat. Then what? She's going to start telling you what to wear, how to act, when you are allowed to fuck. You cannot let that happen. Especially not with a white woman. Those are the easy ones. Those are the practice so that when you go back to a black woman—you know—to get married and so on, you'll be ready. You gotta think about these things man.

SAM: Wait a minute. Aren't you going to marry a white woman?

JEROME: Are you crazy? My mother would kill me.

SCENE 10

SAM's apartment. SAM and MATTIE are in bed.

Note: The entire scene is performed in blackout.

SAM: Oh my God. Oh my God. Oh my God. Oh my God. Oh MY GOD. *(Ad lib orgasm.)* GODDAMN! *(Roars.)* ...That was incredible!

MATTIE: Yeah I used to give lessons to my girlfriends. They called me Obi Wan.

SAM: Oh my God.

MATTIE: Uh-huh.

SAM: Whew... Well okay. Batten down the hatches here I go.

MATTIE: What?

SAM: Periscope down. I'm diving.

MATTIE: Sam.

SAM: Come on, it's your turn.

MATTIE: Nah.

SAM: What?

MATTIE: I don't want to.

SAM: What? Why?

MATTIE: You're not gay are you?

SAM: What?

MATTIE: Forget it! Forget I said that. Look, I don't like it. Okay? I just don't like it.

SAM: You don't like it? Why not?

MATTIE: I don't know. It's just eh... I've never liked it.

(Slight pause.)

SAM: I've never gone down on you have I?

MATTIE: Nope.

SAM: Yeah you always pull me up. Any time I try to go down you pull my head up.

MATTIE: Yup.

SAM: Why is that?

MATTIE: I just don't like it okay? How many times do I have to say that?

SAM: Well it's just a woman not liking that is like a kid who doesn't like ice cream. It doesn't happen.

MATTIE: Well it happens okay. Now come here... What?

SAM: But why?

MATTIE: Who cares?

SAM: I care. That's one of the major weapons in my arsenal man. And you're not even giving it a chance.

MATTIE: Sam I'm fine with the other major weapon in your arsenal. Now come here.

SAM: But why?

MATTIE: Sam—

SAM: What? Is it lapping speed?

MATTIE: Sam—

SAM: Oh you like to keep the little hood thing down don't you? Okay—

MATTIE: Sam—

SAM: Hood up? You're a hood up girl? No problem. Just let me know—

MATTIE: Sam! I am not talking about this anymore!!! All right!?!

SAM: All right! Jesus Christ I'm sorry! God.

(Pause.)

MATTIE: It makes me fart.

SAM: Excuse me?

MATTIE: It makes me fart okay Sam can we end this conversation now?

SAM: It makes you fart?

MATTIE: Yes.

SAM: You mean queef?

MATTIE: No. Not queef. Fart. It makes me fucking fart okay? I don't know why. The doctors don't know why. Nobody knows why. God hates me. Now drop it.

SAM: Okay.

(Pause.)

SAM: Stinky farts?

MATTIE: Oh fuck you Sam I am outta here!!! I am not putting up with you ridiculing my handicap!!!

SAM: Okay no wait! Whoa Mattie! Whoa! Mattie I'm sorry all right! I'm sorry! It's one of my favorite pastimes. It's just that's a little disappointing you know?

MATTIE: You're disappointed? You are disappointed? How do you think I feel? I'm like the weird kid in school who can't get on the roller coaster ride because she barfs all the time. Do you know how humiliating that is? God what I wouldn't give for a deaf man with a poor sense of smell.

SAM: I'm sorry baby—

MATTIE: Why do you care anyway? You get nothing out of it.

SAM: Of course I do. I get the pleasure of watching you cum.

MATTIE: You get that when we have sex.

SAM: I know. And thank you for that. But I'm also concentrating on myself so it splits my focus. Going down on a woman allows me to devote my entire attention to what I think is one of God's greatest achievements. The female orgasm. And there's such a sense of fulfillment. Because it's not easy. Every woman is different. Every woman a new puzzle. Fast, slow, light, heavy, finger, no finger, it's an art form, which must be mastered for each individual woman. And the culmination… the coup de grace… is that beautiful, musical, sensual, graceful, emotional, raw release of uninhibited joy. Takes my breath away every time. Every time.

(Pause.)

MATTIE: Maybe we can light a match?

SCENE 11

MATTIE and KEISHA's apartment. KEISHA is stuffing invitations. MATTIE's doing yoga.

KEISHA: So I met the horses last night.

MATTIE: The horses?

KEISHA: Yeah, Champ and Lucky Lady. You know, to pull my bridal carriage.

MATTIE: Oh yeah.

KEISHA: Yeah. So now is the time I find out that Omar's grandmother is deathly afraid of horses. Some childhood trauma she had when she was like two when her pet rabbits got trampled to death by a wild stallion.

MATTIE: Ugh.

KEISHA: Yeah, apparently it was pretty bad. Cause there were like 150 baby rabbits in the litter and somehow they got into the stable and the stallion was in heat so it just freaked out—and there where like bloody rabbit ears, and fluffy tails all over the place. And supposedly rabbits make the most awful screeching sound when they're dying. It's supposed to sound like a child crying or something like that.

MATTIE: Oh my God.

KEISHA: Yeah. But you would think that after what, seventy-eight years she would have gotten over something like that. Right? I mean come on, she was raised on a farm. She eats fried chicken for Christ sakes. I mean what? Chickens don't make horrible noises when they're getting slaughtered? I bet they do. So they bring out Champ and Lucky Lady, you know, the horses? And my grandmother-in-law-to-be totally freaks out. I mean freaks out. And it was really scary and kinda sad because she's autistic and just had a stroke, so only half of her face works, so it's like a total Dustin-Hoffman-*Rainman* kind of freak-out. I mean she starts banging her head screaming "Bunny!" "Bunny!" "Bunny!" which totally freaks out Lucky Lady who proceeds to take the biggest grossest shit I've ever seen right in front of us. I mean ten pounds of shit just drops out of this horse's ass. Just like that. And I'm like: "Is this normal?" And apparently it is! Horses shit without warning! Dogs squat, cats excuse themselves, but horses? No warning just "Sploosh!" Can you imagine if that were to happen during the ceremony? So to the hell with the horses I'm renting a limo.

MATTIE: Mm-hmm. So what about grandma?

KEISHA: Huh? Oh. I think she's able to talk now. Whatever. I think she blames me for the horse incident. And speaking of horses how's Sam?

MATTIE: Not funny.

KEISHA: Touchy. You must like him.

MATTIE: I just don't appreciate innuendo.

KEISHA: Mm-hmm.

(Pause.)

MATTIE: He does this thing where he blows air through the side of his mouth. And it sounds just like Miles Davis's trumpet. It's uncanny. But he looks like such a goofball when does it. Makes me laugh. He's cute.

(Slight pause.)

KEISHA: Do you think they could starve the horses? Not to be cruel, it's just that I've always dreamt of a horse-drawn carriage at my wedding. Maybe if I paid extra?

SCENE 12

SAM's apartment. SAM and JEROME are playing a video game.

JEROME: Okay so she's in there.

SAM: Uh-huh.

JEROME: The door's closed.

SAM: Uh-huh.

JEROME: What do you do?

SAM: Knock.

JEROME: Yeah but knock and go in? Or knock and wait till she says something?

SAM: I don't know. It depends on what she's doing.

JEROME: You don't know what she's doing. She's just in there. You know she's in there. And you have to go.

SAM: I don't know.

JEROME: Well what do you usually do?

SAM: Like I said I knock.

JEROME: Okay. Okay. And so what if she says "Come in."

SAM: I'd go in.

JEROME: And if she's taking a piss? Or she's in a feminine way?

SAM: What I walk in there and she's taking a piss?

JEROME: Yeah. Yeah. Or some female type shit. You know.

SAM: Why would she tell me to come in then?

JEROME: This is what I'm asking you. Would she? Would she mind?

SAM: Well I guess she doesn't mind if she's telling me to come in.

JEROME: But that's what I'm asking you man. Would she mind? Would you mind? Walking in on her like that? You know. Would you be all embarrassed and shit talking about "Oh my bad baby I didn't know you were douching in here." Or would you just start chatting about what you all are going to do for dinner that evening?

SAM: Man what are you asking me all this for?

JEROME: I'm just trying to see how far gone you are on this chick man. If you all are sharing bathroom time, you're fucked.

SAM: I'm not gone on her. We're just having fun.

JEROME: I'm just looking out for you brother.

SAM: Jerome. I'm cool.

JEROME: All right.

(Pause as they play some more.)

JEROME: Do you shit while she's here? And if you do, do you use the spray or just leave the door open to air it out?

SCENE 13

A bar lounge. SAM, MATTIE, and JEROME sit at a table with drinks.

JEROME: Never?

MATTIE: Never.

JEROME: Never ever?

MATTIE: Never ever.

JEROME: Never ever, ever?

SAM: Jerome—

JEROME: Okay let's say perchance that you were stuck on a deserted island and there was nothing there but a cow. Nothing but sand and a fucking cow. Would you then?

MATTIE: Nope.

JEROME: You would die?

MATTIE: Yup.

JEROME: And if the cow ate you?

MATTIE: The cow wouldn't eat me.

JEROME: How do you know? How do you know this cow?

MATTIE: Cows don't eat meat. They're herbivores.

JEROME: Yeah when it suits them. When it's convenient for them. When they're living the plush pansy cow life chewing cud and getting milked all day. Maybe. But I'm telling you. Put a cow in an extreme situation where it's got to choose between its beliefs and living another day and I'll show you one fucking scary cow—

MATTIE: But cows don't eat meat.

SAM: Mattie you realize you're arguing with a drunk don't you—

JEROME: I'm not drunk—

SAM: Take it easy—

MATTIE: But they physically cannot digest meat do you understand that?

SAM: Baby—

MATTIE: I cannot continue this argument until I least get the proper analogy!

SAM: He's drunk!

JEROME: I'm not drunk.

SAM: Jerome take it—

JEROME: Don't touch me man! …I get it okay? Do I look like I was born on a farm? No! Do I look like a field hand to you? No! I get it now. Thank you. I'll go take the S-A-Fucking-Ts now. Cows can't digest meat. Thank you very much. But *you* can digest meat. Yeah! What if *you* were the cow! Huh? What if you were the cow? What then? All I'm saying is that the difference between choice and instinct is pretty fucking slim in real life applications. When you're there on the edge looking down into the great abyss and you can't see the pretty white light at the end and you can't hear the pretty flute music or smell the pink puffy petunias, instinct takes over… *(Gets up.)* I can see that she's good for you Sammy my man. Good for you. You think I can't see it? I can. *(Derisive.)* Look Winifred… Despite what your parents may say, or the sideways looks you might get. Despite the fact that you're eating this fuck meat crap. Despite the fact that we don't play NBA Live much anymore. Go for it. Fuck it. You're nothing but animals working off instinct… You're a beautiful, beautiful, beautiful, beautiful, man Samuel Malik Williams. *(Tries to kiss SAM.)* I love you.

(JEROME passes out.)

SAM: He's just… Yeah.

SCENE 14

SAM's apartment. MATTIE's in bed sleeping. She wakes up with a sudden gasp. She reaches for SAM who's not there.

MATTIE: Sam? Sam!

SAM: *(Offstage.)* Yeah?

MATTIE: Oh. Nothing.

SAM: *(Entering.)* You okay?

MATTIE: Yeah.

SAM: You sure?

MATTIE: Yes.

SAM: You're shaking.

MATTIE: I'm just cold.

SAM: Want some more blanket?

MATTIE: No I'm fine Sam—

SAM: Are you sure you're all right?

MATTIE: Yes!

SAM: Okay.

(Pause.)

MATTIE: I just had a bad dream that's all.

SAM: Okay… Do you want to tell me about it?

MATTIE: No.

SAM: Okay.

(Pause.)

MATTIE: It was just a weird dream is all.

SAM: Okay.

MATTIE: One of those falling dreams.

SAM: Oh. I hate those. I have those all the time. I always wake up right before I hit. Freaks me out.

MATTIE: I wasn't the one falling. You were.

SAM: I was?

MATTIE: Well I was carrying all this other stuff like the dirt bike with the mag-wheels that my dad got me when I was six, all my old tests and report cards, the bowling ball that I won the Louisville Junior Open with, my old head gear, my baseball card collection, my autographed picture of Scott Baio, the sloppy joes my mom used to make me eat before I went vegan—I mean I just had this mountain of stuff that stretched up to forever. And I was carrying it to who knows where… When I tripped and I was like "Oh shit! Oh shit! Everything's going to fall! Everything's going to fall!" And I was like "Whoooaaa!" You know, trying to keep everything from falling. And I thought it was okay until I looked up in the sky and I could see something falling from the very top of the pile. At first I thought it was Oscar, the ferret that I helped escape from the petting zoo when I was twelve, but as it got closer and closer I could see that it was you.

SAM: So what'd you do?

MATTIE: Well it was either, drop all my shit and catch you or… You know.

SAM: Yeah? So?

MATTIE: I woke up.

SAM: You were going to let me fall?

MATTIE: No— Well I don't know.

SAM: That is messed up. You were going to sacrifice me for some sloppy joes and a picture of Scott Baio?

MATTIE: No I wasn't.

SAM: Wow.

MATTIE: Stop it.

(She leans against him. Pause.)

MATTIE: What do you like about it?

SAM: About what?

MATTIE: It.

SAM: It?

MATTIE: Yeah.

SAM: I like the sounds of it. Not just the vocal ones moaning and groaning and all that. But all the sounds of it. The moist slappy, squishy, slurpy sounds of it. That and the odor of it. I like how it kind of sticks to the back of your throat and tickles the little hairs in your nostrils. That and the taste of it. That taste in your mouth. That's what I like about it. You?

MATTIE: The tussle. The struggle. The push-pull fight of it. The final acquiescence yes. But not without the fight. Not without the tussle.

(SAM kisses her.)

MATTIE: When dogs have sex do they like it?

SAM: I would think so.

MATTIE: And do they like each other as well or is it just the sex?

SAM: I would think they like each other.

MATTIE: So when a dog is humping your leg. You're saying he likes your leg?

SAM: Yeah. I guess not.

MATTIE: Sometimes I wish we were dogs. You know? Life would be so much simpler. Just take a whiff of someone's ass and you know all you need to know about that person. No time wasted in intimacy counseling or anger management sessions. You wanna know how I feel? Smell my ass.

SAM: I just want the skill of licking my own balls.

MATTIE: I gotta go.

SAM: I was kidding.

MATTIE: No I just gotta go.

SAM: Okay.

MATTIE: I'm just making sure we're not crossing the line. Contractually speaking of course.

SAM: Oh. Yeah. Of course not... I mean... You know—

MATTIE: Yeah... I mean... You know—

SAM: I'm cool.

MATTIE: You're cool?

SAM: I'm cool if you're cool.

MATTIE: I'm cool.

SAM: *(Shrugs.)* Cool... Call you a cab?

MATTIE: Okay...

SAM: Okay... Yeah I don't think that dogs actually like each other when they're having sex. I think it's just programmed instinct. Just the right combination of pheromones. Like has nothing to do with it... Then again, I'm not a dog.

MATTIE: Neither am I.

SCENE 15

MATTIE and KEISHA's apartment. KEISHA is trying on her wedding dress.

MATTIE: Okay so there I am on the turnpike. Just me and Mr. Pugglewuck who's driving because it's his turn to drive. And we're driving, flipping through the radio stations. And all of a sudden "Relax" by Frankie Goes to Hollywood comes on! You know that song? *(Singing.)* "Relax! don't do it! When you wanna sock it to it! Relax! Don't do it when you wanna come! Huh!" I love that song. So does Mr. Pugglewuck and it's so funny because we had just been saying ten minutes earlier how cool it would be if we could hear that song. And there it was! I love when that happens. So anyway it's me and Mr. Pugglewuck and we're driving, and singing and blowing bubbles. Roasting marshmallows in the campfire we've got going in the glove compartment. And we're eating kumquats and Skittles and it's funny because Mr. Pugglewuck who's always been a little on the compulsive side, likes to color coordinate his Skittles before he eats them. So he's got them lined up on the dashboard, you know red, orange, yellow, green, blue, indigo, violet and he's eating them one by one. And that's when I notice that the Skittles are lined up in the exact order of the colors in the visible light spectrum. So I go: "Hey Mr. Pugglewuck! ROY G BIV! Get it?" Which I thought was pretty hysterical but apparently was completely lost on Mr. Pugglewuck cause he kinda just looked me and blinked. Which, at the time, I thought that was kinda rude. So I was about to say something when I noticed that instead of arms, Mr. Pugglewuck had fins... And that's when things started to get little weird.

KEISHA: Uh-huh.

MATTIE: Mr. Pugglewuck was actually *the* Mr. Pugglewuck. The sea lion my mother bought me when I was three when my parents and I went to Sea World one summer. Mr. Pugglewuck was my most favorite toy, who I lost on the beach when we went down to the Keys a few years later.

KEISHA: Uh-huh.

MATTIE: And according to my parents I almost drowned trying to swim out to sea in order to find Mr. Pugglewuck who, apparently, I assumed had run away because he was homesick. I was in a coma for three hours. I of course have no recollection of this. But that's not the point. The point is that what I hadn't noticed until after I woke up is that anytime Mr. Pugglewuck spoke… it was with Sam's voice.

KEISHA: Oh.

MATTIE: Yeah.

KEISHA: What do you think that means?

MATTIE: That I should stop seeing him.

SCENE 16

SAM's apartment. SAM and MATTIE languish in bed.

SAM: So what do you want to do now?

MATTIE: I don't know.

SAM: Do you want me to call you a cab?

MATTIE: What?

SAM: A cab.

MATTIE: Do you want me to leave?

SAM: Well I—

MATTIE: Because if you want me to leave I will.

SAM: No I thought you wanted to leave.

MATTIE: What would give you get that impression?

SAM: It's what always happens. I just assumed that—

MATTIE: You assumed?

SAM: Well yeah—

MATTIE: Sam. If I wanted to leave, I would just leave. I would just say "Sam, I'm leaving." And then I would leave. Thus relieving you of the burden of assumption.

SAM: Whatever Mattie. I was just being polite. As in, if you, Mattie want to leave, I will graciously call you a cab Mattie.

MATTIE: What's gracious about calling me a cab Sam? I'm not a retard Sam. I know how to use a phone Sam. I've called a cab or two in my life Sam. In fact I would say I'm pretty darn good at cab-calling Sam. Thank you very much Sam.

SAM: Okay—

MATTIE: Okay so no need for the shroud of chivalry Sam! If you want me to leave, just say leave—

SAM: I never said I wanted you to leave!

MATTIE: So why are you trying to call me a cab?

SAM: Can we just drop the cab!

MATTIE: You brought it up!

SAM: Okay! All right! I'm sorry about the cab Mattie!

MATTIE: I don't want an apology Sam.

SAM: Then what do you want Mattie?

MATTIE: Clarity.

SAM: Clarity?

MATTIE: Clarity.

SAM: Clarity about what?

MATTIE: Clarity on whether or not you want me to leave. Do you?

SAM: No! Do you?

MATTIE: No!

SAM: Fine!

MATTIE: Fine!

(Pause.)

SAM: Are you PMS-ing or something—

MATTIE: Oh my God! That is so fucking typical. Of course you would say that—

SAM: I'm just asking—

MATTIE: *(Mimicking SAM.)* "Are you PMS-ing or something? Are you PMS-ing or something?" Could you at least be a little more creative in your stupidity?

SAM: What is wrong with you?

MATTIE: Nothing. Nothing's wrong with me that's the point! But no! Dr. Sam over here, recent graduate of the University of Assumption specializing in Assumptionology automatically assumes that I am having my period.

(Slight pause.)

SAM: You know what maybe you should leave.

MATTIE: Oh now he wants me to leave. Fine I'm leaving—

SAM: Oh Jesus Christ Mattie what is this about—

MATTIE: Why do you want to know? I'm leaving remember—

SAM: Mattie!

MATTIE: Yes?

SAM: Can you at least tell me what is wrong with you?

MATTIE: Well to do that that would mean I have to stay and since you don't want me to stay I—

SAM: Mattie. Stop it... What's wrong?

MATTIE: Nothing. Oh my God. Am I not being clear? No. No I'm not. I realize that I'm not being clear... Okay, look. I've gotta go. Okay? I promise not to let the door hit my ass on the way out. Heh heh heh. Okay? See ya—I mean bye. Bye. Bye Sam.

SCENE 17

MATTIE and KEISHA's apartment. MATTIE is reading Milestones, *the autobiography of Miles Davis. Phone rings. KEISHA picks up.*

KEISHA: Keisha and Omar 2002? This is Keisha. Yes this is Keisha Jackson. Soon to be Mrs. Keisha Jackson-Johnson. Oh yes, it's about time you returned my call. Yes well there is a problem with the doves. Doves. You know cute little white birds; universal symbols of love and romance? Doves! You rent them! Yes I'll hold... Yes hello. Yes well, I specifically requested twelve white doves. Six for me and six for Omar. Yes Omar, my husband-fiancé. What?

Yes six male doves and six female doves to represent the six years we have been dating and they were to be released from the bell tower as soon as we emerged from St. Mary's. Now you remember? Good. Hold on I've got a beep. *(Clicks over.)* Keisha and Omar 2002? This is Keisha. Jean-Claude? Oui? Non! Non! Non! Non! Pas de crustacae dans le seafood gumbo!

(MATTIE turns up the music a bit.)

KEISHA: De crabe? Mais oui! C'est une crustacae! Shell! Shell! It has a shell! Mon fiancé ne le mange pas. Il est allergic! Quoi? Escargot? Escargot? Mais je ne sais pas. Je vais s'appeller. D'accord— *(Slams the phone down.)* Merde! *(Picks it up, dials.)* Goddamn it I don't know how many times I— Can you turn that down? Mattie?

MATTIE: What?

KEISHA: I'm on the phone. Turn the music down please?

(MATTIE turns it down a bit.)

KEISHA: *(To phone.)* Hello? Omar? Omar? What took you so long to pick up the phone? Where are you? What? *Where* are you? This is Keisha. Keisha? Remember me? What? Uh-huh. Well then where are you? Uh-huh. What are you doing? I said what are you doing? I thought you were at work. I'm just asking a question. You're the one who's getting the attitude— *(To MATTIE.)* Mattie turn the music down! Shit. *(Into phone.)* What? Not you. Mattie's acting up. She just broke up with Sam.

MATTIE: Keisha, that's none of his business.

KEISHA: *(Into phone.)* Sam. Oh I didn't tell you? She's been screwing some brother named Sam. Mm-hmm yeah he's black. Mm-hmm. What? *(Laughs.)* I know she was—

MATTIE: What'd he say?

KEISHA: Oh nothing.

MATTIE: No what'd he say?

KEISHA: Baby can you eat escargot? Escargot. ES-CAR-GO! Snails. Well have you ever tried? You've never tried. So are you allergic? I'm just asking a question. Maybe you'd know without eating it. Look, I really don't need an attitude right now. I have a lot of things that need to get done—

MATTIE: Keisha I really don't think that—

KEISHA: *(To OMAR.)* Because chicken or fish is ghetto! Come on Omar, we may as well get married at Ponderosa. What's wrong with Ponderosa? Are you trying to ruin my wedding?

MATTIE: Keisha.

KEISHA: Mattie I'm on the phone.

MATTIE: Fine I'll wait.

KEISHA: *(To OMAR.)* You know what? I'll just tell Jean-Claude to make a special plate for you so that the rest of the guests can eat the seafood. No you are not eating hot wings at my wedding— You know what? I don't have time for your country black ass right now— I've got a beep. Hello? Who? Uh-huh... *(Pause.)* Oh Yes, the doves! Yes well I saw them yesterday and let me tell you something. Dyed white pigeons from Chinatown do not a dove make! Now, I'm an associate at Piper and Walburg and I will sue you for false advertising, false representation and false indemnification faster than you can spell A-S-P-C-A if you don't get me some real doves for my wedding motherfucker— please hold *(Clicks over.)* Keisha and Omar 2002? This is Keisha... oh hi. Hold on.

(KEISHA holds out the phone to MATTIE. MATTIE gives the "I'm not home" sign.)

KEISHA: Nope sorry you just missed her...

SCENE 18

SAM's apartment. JEROME is rummaging through the fridge. SAM's on the phone.

The line is busy.

JEROME: Wheat gluten. Rice milk. Rice milk? They can get milk outta rice? Ah shit. They putting the cows outta work now. We going to see cows on the welfare lines now. Living up in the projects, eating government soy cheese. Ain't that some ironic shit? Oh thank God, some chicken *(Holding it up to read the label.)* Textured Vegetable Protein. *(Puts it back.)* Goddamn, can a brother get a hot dog up in here? Soy bologna, soy tacos, soy ribs— soy ribs!?! Yo that shit ain't right. This is some offensive shit right here. I mean I'm offended here man. This is three generations of barbecuing heritage talking here. Soy ribs? Man, I'm going to have to revoke your ghetto privileges—

SAM: They're actually not that bad—

JEROME: You tried it—

SAM: Yeah I bought it didn't I?

JEROME: Yeah but I figured that was just for show. You know so you could stay fucking this chick.

SAM: Jerome.

JEROME: I do that shit all the time. It's all about the fucking. Lizzy Lipshitz? Bitch turned me into a matzoh ball eating, beanie hat thing wearing, Sammy Davis Jr. singing motherfucker. Shit I know. I do it too. It's all about the fucking—

SAM: Jerome— *(In phone.)* Hello. Oh hi. This is Sam. Is Mattie there? Okay tell her I called—

JEROME: And let me ask you something? If this Mattie chick doesn't eat meat, doesn't wear meat, doesn't want anything do with meat. Can she still suck your dick?—

SAM: JEROME SHUT THE FUCK UP!

JEROME: What? What'd I say?

SAM: I'm not in the mood for your shit right now.

JEROME: Look at you man. On the phone dialing like a little punk. Come on man. She played you like scrabble man—

SAM: Get out.

JEROME: What?

SAM: You heard me I said get out.

JEROME: Oh stop it man. How many times have I got to tell you about women man? You're like a puppy dog. Ya sweaty bitch.

SAM: *(Taking a step.)* Jerome.

JEROME: *(Takes a step.)* What? What are you going to do?

SAM: Get the fuck out.

(Pause as they stare each other down.)

JEROME: *(Finally backs off a step.)* Whatever.

(JEROME exits.)

SCENE 19

MATTIE and KEISHA's apartment.

KEISHA: Kelly.

MATTIE: Kelly?

KEISHA: Kelly.

MATTIE: Is that her name?

KEISHA: She works out at our gym. She's Norwegian. Size two ass. The bitch.

MATTIE: How'd you find out?

KEISHA: Voicemail.

MATTIE: She left a voicemail?

KEISHA: No he left a voicemail.

MATTIE: He left a voicemail?

KEISHA: Yes. He left a voicemail for her on my cell phone.

MATTIE: He left her a voicemail on your phone?

KEISHA: Yes.

MATTIE: I don't get it.

KEISHA: Keisha and Kelly are not very far apart alphabetically. He must've hit the wrong speed dial button.

MATTIE: Oh my God.

KEISHA: Yeah well the man is *not* really known for his Mensa eligibility.

(Apartment buzzer sounds.)

KEISHA: Tell that motherfucker that I want nothing to do with him.

(MATTIE goes to the door. SAM enters with flowers.)

SAM: Hey—

MATTIE: Hey—

SAM: Just stopping by.

MATTIE: Sam—

KEISHA: Hello there.

SAM: Oh hey you must be Keisha. I'm—

KEISHA: Sam yes of course you are—

SAM: Well it's nice to finally meet you. Congrats on the upcoming wedding.

KEISHA: Thank you.

MATTIE: Sam—

KEISHA: Nice flowers. For me?

SAM: No for Mattie here—

KEISHA: So what is it about white girls Sam? Is it the status symbol that you like or is it that they're so fucking easy?

SAM: Wh-

MATTIE: Keisha!

KEISHA: Can't I ask the man a question? Sam—

MATTIE: Keisha—

KEISHA: Sam. Can I ask you a question—

SAM: Guys—

MATTIE: Keisha stop it!

KEISHA: Sam. Seriously. What is it? You all can't handle us? Do we intimidate you baby—

MATTIE: Stop it!

KEISHA: Oh calm down! Damn Mattie! You're acting like he actually means something to you. Do you have a cat Sam?—

SAM: A cat?—

MATTIE: Don't listen to her—

KEISHA: No cat? You sure you don't have a cat? Hm… I wonder what it could be?—

MATTIE: Keisha don't—

KEISHA: I don't know Sam. There's gotta be something about you that keeps Mattie's attention. What do you think it is?

MATTIE: Sam just leave. Sam. Leave. Please?

SAM: Mattie—

KEISHA: I know what it is! It's your dick! You've got a big dick Sam! A big black dick. Congratulations.

(Pause. MATTIE exits.)

SAM: Nice to meet you.

SCENE 20

A sidewalk. Sounds of cars whizzing by as MATTIE tries to hail a cab. Enter SAM from offstage.

SAM: Hey! Mattie! Hey! Where are you going?

MATTIE: What the hell were you doing?

SAM: What?

MATTIE: Coming over like that? What the hell were you doing?

SAM: I was just dropping by.

MATTIE: Unannounced? You don't call or anything?

SAM: You haven't been returning my calls. So I thought I'd just drop by—

MATTIE: Give me those— *(Grabs the roses and stomps on them.)*

SAM: Mattie—

MATTIE: I'm on to you now you sneaky motherfucker— Taxi!

SAM: What are you talking about?

MATTIE: TAXI!

SAM: Mattie!

MATTIE: TAXI—

SAM: MATTIE!

MATTIE: What!

SAM: Where are you going?

MATTIE: Home!

SAM: You live up the block.

MATTIE: I'm going to my mother's house— TAXI for Christ sakes—

SAM: Your mother lives in Louisville.

MATTIE: No shit Sherlock!—

SAM: Louisville!?! You're taking a cab to Louisville, Kentucky?—

MATTIE: See that's the point! Why do you care where I'm going Sam?

SAM: Why wouldn't I care?

MATTIE: So you admit it? You admit to this caring?

SAM: Of course I do!

MATTIE: Yeah well I'd call that emotional attachment wouldn't you Sam? Flowers? Calling? Caring? Yes. I'd call that emotional attachment. We had an agreement! We signed a contract.

SAM: Oh my God! You cannot possibly be still thinking about that stupid fucking contract—

MATTIE: Stupid fucking contract?—

SAM: Mattie, I think we both know that we've gone beyond the bounds of your little contract.

MATTIE: My little contract? You signed it too! You signed a contract expressly forbidding us to become emotionally attached—

SAM: No, that contract did not forbid anything. It was an exit clause just in case we did become emotionally attached.

MATTIE: Then I'm exiting. Taxi!

SAM: Mattie.

MATTIE: Taxi!

SAM: Mattie.

MATTIE: TA-

(Pause.)

SAM: Mattie? Mattie take it easy. Let's just go home. *(Takes a step.)* Mattie?

MATTIE: *(Steps away.)* I'm going to Louisville.

SAM: Why?

MATTIE: Remember what Keisha said?

SAM: That was garbage.

MATTIE: It was true.

SAM: Mattie come on—

MATTIE: No it was true Sam. It was simple curiosity. That's really what the contract was about. I just wanted a black guy for a couple of months just to have something interesting to put in my diary.

SAM: Bullshit Mattie.

MATTIE: It's true.

SAM: Bullshit.

MATTIE: Sam. Goodbye.

(Pause.)

SAM: Thanks for the ride.

(SAM exits.)

SCENE 21

A bar. SAM sits alone with a drink. JEROME enters. There is an awkward pause. JEROME sits.

JEROME: I knew this Indian chick once. You know, red dot on the forehead and all that shit. Her name was Sipi. Worked at the Foot Locker on Flatbush. She was something. Mad cute in the umpire strips. Little black Converse on. That girl was fine man. Fine ass little Sipi. Sold me a pair of Airwalks, the New Jordans when they came out. A pair of Reebok pumps. Remember Reebok pumps? The fly shit. Right? Sold me all kinds of shit. Socks, tees, my Knicks hat. Damn. I would just go in there sometimes, not even wanting to buy shit. Just check her out. She had this shy smile, the way she looked at me, all shy and shit. I think she was sweating me too. You know. So one time I'm like, "Yo check this out, I'ma roll up in there and ask for her number, and I'ma take her to Coney Island." You know, go slow because you could tell that she was one of those slow girls. Take a whole six months before she'll let you even see her bra strap you know what I'm saying? Probably got to go to some funky ass holy temple and sacrifice a goat or some shit before she'll let you fuck her. You know what I mean? But she looked like she was worth it. You know them Indian people be some freaks behind closed doors. Kama Sutra? 'Nuff said. So I rolled up in there, had my pumps on, had my Knicks hat on with matching Reebok suit. Yeah, you know the deal. And I rolled up in there and I said "A yo Sipi come here girl!" And she was all embarrassed and shit. Talking about "Can I help you sir?" And I was like "Yeah you can help me… what's up with that red dot on your forehead girl somebody poke you or what?" You know, just trying to break the ice and shit. And she looked at me for a second… and started to cry. And I'm like "Naw Sipi baby don't cry I was just teasing. Shit I like the red dot!" And that was the truth. I was cool with the red dot. But she just kept crying like I stole her suede Pumas or something. So the manager, probably her father or some shit comes out and says to me *(Mimicking Indian manager.)* "My friend. You must leave. You must leave right now my friend." And I'm like: "Yo can't I apologize? Can I say I'm sorry?" "No my friend you must leave. You must leave right now my friend. Or I call the cops." Shit what's this friend shit? You ain't my friend motherfucker! You ain't my friend! How are you gonna call the cops on your friend? So anyway, they kicked me out. Banned me from Foot Locker. Imagine that? Ban a brother from Foot Locker? That shit ain't right… I heard through the Foot Locker grapevine that Sipi went to med school a couple of years ago. I knew that girl was smart. Heard she got married too. Some Indian doctor. Two doctors in the house? They must be making bank! Wish I could see her again. Let her know I was cool with the red dot…

SAM: I just got the new NBA Live yesterday.

JEROME: Word?

SAM: Yup… I'll let you play Jordan…

JEROME: Cool.

SCENE 22

Unknown location. MATTIE sits alone as she speaks into a small tape recorder.

MATTIE: You ever wonder what keeps everything going? What is it that binds us? That keeps this whole system moving along you know? I mean there is so much going on at the same time and for the most part it seems to hold together. You ever think why? Like what is it that holds everything together preventing just a complete meltdown of everything? Is it law? Common sense? Fear? God? Whatever it is it seems very tenuous. As if the slightest tug or pull will result in utter collapse. Sometimes I'll just stop in the middle of the street and let the person behind me bump into me. Just to see what happens you know? Watch them walk around me and usually they're all flustered and annoyed and every once in a while apologetic. Like it was their fault. And it always makes me wonder, how through my action of stopping, have I altered their life? You know? Maybe I jarred them out of a moment of self-loathing, or a moment of fond remembrance? Maybe in that split second of stopping them, I caused that person to miss the cab that would eventually get into a horrible fatal accident. Saving his life, and in doing so, maybe I caused the guy that got the cab instead to die in the other guy's place… Maybe we are God and just don't know it… Mattie Winifred Carlson. This moment.

SCENE 23

MATTIE and KEISHA's apartment. KEISHA's on the phone as she rifles through invoices and receipts and phone numbers, etc.

KEISHA: *(Into phone.)* Hi it's me. I just wanted to let you know that I was finally able to get in touch with the DJ and cancel. I'm not getting the hundred dollar deposit back, but that's to be expected. The photographer is a different story. He's trying to argue that he should still get paid, because we— because I didn't give him enough notice and that at least, he should get his plane ticket reimbursed. But I'm like, no way, I mean it's not my fault you bought a nonrefundable ticket. Shit. I mean it's not like he can't apply it to something else— *(Voicemail runs out.)* Hello? Shit. *(Redials.)* Hi sorry, your voicemail cut me off so I couldn't finish. Anyway— Oh I'm still trying to get a hold of Manny at Tux Life to see if maybe I can return the tuxes I had made for you and the groomsmen. If not I guess I'll just throw them out. Oh maybe sell them or— Oh I mean unless you want to hold on to them for some reason? Let me know and maybe we can make a deal or someth- *(Voicemail runs out.)* Hello? Shit.

(KEISHA redials. MATTIE enters. KEISHA doesn't see her.)

KEISHA: Hi, it's me again. Sorry, there's just so much— oh I got an RSVP from

Latrell Parker. Can you believe it? He said he couldn't believe I finally got you to settle down. Isn't that funny? Oh well, I guess I have to call him back… I guess I have to call everybody back— whatever. Your mom called today… Again. I keep telling her that it's not her fault. I mean why would she say that? Why would she think it's her fault? These things— *(Voicemail runs out.)* Goddamn it! *(Redials.)* Okay, I'm just going to make this quick. We— I still owe a thousand dollars to the caterers, another four hundred dollars to the videographer. Two grand to the florists. Oh the rings! I was able to cancel that order without them charging me. I think they let it slide since they'd gotten the "Keisha and Omar Forever" inscription wrong the first time. I wish I had gotten to see them— Hello? *(Slight pause. Then, slamming phone repeatedly.)* MO-THER-FUCK-ER! MO-THER-FUCK-ER! MO-THER-FUCK-ER! HOW DARE YOU DESTROY MY LIFE!!!… *(Pause. She goes to redial.)*

MATTIE: Keisha?

KEISHA: *(Startled.)* Oh my god Mattie you scared the shit out of me.

MATTIE: I'm sorry—

KEISHA: Where've you been? The rent's due. Did you know that? I mean what? You think you can just walk out of here and do what you want and everything'll be fine huh? *(Trying to dial the phone again.)* You just don't walk out on people like that Mattie… You have to take responsibility for your actions. You just don't walk out on people like that—

MATTIE: Keisha put the phone down—

KEISHA: I just need to tell him that— that— I—

MATTIE: Keisha. Put the phone down.

(Pause. KEISHA puts the phone down. MATTIE hugs her.)

KEISHA: I'm sorry.

MATTIE: I'm sorry.

SCENE 24

SAM's place. SAM sits on the bed doing the mouth trumpet noise. The apartment buzzer sounds. SAM goes to answer it.

MATTIE: Hi.

SAM: Hi. What are you doing here?

MATTIE: Just wanted to say hi.

SAM: How's Keisha?

MATTIE: She's okay. We're okay. She told me you stopped by.

SAM: I wanted my CD back.

MATTIE: Oh. *(Pulling out the Miles Davis.)* Here.

SAM: Thanks…

MATTIE: How's Jerome?

SAM: He's fine. Okay you've said your "hi" I've got my CD—

MATTIE: Sam—

SAM: Mattie what are you doing here?

MATTIE: I just wanted to say hi—

SAM: What not enough Negroes in Louisville?

MATTIE: Sam.

SAM: Well you know what they say—

MATTIE: Sam—

SAM: Once you go black you never go back—

MATTIE: Sam! I'm sorry Sam. That was never what it was about. I—

SAM: No?

MATTIE: No.

SAM: So then why did you say it?

MATTIE: I was trying to hurt you.

SAM: No shit. So then what? You're here to say you're sorry?

MATTIE: Yes.

SAM: So say it.

MATTIE: I'm sorry.

SAM: So then great. I guess we're done here. Don't let the door hit your ass on the way out.

MATTIE: Sam—

SAM: Mattie, isn't this a violation of our agreement? We got close. You invoked the exit clause, as per the contract. So what the hell are you doing here?

MATTIE: The contract. I know Sam. It was just— I don't know what I was thinking... It's just that I... Well I realized that the contract wasn't clear.

SAM: It was clear to me—

MATTIE: No. Yes you're right. It was clear enough, but it was too finite. Yes. It was too finite and it didn't give much room for reevaluation. *(She pulls out the contract.)* So I added a couple of amendments that would allow us to reassess the situation at regular intervals as well as room for—

SAM: Mattie.

MATTIE: Yes?

SAM: Can I see that for a second?

MATTIE: *(Handing to him.)* Okay.

SAM: What famous person do you imagine yourself being married to?

MATTIE: What?

SAM: When you daydream. Who are you married to?

MATTIE: Oh. Um. Ewan MacGregor...

SAM: Uh-huh—

MATTIE: Or Harrison Ford—

SAM: Uh-huh—

MATTIE: Russell Crowe. Jeff Goldblum, don't ask me why, Pierce Brosnan, Freddy Prinze Jr. in my more cheesy moments. Why?

SAM: I think of Claire Huxtable.

MATTIE: *Cosby Show.*

SAM: Yeah. I met her once. I was on line at the Food Emporium reading a magazine, and you know how you can feel it when someone's reading over your shoulder? I hate that. So I kinda turned a little to indicate my displeasure and there she was... Mrs. Claire Huxtable.

MATTIE: Did you say anything?

SAM: No. But I remember thinking: "I want to marry Claire Huxtable."

MATTIE: Oh.

SAM: Yeah.

MATTIE: So what is that supposed to mean?

SAM: I don't know.

MATTIE: Are you talking about us? That we aren't meant to be together?

SAM: I don't know.

MATTIE: You want Claire Huxtable? Is that what you're saying?

SAM: I don't know.

MATTIE: Well that's not clear. You're not being very clear Sam—

(SAM rips up the contract. He kisses her.)

SAM: Sometimes things aren't meant to be clear.

(Lights fade as they hug and kiss.)

(End.)

THE NINTH CIRCLE

Edward Musto

EDWARD MUSTO was born in Lynn, Massachusetts. He attended Suffolk University and studied under playwrights Harvey Perr and Leonard Melfi. Other plays he has written include *Genevieve*, *Blood Dues*, *Porter Peace*, *Boston Proper*, and *The Game of Love*. His works have been produced at Actors Outlet, American Theatre of Actors, Creative Place, 45th Street Theatre, Grove Street Playhouse, Harold Clurman Theatre, Main Street Theatre, Neighborhood Playhouse, Raw Space, and Theatre Foray. In 1994, Musto received an Edward Albee fellowship. He is a member of Charles Maryan's Playwrights/ Directors Workshop and lives in New York City.

The Ninth Circle was presented as a staged reading by Tim Corcoran on April 9, 2001, at 29th Street Rep, New York City. It was directed by Tom Herman and had the following cast:

Tom .... Eric Stoltz
Alley .... Elizabeth Elkins
Jane/Doctor .... Paula Ewin
Bartender/Ian .... Benjamin T. Scott
Lara .... Heidi James
Hite .... Don Creech
Upton/Jo-Jo .... Tim Corcoran
Curtis .... Charles Willey
Stevens/Catherine .... Christina McKay
Score/Policeman .... Tony DeVito
Baby .... Moira MacDonald
Projectionist/Julio .... Freddy Dumont

The Ninth Circle was presented by CreZZle Productions on March 26, 2002, at the 45th Street Theatre, New York City, with the following cast and credits:

Tom .... Gene Forman
Alley .... Andrea Maybaum
Jane .... Ann Ruttere
Bartender/Projectionist/Policeman/Ian .... Whalen J. Laurence
Lara .... Heidi James
Marvin/Curtis .... Rick Lawrence
Hite .... John D. McNally
Upton .... Daren Kelly
Stevens/Baby/Doctor .... Sarah Schoenberg
Score .... Stephen Innocenzi
Jo-Jo .... Jay Greenberg
Julio .... Rodrigo Lopresti
Catherine .... Beth Beyer

Directed by: Tom Herman
Set Design: Rick Juliano
Costume Design: Antonio Villareal
Lighting Design: Michael Abrams
Sound Score: Mark Cannistraro
Stage Manager: Wendy Patten
Assistant Director: Judy Brickell
Publicist: Publicity Outfitters

SYNOPSIS OF SCENES

The play opens on November 4, 1980. The action takes place at various venues on the Upper East Side of Manhattan.

ACT ONE
Scene 1: The American Hotel. 5:30 p.m.
Scene 2: Congress. 6:05 p.m.
Scene 3: New Directions. 7:10 p.m.
Scene 4: Bucephalus. 8:23 p.m.
Scene 5: La Brea. 9:41 p.m.

ACT TWO
Scene 1: New York Hospital. 10:34 p.m.
Scene 2: Hite, Upton & Curtis. 11:15 p.m.
Scene 3: Definitions. 11:59 p.m.
Scene 4: Home. 1:30 a.m.
Scene 5: The Inferno. 2:46 a.m.

ACT ONE
SCENE 1

A small dark room at the American Hotel on East 86th Street, New York City. It is 5:30 in the afternoon. The date is Tuesday, November 4, 1980. The only light peeps in from between the slats of a broken set of blinds. Sitting by the window is TOM. Thirty-five years of age. Winsome, boy-next-door looks, though age has begun its descent. He is peering through the blinds. Naked, he turns to take in the bed. ALLEY is facing him, her nakedness hidden by dingy sheets she has drawn up over her. TOM holds up his pack of cigarettes. She nods. He tosses her the pack. It falls onto the bed. She jams cigarettes up, takes one out, then reaches for a small box of wooden matches. She lights her cigarette.

ALLEY: Stay.

TOM: I can't.

ALLEY: Just for fun.

TOM: Wish I could.

ALLEY: Not asking for marriage.

TOM: Good thing. I already am.

ALLEY: Wanna go out?

TOM: Some other time.

ALLEY: Yeah, you're right. What's the point?

TOM: Well, don't be *hurt,* for Chrissake.

ALLEY: Fuck you.

(Pause.)

TOM: Saw a rat in the street today.

ALLEY: A live one?

TOM: Got run over by a car or something. This glop of gray mesh with a splash of red in the middle. It was at the corner of Eightieth and First.

ALLEY: Probably it was a pigeon that got run over.

TOM: No, it was a rat. There was a tail.

ALLEY: You should have brought it. We could have made soup.

TOM: Like they really allow cooking in the rooms.

ALLEY: I'm famished.

TOM: So am I.

ALLEY: Maybe we could go for a bite.

TOM: Got too much on my plate already.

ALLEY: It's just as well.

TOM: Sorry, though.

ALLEY: I *said* it's just as well.

TOM: What time do you have?

ALLEY: Five-thirty.

TOM: I'm sitting here like I have the whole afternoon to piss away.

ALLEY: You already have. It's practically night.

TOM: For your information it isn't practically night.

ALLEY: Evening officially begins at six o'clock.

TOM: Who says?

ALLEY: *TV Guide.*

(Pause.)

TOM: Didn't even get to vote.

ALLEY: Is *that* what you were doing at the school?

TOM: What else?

ALLEY: Thought you might be on the make for one of the kids.

TOM: You did not think that.

(Pause.)

ALLEY: Do you bite your nails?

TOM: Why do you want to know?

ALLEY: Just wondering.

TOM: Kind of personal, that.

ALLEY: Skip it then.

(Pause.)

TOM: No. I don't bite them.

ALLEY: Usually I can tell without having to ask.

TOM: Bite *your* nails, do you?

ALLEY: For years I did. Scraped the enamel right off the corner of one of my front teeth and it came off. You can barely notice it, even if you're up close. A shrink would say I'm eating myself up with something. Try as I may I can't seem to stop. What I used to do with my *nails* I now do with the *cuticles.* Why my fingertips are in such appalling condition. I'd stop if I could. Keep meaning to. But before I realize it my fingers are in my mouth and I'm ripping off big chunks of skin from around the nails. The more I do it, the more I have to. No matter how much it hurts, no matter how much blood I draw. Know what I do sometimes? If it's a large piece of skin I stick it on the end of a match and watch it burn.

TOM: Do you teach first or second grade?

ALLEY: First. Ever watch flesh burning? *(She bites at her nails.)* Look closely now. This patch of skin. It'll catch fire, turn black around the edges, then liquify, bubble, and bloom into ash. *(She blows out the match.)* Wanna go eat?

TOM: Told you. I can't.

ALLEY: Yeah, you're right. I've got things to do, anyway. Grade papers. Plan lessons.

TOM: Mold America's future.

ALLEY: Only got into teaching for all the time off. Out at three every day. Summers off. Spring breaks, too. All the holidays. Leaves me plenty of time for myself.

TOM: And for hotel rooms where they rent by the hour. Creepy smell.

ALLEY: Small price to pay. Cleansing effect of fire and all that. Who did you vote for today?

TOM: No one. There wasn't time. I met you, fell in love. We came directly here.

ALLEY: Who are you going to vote for?

TOM: Don't think I'll be able to. Have to get home.

ALLEY: Who *would* you have voted for then?

TOM: At the office everyone's voting for Reagan.

ALLEY: What do you do?

TOM: I'm a recovering parochial school boy.

ALLEY: Fuck. Don't tell me.

TOM: Corporate outplacement.

ALLEY: What's that?

TOM: The company I work for does corporate outplacement.

ALLEY: But what *is* that?

TOM: Counseling for the unemployed.

ALLEY: How do you make money from *that*?

TOM: Businesses pay us.

ALLEY: So you're like an employment agency?

TOM: The companies that have hired us are the same companies that have fired the people we're counseling.

ALLEY: And what do they get for their money? I assume it costs them plenty. What do they get?

TOM: Peace of mind. *(He lights a cigarette.)* I must've been really hot for you. Got buttons missing. You see, these days it's in the best interests of a company to do everything it can for an exec before showing him the door. Cuts down on hard feelings; cuts down on lawsuits. The process isn't even referred to as anything but an outplacement. Nobody's let go anymore. Nobody's fired, sacked, terminated, or otherwise given the push. Everybody's outplaced. Everybody's happy.

ALLEY: How many companies are there like yours?

TOM: Right now only a handful. And at the top of that short list is Hite, Upton & Curtis, which since 1974 has provided the finest in corporate outplacement. All individual programs feature career counseling, mock interviews on the Betamax with professional feedback, resume preparation, mailings, blah, blah, blah.

ALLEY: Spoken like a glossy brochure.

TOM: We also offer group outplacement, retirement planning, spouse counseling, and seminars on stress management.

ALLEY: Blah, blah, and more blah.

TOM: My watch must be slow. What time have you got?

ALLEY: Seven minutes later than the last time you asked.

TOM: I've got to get home.

(Pause.)

ALLEY: Want my phone number?

TOM: Sure.

ALLEY: Yeah, you're right. What's the point?

TOM: Nothing personal.

ALLEY: I know.

TOM: Just that I rarely go back for seconds.

ALLEY: Same here.

TOM: It was nice, though.

ALLEY: For me, too.

TOM: Maybe we'll run into each other again sometime.

ALLEY: Stranger things have happened.

TOM: Gotta make a pit stop. Get dressed if you want to leave together.

(They dress.)

TOM: Fuck.

ALLEY: What's the matter?

TOM: Damn place is infested.

ALLEY: Better shake out our clothing before we leave.

TOM: Except it ain't roaches.

ALLEY: Place has mice. What a surprise.

TOM: Larger than that.

ALLEY: Well, I doubt you saw a *rat.* They only come out at night. It's only quarter to six.

TOM: Maybe they don't get *TV Guide.*

ALLEY: Rats never come out during the day. They're photophobic. Afraid of the light.

TOM: Give me a cigarette.

ALLEY: What's the magic word?

TOM: Give-me-a-cigarette-or-I'll-kick-your-rotten-head-in.

ALLEY: You're more fun *out* of your clothes than *in* 'em.

TOM: Through yet?

ALLEY: Where's my other shoe?

TOM: I don't see it anywhere.

ALLEY: You aren't even looking.

TOM: Because it's not my shoe.

ALLEY: Such a fuck-head thou art. C'mon. I can't leave without it.

TOM: It's got to *be* here.

ALLEY: Check under the bed.

TOM: Why can't you?

ALLEY: Nice to know chivalry isn't dead.

TOM: Chivalry is *not* what you wanted from me.

ALLEY: Found it.

TOM: Almost ready?

ALLEY: Zip me up.

TOM: *(Slight disdain.)* Anyone'd think we're married.

ALLEY: Perish the thought.

(Pause.)

TOM: Something I said?

ALLEY: Ignore me. Always in a bad mood after I get laid.

TOM: Yeah. Me, too.

ALLEY: *(Taking out a cigarette.)* One for the road?

TOM: Make it quick.

(TOM, in front of a mirror, fastens his tie. ALLEY stares thoughtfully at him for a moment.)

ALLEY: You're actually somebody's husband.

TOM: Hey, we all make mistakes.

ALLEY: Live in town?

TOM: Eighty-fifth and Second.

ALLEY: Children?

TOM: Bite your tongue.

ALLEY: Tell me about your wife.

TOM: Her name is Catherine. She is the perfect woman. Beauty, brains, the works. She manages a marketing research firm, is an accomplished musician, and a gourmet cook. She's good with money, good with people, good with everything.

ALLEY: Who's *she* voting for?

TOM: Often wish I didn't resent her quite as much as I do.

ALLEY: Enjoying the view?

TOM: Mm-hmm.

ALLEY: No false modesty in you, is there?

TOM: Absolutely none, either false or genuine.

ALLEY: Well, you get points for honesty, anyway.

TOM: Something my first grade teacher used to say. No matter how badly you fucked up, she went easier on you if you 'fessed up to it.

ALLEY: *(Squinting her eyes.)* Trying to picture you as a little kid. Having a rough time of it.

TOM: Imagine someone awkward and shy and nothing much to look at. My teacher worried my self-imposed isolation wasn't healthy and determined the best way for me to get over my inadequacies was to force me into a situation that was pregnant with social intercourse. She cast me in the school play. My teacher was way ahead of her time. Must have thought she was going to set progressive education ablaze with this gender-fuck version of *Sleeping Beauty*. In it the Prince of Coldness, a mythical place where it's always winter, angers the evil warlock, who turns him into ice. Only a kiss can save him. He's about to be done in by said evil warlock when in the nick of time he's rescued by a nearby lumber*jill*. She kisses him on the mouth. He melts before her eyes.

ALLEY: And you were the evil warlock?

TOM: I was the ice prince.

ALLEY: Oh.

TOM: Finish up now.

ALLEY: Sure; no problem. Certainly there's no reason why I should hang around *this* dump. I've got my *own* dump to hang around in. Not to mention the usual haunts.

TOM: Plato's Retreat, the Inferno, etc.

ALLEY: You know the Inferno?

TOM: Sure do.

ALLEY: There a lot?

TOM: Once in a while.

ALLEY: Surprised we've never run into each other.

TOM: Who's to say we haven't?

ALLEY: *(Small laugh.)* It *is* pretty dimly lit.

TOM: Adds to the ambiance.

ALLEY: Maybe next time you go I'll be there.

TOM: Never can tell. Got your coat?

ALLEY: I'm all set.

TOM: Shall we, then?

(He moves to kiss her.)

ALLEY: Hey! What are you doing?

TOM: I'm sorry. I was going to kiss you. I forgot I don't know you.

ALLEY: All right. I guess you weren't trying to be familiar.

TOM: Really. I wasn't.

ALLEY: Maybe we shouldn't leave together.

TOM: No, it's okay. C'mon. I'll drop you.

ALLEY: You're taking a cab? I thought you were going home. And isn't that practically around the corner from here?

TOM: Just remembered I told my secretary to meet me.

ALLEY: Where?

TOM: Seventy-third and Lex.

ALLEY: And you're gonna take a *cab*?

TOM: You want a lift or not?

ALLEY: How far can you bring me? My place is way downtown.

TOM: Ten blocks. Take it or leave it.

ALLEY: Never mind.

TOM: Just that I'm already late.

ALLEY: So you said.

TOM: I'd bring you further if it weren't for that.

ALLEY: Maybe I can take the taxi the rest of the way.

TOM: Fine. Let's go now.

ALLEY: Nope. I can't spare the cash. Looks like I'm taking the bus.

TOM: Well, it's been *nice*.

(Pause.)

ALLEY: Yes.

TOM: I mean it.

ALLEY: So do I.

TOM: Really wish I didn't have to go.

ALLEY: Them's the breaks.

TOM: Guess we should say goodbye here.

ALLEY: Please. Not downstairs.

TOM: I know.

ALLEY: Too something... I don't know... creepy.

TOM: Goodbye, then.

ALLEY: See you around.

TOM: What's your name?

ALLEY: Alley.

TOM: Alley.

ALLEY: Yours?

TOM: Tom.

ALLEY: We'll see each other again.

TOM: Think so?

ALLEY: We're bound to.

(Blackout.)

SCENE 2

The bar at Congress, a Lexington Avenue tavern catering to singles; 6:05 p.m. TOM is staring out the window. JANE, seated at the bar, is facing him. Also in attendance is a BARTENDER. When not serving drinks, he is cutting away at sheets of orange construction paper. In front of him is a sign with lettering stenciled on.

JANE: Stay.

TOM: Why should I?

JANE: Because I'm asking you to.

TOM: I'm pissed off.

JANE: No reason to storm out of here.

TOM: All I wanted to do was pick up my notes for tonight's meeting. Simple enough. But no. You have to lay *this* on me.

JANE: Try looking at it from *my* point of view.

TOM: Just bailing out. That's what *I* see. Giving yourself the push without regard to the consequences.

JANE: The company thrived long before I got there; it can survive my absence.

TOM: Tell me why. At least you owe me *that*.

JANE: It's time I left; that's all.

TOM: To go where?

JANE: Someplace else… anyplace else… another life.

TOM: And what about me?

JANE: Nothing will have changed for you.

TOM: You're only my right arm.

JANE: Some minor adjustments and you'll forget all about me.

TOM: There must be *something* I can do.

JANE: My mind's made up.

TOM: Stay till I get a replacement.

JANE: Nothing doing.

TOM: As a favor to me.

JANE: Sorry, but everything's set. I leave in the morning.

TOM: What if I got you a raise?

JANE: It's not money, Tom. I've already told you that.

TOM: We can cut down on your hours, too. All that coming in early, staying late, the weekends. It's taken its toll, hasn't it?

JANE: Not in the way you think.

(Pause.)

TOM: Is it me?

JANE: What do you mean?

TOM: Something I've done. Haven't done.

JANE: No; nothing like that.

TOM: Are you sure?

JANE: I'd do anything for you.

(Pause.)

BARTENDER: How are you folks doing?

JANE: Another, please.

TOM: Don't you think you've had enough?

JANE: That was only my third.

TOM: We're fine, thanks.

BARTENDER: Give a yell if you change your mind. *(He returns to working on the sign.)*

JANE: What do you suppose *that's* all about?

TOM: Some kind of event, I guess.

JANE: But what exactly *is* a "Fires of Passion" weekend?

TOM: Haven't a clue.

JANE: This isn't a hangout of yours?

TOM: Only suggested it because it was equidistant between the office and where I was.

JANE: It's a pickup bar. You probably didn't think I know that, but I did… know that. Now let's go over all this, so I can leave with a clear conscience.

TOM: Put that away for a moment. Jane, you know how dependent I am on you.

JANE: *(To the BARTENDER.)* When you get a chance, I'd like that drink now.

BARTENDER: Coming up.

TOM: I wish you wouldn't.

JANE: Yes, well, the thing about wishes is they don't always come true, do they?

(The BARTENDER serves them.)

TOM: What happened this afternoon?

JANE: Nothing out of the ordinary.

TOM: Something had to have gone on.

JANE: Lots went on. It's an office. Business transpired. Business continues with the day even if you don't. If you know what's good for you, you'll accept my resignation and break in someone new. And "new" means *new*. No luring somebody else's secretary into your corner of Hite, Upton & Curtis. For once, go *against* the grain of instant gratification. Ultimately it'll be better for you if you got someone who *doesn't* know your ins and outs, who doesn't *mind* having to pick up the *slack* when you slack *off*.

TOM: Starting to take this personally, Jane.

JANE: Well, I *am* tired of having to cover for you. Two, sometimes three, afternoons a week.

TOM: Didn't know you minded that sort of thing. Always thought you were vaguely amused by my shenanigans.

JANE: I kept telling you how overloaded I was. All you did was throw your work onto my pile.

TOM: Assignments I thought you could handle. Thought you'd want to have. Most of the other bosses hoard the choicest assignments for themselves. Leave their underlings the grunt work. Honestly thought I was doing you a favor, giving you a shot. In thanks you accuse me of indolence and insensitivity.

JANE: You make it sound like the problem was *me*. My not having understood your motive. Your motive was never the issue. Everything *else* was.

(The BARTENDER approaches, holding up the cutout orange paper strips.)

BARTENDER: Pardon me, folks. May I ask you something? Do you know what these are supposed to be?

JANE: Of course we do. They're teeth.

TOM: Sure. They're waves.

JANE: All right, we give up. What are they?

BARTENDER: Flames.

JANE: I beg your pardon.

BARTENDER: From a fire? Flames. I'm going to line the bottom of this window here, then put the sign up over them. "Fires of Passion."

JANE: Oh, I get it now. Flames. Passion. "Fires of Passion." Got any pretzels or anything?

BARTENDER: But they really don't *look* like flames. Maybe if I put traces of yellow paint on the tips.

TOM: Nah. Then it'll look like candy corn.

BARTENDER: Ready for another?

TOM: Thanks, no.

JANE: I am, yes. Tell us, though. What's the point of the holiday?

BARTENDER: Money is. Lost our lease. *(He returns to his work.)*

TOM: Let's make this your last drink tonight.

JANE: Think they'll raise enough money?

TOM: Not a chance. This place will rise from the ashes as one of those ultra-modern, imported-water watering holes. They'll serve nouvelle cuisine. Little portions.

JANE: You're not drinking, Tom.

TOM: Don't decide anything tonight, Jane. Wait until morning.

JANE: Oh, no. Waiting is all I *do* anymore.

TOM: Talking to you as a friend now.

JANE: I know.

TOM: Not just a boss.

JANE: Yes.

TOM: More than that between us.

JANE: All of a sudden my head is throbbing. I should go home and lie down.

TOM: Put everything on hold until morning. You'll have perspective then.

JANE: You just don't want the aggravation my leaving the office will bring you.

TOM: Not true, I swear.

JANE: Then stop pressuring me.

TOM: Just trying to prevent you from making a terrible mistake.

JANE: Shaking the faith I have in my plans for the future isn't the way to do it.

TOM: You can go far, Jane—if it's what you want.

JANE: Maybe that's it. Maybe I just don't want it.

TOM: It's what you've worked for.

JANE: Five years I've been with the firm. I'm burned out.

TOM: Nothing a week in the Hamptons can't cure.

JANE: But then I'll just be right back where I started.

TOM: That such a bad place to be? Helping people? Reminding them of their own value? Giving them back their self-esteem? We do good work.

JANE: You make it sound like we're missionaries or something. Peace Corps volunteers. How can you fool me when you can't even fool yourself? Face it, Tom. We thrive on other people's misery. We're not social workers; we're parasites. We don't counsel; we just put a shine on the shit.

BARTENDER: And how are we doing down here?

TOM: Just fine, thanks.

BARTENDER: Refill?

JANE: Please.

TOM: No.

JANE: Hey.

TOM: Jane.

BARTENDER: I'll come back. *(Moves to the other end of the bar.)*

JANE: Upton came by.

TOM: Was he looking for me?

JANE: He passed by your office.

TOM: What did he say?

JANE: Nothing, as always.

TOM: Doesn't he pay us a visit every day?

JANE: You know he does.

TOM: So what's the problem?

JANE: It's the way he huffs every time he passes your office and sees you're not there. Today it took on a significance it never did before.

TOM: You're worried because he huffs.

JANE: And shakes his head.

TOM: Let me see if I've got this straight. He passes my office, looks in, sees I'm not there, huffs, shakes his head, moves on.

JANE: Just as he did before he saw to it Neil was let go.

TOM: Anything else?

JANE: He's getting along awfully well with Stevens.

TOM: Stevens.

JANE: The new VP. It seems they belong to the same Rotary Club or some such nonsense. They've discovered they're both liberal Republicans. This weekend they're playing golf. Next thing you know they'll be having barbecues. Sex games by the pool.

TOM: What's your point?

JANE: It crossed my mind Stevens was being groomed as a possible replacement.

TOM: For whom?

(Pause.)

JANE: I'm just saying it's a possibility.

TOM: Based on what, though?

JANE: Look at it from Upton's point of view. Every time he peeks into your office, all he sees is an empty chair. And don't think he doesn't somehow manage to let Hite know his misgivings about you, either. For as long as I've been there he's had it in for you.

TOM: Still don't think there's anything I need worry about.

JANE: You always do that—ask for a report, then disavow it.

TOM: Because you make too much of things. Always a bit too quick to sound the alarm, if you ask me. That how you get your kicks?

JANE: Perhaps your *next* assistant will be more to your liking. I'd better go now. Will you help me get a taxi?

TOM: Wait. Don't go. I'm sorry. I didn't mean that. Sit down just a bit longer. If, for no other reason, just so I can apologize.

(She returns to her seat.)

TOM: I'm mixing it up with you because I think we've been pretty good together. Now you tell me there are things going on you no longer find acceptable. I put on you what's expected of me, slack off, disappear frequently. Your solution is to punish me. Pack it in. Throw the boss into chaos. Jane, you're only hurting yourself.

JANE: This can't be your idea of an apology. May I go now?

TOM: I'm very sorry, Jane, for all of it. If I could take it all back, I would. It's probably futile, but if you did decide to stay with me, I promise things will be different. No more lies, no more goofing off, no more Simon Legree. Say you'll think about it. Even if you don't mean it, say you'll think about it.

JANE: I'll think about it.

(TOM motions to the BARTENDER. At the same time, a woman named LARA enters the bar. TOM continues to converse with

JANE, but finds his attention gradually wandering in LARA's direction. The BARTENDER, watching TOM watching LARA, returns with fresh drinks.)

JANE: Oh, not for me.

TOM: Least I can do, Jane. You've been aces with me and I've been a rat.

JANE: If you want to do something for me, help me get a taxi.

TOM: Wait a second. Haven't we forgotten something?

JANE: Oh! Good thing you remembered. I can't believe I nearly walked out of here with all this.

TOM: Understandable. We did get a little sidetracked.

(She pulls out her notes.)

JANE: Curtis intends to propose a new program for senior execs. Upton got wind of it and insisted Curtis let him fine-tune it before presenting it to Hite.

TOM: Always stealing somebody's thunder, isn't he?

JANE: This is a copy of the proposal.

TOM: Haven't got time to read all that.

JANE: Don't rely solely on my notes. What if I missed something?

TOM: I'm sure they're fine. Any reservations?

JANE: Lots. They're the blue pages there. Major point. It's impossible to increase services to the degree he specifies without adding to the support staff.

TOM: I can read.

(Pause.)

JANE: Help me get a cab now, would you?

TOM: What time's the meeting?

JANE: Eight o'clock sharp.

TOM: I really wanted to get home. How mandatory is attendance?

JANE: Let's put it this way. Hite's had his secretary book the private dining room at Bucephalus. He's also seen to having a television brought in so you can all watch the election coverage.

TOM: But what am I going to do until eight?

(LARA returns TOM's gaze.)

JANE: I'd better get going.

TOM: Yes, well, thanks for everything, Jane. I'll make sure you get credit for all the hard work you've put in here.

JANE: Aren't you coming?

TOM: Might as well use the time to brief myself on all this.

JANE: Think I'll have trouble getting a cab?

TOM: Not at this hour.

JANE: Are you sure?

(He doesn't answer. JANE goes to the door. TOM motions for the BARTENDER. JANE scrutinizes the situation, then abruptly exits. The BARTENDER fixes a drink and brings it to LARA. She looks up quizzically. He points to TOM.)

TOM: Hi.

LARA: Hi.

(Blackout.)

SCENE 3

The main room at New Directions, an art gallery on East 77th Street; 7:10 p.m. An overhead lamp provides the pool of light in the middle of the floor. On the periphery, amidst the shadows, are paintings waiting to be put on display. One is an oil painting of a firehouse in flames. Door at up center. Leaning against a small bar is a sign with the name of the gallery in large letters, with the exception of the last letter, which looks suspiciously like a dollar sign. TOM, in the middle of the floor, is staring out the window. LARA is peering at TOM over a pair of dark glasses. He lights a cigarette. She keeps her distance. He turns, smiles, starts toward her.

LARA: Stay.

TOM: Not going anyplace.

LARA: Don't move from there.

TOM: Any reason why?

LARA: Just for a moment.

TOM: Have to be leaving pretty soon.

LARA: I want to have a look at you first.

TOM: Go on, then. Have your look.

LARA: You're very handsome, aren't you?

TOM: Generally pass through the crowd with a shove.

LARA: Shall I unzip my dress?

TOM: If you like.

LARA: What do you do?

TOM: Anything you want.

LARA: For a living.

TOM: This.

(Pause.)

TOM: What was that?

LARA: What was what?

TOM: That noise.

LARA: I didn't hear anything.

TOM: Thumping of some kind.

LARA: Want a drink?

TOM: I have to be getting home.

LARA: Whiskey all right?

TOM: None for me, thanks.

LARA: Coming right up. You're in luck. It so happens we're out of everything else. The bar needs restocking. Hey! Where do you think you're going?

TOM: Having a look around; that's all.

LARA: Plenty of time for that later.

TOM: Really just wanted to check out some of the paintings.

LARA: I'm flattered, but I would prefer you ask permission before wandering about.

TOM: *(Surprised.)* You did all these?

(She takes out a cigarette, strikes a match across the painting of the fire.)

LARA: Don't I strike you as the artistic type?

TOM: Frankly, no.

LARA: I'll get you your drink.

TOM: Told you. I don't want one.

LARA: Did you say something? You're so far away. Step back into the light so I can *hear* you.

TOM: Aren't there any more lights we can put on?

LARA: Yes, but I don't use them. My eyes are rather sensitive. Too much light and they start to burn.

TOM: Sounded like it came from over here.

LARA: What?

TOM: The noise.

LARA: Most likely what you heard was the heat. Steam coming up through the pipes.

TOM: Except the radiator's down at the other end of the room and the noise was a lot closer than that.

LARA: Someone in the hall. The street door. Rats partying in the garbage cans outside. It could have been anything you heard.

TOM: *(Indicating the door.)* Where does this lead?

LARA: Nowhere. It's a utility closet. Well, sir. Come and get it.

(She beckons him to join her. He returns to the middle of the room. LARA hands TOM his drink, then sips at one she's made for herself.)

TOM: Been a while since I've drunk whiskey.

LARA: Same here. Half an hour at least.

TOM: Forgot how much I like the burn as it goes down.

LARA: It's like a swallow of fire. Sears your throat, warms your belly, rages in your chest. Seconds later, euphoria.

TOM: Cotton balls bombarding your brain.

(They embrace.)

LARA: I like the way you look at me.

TOM: Just seeing what I'm getting into.

LARA: Didn't mean to flare.

TOM: My own fault. Strange places make me feel too much at home.

LARA: It isn't my home, either; not really. I just happen to know the fellow who owns the gallery.

TOM: That right?

LARA: Yes; we're quite close.

TOM: Won't he mind, then?

LARA: About what?

TOM: My being here.

LARA: I see no need to tell him.

TOM: Still he could find out.

LARA: Not terribly likely.

TOM: Think what would happen then.

LARA: I can't imagine. Can you?

TOM: Might he become enraged? Slice us up into luncheon meat?

LARA: Marvin isn't that type.

TOM: No, I guess not. Not with a name like Marvin.

LARA: Don't you make fun of him.

TOM: Wouldn't dream of it.

LARA: He's nearly everything to me.

TOM: Must be quite a guy.

LARA: Once in a while he gets a little peremptory. I oblige him. It's a small price I pay.

TOM: For?

LARA: He gets my work. He gets me.

TOM: Oh, yes. I forgot about your ongoing contribution to the fine arts.

(LARA breaks the embrace.)

LARA: Want another drink? I'm going to.

TOM: Didn't even want *this* one.

LARA: So you got it for nothing. What are you complaining about?

TOM: I've offended you. Didn't mean to.

LARA: Still want to see my stuff?

TOM: A private showing?

LARA: No sense my inviting you to the opening. A week from now we won't remember each other's names. You're already fading.

TOM: Then why bother showing me anything? It's not realistic.

LARA: I've never been fond of realism.

(She surveys the room, then spies a few framed pieces which she brings into the light.)

LARA: This first piece adapts techniques of commercial art. In this work I have taken a familiar object and drawn it in such a way as to comment on the environment we're living in.

TOM: It's a martini glass.

LARA: Yes, but see how I've twisted the stem. I'm trying to show we live in a twisted society. And the critics raved. *(She shows TOM the second piece.)* This collage uses oils and acrylics. For the background I used photographs of the Chicago stockyards. That's my face painted over the face of a cow on a rape rack right before she's inseminated. And the critics raved.

TOM: Always leave your garbage out on the floor?

LARA: That's not garbage; that's an exhibit. Display art satirizing designer goods. I took a wire wastebasket and overflowed it with jeans, T-shirts, and briefs with which I wiped my ass. And the critics raved.

TOM: What's the mousetrap supposed to signify?

LARA: Nothing. That's a real mousetrap. The building's infested.

TOM: Interesting stuff.

LARA: You needn't be polite. I know it's junk. The trouble is it makes money. My serious work they called junk. So now I give them junk and they insist it's art. How lucky I am to be living in a country that values junk. Junk food. Junk merchandise. Junk art.

(Pause.)

TOM: What's that one?

LARA: I don't know what this is doing out here. One of my early drawings. "God's Grandchild."

TOM: Sounds familiar, that name.

LARA: It's from Dante's *Inferno*. "Art, as far as it is able, follows nature, as a pupil imitates his master; thus your art must be, as it were, God's grandchild." But this was another life... before I sold my soul to the Devil.

TOM: And secured your lot in the ninth circle.

LARA: Where the worst sinners go.

TOM: If I get there ahead of you, I'll save you a seat.

LARA: Please do.

TOM: *(Indicating the drawing.)* Time for the unveiling.

LARA: It's not important.

TOM: Don't you want to show it to me?

LARA: Not really; no.

TOM: I would like to see it.

(Reluctantly she shows TOM the drawing.)

LARA: My subject was the duplicity of human nature and the hopelessness of love. The man loves the woman. He takes her hand and presses it to his heart. The woman, you see, has two faces. One looks at the man. The other has already turned to her next lover.

TOM: Feel that way myself sometimes. I never want to be where I am.

(Pause.)

TOM: There it is again.

LARA: What do you mean?

TOM: Same noise I heard before.

LARA: I still don't hear anything.

TOM: Keep quiet for a moment and listen.

LARA: Do you want to take off? Is that what this is about?

TOM: No, no; nothing like that.

LARA: It's all right. Just tell me.

TOM: Something's behind that door.

LARA: That's not possible. I've already told you that.

TOM: Open it.

LARA: We can't.

TOM: Just to be sure.

LARA: I mean it's locked.

TOM: Let me check.

LARA: No! I will. *(LARA goes to the door.)*

TOM: Well?

LARA: I tried to tell you.

TOM: Don't you have a key?

LARA: I never had one.

TOM: Odd. This guy gives you free rein to his place of business, but makes sure you can't get into the broom closet.

LARA: Marvin probably didn't think I'd have a dire need to get at the mops and brooms.

TOM: Well, if it's just mops and brooms, why keep the door locked at all?

LARA: Because that's where the body's hidden!

(Pause.)

LARA: This is so dumb.

TOM: Certainly is.

LARA: All we're doing is wasting time.

TOM: Something I don't have much of.

LARA: Then let's not waste any more of it. Come with me, sir.

TOM: And where are you taking me?

LARA: Not far, I assure you. Just right over here.

TOM: Back into the light?

LARA: Well, you want enlightenment, don't you?

TOM: I'm more comfortable in the dark.

LARA: But then I wouldn't be able to *see* you.

TOM: Now you see me... now you *don't!*

(He swats the overhead lamp. It swings back and forth, throwing alternately huge and tiny shadows of TOM and LARA as they strip off their clothing and roll around the floor. Their giggling gives way to moaning, which is accompanied by a third voice, also moaning, and a loud crash. TOM bolts upright.)

TOM: Don't tell me you didn't hear *that!*

LARA: *Shit!*

(TOM goes to the closet and flings open the door. Inside is a small, timid-looking man on his knees, his pants down around his ankles.)

TOM: Who in hell are you?

LARA: Tom, this is Marvin... Marvin, Tom.

TOM: Don't get up.

LARA: Sorry for the deceit. He likes to watch.

TOM: Oh.

LARA: We thought it might be a problem. Is it?

TOM: Nah.

(Blackout.)

SCENE 4

The private dining room at Bucephalus, a Greek restaurant on First Avenue at 55th Street; 8:23 p.m. Nicely set table. Dinner is a way off, but drinks have been served. A television monitor is off to one side, but the sound's been turned down. TOM is looking toward the door. He's seated at the table along with his business associates, HITE, UPTON, CURTIS, and STEVENS. They are having their picture taken by an obliging WAITER.

HITE: Stay... stay put now, everyone. No one move. Face the camera and don't forget to smile, God damn it.

CURTIS: Is this kid ever going to take the picture?

UPTON: Maybe they don't have cameras in his country.

HITE: As head of the firm, I order everybody to shut the hell up.

UPTON: Think you might join us, Tom?

HITE: What's going on?

TOM: I'm sorry, Mr. Hite. Got a little distracted.

HITE: One picture is not asking too much. So if everyone will just cooperate and smile for the camera, I shall die a happy man.

(The WAITER snaps the picture.)

HITE: Did he take the picture?

CURTIS: Yes, he did, Garth.

HITE: And what was I doing at the time?

CURTIS: Beats me. I was smiling for the camera.

HITE: God damn it! We're going to have to take it again. I had my head turned to one side. I know I did. Plus there was the matter of my arms. I think I had them up to illustrate a point.

UPTON: Well, retakes won't be anytime soon. Our waiter just went to place our dinner orders.

HITE: This is something, isn't it?

STEVENS: It certainly is, sir.

HITE: You've been here how long?

STEVENS: A year. Not even.

HITE: Upton, tell the rookie how many people we had when we started out.

UPTON: There was just the three of us.

CURTIS: One secretary.

HITE: Now we have fifty.

STEVENS: Secretaries?

HITE: Total employees.

UPTON: Of course that's just in New York.

CURTIS: There's another forty in seven field offices across the country.

UPTON: With more to come.

TOM: I didn't know we were opening another office.

HITE: Three. Upton, didn't you tell him?

UPTON: Must have slipped my mind.

HITE: Boston, Minneapolis, and Denver.

TOM: Well, that's a surprise.

UPTON: Sorry for the slipup. I know how important lead time is for you.

HITE: After-hours meetings were held at Burger King. Napkins were used for receipts.

CURTIS: No computers.

UPTON: Right. Just one IBM Selectric.

CURTIS: We couldn't afford the nice frames for transparencies, so Mrs. Hite would make them from Garth's shirt cardboards.

HITE: Those days are long gone.

UPTON: Yes; they sure are.

STEVENS: Ever miss them?

CURTIS: Hell, no.

UPTON: Only romantics can be in love with squalor.

HITE: I have to confess I like being able to afford the best of what's going around. Equipment, supplies, people.

CURTIS: Nothing the matter with that.

HITE: As long as we don't lose our sense of philanthropy. That is what first attracted us.

TOM: *(Aside, to STEVENS.)* Broken hearts.

HITE: Broken hearts. That is our business, after all. Repairing them, that is; not breaking them. I'll tell you how I got into counseling.

UPTON: Waiter, may I have another one of these? No offense, Garth, but I was out of petrol.

TOM: *(Aside, to STEVENS.)* He was two weeks in London.

STEVENS: Have you traveled extensively, Mr. Upton?

UPTON: I've done the continent once or twice. Nothing out of the ordinary, I'm sorry to say; just the major capitals.

TOM: *(Aside, to STEVENS.)* Europe on ten dollars a day.

HITE: Nasty business, travel. Did quite a bit of it myself in the early seventies. Why is it when we go to a foreign country and don't know the language and ignore the customs we're Ugly Americans, but when foreigners come here and don't know the language and ignore the customs we're Ugly Americans?

(The WAITER brings UPTON a drink.)

UPTON: Anyone else want anything?

HITE: Not right now, thanks.

CURTIS: I'll have a refill. Make it harmless, if you would.

UPTON: A harmless one for the man in the bow tie.

TOM: For me, too. Make mine perilous, though. Menacing. Fraught with danger.

UPTON: How about you?

STEVENS: Whatever you're drinking, sir, will be fine.

UPTON: One more of these.

(The WAITER exits.)

CURTIS: If you're going to tell a story, Garth, make it the one about the robin.

HITE: That isn't a story; that's a fable.

CURTIS: Whatever it is, tell it.

HITE: I'm not nearly drunk enough yet. Maybe later.

UPTON: Are we ever going to have the meeting we came here for?

HITE: Oh, not now, Upton. I'm feeling all warm and cozy. It's a mediocre wine I'm drinking, but it's doing the job. *(Tossing a look of acknowledgment to STEVENS.)* Maybe because you're here. Feeling nostalgic. Remembering how I started out. Industrial psychology. For a short time I was pretty hot stuff. Had a good enough reputation in the business to get the call from Cape Canaveral. There was a problem with the technicians down there. They were dropping like flies. No one could figure out why. The answer rested with the President of the United States. It seems the work these guys did was so specialized that there was no place for them to go if they were put out of work. So, every time the President threatened the space program with budget cuts, the men became so anxiety-ridden that they would rupture their own heart muscles. They were dying, quite literally, of broken hearts.

CURTIS: After that, Garth joined Human Resource Management at Harcourt Brace. There he met Mr. Upton and me. A couple of years later we were talking about branching off to form our own company.

HITE: One thing I learned at Cape Canaveral has stayed with me all these years—how the actions of those high up affect so many more down below. That's why I pay such attention to politics.

UPTON: Speaking of which, here's our man coming up on the monitor.

STEVENS: Ronald Reagan.

CURTIS: Just another ad.

STEVENS: I would have figured you for a Democrat.

TOM: *(Aside, to STEVENS.)* Not since the Lincoln-Douglas debates.

HITE: Democrats can only give us what we can't afford. Social programs. Welfare. High unemployment. Inflation.

CURTIS: Twenty percent it's up to.

HITE: Hostages in Iran. Another SALT treaty. Reagan, on the other hand, wants a strong national defense and a hard line against the Soviets.

UPTON: Calm down, Garth. No need to preach to the converted.

HITE: Too late to convert anyone now. Aren't the polls closed?

CURTIS: *(Checking his watch.)* Pretty soon.

HITE: Did we all vote today?

CURTIS: First thing this morning.

UPTON: Right before I came here. Tom, I know you did, too.

TOM: And how do you know that, Upton?

UPTON: I just assumed it since you were so late getting back from lunch.

TOM: This afternoon I was at IBM. There was a demonstration of its new mag card composer, a handy piece of equipment we ought to invest in.

UPTON: Oh, yes. I recall Jane mentioning it a few weeks ago.

HITE: I do wish you'd taken a little time for yourself, Tom. I certainly wouldn't have minded your ducking out for an hour or so. *(To STEVENS.)* Did you vote?

STEVENS: On my lunch hour, sir.

HITE: Glad to hear it.

STEVENS: As long as I don't have to say how I cast my ballot.

HITE: We all know what that means. Oh, well. Maybe by the next election I'll have you voting the right way.

CURTIS: The operative word being "right."

HITE: Regrets already, Mike?

CURTIS: About who I voted for?

HITE: None of my business really. In fact, you can probably sue me just for having asked. *(Spills his drink.)* God damn it! Look what I did. All down the front of my shirt.

UPTON: Let me get the waiter to bring you some club soda.

HITE: Hand me a napkin, would you? Brand-new tie, too.

(UPTON signals for the WAITER. STEVENS hands HITE a napkin. TOM turns to CURTIS.)

TOM: Do you have regrets?

CURTIS: Some apprehension. Not much, but some.

HITE: Was that our waiter hightailing it to the kitchen?

UPTON: I bet he thinks we want dinner hurried up.

TOM: Probably doesn't matter a damn who you vote for.

CURTIS: That's the lazy man's way of thinking. I worry about the consequences of my actions.

TOM: Don't we all?

HITE: *(Placing the napkin back down.)* Thank you very much.

STEVENS: I see our waiter.

HITE: Let's not bother him with this. We'll leave it to the drycleaners to get out.

CURTIS: Naturally, we learn from our mistakes.

TOM: Only to make new ones.

CURTIS: Process of natural selection. Nature swears by it.

UPTON: Garth, let's at least talk about the new OPC program. If for no other reason than to legitimize tonight's expenses.

HITE: Very well. Mind you, I didn't have time to read your proposal in its entirety.

CURTIS: Your proposal?

UPTON: Of course Mike helped out on this, Garth.

HITE: Let me get this straight. A program for executives earning in excess of one hundred thousand dollars per year.

CURTIS: Our current OPC program makes no distinction between lower level executives and higher-ups.

UPTON: We've got outplaced CPAs sitting next to outplaced CEOs, for Chrissake.

CURTIS: This program is the remedy we're looking for. No longer would we have to tell some senior exec he has to wait his turn for a letter he needs typed or that he must sit in the client bullpen.

HITE: Carrels, if you please; sounds nicer.

UPTON: Other perks that come with the program. Unlimited stationery, resumes, mailings. Private phone lines. Private secretaries.

HITE: All this sounds fine and I have no doubt we can sell it. I do question how we are going to pay for it.

CURTIS: There is no reason why our current support staff can't take the overload. All we have to do is consolidate some of our people's functions, do some rearranging of the premises, stretch the workday a bit, and we're home free.

UPTON: Another plus. We charge twenty percent, not the customary fifteen, of the executive's annual base salary.

HITE: You're joking.

UPTON: Some things I do not joke about. Revenue is one of them.

HITE: Tom, you head up Administration. What are your thoughts?

TOM: First of all, there is no way we can accommodate a program like that without adding to staff.

UPTON: At least *read* the proposal before you urinate on it.

HITE: Hold it, you two.

TOM: I read it, Upton, this afternoon. I'll tell you something else. You'll never get that kind of money.

UPTON: Companies pay *headhunters* twenty percent. They pay *employment agencies* twenty percent.

TOM: For people they *want*; not for people they're trying to get *rid* of.

(Slight buzzing sound from the monitor. HITE fiddles with the dials.)

HITE: God damn it! Mike, have a look at this.

CURTIS: What's the problem?

HITE: The cable's gone out or something.

CURTIS: Let me see the manager about it.

STEVENS: Anything I can do to help?

CURTIS: Have a look at the monitor in the bar, if you would. That will at least tell us if the problem's with the set or with the cable.

STEVENS: We'll be right back.

(CURTIS and STEVENS exit.)

HITE: All this cigarette smoke is making me sick. I'm going out for a cigar. Maybe pick up the papers. I'll be back in a few minutes. *(Looking with disdain at the television, shaking his head.) Cable! (Exits.)*

UPTON: Listen to me, fucker; listen good.

TOM: Something on your mind?

UPTON: Go up against me like that again, you're dead.

TOM: Merely expressing an opinion.

UPTON: Fuck you, an opinion; it was an attempt at sabotage.

TOM: An opinion solicited by Hite, who still happens to be running this lousy company.

UPTON: You are way out of line.

TOM: Never did succumb to office etiquette.

UPTON: I mean you overestimate your value to the firm.

TOM: You know dick about what I do.

UPTON: Enough to know you're a liability to us.

TOM: Administration always gets the short end of the stick. Try doing your thing without us to prep for you and clean up afterwards.

UPTON: I'm not talking about that shit. I'm talking about *you*. The extended lunch hours, the unexplained absences, your indifference to work I hear you once took quite seriously.

TOM: Hite, Upton & Curtis. The early years.

UPTON: I don't see it, though. I don't even see the remnants of it.

TOM: Problem with your eyes. They can't see for the dollar signs in front of them.

UPTON: I don't notice you objecting to the dollar sign on your paycheck.

TOM: Earn that in aggravation alone.

UPTON: Which you cause yourself, fighting change that is inevitable.

TOM: I'm not fighting change. I'm fighting you.

UPTON: Believe me, you don't want to take me on. I've got age on my side; knowhow; little bits of guys like you embedded in the lining of my intestinal tract. Fuck with me, Tom, and I'll have you for breakfast, wash you down with my morning decaf.

TOM: All this because I won't endorse your little fee-for-all?

UPTON: Thirty-five's young to be burned out. Way too early for you to be out of your time, but that's what's happened. You're a dinosaur. You're so busy at play you don't see the comet coming, the one that's gonna blast you the fuck off the planet. *(Raising his glass.)* Here's to your good health—in the next life.

(HITE reenters.)

HITE: This does an old man's heart good, the two of you having a drink together. I knew you'd work out your differences. Now, I want both of you to continue making an effort. Is that understood?

TOM: We were doing just that, Mr. Hite. In fact, Upton here was just saying he's going to have me for breakfast some morning. Isn't that right, Upton?

UPTON: Very soon; yes.

HITE: Now *that's* what I like to hear!

(The WAITER reenters. UPTON supervises as he serves. HITE nudges TOM.)

HITE: I've been meaning to speak with you about something.

TOM: Yes, sir.

HITE: The mailroom attendant. His name escapes me.

TOM: Julio.

HITE: That's right. Lot of complaints about him.

TOM: I've been recommending we fire him.

HITE: Much too drastic an action right now.

TOM: Three warnings so far, with no improvement in sight.

HITE: Yes, well, let's just keep an eye on him for the time being.

TOM: As you wish.

UPTON: No, the lamb is for Mr. Hite. He'll be sitting at the head of the table.

HITE: Someone's been going in the executive offices late at night. Once the cleaning lady found some small vials. Evidently she didn't know what they were because she washed them out and neatly placed them on Curtis's desk. He found them in the morning right next to his Week-at-a-Glance.

TOM: I'll keep my eyes open.

UPTON: And the Steak Diane is for me. I'll be sitting next to Mr. Hite. Good.

(The WAITER moves to UPTON's side. He prepares the steak, pouring cognac into a small pan. He ignites it and cooks the meat while UPTON looks on appreciatively.)

HITE: One other thing. Upton. He's a little overbearing, I know, but he's our survival.

TOM: Frightening thought, that.

HITE: Play ball with him.

UPTON: Don't be niggardly with the cognac now. A little more. Yes, that's fine; perfect.

HITE: His is a new regime. We've got to get behind him. It's not unlike the country's having to get behind the new administration. Out with the old and in with the new.

TOM: Yes, sir.

HITE: Good man. Now let's have a fabulous dinner.

UPTON: Television's working again, Garth.

HITE: Oh. So it is. Well, we'd better get Curtis and Stevens.

TOM: I'll take care of it.

(STEVENS reenters. HITE joins UPTON at the table. TOM crosses to STEVENS.)

TOM: I was just coming for you.

STEVENS: Mr. Curtis is on the way.

TOM: Call him Mike.

STEVENS: When he invites me to do so; not before.

TOM: Nobody likes a kiss-ass.

STEVENS: I don't appreciate your disrespect.

TOM: You voted for Ronnie, didn't you? But you led everyone to believe otherwise. They're going to spend so much time trying to convert you. Nice work.

STEVENS: And in the future please keep those little asides to yourself.

TOM: Just trying to let you know you have the freedom to be yourself.

STEVENS: The only freedom I want is to be one of the boys.

(CURTIS reenters.)

CURTIS: Another job well done. Dinner almost ready?

(They join HITE and UPTON at the table.)

UPTON: Very nearly.

CURTIS: Something smells good.

UPTON: Hardly a Greek dish. I think they just indulge me because I spend so much time here.

CURTIS: You mean you spend so much *money* here.

UPTON: Speaking of money—

HITE: No more business tonight, Upton. I'm too hungry, too tired, too drunk.

CURTIS: Drunk enough to tell the robin story?

TOM: Mr. Hite, if you don't mind, I think I'd like to call it an evening. I've got a bit of a headache, so I thought I'd run to the polls before they close, then go straight home.

HITE: Oh, well, I'm sorry you're not feeling well. I told my driver he could run down the street for a cup of coffee. He'll be back any minute and I'll have him drop you wherever.

TOM: Thank you.

HITE: In the meantime, you can listen to the fable for which Curtis harbors such affection. Once upon a time there was a robin who decided to fly north. Winter had already begun, so it shouldn't have been a surprise to the robin when it started to snow. Pretty soon ice formed on his wings and he fell to the ground. He landed in a field where a cow was grazing. Before the robin could get up, though, the cow took a shit on him. The robin hated the smell, but at least it was warm. So warm, in fact, that the ice on his wings melted. The robin struggled to get out of the shit, but couldn't get any more than his head to poke out. Finally, a cat came along and helped the robin get out of the shit. Then he ate him. *(Pause.)* I told you this wasn't a story, but a fable and, like all fables, there is a moral. Not everyone who shits on you is your enemy, not everyone who gets you out of shit is your friend, and if it's more comfortable being in shit…

ALL: Stay there!

(Blackout.)

SCENE 5

La Brea, a porno theatre on First Avenue at 59th Street; 9:41 p.m. Movie screen in front of a row of seats. A film is being run. It's porno, but so far only setup; no hardcore sex on the screen at all. The sound is off. TOM is staring at the screen. Next to him is SCORE, his dealer. They're doing blow.

SCORE: Stay.

TOM: No time.

SCORE: Just a little while.

TOM: A few minutes more; that's it.

SCORE: I can use the company.

TOM: Don't wanna linger too long.

SCORE: It's rare I get to talk.

TOM: Got to get home.

SCORE: Most of the time I'm listening.

TOM: Catherine's going to be pissed.

SCORE: Dealers are like bartenders and shit.

TOM: This stuff is lousy.

SCORE: People tell you things they wouldn't ordinarily.

TOM: Really fucking lousy.

SCORE: It's a one-way deal, though. They talk. You pretend to listen. Like shrinks do.

TOM: Not feeling anything.

SCORE: Primo stuff; the best there is.

TOM: Fuck.

SCORE: I'm telling you.

TOM: Costs more, too.

SCORE: Inflation.

TOM: Paying more for less.

SCORE: Free delivery… and to places like this.

TOM: This is the only part of porno I really like—the first few moves.

SCORE: Stinks in here.

TOM: Atmosphere.

SCORE: Better than those places on Forty-Second Street.

TOM: Much higher class of sleaze in this neighborhood.

SCORE: Ever been in one of those places?

TOM: I've been fucking everywhere.

SCORE: Guys get laid here?

TOM: Sometimes.

SCORE: Chicks hanging out here got to be mostly skanks.

TOM: One man's meat is another man's meat.

SCORE: I got to cut down doing blow.

TOM: Only do it once in a while myself.

SCORE: Where does stuff go on here?

TOM: The lavs.

SCORE: Fuck that shit.

TOM: Behind the screen sometimes.

SCORE: Really?

TOM: Saw a couple going at it once.

SCORE: Were they lying down?

TOM: Standing up.

SCORE: Clothes all off?

TOM: On.

SCORE: I got to cut down doing blow.

TOM: Man, nothing. I might as well be snorting Bisquick.

SCORE: Where's the weirdest place you ever did it?

TOM: I'd have to think. You?

SCORE: Hand job on the Roosevelt Island tram.

TOM: My father's wake, I guess.

SCORE: Get out.

TOM: Food and sex, the only things I could think of.

SCORE: Life-affirming shit.

TOM: Remember walling some willing young thing, friend of my sister's, who kept popping peanut butter kisses into my mouth while I was banging her.

SCORE: You must have had one fucked-up childhood.

TOM: I'm the only person I know who had a happy childhood. One of those perfect New England towns you hear about. The streets are named after shade trees there. People live in old white frame houses surrounded by picket fences. Grandmothers bake pies and can crabapple jelly. Grandfathers subscribe to the *Reader's Digest* and smell of Old Spice after-shave. Mothers and fathers work hard, drink sherry only on special occasions, and only take drugs when they're prescribed by a doctor. They sacrifice everything for children they don't beat, children they don't fuck, children they don't know. I hear the kids there still play kick-the-can. Never quite fit in, as you can well imagine.

SCORE: You got kind of a late start, I guess, hunh?

TOM: From the minute I hit twelve I was getting love pats on my behind. Friends of my mother's, usually, during some social function, would make playful grabs at parts of me. Then there were the woebegone old men who'd follow me into bus depots or sit next to me at the movies. Stuff like that's supposed to traumatize someone like the kid I was supposed to be.

SCORE: Not you, though. Liked fucking too fucking much.

TOM: Didn't get my first fuck until I was sixteen. Beautiful woman, older, younger than the age I am now. Used to hire me for odd jobs. No, it was all good when it finally happened; it was danger, secrets, breathing, sweat, sounds I'd never heard before coming up from inside me, Pandora's box opening up, and me slipping into the rest of my life.

SCORE: I got to cut down doing blow. What do you say we get wasted? Hit some bars.

TOM: Not tonight. I have to get home.

SCORE: Come on. We haven't hung out forever.

TOM: Some other time.

SCORE: How come you're blowing me off?

TOM: I'm doing nothing of the kind.

SCORE: Used to be thick as thieves.

TOM: Were we friends before?

SCORE: Before what?

TOM: You started dealing.

SCORE: Fucked if I know.

TOM: Tend to think it was after.

SCORE: It's a moot point, anyway. Dealing's just what I do; it's not what I *am*.

TOM: That particular might be better served by dropping your nickname, Score.

SCORE: What would I use instead?

TOM: Your real name.

SCORE: There's an idea.

TOM: What *is* your name?

SCORE: Hunh?

TOM: Don't think you ever told me.

SCORE: I had to have.

TOM: No; you never did.

SCORE: Really?

TOM: Yes.

SCORE: I've been in your home.

TOM: Exactly.

SCORE: Fuck.

TOM: Really should get going.

SCORE: Sure you don't want to hang out?

TOM: Positive.

SCORE: *(Indicating the movie.)* I've had enough of this shit.

TOM: Me, too. Very nearly.

SCORE: Catch you another time.

(SCORE exits. TOM watches the screen. In the film a man and a woman begin taking off their clothes. BABY enters. She sits next to TOM.)

BABY: Give me ten dollars.

TOM: What?

BABY: Ten dollars. C'mon now. Hand it over.

TOM: I don't know you.

BABY: A promise is a promise.

TOM: Fuck off.

BABY: Hey, you're talking to a minor.

TOM: Meaning what?

BABY: You could get in so much trouble.

TOM: Recess is over. Time for you to go.

BABY: I'll say you tried to feel me up. I'll say you forced me in here. I'll say you followed me, waited to make your move, were on me before I knew it.

TOM: Move; move your legs. I'm getting out.

BABY: You grabbed me by the arm so tight it hurt. You pushed me in the door of this place and shoved me into a seat. You told me to watch the screen and not say anything. You put your hands on me. You unbuttoned my blouse. You thrust your hands in my panties. There was blood on your hands when you took them out.

TOM: Nothing's on my hands.

BABY: There was. I saw. There was blood on them. Open your hands. You'll see. There'll be blood. You'll see.

TOM: I'm telling you there is no blood. Look.

(He shows her his hands, palms up. She takes out a knife and stabs at them.)

TOM: Crazy bitch! Fuck! Somebody, help! I've been hurt!

(BABY exits. On the screen, the image of a naked man and woman locked in an embrace. Voices belonging to JO-JO and the PROJECTIONIST are heard.)

JO-JO: Frank, get down there!

PROJECTIONIST: What's happening?

(Sound of hurried footsteps. The film freezes.)

JO-JO: Find out what's going on.

PROJECTIONIST: Who's hurt? Someone down there hurt?

TOM: I am.

JO-JO: Do we need an ambulance?

TOM: No. The police, though.

(JO-JO and the PROJECTIONIST enter.)

PROJECTIONIST: There's a phone out front.

JO-JO: No; no cops. Sorry.

PROJECTIONIST: What happened?

TOM: Need a towel or something. I'm bleeding pretty good.

JO-JO: Frank, didn't you turn off the—you know—projector?

PROJECTIONIST: You told me to get down here!

JO-JO: Fuckin' idiot, back upstairs and turn it off! You know the kind of equipment we got! State-of-the-art circa nineteen fuckin' hundred, and you know what happens when you stop the film from running!

(The PROJECTIONIST hurriedly exits. JO-JO looks up at the screen as the sex image is obliterated by flame.)

JO-JO: Fuck.

(The film burns and melts. Screen goes to white.)

(Blackout.)

ACT TWO
SCENE 1

The emergency room at New York Hospital on East 68th Street; 10:34 p.m. A small cubicle defined by a sheet hanging from a rod. There's a bed, not much else; perhaps a cabinet for medical supplies. TOM is sitting on the bed while the DOCTOR works on him.

DOCTOR: Stay put now.

TOM: Right.

DOCTOR: You need to stay still.

TOM: I know.

DOCTOR: This will hurt more if you move about.

TOM: Sorry.

DOCTOR: How did you say this happened again?

TOM: Lunatic stabbed me.

DOCTOR: Any reason in particular?

TOM: Didn't like my brand of after-shave.

DOCTOR: Your own fault.

TOM: Will it be much longer?

DOCTOR: Hard to say.

TOM: Really?

DOCTOR: Because you keep moving about.

TOM: Sorry.

DOCTOR: Apology accepted if you'll just stay put.

(Pause.)

TOM: Are they bad?

DOCTOR: What?

TOM: My injuries.

DOCTOR: I have seen worse.

TOM: Victim of random violence. It's so TV-movieish.

DOCTOR: May I ask who did this to you?

TOM: Never saw her before. I was minding my own business when she sat down beside me. She was muttering about blood on my hands. I showed her there wasn't. Then she stabbed me and suddenly there was.

DOCTOR: Was what?

TOM: Blood on my hands.

DOCTOR: Where did all this take place?

TOM: In a movie theater.

DOCTOR: What was the film?

TOM: It was a love story. I just went in to kill time before an appointment.

DOCTOR: I'd say you got off pretty easy.

TOM: Nine stitches.

DOCTOR: But the tendons and bones weren't touched. Just skin and muscle were slashed.

TOM: Yes, well, lucky old me.

DOCTOR: Please remain still.

TOM: How much longer?

DOCTOR: We're almost through.

TOM: Will there be a scar?

DOCTOR: So tiny you'll barely notice it; very small stitches.

TOM: And my other hand?

DOCTOR: Superficial; scratches mostly. Nothing a little green soap and water can't take care of.

TOM: Will it have to be bandaged?

DOCTOR: If it will make you feel better, I'll be glad to put one on. It's a slow night.

TOM: Didn't know sarcasm was part of the Hippocratic oath.

DOCTOR: Bandaging isn't necessary. I'll probably ask you to soak it in Betadine for the next day or two, though.

TOM: Do I get anything else?

DOCTOR: A lot of discomfort.

TOM: Seriously. This hurts like hell.

DOCTOR: I can give you something for that. There we are. Done and done.

TOM: Curious expression.

DOCTOR: An annoying phrase I inherited from my mother. It just means we're finished. Wait here and I'll get you that painkiller. It should be just a few minutes.

TOM: Good. I *am* in kind of a rush.

DOCTOR: Oh, no, you are here for a little bit. The police have some questions for you.

TOM: I didn't telephone the police.

DOCTOR: Stab wounds must be reported.

TOM: You said yourself these wounds are nothing.

DOCTOR: It's not up to me.

TOM: How long will it be?

DOCTOR: Relax. Have a seat. They'll be with you as soon as they're free.

(JO-JO enters.)

JO-JO: Excuse me.

DOCTOR: Yes?

JO-JO: I don't know if I'm supposed to be back here.

DOCTOR: Depends on who you are.

JO-JO: I'm looking for the fellow who was—you know—stabbed earlier.

TOM: At the theatre?

JO-JO: Oh, hi.

DOCTOR: Please wait for him outside.

JO-JO: I promise I'll just be a—you know—minute.

DOCTOR: Very well. Make it fast, though.

JO-JO: Promise.

(The DOCTOR exits.)

JO-JO: So, how are you doing?

TOM: They say I'll live.

JO-JO: Gonna be all right going home?

TOM: Yes.

JO-JO: Because it's no trouble if you want me to get you a—you know—cab or something.

TOM: That's all right.

JO-JO: Least I can do. This your chart here?

TOM: Beats me.

JO-JO: All the vital info and stuff. Name, injury, next of kin.

TOM: I guess so.

JO-JO: Used.

TOM: Yes.

JO-JO: That's an unusual name.

TOM: Sounds made up, doesn't it?

JO-JO: I just figured it was—you know—short for something. You don't mind my coming here, do you?

TOM: Not at all.

JO-JO: I just wanted to see how you were.

TOM: Very nice of you.

JO-JO: Hey.

TOM: At some point you'll tell me who you are, yes?

JO-JO: I thought you saw me at the—you know—movie house.

TOM: Sorry, but it was very dark there and I was preoccupied at the time.

JO-JO: Understandable.

TOM: Thanks for coming by. As you can see, though, I'm fine.

JO-JO: Listen, just so you'll know, your bill is coming straight to me and I'll see it's—you know—paid.

TOM: There's no need for that.

JO-JO: Your hands are gonna be all right. I mean there's no permanent damage or anything. I just wondered because you're wincing and—you know—holding 'em funny.

TOM: They're very sore; that's all.

JO-JO: The doctor gave you something for that, though, didn't she? She should, if they're that—you know—painful and everything.

TOM: She's getting me something right now. So, if you'll excuse me—

JO-JO: The name's Swift. Jonathan Swift. Yeah, just like the famous one 'cept everybody calls me Jo-Jo. I manage La Brea. I rushed down here because I feel—you know—bad about what happened.

TOM: It wasn't your fault.

JO-JO: No, but it was my place of business where you got—you know—cut. I wanted to catch you so we can talk about what happened before you speak to the—you know—police, if you plan on speaking to the police, that is.

TOM: If I didn't have to, I wouldn't.

JO-JO: Cops aren't exactly my favorite people, either. Not that cops are bad. I found that out even before I opened up La Brea. Hey, you wanna know where I got that name?

TOM: Not really; no.

JO-JO: From a picture in one of those Little Golden Books you read when you're a—you know—little kid. Dinosaurs at play in the tar pits. A brontosaurus, trapped in the tar pit, 'bout to have a huge bite taken out of his side by a tyrannosaurus—also trapped, sinking fast, 'cept he doesn't seem to know it. I thought they were playing because I was at the time just a—you know—little kid. What were we talking about?

TOM: Cops.

JO-JO: And how much of a nuisance they can be. Especially when they're carrying out an agenda.

TOM: Mr. Swift, all this is very interesting, but I'd appreciate it if you would get to the point.

JO-JO: It's about what you say to the police.

TOM: Be more specific.

JO-JO: When you talk to them, tell them *how* you got hurt, but don't tell 'em *where*.

TOM: Why should I lie? There's no need to.

JO-JO: They're gonna close me down. All they need's an excuse. See, something awful's happening to the neighborhood. Gentrification. They wanna upscale, so they're kicking me out.

TOM: Against the law. They can't.

JO-JO: Oh, they're not saying I got to close down 'cause of *porn*. That'd be censorship. It's other stuff. Zoning laws, they say. But we both know what it really is. High crime rates, low property values, violence against women, juvenile delinquency. Dirty movies are to blame.

TOM: Quite a bit on your plate, I grant you.

JO-JO: The thing is, your—you know—misfortune's gonna put my porno theatre in a bad light. Follow me. If a prostitute working my establishment gets beaten by some psycho—it's happened—no harm done; it's just a hooker. If some fag gets pickpocketed while he's doing some number in the men's room—it's happened—that's okay, too; he got just what he deserved. But if the victim is you, pal—if the victim is white, male, heterosexual, young, professional, comfortable in J. Press suits—that's a whole other ballgame. They'll come after me big time, gnaw like rats till La Brea's a fossil of its former self.

TOM: You have a very specific agenda here.

JO-JO: And you don't?

TOM: None that I'm aware of.

JO-JO: I would guess you are a man of—you know—principle. Your wife must admire that about you. Catherine, isn't it? She must be a very—you know—understanding woman. Gotta be. She understands her husband's need to duck into the dirty movies every now and then, have it off with some—you know—gray thing, then come home to her. Most wives it would kill—if they knew.

(The POLICEMAN enters.)

POLICEMAN: You the stabbing?

TOM: That's me.

POLICEMAN: I need to ask you some questions.

TOM: Yes; the doctor said.

POLICEMAN: The basic information I got from the hospital.

TOM: Do you need me to verify it?

POLICEMAN: And to tell me what happened earlier.

TOM: Not much to tell. I was on my way home from a business dinner.

POLICEMAN: What time was this?

TOM: Little more than an hour ago.

POLICEMAN: Go on.

TOM: I was walking north on First Avenue. Girl came up to me. I heard her voice. Didn't realize at first she was even talking to me. She asked for ten dollars. I assumed she was panhandling.

POLICEMAN: Mm-hmm.

TOM: She went on about how there was blood on my hands. I showed her there wasn't. That's when the knife appeared.

POLICEMAN: Can you describe her?

TOM: Fair-skinned, blonde, slim. Young; late teens.

POLICEMAN: I was under the impression this incident took place in a theatre.

JO-JO: Well, it did happen near where *my* theatre is. La Brea. It's on the—you know—west side of the street. I'm the manager there. The name's Swift. Jonathan Swift. Yeah, just like the famous one 'cept everybody calls me Jo-Jo.

POLICEMAN: You know anything about this?

JO-JO: I saw this guy in trouble and came to give him a—you know—hand.

TOM: That's right.

POLICEMAN: Anything else about the assailant you can tell us?

TOM: It all happened so quickly.

JO-JO: She was no youngster, though. That much I remember.

POLICEMAN: Would you say you got a good look at this girl?

JO-JO: From the ticket booth; yeah. Approximately thirty years of age; dark skin; jet-black hair; very short, very wide, very freaky.

POLICEMAN: Get a look at her eyes?

TOM: Too dark to see.

POLICEMAN: Weren't the street lights on?

TOM: Probably, but I was just coming out from the shadow of the bridge.

POLICEMAN: Would you recognize her if you saw her again?

TOM: I doubt it.

POLICEMAN: Yet *you* got a *very* good look at her and you had to have been at least fifty feet away.

JO-JO: The gas station across the street is pretty well lit.

TOM: I'm sorry I'm not able to be of more help.

JO-JO: Her eyes *were* kind of funny now that you mention it.

TOM: They were?

POLICEMAN: Go on.

JO-JO: Wild. Rolling around her—you know—head.

TOM: Why do you ask?

POLICEMAN: Occurred to me she might be on drugs.

JO-JO: 'Course! That's it! The chick was a druggie. Oh, well. Case closed on this one. Why didn't we think of that before? Drug trash. Sure. Got to be.

TOM: We don't know that.

JO-JO: It's possible, though, and the whole drug thing is getting out of hand. Isn't that right?

POLICEMAN: Certainly there's pressure from very high up about it.

JO-JO: That's everything, then?

POLICEMAN: Pretty much.

TOM: So it's all right for me to go.

POLICEMAN: If it's all right with the hospital, it's all right with me. I would like to get a statement from you, too, Mr. Swift.

JO-JO: Sure, sure; no problem. Let's just step out here because I—you know—promised the doctor.

POLICEMAN: Take care now.

(JO-JO and the POLICEMAN exit, standing for a moment behind the sheet that demarcates the cubicle TOM is in from the rest of the emergency room. The DOCTOR joins them.)

DOCTOR: Finished?

POLICEMAN: He's all yours.

DOCTOR: Awful story, isn't it?

POLICEMAN: Pretty bad.

DOCTOR: You don't believe it?

POLICEMAN: Sir, why don't you take a seat? I'll be right with you.

JO-JO: Oh, sure, I got—you know—time.

(JO-JO exits. TOM rolls down his sleeves and puts on his jacket, while listening to the conversation going on behind him.)

DOCTOR: So what do you think this was?

POLICEMAN: Drug deal that went wrong.

DOCTOR: Really?

POLICEMAN: It's almost always drugs.

DOCTOR: Ah, yes. Drugs. Gonna be the death of us all. I'm kidding.

POLICEMAN: I'm not.

(The POLICEMAN exits. The DOCTOR reenters.)

DOCTOR: Here are the pills I promised you.

TOM: Thank you.

DOCTOR: One every six hours for pain.

TOM: Not recreation.

DOCTOR: That's right. You spoke with the police?

TOM: Oh, yes.

DOCTOR: Well, you're finished, then.

TOM: Done and done.

(The DOCTOR pulls the sheet to one side, revealing the end of a wide corridor. Painted on the wall are the words "FIRE ESCAPE" with an arrow pointing to stage left. TOM walks down the corridor. He exits, right.)

(Blackout.)

SCENE 2

TOM's office at Hite, Upton & Curtis on the twenty-sixth floor of the Chemical Bank Building on Park Avenue; 11:15 p.m. Standard office setup: desk, chair, credenza, a filing cabinet or two. Overhead fluorescents are off; only some dim city lights seep in through the blinds. TOM is looking out the window. All of a sudden, the lights come on. This startles TOM, and he turns to see JULIO standing in the doorway. He is a young man, perhaps eight years TOM's junior, very well dressed. He is freebasing.

JULIO: Stay, no problem; right where you are.

TOM: Julio.

JULIO: Is only me. No need to get all upset.

TOM: What are you doing here?

JULIO: Could be I'm working late.

TOM: Ha and ha.

JULIO: No, it could be that I am.

TOM: By the way, a word of advice. Stop using the office as your private opium den.

JULIO: I don't know what you mean.

TOM: Whole floor smells like burning plastic.

JULIO: That wasn't my doing.

TOM: Don't know how the fuck you stand it.

JULIO: Stand what?

TOM: Inhaling that stuff.

JULIO: That is too bad for you if you think I do drugs and shit.

TOM: You can say that and keep a straight face.

JULIO: Are you accusing me?

TOM: What's in your left hand?

JULIO: Nothing.

TOM: And in your right?

JULIO: Nothing.

TOM: What's that smell?

JULIO: I don't know.

TOM: The police would.

JULIO: Call them.

(TOM reaches for the phone, but thinks better of it. JULIO fires up a small butane torch, inhales deeply.)

JULIO: What happened to your hand?

TOM: Nothing.

JULIO: You hurt it?

TOM: I don't know.

JULIO: How come it's all bandaged and shit?

TOM: That wasn't me.

JULIO: What are you doing here so late?

TOM: Came to give notice.

JULIO: About what?

TOM: It means I'm quitting.

JULIO: How come?

TOM: Not worth talking about.

JULIO: Who's going to do your job?

TOM: I don't know.

JULIO: Maybe me.

TOM: Really think they'll do that?

JULIO: Sure; is possible.

TOM: Qualified, are you?

JULIO: To do what you do is not so hard. Boss people around. Sign your name to papers.

TOM: Go for it, kid; give it your best shot.

JULIO: You recommend me.

TOM: Forget it.

JULIO: Think you can't be replaced by me. Is stupid on your part because anyone can replace anyone. That is what I have learned here. All you have to do is make everyone think you are busy when you are not.

TOM: Don't even know why you'd *want* this job.

JULIO: Is so hard to understand. A job with more money and being out from under someone's thumb.

TOM: Julio, it's not going to happen.

JULIO: Maybe it will.

TOM: How many warnings have you got on your record?

JULIO: A couple.

TOM: Try again.

JULIO: Is three warnings.

TOM: Simply put, you're the worst worker this company's ever had. You are chronically late, take too much time for lunch, sneak out early.

JULIO: I learned from the best.

TOM: Only two runs a day, yet nobody ever gets the mail on time. Boxes conveniently disappear whenever you're too lazy to deliver them. You order supplies we don't need, then do a half-assed job on the invoices, which we do need. You lie, always get caught, tell bigger lies. As unsuitable employees go, Julio, you are the cream of the crap.

JULIO: Then why don't you fire me?

TOM: Hasn't been for a lack of effort.

JULIO: Is because I am Hispanic... is because I am a minority. They are too afraid to fire me. They are afraid I will complain and they will have a discrimination lawsuit to face.

TOM: You really *aren't* as dumb as you look, are you?

JULIO: What a company this is! They make money telling other companies how to fire people, but they don't know how to get rid of me!

TOM: And so you keep pushing that envelope.

JULIO: I didn't wreck any envelopes, so don't try and say that I did!

TOM: Only mean you've gone just about as far as you can.

JULIO: We'll see about that, my friend.

TOM: Your crowning glory, though, was that attempt at credit card theft.

JULIO: Wasn't me.

TOM: Using a client's American Express card number to order jewelry for your girlfriend.

JULIO: Wasn't me.

TOM: Moronic to think you could have gotten away with something like that.

JULIO: They never proved a thing.

TOM: Had they proven it, had they *pursued* it, you would have been up on two counts at least. Grand larceny and tampering with the U.S. mail.

JULIO: Makes you wonder what you have to do to get fired from here.

TOM: Excuse me, but I have work to do. *(TOM sits at his desk.)*

JULIO: You are writing your resignation?

TOM: Not immediately. First thing I plan to do is fire you.

JULIO: Is fine by me.

TOM: You don't have a problem with that.

JULIO: Oh, no. If you fire me I am eligible for the unemployment. I can go for months on that... get another job only not tell them. Is good, they tell me, for twelve weeks at least... and someone else tell me maybe it goes up to twenty-six weeks. Fire me and you only do me a great favor.

TOM: You're right. *(He tears up the paper.)*

JULIO: What are you doing?

TOM: Promoting you.

JULIO: I don't think I heard you right.

TOM: Yes, you did. *(Takes out a fresh sheet of paper, begins writing.)* Management's been laboring over how to get rid of you. This is the answer.

JULIO: You are so full of shit.

TOM: Makes perfect sense. You take over, fuck up, get fired. The company gets rid of you, acquiring a few brownie points in the process. Hiring minorities. Promoting internally.

JULIO: Is of no importance what kind of job they fire me from. I can still collect. Management gets nothing this way.

TOM: It gets to knock that chip off your shoulder. It gets to stick a pin in that swollen self-esteem. It gets to watch the quicksand swallow you whole. Congratulations, Julio—and welcome to management.

JULIO: Fuck you, I can do this job.

TOM: Then they'll have no reason to fire you, will they?

JULIO: Jane will take care of me.

TOM: Another surprise. Jane quit this afternoon.

JULIO: I can turn the promotion down.

TOM: You won't, though, will you? It's too mouth-watering an opportunity.

JULIO: Or just quit altogether.

TOM: *Are* you quitting?

JULIO: Is sad you think so little of me... think I can't do your job... think you are so superior.

TOM: Not me, but wait until you have Upton breathing down your neck. Don't worry. He isn't prejudiced. He's an equal opportunity abuser.

JULIO: Fuck you!

TOM: Are we going to fight? It's all right, I guess; we're both covered by workman's comp.

JULIO: Everything you find so contemptible!

TOM: Sadly, yes.

JULIO: And you look down on me because I am the same as you!

TOM: Lose that. We are nothing alike.

JULIO: More than you think.

TOM: You've never committed to a single day's work.

JULIO: So you think is all it takes is to be dedicated and working hard. Maybe you are right. Let us suppose I become all these things you say I must be. Tell me how much of a chance I have to climb up to where you sit. There are how many Hispanics working that high up? There are how many Hispanics working here in total? Present and accounted for. I deliver mail.

TOM: Do you really believe you aren't taken seriously because of your ethnicity?

JULIO: Is why you are offering me a promotion.

TOM: I'm offering you a promotion because you're a lousy worker!

JULIO: The secretaries, they don't even pronounce my name correctly. *(Using a hard "J".)* Julio. Helio. Many times I have told them the way it is pronounced. They do not bother to remember; it is not important enough for them to. *I* am not important enough.

TOM: Well, you are now. Come. Sit.

(TOM rises. JULIO crosses to sit behind TOM's desk.)

JULIO: Now what?

TOM: Let's see what I can teach you.

JULIO: Invoices. I must sign off on the invoices.

TOM: We already know how poorly you perform that function. Let's see if you can perform a different task equally poorly.

JULIO: Like what?

TOM: Here are some files that will help you out. What I do and how. Made them up for Jane last year when I went on vacation.

JULIO: So many papers.

TOM: Let's start with something easy. We're opening three new field offices. They need setups. Each office receives twenty copies of all three OPC manuals for general stock, plus an information booklet that goes to the office manager. Make sure the stuff is shipped UPS, not FedEx. Hite's on the warpath about expenses.

JULIO: I don't think I like this job.

TOM: Your tough luck.

JULIO: Fuck you. I can always quit.

TOM: And no one will stand in your way.

JULIO: But then I would not be able to collect the unemployment. I will make a deal with you.

TOM: What kind of deal?

JULIO: Counsel me like we do for the big executives. This will enable me to get work elsewhere. In return, I will quit my job here. This way everybody is happy.

TOM: You want the company to outplace you.

JULIO: Is not a bad offer I make. The company must not know, however. You will be my counselor, but on the sly.

TOM: You'll resign.

JULIO: Deal?

TOM: Deal.

(They shake hands.)

JULIO: Let us start with the training that will benefit me when I go into an interview.

TOM: Got one already lined up, haven't you?

JULIO: Perhaps, but is not your concern.

TOM: Sit here. Pretend you're applying for a job.

JULIO: I do look my best all the time, so that is not a problem.

TOM: Appearance isn't everything.

JULIO: Professional appearance maybe is.

TOM: Now, first of all, and you won't find this in our instructional manuals, it's generally not a good idea to freebase during a job interview. Sends a prospective employer the wrong message.

JULIO: What else?

TOM: Your employment history. Don't make things up. Don't give yourself skills you don't have or degrees you haven't earned.

JULIO: Get to the important stuff.

TOM: Don't be impatient. We just started.

JULIO: Is so boring.

TOM: Stop fidgeting in the chair, too; sit still. Now, the interviewer will probably ask you some difficult questions.

JULIO: Such as what?

TOM: What your weaknesses are.

JULIO: Haven't any.

TOM: That's exactly what you *don't* say, Julio. You'll say something along these lines. "Well, sometimes I'm *too* punctual." Pay attention now. "Sometimes I pay *too* much attention to detail." The idea is to take a negative and turn it into a positive.

JULIO: This is shit.

TOM: Julio, we've been at this for all of two minutes.

JULIO: Appearance isn't everything, you tell me, but all you're giving me is a way to appear. You are teaching me nothing. The deal is off.

TOM: Calm down now.

JULIO: Fuck you, calm down. Is not your tomorrow you need to worry about. I tell you this. I am not going to quit here. You are going to fire me and that is all there is to it.

TOM: We had an agreement, Julio.

JULIO: I cannot quit. I need to collect unemployment. If I quit, I cannot collect.

TOM: Forget it; not going to happen.

JULIO: Company man! How much ass you got to kiss to become like you?

TOM: I'm not going to fire you! If you're unhappy here, quit!

JULIO: I cannot quit—and you will fire me!

TOM: There's nothing you can do to make me change my mind.

(JULIO stands on TOM's desk. He unzips his fly and urinates on the papers strewn across the desk.)

TOM: You win. You're fired.

JULIO: Knew you would see it my way.

TOM: Pleasure doing business with you.

(Blackout.)

SCENE 3

The sauna at Definitions, a health club on York Avenue between 82nd and 83rd Streets; 11:59 p.m. An enclosure of dark wood. A bench on the floor, plus a level or two built up into the wall. Small firebox heating the room runs on electricity. Fiery glow visible through a metal grate. Control switch nearby. Minor buzzing in the background. TOM is sitting on the level, sweaty, barely able to stay awake. On the bench, IAN, about TOM's age, is equally exhausted. Their eyes are shut. Naked, they have towels draped across their laps. The buzzing stops. Light from the firebox begins to dim. TOM moves for the control switch.

IAN: Stay.

TOM: Huh?

IAN: I'll get it.

TOM: Thanks.

IAN: Always want to help the handicapped.

TOM: What? Oh.

(IAN works the switch. Immediately the buzzing starts up again. Light inside the firebox brightens. IAN moves to sit next to TOM.)

IAN: All set.

TOM: Terrific.

IAN: Fifteen minutes should do it.

TOM: Got to get home, anyway.

IAN: They'll want us out soon.

TOM: Is it that late?

IAN: Already'd begun closing.

TOM: What's the time?

IAN: Midnight or so.

TOM: Surprised they even let us in.

IAN: Had to slip the guy something.

TOM: A lot?

IAN: Twenty bucks.

TOM: Did you come in after me?

IAN: Before.

TOM: Owe you a note of thanks.

IAN: Skip it.

TOM: Wanna turn up the heat?

IAN: Your funeral.

TOM: Point is to perspire as much as possible, so the poisons can leave you. I always do this before I go home.

IAN: What's your name?

TOM: Tom.

IAN: Ian.

TOM: Hi.

IAN: Hi.

(Pause.)

IAN: Wanna fuck?

TOM: Sure.

IAN: Great.

TOM: Kind of tired, though.

IAN: You and me both.

TOM: Haven't seen you before.

IAN: I'm new here.

TOM: This isn't a gay club.

IAN: I know.

TOM: Thought you might not. Felt you *should* in case you didn't.

IAN: Appreciate it.

TOM: Wouldn't want you suffering the consequences for trying to mold the wrong piece of clay.

IAN: Took out a membership here strictly for working out. Already know where to go for sex.

TOM: Anywhere.

IAN: Right.

(Pause.)

TOM: Anytime you want to start.

IAN: You start.

TOM: I can't.

IAN: Neither can I.

TOM: So fucking tired.

IAN: No energy whatsoever.

TOM: First time.

IAN: What.

TOM: That I'm too tired to do anything.

IAN: It happens.

TOM: Never to me.

IAN: You're all fucked out.

TOM: So to speak.

IAN: Are you a fag?

TOM: No.

IAN: You've tried it, though.

TOM: Been there; sure. It's okay. Don't want a steady *diet* of it. Once in a great, great while.

IAN: Like me with women.

TOM: That right?

IAN: Just often enough to clear the palate.

TOM: Never heard it put that way.

IAN: Am I wrong?

TOM: Nope.

IAN: I don't admit that to many people.

TOM: That you fuck women every so often?

IAN: Bisexuality has become unhip.

TOM: Have you a lover?

IAN: Not exactly.

TOM: Meaning what?

IAN: I have a boy who comes in.

TOM: He's trade?

IAN: No.

TOM: Still too young to be paying for it, aren't we?

IAN: This kid hasn't come out yet. He lives with his parents in the apartment directly below mine.

TOM: Convenience is everything.

IAN: Well, it used to be.

TOM: I have to tomcat around. You get free deliveries.

IAN: Looks good on paper, I'll admit.

TOM: No strings; perfect.

IAN: There is a balance of power. He's got youth and beauty. I've got my own apartment. Feel like I'm on alert twenty-four hours a day, though. Four in the morning this kid's rapping on my door, coked up, expecting to get fucked. Momentary satisfaction never used to take up so much of my time.

TOM: Everyone should have such problems.

IAN: Are you married?

TOM: Not very.

IAN: Does your wife know that?

TOM: Probably suspects.

IAN: What do you do?

TOM: Nothing anymore.

IAN: You're out of work?

TOM: By my own hand. Quit my job about an hour and a half ago. Typed up a snappy little resignation. Left it on my boss's desk.

IAN: Something will turn up.

TOM: I'm not sure I want it to.

IAN: Reagan's our next president. The economy's going to take off.

TOM: How do you know?

IAN: I'm an economist.

TOM: Hate thinking about the future. Until recently it was never a subject for consideration. Now. That was the only thing I ever believed in.

IAN: What happened?

TOM: Today did. Now turned into later.

IAN: Bummer.

TOM: It crossed my mind to kill myself, but I'm thirty-five.

IAN: Too old to die young.

TOM: Precisely.

(Pause.)

IAN: Anytime you want to start.

TOM: You start.

IAN: I can't.

TOM: Breathing takes so much out of you.

IAN: Like keeping your eyes open.

TOM: Hard to believe you're an economist.

IAN: I could show you my paper on supply-side economics.

TOM: Never quite grasped what that was.

IAN: Easy to understand. You cut taxes to get people to save more, spend more, invest more. The economy burgeons. Tax revenues flourish.

TOM: Makes sense.

IAN: Looks good on paper, I'll admit.

(Pause.)

TOM: What's he want?

IAN: He?

TOM: Your whatever; the boy downstairs.

IAN: His next fuck on standby.

TOM: Might be easier just to fuck him than to explain why you don't want to.

IAN: Very often the case.

TOM: Sounds like a perfect setup.

IAN: It was. And the reward for perfection is decay.

(Pause.)

TOM: Some bruise you've got there.

IAN: Really?

TOM: On your shoulder. No, no; the other one.

IAN: The skin isn't broken, is it?

TOM: Discolored; sort of a bluish-purple.

IAN: Feels normal.

TOM: Did you bump into something?

IAN: Not that I recall.

TOM: Looks painful.

IAN: It isn't.

TOM: Probably nothing.

(Pause.)

TOM: Anytime you want to start.

IAN: You start.

TOM: I can't.

IAN: Feel so drained.

TOM: Rigor mortis is setting in.

IAN: This heat isn't helping any, either.

TOM: I'm as helpless as—ice.

(Blackout.)

SCENE 4

TOM and CATHERINE's apartment in a high rise on East 85th Street; 1:30 a.m. Small living area stripped bare, except for a television and a Betamax perched on a makeshift cart. A tape measure lies amidst some decorating magazines strewn in the middle of the floor. TOM and CATHERINE are eating in stony silence. Just some Chinese takeout cold from the fridge. CATHERINE spots something on TOM's collar, examines it.

CATHERINE: Stay.

TOM: What?

CATHERINE: This thing staring at me; made of plastic, comes to a point at one end. I just realized it's one of the stays from the collar of your shirt poking out.

TOM: Oh.

CATHERINE: Remember to leave it out, so I can fix it.

(Pause.)

CATHERINE: How's your hand?

TOM: Acting up a bit.

CATHERINE: Take one of your pills.

TOM: Plan to.

CATHERINE: Let me get you some water.

TOM: Don't bother. *(He exits.)*

CATHERINE: The new furniture comes tomorrow. I wound up ordering the loveseat I told you about, but I'm not sure I should have.

TOM: Catherine, where'd you move the glasses?

CATHERINE: Aren't they where they always are?

TOM: Where's that?

CATHERINE: In the cabinet over the sink.

TOM: They're not there.

CATHERINE: Facing the sink... to your *left.*

TOM: Oh.

(Pause.)

CATHERINE: Hear what I said about the love-seat?

TOM: *Goddamn it!*

CATHERINE: So I guess you would be in the *anti*-love-seat contingent.

TOM: Damn glass slipped out of my hand.

CATHERINE: Want some help?

TOM: Relax. It's just some spilled water. I *think* I can handle it.

CATHERINE: I just thought it might be difficult with your hand still sore.

TOM: Where are the towels?

CATHERINE: On the inside of the cabinet door.

TOM: Which one?

CATHERINE: Below the sink.

TOM: Oh. *(TOM reenters.)*

CATHERINE: That was fast.

TOM: The quicker picker-upper.

CATHERINE: Didn't it break?

TOM: Plastic glass.

CATHERINE: Bloomingdale's is delivering the living room set tomorrow morning. Any chance you can be *here* instead of the office?

TOM: No problem.

CATHERINE: Really? Well, that's a relief. One less thing *I* have to worry about.

TOM: What's the tape measure doing out?

CATHERINE: I think I miscalculated. There may not be room for that love-seat.

TOM: Should have done the measuring before you bought it.

CATHERINE: We all make mistakes, Tom. Haven't you?

(Pause.)

CATHERINE: Look at us. It's like we've come full circle, isn't it? When we first moved in, we had *nothing* in here, remember? No furniture. Our cartons hadn't arrived. For a solid week all we had was my Betamax on a milk crate. And we lived on Chinese takeout.

TOM: Just the essentials.

(Pause.)

CATHERINE: Think if we position the love-seat against the *wall* instead of facing the *window* we'll have a little more room?

TOM: Your guess is as good as mine.

CATHERINE: It's so relentlessly beige in here. The new furniture should help some. The sofa and chairs are pale green and white Victorian chintz. The coffee table's mahogany and there are two matching end tables. I bought a small worktable for the kitchen. But that's coming from Conran's sometime tomorrow afternoon.

TOM: Wanna go out?

CATHERINE: Now?

TOM: Still early. Nothing starts closing up for another couple of hours.

CATHERINE: You just got *home*. Now you want to go *out* again?

TOM: Yeah, why not?

CATHERINE: I'm not as young as you think *you* are.

TOM: There was a time when we wouldn't even get *back* to my place till after sunrise. We'd scarf down some breakfast, then sleep till noon. Nod off to the sounds of all those suckers scurrying to work.

CATHERINE: That was a *lifetime* ago. We've other things now.

TOM: I know. Tables from Conran's.

CATHERINE: Usually men take *interest* in their homes, even if it's just to secure their creature comforts. The perfect easy chair to burrow in after dinner. The best sound system for those old forty-fives they refuse to throw out. The biggest television they can get for what they can afford to pay. Not you, though.

TOM: Staying-at-home stuff is pretty overrated.

CATHERINE: And you know this *how*?

TOM: Don't tell me that was the plan for tonight. Impromptu nostalgia, then some snuggling by the fire.

CATHERINE: Anything's possible.

TOM: You *do* realize we don't *have* a fireplace.

(CATHERINE angrily hits the remote to the Betamax. There is the sound of a crackling fire, and the room takes on a burning radiance.)

CATHERINE: Courtesy of one of our distributors. It's a *video* of a fire in a fireplace. They tell me it's going to be the next big craze.

TOM: Sure you don't want to go out?

CATHERINE: Why don't you ever want to stay in?

TOM: Beats me. I get restless.

CATHERINE: We haven't finished eating.

TOM: Coffee shop's open all night.

CATHERINE: I'm not dressed.

TOM: Easily rectified.

CATHERINE: And tomorrow's jam-packed.

TOM: Screw tomorrow.

CATHERINE: You said you'd *be* here, remember.

TOM: Oh, right. Tables from Conran's. Tables from Conran's.

CATHERINE: *Table* from Conran's. Just the one.

TOM: Sofa and chairs from Bloomingdale's. Rug from Bon Marché. Linens from Porthault. Assorted extras from various chichi Madison Avenue boutiques. That pretty much it?

CATHERINE: Still acting up? Your hand, I mean.

TOM: No.

(Pause.)

TOM: Finished?

CATHERINE: Oh, yes, I think so.

TOM: Let me help you clean up.

CATHERINE: I'm not going out.

TOM: Suit yourself.

CATHERINE: Tom, if you weren't out so much, I could plan things better. Meals and such. I wouldn't be serving *scraps* all the time.

TOM: Have I ever complained about anything at home? No.

CATHERINE: No. No, you're very easy to please. I often wish you weren't. Think it's easy being tied to someone who never wants a say in anything? Sometimes I wonder why you married me. Sometimes I wonder why you married.

TOM: Seemed like a good idea at the time.

CATHERINE: And when did it *stop* being a good idea?

TOM: People change. That's all I'm saying.

CATHERINE: What are you *talking* about? You haven't changed in the *least*!

TOM: I know. *You* have.

(Pause.)

TOM: Way back when, and not so long ago, we were of like minds. Two live-for-the-moment people who'd found each other. But the joke was on me. You were an amateur. Whatever bacchanal spirit I saw in you was merely youth, rebellion, adventure. Things you would grow out of. By the time I realized that, it was too late. You were coming down the aisle, wedding bouquet in hand. Four hours later I committed my first act of adultery. I'll spare you the details. You were so busy planning our future, it never occurred to you I wouldn't be part of it. Of course that hadn't occurred to me, either.

CATHERINE: And what did you think was going to happen, Tom? Let me guess. We'd drift into separate lives. Plenty of slack in that thread tying us together. Works for some; open to anything, lots of freedom.

TOM: Something like that.

CATHERINE: Lately you've come to remind me of that fellow you regret having invited to a party. Oh, you know the one. He refuses to acknowledge the party's over. Guests are getting into their coats, the host is putting out lights, the hostess is tidying up, but he insists the night's still young, continues pouring drinks, and having fun all by himself. His car is always the *last* to pull out of the drive and head home.

(Pause.)

CATHERINE: Where are you going?

TOM: Out.

CATHERINE: At this hour?

TOM: Just for some air.

CATHERINE: Will you be long?

TOM: Does it matter?

CATHERINE: If there's any point to it, I'll wait up.

TOM: Can't think of one. Can you?

CATHERINE: No.

TOM: Anything else?

CATHERINE: You're free to go.

(Blackout.)

SCENE 5

The Inferno, a private club on Third Avenue near 86th Street; 2:46 a.m. A patch of bare floor. Out of sight, built into the floor, blowers on high speed facing up toward the ceiling. Ribbons attached in such a way as to suggest fire. Garments strewn about the middle of the room. TOM has a woman up against the wall. Some fierce lovemaking coming to an end. He draws away from her. It is ALLEY. He reaches out to touch her face. She pushes his hand away, moves for her clothes, gets dressed.

ALLEY: Go.

TOM: Fuck you.

ALLEY: You just did.

TOM: What's the problem?

ALLEY: No problem.

TOM: Yet you're acting like there is.

ALLEY: So what.

TOM: Blood.

ALLEY: Huh?

TOM: My lower lip. Blood.

ALLEY: Accidents happen.

TOM: Like inept teenagers.

ALLEY: Pipe down about it.

TOM: Hurts, though.

ALLEY: It won't last.

TOM: No; I suppose not.

(Pause.)

TOM: You look familiar.

ALLEY: Really.

TOM: Have we met before?

ALLEY: Awfully cute.

TOM: I'm serious.

ALLEY: Cigarette?

TOM: Sure.

(They light cigarettes.)

TOM: Well, have we?

ALLEY: Have we what?

TOM: Met.

ALLEY: We may have bumped into each other.

TOM: Wait a minute. I know. This afternoon. You're the schoolteacher.

ALLEY: One gold star coming up.

TOM: Should have said something.

ALLEY: I have to go.

TOM: What's the rush?

ALLEY: Nothing to hang around *here* for.

TOM: Plenty to hang around here for.

ALLEY: This is it for me.

TOM: We can rustle up some people, if you want; continue partying.

ALLEY: I mean for good.

TOM: Yeah?

ALLEY: No more bars, no more clubs, no more letting in strangers. I always know when the party's over and when it's time to find something else.

(Pause.)

TOM: Still tasting it.

ALLEY: What?

TOM: Blood. My lip keeps splitting open.

ALLEY: Take me to court.

TOM: I might just do that.

ALLEY: Nice running into you. *(She starts to go.)*

TOM: Music's pretty bad, hunh?

ALLEY: Long as you can move to it. Do you dance?

TOM: Only in the shower.

ALLEY: Non-skid decals. For your sake I hope you believe in them.

TOM: Scarcely believe in anything else these days.

ALLEY: Wanna slow dance? C'mon. Hey, what's wrong?

(They dance.)

TOM: Been a hell of a day.

ALLEY: For all of us… the entire *country*.

TOM: That's right. I completely forgot.

ALLEY: Don't you want to know who won?

TOM: Ronnie-baby.

ALLEY: Fair and square.

TOM: Accent on the square.

ALLEY: It's like I said. The party is definitely *over*.

(The music fizzles to a stop. They continue dancing.)

TOM: Man, it's hot in here.

ALLEY: Hence the name. The Inferno.

TOM: Think it was meant to be?

ALLEY: What.

TOM: Reagan getting in. This step backwards.

ALLEY: Once he claimed we had with him a "rendezvous with destiny." It *is* possible to step backwards and still go forward. We're always progressing. Everything contributes to the evolution of our souls.

TOM: Don't tell me you're religious.

ALLEY: Spiritual as opposed to religious.

TOM: Translated, you've turned to the East. Reincarnation. Past lives. Lives to come. I won't follow you there.

ALLEY: Will you follow me home?

TOM: I *am* home.

ALLEY: You've a wife. I don't remember her name.

TOM: Neither do I.

ALLEY: What happened?

TOM: Had to get out.

ALLEY: Anything else to report?

TOM: Gave myself the boot at work.

ALLEY: And God said burn away the old world and let a new one rise from the ashes.

TOM: Did God really say that?

ALLEY: Are you intimating He was misquoted?

TOM: Just misunderstood.

(They kiss.)

ALLEY: Tell me one thing you believe in.

TOM: I believe in here-and-now.

ALLEY: That's two things.

TOM: Not if you hyphenate them.

ALLEY: Bucking for another gold star?

TOM: C'mon. Stick around a while.

ALLEY: I *promised* myself.

TOM: Fun and games. You have time for fun and games.

ALLEY: We've *had* our fun.

TOM: I'm going to tell you my name.

ALLEY: Why?

TOM: Don't you want to know it?

ALLEY: Okay.

TOM: Tom.

ALLEY: Alley.

TOM: I know.

ALLEY: You did not.

TOM: I might've.

ALLEY: Do you smell something burning?

TOM: Let's go upstairs and have a couple of drinks. You don't want to leave. You're like me. The minute you get home, you want to go out again.

ALLEY: Has it always been like that?

TOM: For as long as I can remember.

ALLEY: I really have to go.

TOM: Stay.

(Pause.)

TOM: I know you said this'd be your last night. But the night isn't over. Tomorrow hasn't come yet.

ALLEY: Tomorrow began at midnight.

TOM: Tomorrow comes at six a.m.

ALLEY: Who says?

TOM: *TV Guide.*

ALLEY: I'm so easily seduced.

TOM: Good. I like that in a woman.

ALLEY: Up for playing around some more, are you?

TOM: Why don't you come over here and find out?

(He pulls ALLEY to him. She submits to his embrace.)

ALLEY: You *are*! You *are* up for some more playing around!

TOM: Satisfaction guaranteed!

(Suddenly the music comes on again. But mingled with it are sounds of a disturbance. Voices raised in fear. Hurried footsteps. TOM breaks the embrace.)

ALLEY: Did you hear that?

TOM: Someone yelled there's a fire.

ALLEY: I smell smoke.

TOM: Come on. We'll head up to the ground floor.

(Smoke billows in. Fire alarm goes off.)

ALLEY: We can't get out this way!

TOM: There's a door at the end of the passageway.

ALLEY: It's upstairs! The fire's upstairs!

TOM: C'mon!

ALLEY: We've got to go back!

TOM: The door won't open! Something's blocking it on the other side!

ALLEY: Our only chance is go back the way we came!

TOM: You'll never make it!

ALLEY: I'm getting out!

TOM: I can't! I can't! *I can't move!*

(ALLEY exits. TOM tries to follow, but can't bring himself to do it. He looks up fearfully. Fiery glow descends upon him. He cries out as the light on him burns hot, then slowly fades.)

(Blackout.)

(End of play.)

THE DOCTOR OF ROME

A sequel to Shakespeare's *The Merchant of Venice*

Nat Colley

NAT COLLEY was born and grew up in Sacramento. He received bachelor's and law degrees from the University of Michigan. He is a practicing lawyer who lives in Los Angeles. His first job in the theatre was as assistant director to Luther James on August Wilson's *Joe Turner's Come and Gone* at Sacramento Theater Co. Since then, Colley has written *The Shoebox*, presented at Lorraine Hansberry Theater, San Francisco, in 1993; *A Sensitive Man*, presented at Moving Arts, Los Angeles, in 1996; and *The Dangerous Minute*, also presented at Moving Arts in 1997. He wrote *Seat Selection*, which he then directed at the Los Angeles Museum of Contemporary Art in conjunction with Cornerstone Theater in 1997; earlier, he had directed his play, *The Abortion of Mary Williams*, at the Ivar Theater in Los Angeles. Colley also directed the film version of that play, which was selected for inclusion in the Showtime network's black filmmaker's showcase and broadcast in 1998.

The Doctor of Rome was first presented by Revolving Shakespeare Company (Ralph Carhart, Artistic Director; Daniel Colb Rothman, Producing Director), on May 15, 2002, at the Greenwich Street Theater, New York, with the following cast and credits:

Merchant 2/Rabbi .... David Arthur Bachrach
Rachel .... Bethany Butler
Merchant 3 .... Trevor Davis
Tubal .... Mike Finesilver
Bellario .... Michael Hardart
Merchant 1/Guard .... Rob Langeder
Duke of Venice .... Brian Linden
Portia .... Lanie MacEwan
Largo .... Lawrence Merritt
Daniel .... John Peterson
Bassanio .... Miles Phillips
Jessica .... Dara Seitzman

Director: Daniel Colb Rothman
Set Design: Sebastien Grouard
Lighting Design: Andrew Dickey
Costume Design: Jim Parks
Graphic Design: Antonio Pendones: GraphAct.com
Fight Choreography: David Mason
Stage Manager: Laura Maag

"A Daniel come to judgement! yea, a Daniel."
—*Shylock,* The Merchant of Venice, *Act IV, Scene I*

CHARACTERS

DANIEL: Shylock's grandson by Jessica, 15

TUBAL: Shylock's friend and executor

JESSICA: Daniel's mother, Shylock's daughter

PORTIA: Wealthy heiress of Belmont, Daniel's godmother, and Shylock's nemesis; the Doctor of Rome (BALTHAZAR)

BASSANIO: Her husband

RACHEL: Portia's half-Moor handmaid, daughter of Shylock's former servant Launcelot Gobbo, 15

DUKE: The Duke of Venice

BELLARIO: A Doctor of Padua and Portia's cousin

RABBI: Spiritual leader of the Venice Synagogue

LARGO: A wealthy Merchant of Rome

MERCHANTS 1, 2, and 3: Other traders on the mart at Venice

GUARDS: As needed

Note: BALTHAZAR and BELLARIO are civil doctors, i.e., doctors of the law.

SETTING

Belmont, Venice, and their environs.

TIME

A scant fifteen years since the close of *The Merchant of Venice.*

SYNOPSIS OF SCENES

SCENE ONE: A Merry Bond
SCENE TWO: These Naughty Times
SCENE THREE: On the Rialto
SCENE FOUR: Since I Am a Dog…
SCENE FIVE: A Hot Temper Leaps over a Cold Decree
SCENE SIX: A Wilderness of Monkeys
SCENE SEVEN: The Quality of Mercy
SCENE EIGHT: The Trial of Caskets
SCENE NINE: If You Prick Us…
SCENE TEN: Better the Instruction

SCENE ONE
A Merry Bond

Setting: Belmont; 15 years later. At rise: PORTIA enters, a study in frenetic movement, and a few steps behind her, trying to keep up, RACHEL.

PORTIA: Are you sure everything is ready?

RACHEL: I have checked everything three times, madam, each time you have asked.

PORTIA: What is that smell?

RACHEL: One whole pig and a turkey, madam.

PORTIA: Did you tell…

RACHEL: Yes, madam, elderberry wine sauce, as you requested.

PORTIA: *(Wiping the furniture with her fingers.)* And the rooms?

RACHEL: Swept and polished.

PORTIA: Excellent.

RACHEL: No, it isn't, my lady. *I* did most of the dusting. Some of your servants seem quite useless.

PORTIA: My dear Rachel, that's why I have you to keep after them.

RACHEL: Tending to you is my first duty.

PORTIA: Your duty is whatever I say it is.

RACHEL: *(Referring to PORTIA's hair.)* This won't do.

(RACHEL begins to restyle PORTIA's hair.)

PORTIA: Dear girl, you are more nervous than I am.

RACHEL: Please, madam, let me tend to my responsibilities.

PORTIA: All right. It is one thing you do better than any servant I have.

RACHEL: Aye, and they resent me for that, as well.

PORTIA: It takes a deft hand to make sure a command is followed, specially if it be not one's own.

RACHEL: I thank my lady for her confidence in me, and for all she has done for this simple girl. It will do me well when I am a married woman with a household of her own to care for.

PORTIA: Time enough for that, my dear. You are still quite young.

RACHEL: Still, I do wonder about it, when I watch you and Lord Bassanio together, it is as if you had just met.

PORTIA: It has been wonderful, our time together. My only regret is that I have not borne him children.

RACHEL: Fret not for this, Lady Portia. God has found so many other good things for you to do.

PORTIA: Sweet Rachel, don't you understand, a woman is judged on the size and quality of her home and family, no matter what else she may have accomplished? *(A pause, then, ruefully.)* All the more so if no one *knows* what she has accomplished.

RACHEL: The fault may not lie with you, my lady.

PORTIA: How is that, my dear?

RACHEL: Perhaps it is Lord Bassanio that can't… have children.

PORTIA: I'll not have you say a word against Bassanio! Not even in my own defense!

RACHEL: Yes, madam.

PORTIA: Besides, Daniel is my son.

RACHEL: No doubt Jessica would disagree.

PORTIA: *(Disdainful.)* She is only his mother. *I* have educated him. *Schooled* him. *Cultured* him. *(Proudly.)* He is a fine work.

RACHEL: *(Wistfully.)* Ahh… indeed.

(PORTIA looks suspiciously at RACHEL, who catches herself and changes the subject back to BASSANIO.)

RACHEL: But… if it is permitted, may I ask why my lady would not suffer to hear this humble servant's suggestion regarding Lord Bassanio, since it may at least ease your own guilt?

PORTIA: It is a wife's place to always put her husband first. A wife is to be in subjection in all things. And it is a small price to carry this burden that he may be relieved of it.

RACHEL: But my lady, it is not the same thing at all. To be in subjection is not to take on things that are not of your doing.

PORTIA: But it is of my doing. I loved him. I married him, and were it not for my father's clever devices, which Bassanio overcame, I would have chosen him over all. That being so, Rachel, I must take all that comes with it, for good or ill.

RACHEL: *(Stops working on hair, and kneels beside her mistress.)* Would he do the same for you?

PORTIA: Of course.

RACHEL: Have you ever tested him?

PORTIA: I need not stoop to such devices. I trust Bassanio completely, and he has never given me reason to doubt his love. Besides, men such as Bassanio are tested every hour of every day.

RACHEL: How so?

PORTIA: With lovely young maidens such as yourself about the house all day. They whisper words of love, but it isn't love, only a fleeting need for passion.

RACHEL: My lady, Lord Bassanio has never…

PORTIA: There! You see? You have acquitted him yourself.

RACHEL: But how can a woman know, before marriage, I mean?

PORTIA: What has God said? By their fruit ye shall know them. A man is to love his wife, even as Christ loved the church.

RACHEL: I am not so young that I have not learned that what God has said and what a man does do not always agree.

PORTIA: Then you are wise beyond your years.

RACHEL: Help me be wiser still. How am I to know? To really know?

PORTIA: I cannot help you. No matter how kind, or thoughtful, or gentlemanly he may seem, you can never know. Even if he is true at the beginning, he may change. The woman must simply wait in faith, hoping that in such moments of testing he will show himself true to her. Meanwhile, she must always remain true herself. But why do we talk of such things? I am not about to lose yet another maid to marriage!

RACHEL: But my lady, there *is* one who has whispered words of love to me.

PORTIA: What's this?!

(Sound: the door.)

RACHEL: I'll get it.

PORTIA: We will talk of this again.

(RACHEL opens the door, and JESSICA enters with DANIEL.)

PORTIA: And here he is, the subject of our labors!

DANIEL: Sweet Portia.

PORTIA: And Jessica... What? No Lorenzo?

JESSICA: Gratiano was detained in Genoa. Lorenzo went to aid him.

(PORTIA takes JESSICA aside, they speak in stage whispers. Consider running this dialogue simultaneously with the RACHEL and DANIEL dialogue that follows.)

PORTIA: What, has another venture misfired?

JESSICA: Indeed so.

PORTIA: Bassanio has neither the luck nor the skill of old Antonio. He's already lost most of what was left to him.

JESSICA: Why do these men persist? You have more wealth than even *Bassanio* could spend.

PORTIA: That they are men, driven to prove themselves in conquest and rivalry is explanation enough.

JESSICA: They say the time of genteel leisure has passed.

PORTIA: *(Scoffing.)* Ridiculous! If man were made to grasp at profit as do these merchants, we would hardly be civilized at all, but mere wolves. Aagh! This new capitalism will be the death of us all.

JESSICA: Daniel and I have suffered as much under Lorenzo's lack of thrift, but without your inheritance to fall back upon. *(Looks to make sure they are not overheard, still whispering.)* Are you sure this plan is right? A merchant can make a good living, and Daniel may yet prove more skilled in these matters than our husbands.

PORTIA: Steel yourself, Jessica. We've worked too long and hard to bring these events about. Bassanio and Lorenzo are failures at merchandise. If they refuse to act like gentlemen, so be it. But I'll not have them drag Daniel down to being a grubby merchant with them. No! He will have an honorable and learned profession at law. Daniel will meet Bellario this afternoon and be off to Padua as his clerk before sunset!

JESSICA: How can you be so sure Daniel will agree?

PORTIA: *(With an air.)* We shall be most persuasive. And considering our opposition I am sure we can prevail.

JESSICA: What of Bassanio?

PORTIA: I assure you, my dear, Bassanio will be in no *condition* to prevent us.

(She continues off JESSICA's look of uncertainty.)

PORTIA: Jessica, I love Bassanio, just as you love Lorenzo. But we've tolerated their prodigality for far too long, and if we love Daniel then we must rescue him from their ways. You have the most to benefit from this plan.

JESSICA: Yes, yes, you are right. Daniel will be well able to care for me in my old age if our plan succeeds. Has Bellario arrived?

PORTIA: Not yet. Come, let us sit in the back. Do you like elderberry wine sauce?

JESSICA: It makes me ill.

(They exit.)

DANIEL: *(With a look of dazed infatuation.)* How is it that a child of Launcelot Gobbo could be both diligent servant and beautiful maid?

RACHEL: How is it that you never cease your dotage upon me?

DANIEL: But why should I? You are glorious to look at.

RACHEL: If you wish to stare at something there are many fine paintings in this house.

DANIEL: Paintings, yes, but none that will gaze back at me with your look of love.

RACHEL: I've given you no such look.

DANIEL: Pictures without the warmth of your body.

RACHEL: Behave yourself!

DANIEL: Portraits without the smell of your precious skin.

RACHEL: You are going to get us both in trouble.

DANIEL: There is no art in this house, nay, in all the world more beautifully framed than that which I now behold, and I would trade them all to possess this one gracious sculpture. *You* are God's work of art.

RACHEL: You say that in spite of the dark canvas he has used?

DANIEL: Dark, but lovely, like the tents of Kedar. It is in the background, so that I see only your fair half.

RACHEL: *(Irritated.)* You can quote Solomon but you lack his wisdom. The dark is there just the same. Perhaps that is why you tease me, since you know none else will have me.

DANIEL: They know not where to find you, for you are safely ensconced here at Belmont.

RACHEL: Still, though you speak otherwise to please me you know I am but a half-breed, an oddity. And what if I prove more dark than fair?

DANIEL: *(Approaching to comfort her.)* When in service of Bassanio and Antonio my father took us to Naples, I did see many peoples there in all manner of trades and from all over the world. Mostly they were kind, and enriched me by their charity. And so I still find myself drawn, childlike, to that which is different from myself.

RACHEL: *(Softening toward him.)* There could be danger in such adventures.

DANIEL: Ahh, but what I might learn along the path could more than compensate.

RACHEL: If indeed you lived to tell the tale.

DANIEL: That shortened life would be all the richer for your presence in it.

RACHEL: *(Laughs.)* Those with a soft life such as Lady Portia has given you live long and peaceably and at ease.

DANIEL: *(Taking hold of her.)* Don't mock me. I would work seven plus seven years, all the fourteen years of my life to have you, just as Jacob in the Bible worked for his Rachel.

RACHEL: He worked for Leah first.

DANIEL: That was God's will, not Jacob's desire. Besides, there is no Leah betwixt you and me. And all of those years seemed but a few days to him, because of his love for Rachel.

(She is taken with him, and he is about to kiss her, but she pulls back.)

RACHEL: We'll both be hung by the neck if we're caught.

DANIEL: Then let us not be caught.

RACHEL: *(Breaking away from him.)* Daniel! That is *not* the right answer! Do you love me?

DANIEL: Yes.

RACHEL: Enough to let them find out?

DANIEL: I don't care if they find out.

(They come close again, as if about to kiss. BASSANIO enters, licking his fingers, and the lovers immediately pull away from each other.)

BASSANIO: What, Daniel? When did you arrive?

DANIEL: Only now, Lord Bassanio.

BASSANIO: *(Terse, to RACHEL.)* Why wasn't I called? Leave us.

RACHEL: Yes, my lord.

BASSANIO: And Rachel?

RACHEL: Yes, my lord?

BASSANIO: What is this sauce they've made in the kitchen? It is delicious.

RACHEL: I'm sure I don't know, my lord.

(She exits, slowly, looking expectantly to DANIEL, who looks longingly back, but says nothing. Finally, she stomps out.)

BASSANIO: What's the matter with her? *(Not waiting for an answer.)* Come Daniel, what word from Genoa?

DANIEL: Good Lord Bassanio, must I deliver the news?

BASSANIO: What? Have my friends disappointed me again?

DANIEL: Not your friends, sir, for even now is my father on his way to aid Gratiano, but your buyers. Verazano has reneged, saying the goods were not to his standard. Gratiano was hopeful that my father may yet persuade him to reconsider.

BASSANIO: Your father is as faithful as Verazano is devious. Perhaps they will succeed. But no matter.

DANIEL: No matter? If this fails, you will have lost the last of what Antonio left you.

BASSANIO: Not all.

(He pulls out some papers and shows them to DANIEL.)

BASSANIO: Look Daniel, on this. There is coming to the Rialto a prominent merchant from Rome, one Largo. By great fortune I was able to learn in advance of his venture, and determine what he seeks.

DANIEL: Which is?

BASSANIO: Pork!

DANIEL: Pork?

BASSANIO: Pork, Daniel, and in great quantities. It seems there is a shortage in Rome of this animal for which the nobility has developed quite an appetite. And I am ready to supply them. I have purchased as many of these animals as there are in all this part of Italy.

DANIEL: But the cost!

BASSANIO: I have only made a deposit on each for the promise not to sell them to another. I need not pay the balance until I come to claim the hogs. And when I do, it will be with profits from the deal with Largo.

DANIEL: But what if he should go elsewhere?

BASSANIO: No one else will be able to supply him. He will have to deal with me.

DANIEL: I hope it goes well.

BASSANIO: It must, Daniel. I will show myself a master of something at last, and not a mere appendage to Portia's inheritance. And since your father is away, you shall accompany me.

DANIEL: Sir?! Is it true? Am I at last to see the mart at Venice?

BASSANIO: It is past time you made appearance there.

DANIEL: But Mother…

BASSANIO: You are a man, now. It is time you find yourself in the world. *(BASSANIO becomes unsteady on his feet.)*

DANIEL: Are you all right?

BASSANIO: Just a little dizzy. I'm fine. Come, I will show you the hogs I have already.

DANIEL: But…

(BASSANIO takes him by the arm and they exit. RACHEL reenters with a food tray. PORTIA follows.)

PORTIA: Hold, Rachel, my dear.

RACHEL: Did I forget something, my lady?

PORTIA: No, no, dear, I just wanted to continue our talk.

RACHEL: Madam?

PORTIA: Don't be coy with me. When we were interrupted?

RACHEL: Oh yes, we were talking about Daniel. *(Covering her mouth.)* Oops.

PORTIA: No, dear, you were talking about some young man who seeks your favor… What's the matter?… *(She suddenly makes the connection.)* No!

RACHEL: Please don't be angry, my lady!

PORTIA: This cannot be! He is to take a career, not a… How far has this gotten?

RACHEL: He seems quite taken with me, and I cannot say I do not return the feeling, but we've not dishonored ourselves, my lady.

PORTIA: *(Trying to calm herself.)* Thank God for that! Rachel, my dear, Daniel is a young man, and young men, as do old men, often have desires towards young women which are not at all long lasting, but matters of passing interest. You would not wish to find yourself in such a position.

RACHEL: My lady is certainly right in that. But what if his intentions are honorable?

PORTIA: Rachel, do not misunderstand me, Daniel is an honorable young man. But he is merely a visitor to Belmont. He will hence depart his parents' home and on to the books of law at Padua. That is the plan. You know that. You will not accompany him there. He will meet many others in these cities who are more suited to the place in life he will attain.

RACHEL: I sense a kindness of intent, but still your words wound me.

PORTIA: Has he offered you some token as a pledge?

RACHEL: No, my lady.

PORTIA: *(Visibly relieved.)* There, you see? He is not serious. Now, I don't want to hear any more about this. I will speak to Daniel at the earliest opportunity, but in the meantime, if he approaches you, you must reject him.

(She reacts to RACHEL's downcast look.)

PORTIA: Think not too much on all of this. Let time pass, but be a keen observer of it. I love Daniel, but he is a man. You will see that this interest of his will fade, and sooner should you pledge to keep your honor. But now I must find Lord Bassanio.

RACHEL: *(Pointing offstage.)* He is there, with Daniel.

PORTIA: Ah, I will bring Jessica.

(PORTIA exits. DANIEL returns.)

DANIEL: Ah, to gaze my way into rapture again.

RACHEL: I am the one who needs to see clearly.

DANIEL: What's this?

RACHEL: How long shall I hear your sweet words?

DANIEL: For as long as you desire.

RACHEL: It is the length of *your* desire that is in question.

DANIEL: But why?

RACHEL: Perhaps you will be silent once your desire is fulfilled?

DANIEL: I will never be quenched of drinking from your fountain.

RACHEL: And when my fountain runs dry of youth and beauty?

DANIEL: What has troubled you?

RACHEL: Nothing that has not troubled a million women before me. How do I know your words are true? How do *you* know your words are true?

DANIEL: I am a *paladin* of truth. By the hand of God, let no prevarication ever escape my lips. Not only to you but to all the world, yes, to the devil himself, will I always have the courage to speak the truth, no matter what the cost.

RACHEL: Indeed. And do you love me?

DANIEL: I do.

RACHEL: And do you want my hand?

DANIEL: Forever.

RACHEL: Then you have but to put a ring upon it, declare your troth publicly, and it shall be yours.

(DANIEL is taken aback.)

RACHEL: What is it, Paladin? Has my knight lost his breastplate of courage?

DANIEL: Precious Rachel, I have no ring.

RACHEL: Then you have not me, either.

DANIEL: Rachel...

RACHEL: I'm serious, Daniel. I'll have no part of death and foolishness like those people in Verona. If you wish to embrace me then you must embrace the truth, and do it openly, taking whatever comes of it, for good or ill.

(PORTIA, BASSANIO, and JESSICA enter.)

JESSICA: What goes on here?

DANIEL: Sweet ladies, I find myself in need.

PORTIA: Of what? You have but to ask, you know I can deny you nothing.

DANIEL: Mother, have you a trinket, a jewel I might use?

JESSICA: You know I wear not such things.

DANIEL: Then perhaps you, Lady Portia?

PORTIA: I have many. Which pleases you?

DANIEL: A ring... such as you wear there.

PORTIA: This?... There you have caught me in a falsehood, for I cannot part with this ring.

DANIEL: I do but need it for a short time, 'til I can acquire one of my own.

PORTIA: Give up your suit. I have pledged my love that this ring shall never part my finger.

BASSANIO: What ring do you speak of, my lady?

(BASSANIO and PORTIA extend their hands.)

RACHEL: Look, Daniel, they match!

PORTIA: I gave Bassanio his ring when we were married, and had him vow never to part with it. Then, when he had the audacity to let slip that vow, I forgave him, and he quickly had another one made, and upon giving it to me extracted the same pledge from me as well.

BASSANIO: It has never left my hand, in all the many years since last I put it on. I would sooner die.

PORTIA: And I would sooner assist you were you to part with it.

BASSANIO: And would you part with yours?

PORTIA: Never, my love.

BASSANIO: It is our merry bond.

DANIEL: Such love as this is what the world seeks after, to hold if only for the briefest moment.

PORTIA: This is well said. For what do you need this ring?

DANIEL: You said I had but to ask.

PORTIA: *(Eyeing RACHEL.)* And wisdom says I should inquire further where love would not. Wherefore this ring?

DANIEL: Portia, Bassanio, and most of all, Mother… I have asked Rachel to marry me.

JESSICA: *WHAT?!*

PORTIA: Rachel, you've refused him!

RACHEL: No, my lady, I have not.

JESSICA: I forbid it. This isn't the hour.

DANIEL: What time piece can one consult as to marriage?

BASSANIO: Daniel, this is absurd. You know nothing of the world.

DANIEL: Nothing of the world? I have been all over Italy for as long as I can remember, sitting at the feet of you and my father while you traded with merchants from *everywhere* in the world.

BASSANIO: Genoa and Naples are not the world, lad. You've not seen Venice.

DANIEL: Because you have yet to take me there.

JESSICA: I have forbidden it!

DANIEL: But I *am* ready, and Bassanio will guide me.

PORTIA: But now it is time for you to take your own place in this world.

DANIEL: And I shall.

JESSICA: Not with her.

DANIEL: But why not?

JESSICA: She is a servant.

PORTIA: She will not fit with your place in the world.

DANIEL: My place? What is my place in the world?

(The door sounds. There is an awkward silence. The knock comes again, and RACHEL, sighing and rolling her eyes, goes to answer it.)

PORTIA: Bellario!

BELLARIO: Portia, my dear. *(Sensing the tension in the room.)* Have I come at a bad time?

PORTIA: No, not at all. Your arrival was most timely. How was your journey?

BELLARIO: Fine.

BASSANIO: You have been too long from Belmont. What news from Padua?

BELLARIO: I have too much work and not enough capable hands to aid me.

PORTIA: How terrible for you. Daniel, this is my cousin, Doctor Bellario of Padua, the most respected civil doctor in all of Italy.

DANIEL: I am honored, sir.

BELLARIO: I have heard many good things about you, young man.

DANIEL: Lady Portia has always exaggerated my fine points in order to hinder notice of my deficiencies. I hope you will not be greatly disappointed.

PORTIA: This is not a time for modesty, Daniel. One would do well to spend time in Bellario's company, but he's not likely to do so willingly with one who holds back.

DANIEL: No doubt your cousin's exuberance is something with which you are already quite familiar, Doctor Bellario.

BELLARIO: Not like this, young man. She is quite fond of you.

DANIEL: She has always been like a mother to me.

(DANIEL reaches out to JESSICA.)

DANIEL: But good sir, let me introduce my real mother to you.

JESSICA: I am Jessica.

BELLARIO: Madam, it is my pleasure.

BELLARIO: Well young man, have you as much promise as my cousin foretells me of you?

DANIEL: Time will soon reveal it, sir. For good Bassanio here has offered to take me with him to Venice to conclude a great bargain there.

BELLARIO: Indeed. Is that what you wish for yourself?

DANIEL: I have spent my life among merchants. It seems only right that now I practice what I have observed from them.

BELLARIO: What about the law?

BASSANIO: What's that?

PORTIA: It is just a thought, my dear. Bellario too has need of an apprentice.

DANIEL: I know nothing of the law.

JESSICA: Perhaps good Bellario could teach you.

PORTIA: You know, Daniel, any skilled dealer can operate upon the mart. But a keen mind is required of a civil doctor, and they too may live handsomely, if they are diligent. I should leap at the chance to work with one as learned and respected as Bellario.

(Note: The argument that follows is spirited and lively, but loving and completely without malice.)

DANIEL: Portia, of all women you are the most adept, and you are a zealous advocate of your cause, but now you go too far.

PORTIA: How so?

DANIEL: A woman may never be a civil doctor.

PORTIA: That is merely a custom that we have chosen to consent to, but I assure you, we have the ability.

DANIEL: Certainly you have the ability, dear lady, but you also have a husband, a home, and a household. How could you think to suggest such a thing?

PORTIA: If a man has a wife, a home, and a household, you would not think twice of his being a civil doctor.

DANIEL: Think of the implications of what you are saying. I know you, you would not stop there. Women would be everywhere, in every profession and occupation. No doubt you would include them in the priesthood, and what of celibacy then? You may as well turn the world upside down. You advocate anarchy.

PORTIA: I advocate nothing, but only to point out that women are capable of far more than you realize.

DANIEL: I know full well what women are capable of. Their judgments would not follow law at all, but feelings of love and pity and terror. Such is not what justice is made of.

PORTIA: If justice is not concerned with love and pity, nor in terror of what law can do to those who stand before it, with what shall it be?

DANIEL: With truth. It is rare that there is doubt or confusion as to what law applies to any given case. Rather, it is in the quest for truth, to find what really happened and where the fault lies, that we have courts and laws. For it is in terror of law and justice that many do perjure themselves both in and out of the court. Therefore, the search for truth must be paramount, and without regard for feelings of tenderness and mercy, for these things will pervert the course of law. And a woman is far more subject to such feelings than a man. I say there can be no justice without truth.

PORTIA: Truth is a harsh judge. Do you really contend that there is no place in justice for mercy and forgiveness?

DANIEL: Not at all. But their place is later, after judgment.

PORTIA: Then there is no disagreement.

DANIEL: The disagreement is what would happen if a woman were to determine the cause. She would bring mercy and forgiveness in before the matter was concluded.

PORTIA: Better too early than too late.

DANIEL: No. The truth cannot be compromised. The whole matter must be known first.

PORTIA: Knowing the whole matter may make forgiveness impossible. No doubt this is why we are admonished to forgive and forget.

DANIEL: That admonition is not in scripture.

PORTIA: Not in as many words, but the essence is there.

DANIEL: Where do you find support for such statements?

PORTIA: Well, what of St. Paul, "forgetting that which lies behind, I press toward the mark..."

DANIEL: He speaks of his own sins.

PORTIA: We would hardly be considered holy if we forgot only our own sins. And we are told that love keeps no account of wrongs.

DANIEL: We are also told that love rejoices in the truth.

PORTIA: But above all things we are to love as God has loved us, is this not true?

DANIEL: Certainly.

PORTIA: And has not God promised to separate us from our sins as far as the east is from the west? How then can we recall them if God has seen fit to put them asunder?

BELLARIO: Hah! She has you there, young man. But a fine argument, just the same.

DANIEL: Portia has always managed to have the last word.

PORTIA: I have loved every word of every debate with you, Daniel. Your mind grows and keeps me ever challenged.

DANIEL: I am only grateful that these debates are for entertainment and not substantial.

(There is another knock at the door. RACHEL, visibly shaken but still dutiful, opens, and in steps an old Jew. It is TUBAL.)

BASSANIO: Hail, old Jew. What have you here?

TUBAL: I seek Lord Bassanio.

BASSANIO: I am he.

TUBAL: I am Tubal.

BASSANIO: *(Pausing a moment to think.)* Shylock's friend?

TUBAL: The same. I ask that you help me to find Jessica.

BASSANIO: For what purpose?

TUBAL: I have grave news that must be delivered personally.

(BASSANIO looks to JESSICA, who comes forward.)

JESSICA: *(Coldly.)* I am here, Tubal. Why have you sought for me?

TUBAL: *(Reacting to her tone of voice.)* Very well, we'll not delay the time with pleasant talk and false remorse of times we have missed. Shylock is dead. I have come to bring you this news, and to give over to you all that was left of his estate.

JESSICA: *(Suddenly elated.)* What does it contain?

TUBAL: The house in Venice, and furnishings. Some money, enough to care for you and perhaps to set your child up in business, if he so desires. This was Shylock's wish.

JESSICA: Shylock's wish? He's dead, thank God. And how well timed. The money will serve us all well.

TUBAL: *(Disgusted.)* Not even the pretense of grief?

JESSICA: I had grief enough in that house when it was his. Now it is mine, and it shall be a house of joy.

TUBAL: You will come to Venice, then?

JESSICA: Yes.

TUBAL: I have a carriage.

JESSICA: No. I'll not leave now, nor will I ride with you.

TUBAL: The house sits empty.

PORTIA: Jessica, let us help. We can send a servant ahead of you, in the company of this gentleman, who can take control of the property until you arrive.

JESSICA: Very well, tarry a moment, Tubal, and we shall have someone ride back with you presently.

DANIEL: Mother, who is this Shylock that he leaves such bounty to you, and why should he have a Jew as his executor?

JESSICA: He... was a man of many unfortunate and peculiar habits. *(To TUBAL.)* You may wait outside.

DANIEL: Yes, but to entrust one's wealth to one of that tribe goes beyond peculiar.

It is utter folly. We shall never know how much was stolen.

TUBAL: Does the boy not know?

JESSICA: You may wait outside!

DANIEL: Know what, Jew? I know that twice already my mother has asked you to wait outside, yet your stench is still present.

TUBAL: *(To JESSICA.)* How could you do this? For fifteen years, you've told him nothing of the truth?

DANIEL: My mother is a good Christian woman, in whom truth like all other virtues resides most heavily. You will not speak to her this way and you will leave as she has requested and I now demand.

TUBAL: Very well, my proud young Christian. You say you value truth, then know this: Your mother was born a Jew. This Shylock was her father, your grandfather, a member of my synagogue, and my dear friend. That is why I am his executor.

DANIEL: Cursed dog! How can you say such things?! My grandfather was dead before I was born.

TUBAL: Sadly, in many ways that is also true. *(To JESSICA.)* Tell him I speak the truth.

DANIEL: A Jew's truth is always half a lie. You twist words in whatever direction lies profit.

TUBAL: Tell him!

DANIEL: My mother need not vouch for your raving! My grandfather was a Christian!

TUBAL: Under penalty of death!

DANIEL: What do you say?

TUBAL: Ah! Have I reached you? If your mother will be silent then inquire of your friends there. They know the truth. They all know it.

DANIEL: Mother, Mother, confront this man. Refute him! Why do you remain quiet in the face of these horrible sayings?

JESSICA: *(To TUBAL.)* Damn you! *(She walks away.)*

PORTIA: Daniel, understand. Your grandfather was a man of hellish cruelty. When your mother found God, it was only right that she sought to separate herself from Shylock's evil, just as far as the east is from the west.

DANIEL: What? Is it true, then? Has my mother deceived me for all of my life?

PORTIA: Only as she thought necessary. Calm your feelings, Daniel. It is your Christian duty to forgive and forget. Many sins are well intentioned, and certainly those of a mother.

DANIEL: To forgive, it is too soon. To forget, I must know what it is I am not remembering. *(Looking to PORTIA, then to TUBAL.)* Tell me, am I a Jew?

PORTIA: No, of course not.

DANIEL: But it is in my blood.

PORTIA: Christianity is the blood of Christ, which overrides the blood of man. All the more in this case, since it was only half-Jewish blood, and that washed away with your mother's faith before you were born.

DANIEL: But still, it is in my blood.

RACHEL: Perhaps then we shall see only your Christian half?

(DANIEL winces.)

PORTIA: Yes, that's right. We are under grace, not controlled by law as they are.

BELLARIO: She is right. You would do well to come with me to Padua to be my clerk. There you could study to use the law, rather than be controlled by it.

DANIEL: You would still have me, sir?

BELLARIO: Indeed, and consider myself fortunate for the experience. I would aid your study, and you would become a fine doctor yourself.

BASSANIO: But what of the mart, and of fortunes made upon exchanges there? I need your help, Daniel, and your companionship. *(BASSANIO becomes woozy.)*

DANIEL: Good Bassanio, are you well?

BASSANIO: No, not at all.

PORTIA: *(Winking at JESSICA.)* Here, let me take you to bed. I guess we shall have to cancel your trip to Venice.

BASSANIO: No! Too much depends upon it.

PORTIA: It can't be helped. You are in no condition to go.

BASSANIO: Daniel, did you mean what you said about the world? Do you think you are ready?

DANIEL: I do, sir.

BASSANIO: Then do this for me. Go to the Rialto, and conduct the business I propose with Largo. Much depends on this for me.

PORTIA: But he is going to Padua!

DANIEL: I will do it, Lord Bassanio. Take you to bed and worry not. Good Bellario, grant me leave to aid this man in his hour of need, and after I will come straightaway to Padua.

BELLARIO: Very well, since it is a matter of aiding a friend in need. I will give you some books to study on your travels.

DANIEL: Since I must to Venice, I will look into this property for you, Mother.

JESSICA: Daniel, Venice is a haughty and savage place.

DANIEL: I can handle it, Mother. It is time I find myself in the world.

JESSICA: I fear that my son shall not return to me. Be careful.

DANIEL: I shall. Help Portia look after good Bassanio.

BASSANIO: Bless you.

(BASSANIO, PORTIA, and JESSICA exit.)

DANIEL: *(To TUBAL.)* Tubal, I would be the servant with you to Venice.

BELLARIO: I shall retrieve the books from my carriage.

(TUBAL and BELLARIO exit.)

RACHEL: *(Weeping.)* It's true, Portia was right.

DANIEL: No…

RACHEL: You've forgotten all about me!

DANIEL: I have not!

RACHEL: You swore to uphold the truth, and then forgot what truths you spoke to me.

DANIEL: Rachel, do not feel this way. This is good for us. My mother's inheritance and the commission Bassanio pays me will get us started handsomely, and then I will send for you to join me in Padua, where a glorious ring shall await you.

RACHEL: How is it that the son of Lorenzo thinks he can do any better at the marts of Venice?

DANIEL: Have faith.

RACHEL: I will never see you again. Portia and Jessica are against it.

DANIEL: I love them both, but they do not control me.

RACHEL: You are naive, my Paladin. The only reason they consent to your going to Venice is to part you from me. The venture there is sure to fail, they all do. And then you shall have no choice but Bellario. Think you that Bassanio's illness was an accident? They plotted it to keep him from interfering in their plan to send you off to Padua, and that is what is happening.

DANIEL: What are you saying?

RACHEL: I spoke plainly enough.

DANIEL: I am stunned.

RACHEL: I am sure it is not the last time.

DANIEL: Rachel…

RACHEL: You have failed the test of love. Go now. The world awaits you.

(She leaves him standing there.)

SCENE TWO
These Naughty Times

Setting: A cemetery in Venice. At rise: TUBAL and DANIEL enter, walking carefully over the graves.

TUBAL: Here it is. The fresh one.

(DANIEL sighs heavily; he ponders the grave.)

DANIEL: What did he die of?

TUBAL: Time. As I will, soon.

DANIEL: You seem well enough.

TUBAL: You do not.

DANIEL: Thank you for accompanying me. I would not have been able to find it without you.

TUBAL: Why did you come?

DANIEL: To see for myself. To confront the truth.

TUBAL: And what is the truth?

DANIEL: That I am a Christian. That I have nothing to fear from… this man.

TUBAL: Fear? Did you expect that he should take hold of you from the grave?

DANIEL: I was not sure what to expect. But now… I am content. Perhaps I have treated you badly. I am sorry for that. You have been most gracious.

TUBAL: It is… accepted. Let me also say that I have received a benefit in your company.

DANIEL: How so?

TUBAL: To be in the company of my friend's grandson is a great thing.

DANIEL: You flatter me.

TUBAL: I tell you the truth. Only to have him here, alive to see you with his own eyes, would be greater. We sought for you before you were born.

DANIEL: *(Stifles a cynical laugh.)* Indeed, and why is this? Am I a messiah, that you should seek me so?

TUBAL: When your mother left Shylock's house, I went in search of her, but was never able to find her. We did hear, from time to time, of her doings, and eventually, of your birth. We did pray for you.

DANIEL: A Jew and Christian praying together… *(Nods in disbelief.)* Well, I am grateful for your sincerity, nonetheless.

TUBAL: May I tell you the truth?

DANIEL: Truth is all I desire. Say on.

TUBAL: It is not so.

DANIEL: What do you mean?

TUBAL: After the baptism, we shunned him publicly. We had to. We treated him like mishumid. But it was for his own safety. If anyone thought otherwise, we would be put to death for proselytizing. There was great danger. But in secret, we did pray together, and study, and wear the tallit.

DANIEL: His conversion was a lie?

TUBAL: Shylock would gladly have lived publicly as a Jew. It took all of my power to persuade him to remain alive, and not to give up in his despair.

DANIEL: How did this conversion come about?

TUBAL: Did you know Antonio?

DANIEL: A fine man. I remember him favorably.

TUBAL: He was indebted to Shylock on Bassanio's account.

DANIEL: Bassanio? Was he a spendthrift even then?

TUBAL: I understand this is how he financed his courtship of Portia.

DANIEL: Indeed?

TUBAL: When Antonio could not pay, Shylock brought him before the Duke to enforce the penalty of the bond.

DANIEL: This is not uncommon, though I find it hard to believe Antonio was ever so destitute.

TUBAL: The penalty… was a pound of Antonio's flesh.

DANIEL: What? Do you mean to say that Shylock intended to cut off a piece of Antonio's body? That is too barbarous to believe.

TUBAL: Precisely! It was a bargain made in sport, for Shylock wanted only Antonio's love.

DANIEL: For love he could have made a gift of the money, rather than a loan on such absurd terms.

TUBAL: Cheap love is never appreciated. *(Beat.)* But by then, Jessica had fled with Lorenzo, and taken money and jewels to underwrite her elopement.

DANIEL: Hold there, Jew. Are you saying my mother is a thief?

TUBAL: These are the facts. Neither she nor Lorenzo had anything of their own.

DANIEL: Took she anything of great value?

TUBAL: Money, and other costly items. But only one thing of great value.

DANIEL: What was this?

TUBAL: A ring. A turquoise, given to Shylock by your grandmother before they were married.

DANIEL: As a pledge of their love?

TUBAL: Of course.

DANIEL: I have not seen Mother with such a ring.

TUBAL: Certainly not. It was one of the first things she spent.

DANIEL: Spent? Her parents' ring? She

did not wear it herself, or give it as a pledge of love to Lorenzo?

TUBAL: She exchanged it for a monkey.

(DANIEL reacts to the irony.)

TUBAL: Shylock was brooding, hurt, and angry. He had extended himself to the Christians and they had mocked him. For Lorenzo was long an associate of Bassanio and Antonio. They knew, they all knew of her plot with Lorenzo. So he sought revenge. He brought Antonio before the Duke to seek the penalty of the bond. There came to the court a doctor of Rome, one Balthazar, who rendered judgment that by pressing his demand for the pound of flesh, Shylock was seeking the life of a citizen, and was therefore liable to be punished by death and to have his property confiscated. *(Beat.)* He was saved from this fate when they compelled him instead to become a Christian, to give half his property to Antonio, and to bequeath that of which he died possessed to your mother. We were able to save this house by paying in fines to the state most of what was left. It was hard, but he endured.

DANIEL: You admit, sir, that your friend sought the life of a Christian?

TUBAL: 'Tis true.

DANIEL: Then soften not the blow for me. *(Beat.)* There is much here to consider. But it seems there was evil enough on all sides. One thing I do thank you for, Jew. I believe you have been honest with me, even in things which do not reflect kindly on Shylock.

TUBAL: I love you as I did your grandfather, therefore I have told you the truth. And I have perceived that you value truth greatly, perhaps above all other things.

DANIEL: It is only by knowledge of the truth that one knows properly how to act. *(Studies the grave.)* What of his wife, my grandmother?

TUBAL: A wonderful woman.

DANIEL: Did she love Shylock, in spite of his flaws?

TUBAL: His flaws, as you put it, were not so noticeable during her lifetime.

DANIEL: *(Smiling.)* What other purpose is a woman's love? Where is she buried?

TUBAL: On the other side.

DANIEL: Why not here, beside her husband?

TUBAL: She died a Jew. Jews and Christians are not buried together.

DANIEL: What of that? She was his wife.

TUBAL: No matter. In the eyes of the world, they were as different as jet and ivory.

DANIEL: This is madness!

TUBAL: This is the law.

DANIEL: And what of me, then? When I die, shall they cut me in half, casting one part hither and the balance yon?

TUBAL: You accept your Jewish half, then?

DANIEL: I accept the fact that it forms my history. It is only this moment a part of my present and shall have nothing of my future. *(He looks back to the grave.)* The world has a natural order, Tubal. And we humans shun it at our peril. But to separate a man from his better half for a difference that matters not between them… *(Sighing.)* These are naughty times that separate owners from their rights. What was her name?

TUBAL: Shylock's wife?

DANIEL: My grandmother.

TUBAL: Leah.

DANIEL: *(Shocked.)* What?

TUBAL: Leah.

DANIEL: So. A Leah lies betwixt us indeed. What sign of mischief lies in this?

TUBAL: What are you talking about?

DANIEL: Will you take me to her grave as well?

TUBAL: This way.

SCENE THREE
On the Rialto

Setting: The mart in Venice. At rise: A small crowd of men is already onstage, talking amongst themselves. DANIEL enters, looking all around him, wide-eyed, and a little out of place.

DANIEL: Excuse me, sir, I am looking for one Largo.

MERCHANT 2: As are we all, boy. What have you to do with him?

DANIEL: I've come to bargain with him.

(General mocking laughter.)

MERCHANT 2: Ha! You? You're barely old enough to be an apprentice.

DANIEL: I am of age.

MERCHANT 3: And what have you got to offer him, boy?

DANIEL: That is for me to discuss with him.

MERCHANT 2: You are less than an apprentice. Think that you can keep any secret long on the Rialto? You'd do better to shout it from the rooftops.

DANIEL: That may be, but when I shout it will be in Largo's ear.

(He goes aside, where he is befriended by MERCHANT 1.)

MERCHANT 1: Strong words, these. A storm, lad?

DANIEL: Nay, but a strong gust with no sail to make it productive.

MERCHANT 1: You do well not to mix with such. They are lovers of trouble.

DANIEL: Well said.

MERCHANT 1: I've not seen you here before.

DANIEL: It is my first venture upon the mart.

MERCHANT 1: And not your last, I assure you. The Rialto can be vicious and cruel, but it is also exhilarating, and eminently rewarding. Not unlike a woman.

DANIEL: Your humor is strange, my friend.

MERCHANT 1: How so?

DANIEL: I am the one who has been cruel to my lady. And she is certainly not vicious.

MERCHANT 1: *(Laughing.)* And you are certainly not married.

DANIEL: No… But I should be.

MERCHANT 1: Then why aren't you, lad?

DANIEL: I lack the means. Perhaps I also lack the courage.

MERCHANT 1: Lack of means has made a coward of many a man. *(Beat.)* Is this also what makes you cruel?

DANIEL: It is.

MERCHANT 1: It's not you, lad. It's poverty that's cruel. *(Beat.)* Mark you well. You will see it all here. The bitter, defeated traders, with their evil, jealous sulk. And then the victors, swaggering in their newfound wealth.

DANIEL: But if one has what another needs, and the same is true in return, then cannot both be victors?

MERCHANT 1: For every two such victors, there are half a dozen left outside the bargain. *(Beat.)* Do you trade on your own account?

DANIEL: No, for another.

(LARGO enters, MERCHANT 1 rises.)

MERCHANT 1: One last piece of wisdom, then. Charge a fat commission.

DANIEL: I shall. Thank you.

DANIEL: Where are you off?

MERCHANT 1: Here is the man I've come for.

(The other merchants flock around LARGO, who is dressed more sumptuously than they.)

MERCHANT 2: Bless me! It is Largo, great merchant of Rome.

MERCHANT 3: Good sir! And how is Rome?

LARGO: I've seen not Rome for many weeks. I go there hence.

MERCHANT 1: With great pains we have awaited your arrival.

MERCHANT 2: And with great pleasure we would supply your wants and speed you on your way to Rome.

LARGO: You would give me great pleasure if you could but supply my needs. Rome awaits the spoils of this fruitless journey.

(DANIEL rises and approaches, but can't get near LARGO because of the other three.)

MERCHANT 3: *(With a flourish.)* Then let Rome await no longer! For here I have the spices of the Orient, every seasoning to spice the appetite of every seignior in all of Rome. And look! See how conveniently they are encased in these artful flasks. These porters of taste are themselves well worth the price.

LARGO: Perhaps, had I the meat delicacies I favor, such an offer might tempt me. But for now…

MERCHANT 2: *(Displaying his wares.)* But for now, you have need of fine silks and other gracious materials to comfort your frame while yet gilding it as is required of a man in your station. Here, feel this fabric.

LARGO: What you have to sell is not what I seek to buy.

MERCHANT 3: Does he offend our goods?

MERCHANT 2: They are of the highest quality!

LARGO: Have you no sense?

MERCHANT 2: Must you drive a hard bargain at all accounts?

MERCHANT 3: Well said! And what price would you have?

LARGO: I seek not these things! Your words cannot change me. Is there not one of you who understands that?

DANIEL: Largo!

LARGO: And who might you be, lad?

DANIEL: I am Daniel, come to you on behalf of Lord Bassanio of Belmont.

LARGO: What's this? Does my commerce offend so that he sends a child to greet me?

DANIEL: Sir, I am of age, and it is because of his confidence in me and his desire for your custom that we meet this way.

LARGO: I'll be the judge of his confidence... and of whether you shall have my custom.

MERCHANT 3: Never mind the lad, my lord, what would you have of us?

MERCHANT 2: Yes, tell us and we shall straightaway acquire it for you.

MERCHANT 3: At a fair price.

MERCHANT 2: Of course. The markets of Venice seek only to serve you.

LARGO: You cannot serve me with that which I do not require.

MERCHANT 1: What you require, sir, is meat.

DANIEL: Specifically, hogs.

(DANIEL and MERCHANT 1 eye each other; they realize they are competitors.)

LARGO: Here are merchants worth my time if not my custom. I see that you two at least bother to know my needs.

MERCHANT 1: I know that there is a plague among the hogs at Rome.

DANIEL: And I know that they are a favored food of great hosts like yourself.

LARGO: Then take me to your stockyards, gentlemen, so that I may choose my hams carefully.

DANIEL: Good sir, I cannot, for my stock is held mostly at Belmont, and in nearby places.

LARGO: I've not time for a side trip to Belmont. I am sorry, lad, but this is a bargain you have lost.

MERCHANT 1: Alas, Largo, I too have not the merchandise nearby.

(LARGO reacts with disgust.)

MERCHANT 1: If you could but wait a short while...

LARGO: I cannot wait. I must urgently return to Rome. Therefore we shall conclude the matter now, and the seller I choose shall send the hogs after me straightaway.

DANIEL: It shall be done.

LARGO: It shall be done according to the laws of Venice. I warn you, young man, and you as well, merchant, if these hogs are not of good health and quality, then by the laws of Venice I shall have my damages trebled from you! Is that understood?

DANIEL: Yes, sir.

MERCHANT 1: It is what the law requires. I warrant you no less.

LARGO: Then tell me of your stock.

MERCHANT 1: A fine herd of portly animals, well fattened upon the finest grains to give forth succulent hams and excellent roasts to satisfy the wants of your estimable class and society.

LARGO: And yours, young man?

DANIEL: *(With a shrug.)* They are hogs, my lord.

MERCHANT 1: The heads are of such size and stature as to make pageant of any banquet table upon which they may be served, suitably poised, with an apple clutched upon the fangs.

(LARGO and MERCHANT 1 both look at DANIEL.)

DANIEL: *(Uncertain what to say.)* They are nice hogs?

LARGO: What is your price?

MERCHANT 1: Seven ducats.

LARGO: *(Outraged.)* A head?!

MERCHANT 1: It is a fair price.

LARGO: I'll take this man's silk upon my table and season it with that one's spices before I'll pay such a price!

(MERCHANTS 2 and 3 come closer.)

MERCHANT 2: The silk is all natural.

MERCHANT 3: And the spices are nutritious.

MERCHANT 1: Six, then.

LARGO: Hah!

MERCHANT 1: I'll not bargain against myself.

LARGO: Why not? You bargain alone now.

DANIEL: I can go four ducats.

MERCHANT 1: What's that?

LARGO: I heard him plain enough. Four ducats.

MERCHANT 1: He can't deliver for that price.

DANIEL: I can. Four ducats a head.

MERCHANT 1: You can't obtain a hog in all Italy for that price. I know. I've searched. They're not to be had. You're lying! You have no hogs at all.

DANIEL: I do, sir. My principal has made arrangements to secure what hogs he could find in all these parts.

MERCHANT 1: So it was you who blocked my market.

DANIEL: I have a shrewd principal, sir. But whence are your hogs?

MERCHANT 1: Dalmatia.

LARGO: Dalmatia?

DANIEL: And how would you deliver these hogs? And what guarantee has this gentleman of their condition? I, at least, have seen my hogs with mine own eyes.

LARGO: Trouble yourself no more, lad. We have a bargain at four ducats a head.

MERCHANT 1: *(Storming angrily off to one side.)* And to think that I did comfort you.

MERCHANT 2: Congratulations, young man. We shall not underestimate you again.

MERCHANT 3: Henceforth, we shall treat you like the man you are.

(MERCHANTS 2 and 3 join MERCHANT 1. LARGO and DANIEL shake hands on their deal, and, as they do, DANIEL notices the ring on LARGO's finger.)

DANIEL: That is a most wondrous ring, sir. May I see it?

LARGO: *(Holding it out but not taking it off.)* Surely. I have had it many years. It has been admired all over the world.

DANIEL: How did you come by it?

LARGO: A poor sailor, down on his luck.

DANIEL: I'm told my grandfather had such a ring once.

LARGO: They could be one and the same, for I have never seen another like it.

DANIEL: It is very much as described to me. It would make a fine wedding gift.

LARGO: Aye, and you a fine husband and provider, if you continue on the mart as you have started. Lord Bassanio has chosen his apprentice well. I would take you, were you not spoken for.

DANIEL: I thank you, sir.

LARGO: Come, let us dine together while we plan the delivery of the animals.

DANIEL: Yes, sir!

LARGO: *(Eyeing him carefully.)* But... this sailor was too young to be your grandfather.

DANIEL: Indeed. My grandfather did commerce here, once, as we do.

LARGO: A merchant would not let such a ring slip through his fingers lightly.

DANIEL: No, sir. It was stolen.

LARGO: Ah, then Justice, in her providence, has brought it back to your family... for a price, of course.

DANIEL: A ring is not a king, and a fair price is not a ransom.

LARGO: Perhaps, when Justice has come full circle, you will meet with the thief and thereby gain restitution.

DANIEL: Oh, I know the thief.

LARGO: Ho-ho! There is one for the gallows, eh?

DANIEL: No, it was my mother.

LARGO: What? Your mother? Lad, for the price of *that* story, I'll buy you *two* meals.

DANIEL: I pray you find your curiosity worth your generosity, for the story is short enough. My mother ran off with my father, a suitor her father did not approve of, and she financed her escape in part with this ring.

LARGO: Did not he go after her?

DANIEL: It was to no avail.

LARGO: And how do you sit between the two?

DANIEL: My position is secure. Grandfather is dead, and I am set upon my own career, emancipated.

LARGO: Ah well. Let us eat, then. I am a man of my word.

DANIEL: Still, I would know your price for the ring.

LARGO: I think, lad, that you have not the means of fair price for such a ring.

DANIEL: I could earn it.

LARGO: You have skill and wit. They will merit you such good fortune in time that you will name your price to have any bauble your lady fancies. What name had your grandfather? I have traded upon this mart at least as long as you have upon the Earth. Surely I knew him.

DANIEL: His name was Shylock.

LARGO: The Jew?

DANIEL: You knew him, then?

LARGO: Was not a sharper financier in all Italy. *(LARGO takes another look at DANIEL.)* Regard yourself a Jew?

DANIEL: Not at all, sir.

LARGO: But you speak so freely of it.

DANIEL: It is the truth.

LARGO: A truth a wiser man would sooner hide.

DANIEL: But *I* am not a Jew, sir. My mother converted to Christianity before I was born.

LARGO: Come now, don't proclaim your blood and then deny it!

DANIEL: I only knew of this two days ago!

(Hearing their raised voices, the rejected MERCHANTS come back over.)

MERCHANT 2: *(Greedily.)* What's this? What's this? A spat, a quarrel?

MERCHANT 3: A deal gone awry?

MERCHANT 1: Is there hope for us yet?

LARGO: No, no, our dispute is not for merchandise.

MERCHANT 3: *(Walking away.)* Ahh, pity.

MERCHANT 2: *(Pulling MERCHANT 3 back, whispering to him.)* Any spat's a schism, and any schism a parting, and any parting an opening, and any opening...

MERCHANT 3: *(Catching on.)* ...an opportunity!

MERCHANT 2: Indeed. *(To LARGO and DANIEL.)* Pray tell, what is this dispute? Perhaps, since we have nothing to gain thereby, we may be the arbiters of peace between you good co-venturers.

LARGO: It is simple enough. I say he is a Jew.

MERCHANT 1: *(Genuinely shocked.)* A Jew?!

DANIEL: *(Insistent.)* I am *not* a Jew!

MERCHANT 2: Don't raise your voice to us, Jew.

DANIEL: I shall raise more than my voice if you call me that again!

MERCHANT 3: *(Mirthful.)* Perhaps he will answer to dog!

MERCHANT 1: *(Deadly serious.)* Or cur.

MERCHANT 2: Aren't the Jews forbidden to trade upon the mart?

LARGO: I see no reason. They may lend money.

MERCHANT 2: Perhaps in Rome.

MERCHANT 3: Aye, for they are fit for charging interest on filthy lucre. But to handle goods and compete with Christian merchants, that is another thing.

MERCHANT 1: Aye, another thing indeed.

MERCHANT 2: We'll have to look into this question.

MERCHANT 3: And look at what he sells! Pork, the very thing they won't eat themselves!

MERCHANT 2: Now, there *is* a strange thing.

LARGO: If there is anything wrong, there will be satisfaction from the courts of Venice, I assure you. But I am in no position to repudiate the bargain. I have given my word.

DANIEL: I thank you for that, sir. You are an honorable man.

MERCHANT 1: Fiendish Jew! Did you think a Christian gentleman could be otherwise?

DANIEL: I only meant...

MERCHANT 3: We know what you meant, Jew!

MERCHANT 2: Yes, indeed we do.

MERCHANT 1: I had need of this bargain, Jew, to feed a Christian wife and family! Take your stench from here so we may work in peace.

DANIEL: I demand you respect me, sir.

MERCHANT 1: What outrage! What have you that a Christian need respect? Here is my respect!

(He spits on DANIEL, who is stunned to temporary inaction. Then, as he advances on MERCHANT 1…)

MERCHANT 2: Here, Jew, I pay my respects!

(He also spits on DANIEL.)

MERCHANT 3: And mine as well!

(He too spits on DANIEL. When DANIEL turns to MERCHANT 3, MERCHANT 1 rushes him, and shoves him violently into MERCHANT 2.)

MERCHANT 1: Cur!

(MERCHANT 2 pushes DANIEL onto MERCHANT 3.)

MERCHANT 2: Jew!

(MERCHANT 3 pushes DANIEL onto MERCHANT 1.)

MERCHANT 3: Dog!

(And the cycle is repeated.)

MERCHANT 1: Cur!

MERCHANT 2: Jew!

MERCHANT 3: Dog!

DANIEL: *(To LARGO.)* Sir, won't you help me?

MERCHANT 1: Yes, good sir! Help us all!

(MERCHANT 1 takes off his coat and lays it at LARGO's feet. MERCHANTS 2 and 3 follow suit. MERCHANT 1 then strikes DANIEL, hard, with his fist. DANIEL puts up his fists. MERCHANT 3 grabs DANIEL from behind.)

MERCHANT 3: Ho! He wants a fight, this one does!

(MERCHANT 1 then strikes the helpless DANIEL several times. MERCHANT 3 releases him, and DANIEL crumples to the ground. Not satisfied, MERCHANT 1 kicks him savagely. MERCHANTS 2 and 3 follow suit. Each kick leaves a sickening, dull thud, and they continue to take turns kicking and stomping on the prone DANIEL. The lights fade to black, yet we can still hear the kicking, and DANIEL's agony, for several distressing seconds.)

(Intermission.)

SCENE FOUR
Since I Am a Dog…

Setting: Shylock's house in Venice. At rise: TUBAL and JESSICA are binding DANIEL's wounds. BELLARIO is also present. They are silent, except for an occasional whimper from DANIEL.

JESSICA: You see, Doctor Bellario, that you have escorted me to Venice in time to see the violence it has done to my son.

BELLARIO: Bind him up, madam, and I shall carry him on safely to Padua.

(BELLARIO exits. Slowly, TUBAL and JESSICA begin to compete with one another to care for DANIEL's various injuries. They become more and more aggressive, until…)

DANIEL: *(Leaping up, moving away.) Owwww!*

JESSICA: We're trying our best, Daniel.

TUBAL: Come back, sit down.

(Inspecting DANIEL's mouth.)

TUBAL: How is it you have not lost any teeth?

DANIEL: After the first blows, I decided to keep my mouth closed.

TUBAL: Wisdom gained late is yet wisdom.

JESSICA: Father was spat upon on the mart, but he was never beaten.

TUBAL: Shylock had restraint. He knew his limitations as a Jew.

DANIEL: *(Leaping up again, angry.)* Pardon my inexperience! I've never been a Jew before!

JESSICA: Stop saying that! You are not a Jew.

DANIEL: Aren't I, Mother? Tell that to those good Christian gentlemen on the mart. If they made nothing else clear, it was that. *(Pointing to his various bruises.)* Do you see these, Mother? Don't think they are bruises, oh no, each is a separate proclamation, like the town crier, shouting Jew! Dog! Cur!

JESSICA: Your wounds will heal once you get to Padua. And when that happens, say nothing of this. No one will be the wiser.

DANIEL: Because I have a light canvas.

JESSICA: What?

DANIEL: You wouldn't understand, Mother. I didn't, until now. *(Looks to TUBAL.)* Nor do I understand you.

TUBAL: Me?

DANIEL: You put yourself at risk to pull me from the mart.

TUBAL: I've given you answer enough for that.

DANIEL: That you loved my grandfather. So it would seem. What of you, Mother?

JESSICA: *(Trying to shift focus.)* Everything appears to be in order. It is amazing how little the house has changed.

(TUBAL, not wanting to be in the middle of the family fight and mildly disgusted by JESSICA's graceless attempt to change the subject, exits.)

DANIEL: Mother, I have learned much in the last few days, things that have both thrilled and offended. Why couldn't I have learned them from you?

JESSICA: When I left this place I wanted no more to do with any of it. I wanted no reminder of my past as an infidel.

DANIEL: And this is why we never came to Venice?

JESSICA: Yes. Have you now evidence enough of the correctness of my decision?

DANIEL: But didn't you think that I had a right to know these things, Mother? It is such a strange feeling, recalling how I have mocked Jews, not knowing I was one of them.

JESSICA: You are a Christian. You were born of Christian parents, baptized and christened in the church, taught catechisms. You are a Christian.

DANIEL: But you were not born a Christian, Mother.

JESSICA: Neither were many of the saints.

DANIEL: But did they conceal their pagan past, or did they point to it with joy and celebration that they had come out of it? Why have you lied to me, Mother?

JESSICA: Don't speak to me that way!

DANIEL: How should I speak to you, Mother? I am in shock. I don't know what to feel or what to think. You, my loving, doting, Christian mother, have lied to me about who you are, who your father was—who *I* am. How should I speak to you, Mother? Should it be tenderly, like an infant tucked into bed with lullabies and fairy tales? Or should it be stoutly, like the eight-year-old trying to be a man when his father would go away to work for a man who spat on my grandfather?

JESSICA: Many families are divided, Daniel. Unfortunately, ours is one of them. There can be no reconciliation between the Jew and the Christian. The one must destroy the other. This is why they are forever separated.

DANIEL: You have practiced purity and separation all of my life. But what of truth?

JESSICA: Again you call me a liar.

DANIEL: You have not told me the truth.

JESSICA: It is a mother's duty to protect her children.

DANIEL: Look at me, Mother! Am I protected? *(Beat.)* No greater harm would have come to me from knowing Shylock.

JESSICA: You don't know that.

DANIEL: You've seen to that.

JESSICA: Very well. Perhaps you have spent too much time with Tubal after all. No matter. This will soon all be buried once again.

DANIEL: What do you mean?

JESSICA: I mean to sell this house, and everything in it.

DANIEL: You can't do that.

JESSICA: I can and I shall.

DANIEL: But there is so much here.

JESSICA: And I want none of it.

DANIEL: This is nothing more to you than a place to loot.

JESSICA: Daniel!

DANIEL: Yes. To loot. You're doing it again, just as you did the last time you were here. You are a thief as well as a liar.

JESSICA: I warn you, Daniel. You are in no position to judge me.

DANIEL: Do you threaten me? Fine, I shall give you cause. When I collect my commission, I shall send for Rachel.

JESSICA: No! I forbid it.

DANIEL: You forbid it? On what grounds?

JESSICA: She is beneath you. A servant, the child of a fool and his folly.

DANIEL: No. She is kind, and the vital link of that house.

JESSICA: She is a Moor.

DANIEL: And you? You married outside your own kind.

JESSICA: There is a great difference. My love could save me from hellfire. She can only debase you.

DANIEL: How dare you speak of debasing after what you did? Perhaps Shylock was not a great man, as you say, but he cared for you after your mother died. And what of Leah? Did she deserve what you have done to them?

JESSICA: Leave my mother out of this!

DANIEL: No! I want her in it. In fact, I insist that she be in it! Wasn't it enough that you had your own way in marriage? Why did you also lay waste to the token of their affection?

JESSICA: Insolent child! Infidel!

(DANIEL prepares to leave, and, in his anger, he speaks as much to himself as to JESSICA.)

DANIEL: Truth and right should dwell together. And if one is a paladin of truth he should also be a squire of right. Wherefore, I must work my portion for Leah.

JESSICA: Know this. If you marry this girl, and you fail to repent of your sins against me here today, you shall pay dearly.

DANIEL: *(Extending his fingers.)* How, Mother? I have no wedding ring for you to steal!

JESSICA: *(Furious.) Get out!*

SCENE FIVE
A Hot Temper Leaps over a Cold Decree

Setting: Venice, the DUKE's chambers. At rise: DANIEL enters, followed by TUBAL and BELLARIO. The DUKE and LARGO are already present.

DANIEL: So, you are here, my friend?

LARGO: I have no friend save my next bargain. I come here to pay my respects to the Duke before returning home.

DANIEL: Your grace, I was this day viciously assaulted upon the Rialto. This man was there.

LARGO: I laid not a hand upon you, sir.

DANIEL: Nor did you raise a hand in my defense.

LARGO: *(Referring to TUBAL.)* Your countryman there did come to your aid.

DANIEL: Would it have so offended to help one with whom you had just made a bargain?

LARGO: Our bargain is secured by the laws of Venice. Aiding you would not have changed that in the slightest.

TUBAL: There are higher laws than those of Venice.

LARGO: Aye, but have you access to them?

DANIEL: Your grace, I demand justice. Seize these men that have so violated me.

DUKE: Who are these men?

LARGO: Fellow merchants, your grace.

DUKE: Were these men the losers in your trade?

LARGO: That is true also, your grace, but by my witness that is not what provoked the matter. It seems this young man is a Jew. And a brazen one at that.

DUKE: Are you a moneylender?

DANIEL: No, your grace. I am too poor for such a trade.

LARGO: Aah, that reminds me.

(He hands DANIEL money.)

LARGO: Here is your price, as we agreed. Make sure the hogs are delivered to me in Rome straightaway. The Duke is my witness.

DUKE: It shall be done.

DANIEL: Your grace, what of my attackers?

DUKE: They shall be warned to restrain themselves.

DANIEL: *(To BELLARIO.)* Can you get me no justice?

BELLARIO: Your grace, you cannot allow unrest and disorder upon the mart.

DUKE: Nor can I have Jews disturbing the merchants. Very well. I shall send a bailiff to look into it.

BELLARIO: Thank you, your grace.

DANIEL: I have one thing more to ask of the justice of Venice.

DUKE: And what would that be?

DANIEL: That you grant me permission to move my grandfather.

DUKE: Move him?

DANIEL: Exhume and rebury him, your grace. It is my desire that he be laid to rest next to my grandmother, his wife, according to the traditions of his heritage.

DUKE: Why was this not done in the first instance?

(TUBAL is becoming nervous.)

DANIEL: Because he was buried as a Christian.

(TUBAL is now very *nervous.)*

DUKE: Who is your grandfather?

DANIEL: Shylock.

DUKE: Shylock? But he was a Christian.

DANIEL: No, your grace. He was not. His conversion was coerced, as you well know. It was an offense, to both law and Heaven.

BELLARIO: Hold, Daniel. You go too far. It is no offense to save a man's soul.

DANIEL: A man's soul is for himself to save. And a wife is for him to lay by. *(To DUKE.)* Will you grant my request?

DUKE: The answer is no.

DANIEL: On what ground?

DUKE: Shylock's conversion was part of a case settled before this court long ago. The laws of Venice must always be constant. Much trade depends upon the reliability and consistency of those laws. Shylock understood that. There is nothing in what you have said that would change the decision in even the slightest part.

DANIEL: But he was not a Christian.

DUKE: And how would you know that? What, are you telling me the Jews made a mockery of me behind my back? Who sent you? I'll have them before me in moments to answer for this.

DANIEL: Please, your grace. I seek only to lay my ancestor beside the woman he loved, and with the ceremony of his true heritage. Is this so much to ask, that the justice of Venice accord with the truth?

DUKE: The truth, young man, is that such conversions take place all the time. Nowhere have I heard of them being challenged, and certainly not after death. It is now a matter for a court beyond this one.

DANIEL: Sir, it is within your power to do this.

DUKE: The church would not like it.

DANIEL: You made the order without the church.

DUKE: What think you, Bellario?

BELLARIO: The Duke is certainly correct. *(To DANIEL.)* Had I known that you would add this matter to your agenda, I would most stringently have advised against it.

DANIEL: Of course. It was your compatriot Balthazar who engineered this injustice. And how fitting that you should witness this, Largo, the handiwork of your countryman. You call this justice? Fie on your law!

LARGO: What countryman is this you speak of?

(Now it is BELLARIO who gets nervous.)

DANIEL: Balthazar, Doctor of Rome. It was he who presided over Shylock's conversion.

LARGO: A civil doctor, you say?

DANIEL: Yes.

LARGO: From Rome?

DANIEL: Yes, yes!

LARGO: There is no such person.

DUKE: What's that?

DANIEL: Say again?

LARGO: There is no civil doctor of Rome named Balthazar.

BELLARIO: This was many years ago, sir.

LARGO: How many years ago?

DUKE: Fifteen.

LARGO: I have traded upon the mart at Rome for more than twenty years. In all that time I have had ample opportunity to plead my case before every civil doctor that practices there. I tell you there is no such person, and never has been.

BELLARIO: You are mistaken.

LARGO: I am *not* mistaken, sir! And I shall tell you another thing I am not mistaken about. It now appears that judgment in Venice may be administered by any perjurer able to ply his trade here. What, then? Where is the justice of Venice? And where is the security of foreign traders like myself, that our contracts will be honored and our goods protected?

DUKE: I am stunned.

LARGO: You shall be bankrupt if we take our trade away!

DUKE: I assure you, we shall get to the bottom of this!

LARGO: I assure you, you shall! How did this Balthazar come to your court?

DUKE: He was sent to me, referred... *(Remembering.)* ...by *you*, Bellario.

BELLARIO: My lord! Surely you cannot accept the word of foreigners and Jews!

DUKE: The whole trade of Venice depends upon such foreigners. Explain yourself!

BELLARIO: It is a trick, a devilish machination of Jews to pervert the justice of Venice.

DUKE: It would appear that the justice of Venice has already been perverted, and that with your help. It was your letter that recommended this Balthazar, or whatever his name is, to me.

DANIEL: My lord, would that not make him also guilty of the fraud?

DUKE: As you well know it would.

BELLARIO: My lord, you cannot do this.

DUKE: I can, and I will. I will adjourn this matter to another day, to give you a chance to defend yourself, Bellario. But if I find that you have deceived me, and imperiled the reputation of Venice before all the world, then indeed, you shall pay heavily. Guard!

(The GUARD enters, and, at the DUKE's gesture, escorts BELLARIO away.)

DUKE: Largo, I must delay your departure, for it seems I will need your testimony.

LARGO: As you wish, my lord.

(DANIEL and TUBAL prepare to leave.)

DUKE: Hold, Jews. This matter is not yet resolved, and may not turn out as you hope.

DANIEL: I seek only truth, your grace.

DUKE: Some may die of the truth.

DANIEL: I seek the life of no one, my lord.

DUKE: Then take care. Others may not say the same of you.

SCENE SIX
A WILDERNESS OF MONKEYS

Setting: Belmont. At rise: RACHEL opens the door. It is DANIEL. They embrace.

RACHEL: I have been so worried for you.

DANIEL: And I have missed you dearly.

RACHEL: Let me see your wounds.

DANIEL: How did you know of them?

RACHEL: Bellario sent an urgent letter.

DANIEL: Ah, Bellario! How has Portia taken the news?

RACHEL: She is upset, of course.

DANIEL: Yes, of course.

RACHEL: Why did you do it, Daniel?

DANIEL: I did it for Leah.

RACHEL: Leah!?

DANIEL: Yes, for Leah, and for you.

RACHEL: You speak of Jacob's Leah?

DANIEL: No, but of my own. She was Jessica's mother, my grandmother. I saw her. She called out to me from the grave.

RACHEL: And what did she say to you?

DANIEL: That I should ease her loneliness. That I should right a wrong done to her in which she had no fault. And so I shall. And if I do this for Leah, whom I have not known, how much more, then, shall I fulfill the wishes of Rachel, whom I love?

RACHEL: Oh, Daniel.

DANIEL: If she will still have me.

RACHEL: Yes, yes of course!

DANIEL: Dearest Rachel, I shall never wrong you again.

RACHEL: Then I shall not leave your side.

(BASSANIO enters.)

BASSANIO: Daniel! Come you to Belmont?

DANIEL: My lord and friend, I have indeed returned, to settle accounts and collect my bride.

(DANIEL hands money to BASSANIO.)

BASSANIO: I see. You have done well, and are a man of honor—in spite of your recklessness.

DANIEL: Recklessness?

BASSANIO: Yes, reckless.

DANIEL: I have done nothing to deserve such a label.

BASSANIO: It would seem everything you have done since last you were here should be labeled such. *(He raises the money.)* Starting with this.

DANIEL: It was a great triumph to outwit my adversaries on the mart, all the more so now, since they hate me.

BASSANIO: Why did you tell them of your Jewish blood?

DANIEL: Because it never occurred to me to lie.

BASSANIO: And why pursue the question at all?

DANIEL: It is a matter of principle.

BASSANIO: Jewish principle?

DANIEL: No. Personal principle. I must not fear the truth but know it.

BASSANIO: And when you know the truth, what then?

DANIEL: Then I will not be deceived. I will know myself.

BASSANIO: *(Angry.)* Enough of truth. What of discretion?

DANIEL: *(To RACHEL.)* Go now, make ready for our wedding trip.

(She exits.)

BASSANIO: And there goes folly still. How will your place with Jessica be restored if you marry Rachel?

DANIEL: I do not know.

BASSANIO: Daniel... foolish, impulsive Daniel.

(Takes hold of DANIEL.)

BASSANIO: Is it too late? Can I yet awaken you from this stupor that blinds you?

DANIEL: I am in no stupor, Bassanio. Indeed, I see clearly now as I had not before. I do not wish to go to law at Padua, but to continue with you on the mart.

BASSANIO: And yet another bad match! It was foolish of me to send you in my distress. And yet more foolish for you to speak so freely of your Jewish blood. I can't send you back there now.

DANIEL: I had success there.

BASSANIO: You were beaten there! And they will intimidate you with it should you return again. Your fear will bar a repeat of your success.

DANIEL: Now you do me wrong, sir. I have more courage than you think.

BASSANIO: Why is it that you cannot understand? Did they beat the sense out of you as well? A Jew cannot trade upon the mart.

DANIEL: You do me wrong again. You well know I am not a Jew.

BASSANIO: There is not a merchant on the mart who would agree with you.

DANIEL: Nor you, my friend?

BASSANIO: You are of no use to me.

DANIEL: I see. Then I shall take my bride and my leave. First let me greet Portia.

BASSANIO: I would not, were I you.

DANIEL: Do you command me?

(PORTIA enters.)

BASSANIO: I advise you, but my wisdom is nullity where your passion is stirred.

DANIEL: Then I will see her.

PORTIA: I am here, Daniel.

(DANIEL goes to her, but she stops him.)

PORTIA: Why, my beloved, have you so wounded me?

DANIEL: I have done you no harm, sweet lady.

PORTIA: When you betrayed my cousin, and turned on your master, you did wound me more grievously than those bruises which you now bear.

DANIEL: I did not know that he would be implicated in any wrong when I went before the Duke.

PORTIA: And why did you not take him into your confidence, since he was to be your sponsor at law?

DANIEL: If I had, and he had dissuaded me, the truth would not come out.

PORTIA: Indeed. And my cousin would be a free man.

DANIEL: What of Venice?

PORTIA: I do not love Venice.

DANIEL: Sweet Portia, it is from you that I have learned the virtues of truth and justice and beauty and grace. You who freed me from Jessica's rigid authority and opened my mind to see the wonders in the world around me. How I chafed under her hand, longing for the time when we would return here, to you, at Belmont, for Mother ever cowered before you. I never understood until now. She is ashamed of whence she has come, and curried your favor as proof of her acceptance. But you have made sure that my soul was never so withered. Would you have me turn a blind eye to these, even for a kinsman?

PORTIA: My love, especially for a kinsman, whom I love.

DANIEL: You know I cannot do that.

PORTIA: I did not. But now I do.

(RACHEL returns.)

DANIEL: So this is where it stands?

(He reaches for RACHEL, she stands beside him.)

DANIEL: We take our leave of you, dear lady. *(To BASSANIO.)* And of you, sir. Regardless, we shall not forget your kindness heretofore.

(DANIEL and RACHEL exit.)

PORTIA: It would seem, husband, that the Jew whose death we were recently told of in this very house has been resurrected in the form of our very own godson.

BASSANIO: We must find a way to deal with him.

PORTIA: Indeed we must. But I'll not have Daniel harmed.

BASSANIO: Has your love blinded you to what has happened? What if Bellario, to save himself, reveals who Balthazar really was fifteen years ago? He may not hang, but you most surely shall, for you are not only not a civil doctor, but a woman, at that.

PORTIA: What you propose solves nothing. The Duke may yet press his case against Bellario.

BASSANIO: Lose a cousin you might, but if the choice lies between Daniel and my bride, then it is for me no choice at all.

PORTIA: You shall not be put to such a choice, husband, nor will I accept a choice between Bellario and Daniel.

BASSANIO: You have a plan?

PORTIA: Indeed, my dear husband, as you have quite rightly noted, I am a woman and as such can do nothing. But Balthazar can in his wisdom save the day.

BASSANIO: You would recreate the very thing which now puts us in peril?

PORTIA: It is the only way to save Bellario.

BASSANIO: I cannot allow it. It is far too dangerous.

PORTIA: I've done it before, even you did not recognize me. If God is on my side, I can succeed again.

BASSANIO: How will you explain your sudden reappearance as Balthazar?

PORTIA: Leave it to me.

BASSANIO: Bellario will understand. Perhaps he will keep quiet.

PORTIA: You can't be serious. I'll not abandon my cousin to the gallows any more than you could leave Antonio to Shylock's knife.

BASSANIO: No. I am your husband. I forbid it.

PORTIA: Please, Bassanio, this matter calls for sober thought.

BASSANIO: You mock me.

PORTIA: Bassanio, I love you, but come to your senses!

BASSANIO: I cannot allow you to be destroyed.

PORTIA: I will find a safe path. Daniel spoke so eloquently of Jessica's soul. But it is his that concerns me. I shall not give up hope of redeeming Daniel's soul as well as Bellario's life. God will point the way.

BASSANIO: And no doubt you shall steady his hand.

SCENE SEVEN
The Quality of Mercy

Setting: Venice; a synagogue. At rise: A RABBI putters in the background. DANIEL and RACHEL enter.

DANIEL: Rabbi?

RABBI: Yes?

DANIEL: I am Daniel. Tubal sent me.

RABBI: Ah, yes, he told me of you. Come in.

DANIEL: This is Rachel.

RABBI: *(Acknowledging her.)* My dear. *(To DANIEL.)* And what may I do for you?

DANIEL: We wish to marry. And to join the synagogue.

RABBI: You have it backwards. If I am to marry you, you must become Jews first.

DANIEL: Tubal has given me many books to study. I am ready.

RABBI: Indeed. We shall see. Is it of your own free will that you take this vow?

DANIEL: It is.

RABBI: And do you understand that you are making a fundamental change in your relationship, both to God and to man?

DANIEL: I do.

RABBI: Why?

DANIEL: *(Perplexed.)* Why?

RABBI: Yes, why do you wish to become a Jew?

DANIEL: But I am a Jew. All this is but a formality.

RABBI: A formality?

DANIEL: My mother was a Jew.

RABBI: Yes, but it is so rare that I have this opportunity, I'll not let it pass.

DANIEL: What do you speak of?

RABBI: So many of our children see Judaism as nothing more than an accident of birth, a thing that one is, not a life that one leads.

DANIEL: I have read the books of Moses.

RABBI: Is that all?

DANIEL: Tubal has told me a great deal. I know full well the danger, and what I leave behind. This is what I want.

RABBI: What is it you leave behind?

DANIEL: The Christian world. A wilderness of hate.

RABBI: Why?

DANIEL: Still more questions?

RABBI: Answer me.

DANIEL: They have rejected me.

RABBI: Because of your Jewish blood?

DANIEL: Yes.

RABBI: And so you wish to become a Jew…

DANIEL: Yes.

RABBI: …because the Christians have told you to do so.

DANIEL: No. Wait. Is this not true? Am I not a Jew?

RABBI: You are rightfully angry about your abuse upon the Rialto. But anger is not what makes a Jew, any more than hating Jews makes one a Christian. I will give you some things to look at. When you are ready, we may talk again.

DANIEL: Everyone gives me books to read.

RABBI: How else does one learn?

DANIEL: By experience.

RABBI: The lessons of experience can be quick, but very painful.

DANIEL: Then you will not marry us?

RABBI: Not yet. Study. Both of you.

(RABBI exits. DANIEL's disappointment shows.)

DANIEL: We are lost in a wilderness of rejection.

RACHEL: Fret not, my love.

DANIEL: Fret not? My own people won't even accept me!

RACHEL: I have accepted you.

DANIEL: Perhaps you were mistaken to forgive me.

RACHEL: I think not. But the Rabbi is right, Daniel.

DANIEL: What are you saying?

RACHEL: You're not ready. You are so bitter, and filled with vengeance.

DANIEL: They have wronged me. All of them.

RACHEL: I cannot tell if you are more angry about their wrongs, or the fact that now you are a Jew.

DANIEL: It is a fall from grace.

RACHEL: This same self-loathing is the cause of every war and murder on the face of the Earth. The Rabbi will accept you. But you must accept it, before the hatred of others consumes you. You seek to destroy them, but you may only destroy yourself.

DANIEL: Sweet Rachel, when did you become wise as well as beautiful?

RACHEL: I was always wise. You were not looking at my brain.

DANIEL: *(Handing her one of RABBI's books.)* Let us begin our study, then.

RACHEL: *(Refusing book.)* Daniel, can we talk?

DANIEL: What is it?

RACHEL: I'm not sure I want to do this.

DANIEL: What are you talking about?

RACHEL: I am not sure I am ready to become a Jew, or that I should.

DANIEL: How can you say this? After all we've been through!

RACHEL: No, Daniel, after all *you've* been through. You are wrestling with God on these matters. I've done none of that. I am merely following you.

DANIEL: Are you saying you don't wish to follow me?

RACHEL: No, Daniel, I am not saying that. You have searched it all out. You are finding yourself, tracing your blood to find your heritage. Before I become your wife, I should do the same.

DANIEL: And you can. I will teach you everything. We will learn together.

RACHEL: Daniel, I will gladly learn from you, anything you wish me to know, but there is something I must learn that you cannot teach me. I must trace *my own* blood to find myself.

(RACHEL reacts to DANIEL's bewilderment.)

RACHEL: All my life, I have waited in frustration for Europe to embrace me, to love me, and all the while, there is another half of me I have not even thought to ask until now.

DANIEL: Tell me what this means.

RACHEL: There are Moors right here in Venice. I have family among them I have never met. My cousin is even a nobleman here. Solomon says I am dark, but lovely, as if he is startled to discover that darkness does not exclude loveliness. But this is God's word. And I wish to know more about that which is lovely in that which is dark. Come with me, and we will see that Hagar and Ham have many beautiful children, just as Jacob does.

DANIEL: How do you know they will accept us any more than the Christians or the Jews?

RACHEL: They are family, and I want to see them.

DANIEL: Perhaps they will be kind to you, but not treat me well.

RACHEL: They will be as kind to you as you are to them.

DANIEL: I know even less about Moslems than Jews. What if I offend without realizing it?

RACHEL: I know a few things.

DANIEL: Are you sure?

RACHEL: Yes.

DANIEL: I still must prepare for Bellario's trial.

RACHEL: Are we back to vengeance again? Very well. Come, my angry little Star of David, and I will tell you tales of Scheherazade before you throw your stones.

SCENE EIGHT
The Trial of Caskets

Setting: Venice, the DUKE's court. At rise: RACHEL, DANIEL, LARGO, and BELLARIO are present. The DUKE enters, with GUARDS.

DUKE: Let us begin.

DANIEL: Have you a civil doctor to aid us?

DUKE: After all that I have been through on account of lawyers? No, I will judge this matter myself.

DANIEL: As you wish. Bellario, I have here retrieved from the Duke's own files a letter. Do you recognize it?

BELLARIO: It is faded and the paper fragile.

DANIEL: Come sir, is it not the letter that you yourself sent to this very court, recommending one Balthazar in your stead?

BELLARIO: I do not recall. Perhaps my secretary wrote it.

DANIEL: Indeed. And do you have with you any member of your staff who was with you fifteen years ago?

BELLARIO: Only Luisa, my housemaid.

DANIEL: Then, may it please the court, I should send to Padua for Luisa, to inquire if her master was ever so sick he could not travel to this court himself, or ever had a visitor named Balthazar.

(PORTIA enters, dressed as a civil doctor, with BASSANIO.)

PORTIA: That will not be necessary. I am Balthazar.

DANIEL: Impossible. Balthazar does not exist.

PORTIA: Then touch me if you must, you will find I am substantial enough.

DANIEL: Bassanio! What part have you in all this?

BASSANIO: Only to witness, and to see what shall become of my friends, Daniel and Bellario.

DUKE: You take no sides?

BASSANIO: Only to hope that the matter be dropped.

LARGO: It is too late for that.

BASSANIO: Then I pray no harm comes to anyone.

DANIEL: It is too late for that, as well. Ask Shylock. *(Referring to BALTHAZAR.)* Your grace, I would beseech on behalf of the justice of Venice, that the complaint be enlarged, and that this person, whoever he is, be equally charged with Bellario.

DUKE: It is done.

DANIEL: Who are you really?

PORTIA: I am Balthazar, Doctor of Rome.

DANIEL: Very well. You are acquainted with the other defendant?

PORTIA: Indeed.

DANIEL: And you, Bellario, do you recognize this man?

BELLARIO: It is, as he says, Balthazar.

DANIEL: Then tell me, sir, how is it that you happened to come to this court today?

PORTIA: There is no lawyer better known or respected than Bellario in all of Italy. When I heard of his distress, I came hence immediately to help.

DANIEL: How fortuitous that word has traveled to you so quickly. *(Referring to LARGO.)* Perhaps then you can also explain why it is that this merchant of Rome has never heard of you?

PORTIA: My tenure in Rome was brief, the records poor. I did fall ill, and there was little hope for me. I quit the law and went off to the Sicilian coast to die. But I did not die. Instead God was merciful and I recovered. But I reasoned that the law had made me ill, and I vowed not to return to it, and spent these last few years traveling. It is no wonder that after fifteen years there would be scant memory of me.

LARGO: I have made a sworn statement.

PORTIA: And you have me, standing before you in the flesh. You are mistaken. I shall demonstrate.

LARGO: How so?

PORTIA: Have you always traded from Rome?

LARGO: I have.

PORTIA: But have you not traveled, sir? To Spain, and Tunis, and other distant parts?

LARGO: Aye, and often.

PORTIA: And these trips have taken much time, have they not?

LARGO: Yes, of course.

PORTIA: Then is it not possible that we have simply missed each other?

LARGO: Yes, I must concede that is possible.

PORTIA: Indeed, it is even possible we have met, yet you do not recall me.

LARGO: That could be so.

PORTIA: Your grace, I submit to you that this good merchant is merely mistaken. There is no need to be concerned for the justice of Venice. It is secure.

DUKE: Very well.

DANIEL: Wait! Even if you are who you say you are, what you did in this room fifteen years ago was not justice.

PORTIA: You have been told, have you not, that the laws of Venice must be constant?

DANIEL: I have.

PORTIA: Then what grounds are there to disturb a judgment settled fifteen years ago?

DANIEL: None but the truth.

PORTIA: My lord, you have enlarged the charges to include me, and you were within your rights to do so, since you had not heard from me. But now I should like to bring charges against this man.

DANIEL: Me? On what grounds?

PORTIA: I shall enumerate. First, laches, since a judgment must surely be final at some point in time, and not subject to forever being reopened by aggrieved litigants. You have said you were concerned with the justice and reputation of Venice. I submit you do upset that which you seek to defend when you reopen this case fifteen years after the fact. Witnesses are dead or scattered, memories old and faded. It is only by the grace of God that I am here to defend myself and Bellario. Were these charges brought fifteen years ago, I could have brought forth legions of witnesses from Rome to assert my credentials, but what more could this Jew have brought forth? And this leads me to my second charge. This man was not even alive at the time of these events. Further, though it was his ancestor Shylock who was tried, he has not the right to raise any claims on behalf of Shylock, since he is neither the executor nor the beneficiary of his estate. He has no standing to bring this matter before this court, even were it a timely claim.

DUKE: Who is the beneficiary?

BELLARIO: Jessica, his mother, a Christian woman, who, I can assure the Duke, would not stand for what this man is doing here in this court.

BASSANIO: Aye, she may yet disown him. *(To RACHEL.)* How can you attach yourself to this... Jew?

RACHEL: You are all white, to me.

DUKE: What of the executor?

DANIEL: Tubal, I can bring him.

PORTIA: Has the estate been conveyed?

DANIEL: Yes, when Mother came back from Venice...

PORTIA: It is out of his hands. Only the beneficiary may act now.

DANIEL: Then I am lost.

PORTIA: There is more. Since you are without standing to bring this matter, I charge that you have done so maliciously, to upset the stability of the state, and to ruin the good name of the Christian community in your own quest for vengeance. You have set out to ruin and defame us, for which damage you shall pay dearly.

DANIEL: I have nothing.

PORTIA: Perhaps a time of indentured servitude would suffice.

BELLARIO: Aye. Fifteen years might be enough.

BASSANIO: Fifteen minutes on the gallows would be better.

PORTIA: What do you say, Jew?

RACHEL: Daniel, say nothing.

(She takes him aside.)

DANIEL: What am I to do? How did this happen?

RACHEL: Courage. You must take time, calm yourself, and think. What are your options?

DANIEL: I have none. I am no lawyer. I am outnumbered and outmatched. I shall die or be enslaved. Sweet Rachel, think of me, as you look upon the beautiful sons of Ham.

RACHEL: I will not abandon you.

DANIEL: My love, I do not deserve you.

RACHEL: Nor I you, but here we are.

DANIEL: *(Addressing the court.)* What will you do with me?

PORTIA: If it please the Duke…

DUKE: Say on.

PORTIA: A time of solitude would suffice. A long term of isolation in a monastery, where he can renounce his Jewish flirtations and learn all he can of the one true God. Then, when the monks think him ready, he may be released, to start his life over again.

DANIEL: Good sir, what of Rachel?

PORTIA: There are no women in the monastery, young man. And you needn't ask if she will wait for you, for I shall add the further condition that you never see her again.

RACHEL: Oh no!

DANIEL: Good sir, give me your hand.

PORTIA: *(As she does so.)* Do we this to signify your agreement?

DANIEL: We do this so that you may feel my flesh, look into my eyes, be aware of my passions, my life. I am a human being, like yourself. You talk of Christian mercy, have it yet for me. Set me free to go away from here with my fiancée, to live our own lives.

PORTIA: *(Starting to move away.)* I save you from yourself.

DANIEL: *(Holding more tightly to her hand.)* I beg of you! Shall I humble myself? I treat you as the Pope, for you have as much power over me.

(DANIEL goes to kiss the ring on her finger, and stops short, recognizing it. He is struck with horror and confusion. PORTIA realizes what has happened, and snatches her hand away.)

DUKE: What is it?

LARGO: What's happened?

PORTIA: Nothing. The Jew's pleas do reach me. I say we let him go.

LARGO: *(Standing before DANIEL.)* What have you done to him? Have you cast a spell? Are you a witch as well?

DANIEL: *(Struggling for words.)* I... have done nothing.

DUKE: What did he do to you?

PORTIA: Nothing! Nothing, I say. Let him go!

LARGO: The truth, lad. You who have boasted all this time of truth. What happened just now?

DUKE: Out with it! Answer us!

DANIEL: It is the ring.

DUKE: The ring? What of it?

DANIEL: *(To PORTIA.)* I am amazed.

DUKE: What is he talking about?

(LARGO approaches PORTIA, and examines the ring.)

LARGO: What is the meaning of this ring?

PORTIA: It is a token of my love.

LARGO: Indeed.

BASSANIO: Your grace, this has nothing...

DUKE: *Silence!*

LARGO: Have you a wife?

PORTIA: I do not.

(LARGO walks to DANIEL, and examines his hands. Finding nothing, he has an idea. He goes to RACHEL, but her hands are unadorned as well. He shrugs in frustration toward the DUKE. BASSANIO glowers at DANIEL.)

DUKE: Young man, you have come this far in your suit. Why do you hold back now?

DANIEL: For love, your grace.

(The DUKE and LARGO look at each other. They are determined to figure this out. The DUKE gestures to RACHEL.)

DUKE: Is not this your love?

DANIEL: She is, your grace.

DANIEL: Yet she wears no ring, and neither do you.

DANIEL: 'Tis true, your grace.

DUKE: Does your love exceed the truth and justice of your suit?

DANIEL: It is indeed precious, your grace.

(The DUKE circles the room, looking intently into the faces of the participants, seeking a clue. He stops at RACHEL.)

DUKE: And if it cost you your love, would you still seek truth and justice?

DANIEL: Your grace does not understand.

DUKE: I understand that some here have interfered with the justice of Venice, which I love. So I ask you again, if I take your love, will justice be done, though I know not how?

(DUKE signals for GUARDS, who approach RACHEL, menacing. DANIEL looks from RACHEL to PORTIA and back again.)

DANIEL: Your grace, take not my bride from me, for I shall tell all.

(With that, BASSANIO leaps at DANIEL, who does not resist. The GUARDS pull BASSANIO off DANIEL.)

DANIEL: I blame you not, Bassanio.

DUKE: *Tell us!*

DANIEL: These two are husband and wife. The ring betrays them.

DUKE: What?!

(LARGO approaches BASSANIO, and examines his hands. Then he goes to PORTIA, and looks at her hands again. He takes off her disguise.)

LARGO: A woman? This is an outrage!

PORTIA: I am Portia.

DUKE: The Lady of Belmont?

PORTIA: The same.

DUKE: *(Stunned.)* And… were you Balthazar fifteen years ago?

PORTIA: I was.

LARGO: This is incredible!

DUKE: But how, why?

BASSANIO: Your grace, I am at fault.

PORTIA: Bassanio, please…

BASSANIO: *(Angrily.) Be silent, Portia! (Beat.)* Be silent, and let me be your husband, and all that that means.

PORTIA: *(Shocked.)* Yes, my lord.

BASSANIO: Your grace, she is my wife, and I am responsible for all her actions. You will recall that it was my own kinsman Antonio for whose benefit she did render judgment here. I tricked Bellario to get the letter introducing Balthazar to this court. I planned the whole thing. But I did love my kinsman Antonio, and would do anything to save him, just as I have tried here to save Bellario. She is faultless. Let her go, and let the punishment fall solely on myself.

DUKE: Do you know what you ask?

BASSANIO: It is a hanging offense.

DUKE: You are a brave and noble man, Bassanio. But tell me, who else was involved in this conspiracy?

BASSANIO: No one, your grace.

DUKE: What of your friends, Gratiano and Lorenzo?

BASSANIO: They only learned of it after the fact, my lord.

DUKE: *(Turning to PORTIA.)* But you did not come alone. Who was it played your clerk?

PORTIA: It was Nerissa, my maid at the time.

DUKE: And now Gratiano's wife, as I recall. No doubt she too was acting under your orders.

PORTIA: She was, your grace.

DUKE: I am amazed. *(Turning to DANIEL.)* I thank you, young man, for your devotion to truth has done a great service to Venice this day. You and your fiancée are free, and since the judgment of fifteen years ago is clearly invalid, you may move your grandfather as you requested.

DANIEL: I thank you, your grace. But what shall become of these?

DUKE: *Guards!*

(The GUARDS approach.)

DUKE: They must hang.

DANIEL: What?

DUKE: All of them, together with their wives.

DANIEL: But sir, what of mercy?

DUKE: I am not the Duke of mercy, young man, but of Venice. And it is Venice I must protect, and its markets I must defend. All the world must know that in Venice they may trade freely and safely. The economy of the entire city depends upon it.

DANIEL: But the women...

DUKE: All those who would corrupt the course of capitalism, or fail to turn them in once known, must be penalized, quickly, publicly, and severely, to discourage others. *(To the GUARDS.)* Take them away.

(The GUARDS hustle PORTIA, BASSANIO, and BELLARIO away. The DUKE and LARGO exit. DANIEL falls weeping into RACHEL's arms.)

SCENE NINE
If You Prick Us...

Setting: The Venice gallows. At rise: JESSICA, BASSANIO, and PORTIA await execution. RACHEL and DANIEL enter from the side nearest JESSICA. RACHEL speaks to the other prisoners, as if offstage.

RACHEL: Bellario, Lorenzo, Gratiano, Nerissa, may God have mercy on your souls.

(JESSICA turns away at their approach.)

DANIEL: Mother? Mother, won't you speak to me, even in this last hour? Must we end this way, in harshness? Mother? It is useless.

RACHEL: You made the effort, Daniel. It is between her and God, now.

BASSANIO: Well, have you married yet?

DANIEL: No. This seemed not the time for such a celebration. But soon.

BASSANIO: It is a fine thing, but costly. You have chosen well, Daniel, if you have chosen for love. So regret nothing, for to chose love is to risk and hazard all.

DANIEL: I shall remember. *(Turning to PORTIA, beginning to weep.)* I would never have wished this upon you, sweet lady.

PORTIA: Nor I you, my love. There is pain and wrong enough for us all. We are paying for our sins.

DANIEL: Do you remember that psalm that you tried to teach me once? I could never get it right.

PORTIA: "Truth and mercy have met together..."

DANIEL: "...righteousness and peace have kissed."

(DANIEL reaches out to RACHEL and takes her by the hand.)

DANIEL: Farewell, sweet lady.

PORTIA: Farewell, my love.

(DANIEL and RACHEL move to the far side of the stage, as darkness falls on the others. Sound: The loud, sudden, violent sound of the floor being pulled out from under the prisoners.)

(Blackout.)

SCENE TEN
Better the Instruction

Setting: Shylock's (now DANIEL and RACHEL's) house. At rise: DANIEL and RACHEL are going through things at the house. She is garbed in Moslem robes. There is a knock, and DANIEL opens the door. TUBAL enters, carrying a package.

DANIEL: Hail, Tubal, my friend. What's this?

TUBAL: They were your grandfather's.

(DANIEL opens the package. It is a yarmulke and tallit. He seems unsure, both attracted and apprehensive. RACHEL stands behind him, touching him. He looks to her, then back to TUBAL. Slowly, he takes the yarmulke and puts it on and reverently returns

the tallit to the box. There is another knock. RACHEL opens the door, and the DUKE and LARGO enter. TUBAL steps aside. RACHEL and DANIEL are cool, but proper.)

DUKE: Good day.

RACHEL: Your grace.

DANIEL: What brings you hence?

DUKE: The good merchant and I have come to ask a favor of you.

RACHEL: Of us?

DANIEL: What kind of favor?

DUKE: Because you hold now both the House of Shylock and the House of Belmont, you are one of Venice's most wealthy citizens.

DANIEL: If we remain in Venice.

DUKE: This is why I come. I heard you had plans to leave us.

RACHEL: We are not welcome here.

DUKE: That is not true, my lady. You would be quite welcome here; indeed, you are indispensable.

DANIEL: How so?

DUKE: With your great wealth, you could serve the needs of commerce quite well.

DANIEL: You mean I could be a financier, a moneylender, like my grandfather.

DUKE: It is a profession to which you are most nobly suited, sir. You would be free to set your own terms. And I would make sure that you and your wife were well treated and protected, on the mart, or anywhere in the city, should you feel it necessary.

DANIEL: You and your justice have robbed me of nearly all that I love. And now I would help you?

(DANIEL walks away, RACHEL goes after him.)

DANIEL: I will not enrich their villainy.

RACHEL: You could not foresee what would happen. And if we leave, we shall have to sell all.

DANIEL: It is proper, so we are not reminded of our griefs here.

RACHEL: But if we stay, we can honor those we have lost.

DANIEL: How so?

RACHEL: With my family's influence and your clever financing, we may yet teach Venice to season justice with love and mercy.

(A beat while DANIEL mulls this over.)

RACHEL: Did you not tell Rabbi that you would foreswear vengeance when he admitted you to the synagogue?

DANIEL: It is a hard lesson.

RACHEL: But we have learned it. Perhaps they can as well. *(Beat.)* Let us try it.

DANIEL: *(To the DUKE.)* We'll stay.

DUKE: Excellent! And for your first transaction, this fine merchant, who you know well, lies in need of your help.

LARGO: Because I have stayed over all this time, I have run out of funds with which to return home, and I have urgent business there to look after, or I shall lose even more.

DANIEL: How much do you need?

LARGO: Three thousand ducats would be sufficient.

(RACHEL comes forward, and counts him out the money.)

LARGO: Thank you, dear lady.

DANIEL: When shall we receive payment?

LARGO: In three months' time. The Duke is my witness. And what shall be the interest?

DANIEL: This time, I shall only take your ring.

LARGO: The turquoise? But surely you would rather…

DANIEL: The ring!

(LARGO struggles to take the ring off, and hands it to DANIEL. The DUKE and LARGO exit. DANIEL spits on the ring, and wipes it clean it inside and out. Then, turning to RACHEL, he kneels before her, and places the ring on her finger.)

(The end.)

GALAXY VIDEO

Marc Morales

MARC MORALES was born in Manhattan in 1970 and raised in Yonkers, New York. His father is a retired New York Police Department sergeant and his mother a hospital administrator. He studied acting with Sir Mort Clark and voice with Michael Forman. Morales also studied modern dance with Molly Franz Blau and was a member of her company, Danceworks, for five years. His previous writing/directing credits include *Edge of Insanity*, *Edge of Insanity 2*, and *A New Beginning*. He recently wrote and directed *The Lounge* at the St. Marks Theater where he is an artist-in residence for the Horse Trade Theater Group.

Galaxy Video was first presented by Edge of Insanity (Marc Morales, Artistic Director) in association with Horse Trade Theater Group on March 7, 2002, at the Red Room Theatre, New York City, with the following cast and credits:

Scott .... Josh Adler
Angry Employee .... Kerry J. Agate
Chris .... Larry Brenner
Melody/Ninja .... Nina Capelli
Manny .... Joanna H. Clay
Simon/Bathroom Man .... Christopher Frankie DiGennaro
Beth .... Wynn Everett
Erick/Michael .... Charles Paul Holt
Barnaby Franklin/Jason .... Jeffrey McCrann
Jerry .... Josh Mesnik
Russel .... Braden Moran
Marissa/Ninja .... Daisy Payero
Shelly/Freddie .... Roxane Policare
Jamielee/Shelby .... Shira Zimbeck

The Insane Production Team (responsible for the MADNESS)
Director: Marc Morales
Stage Manager: Joanna H. Clay
Assistant Stage Manager: Jennifer Lieberman
Scenic Designer: Bradd Baskin
Lighting Designer: Christina Saylor
Producer: Kari O'Donnell
Publicist: Scott Makin

Galaxy Video was subsequently produced in a return engagement on April 26, 2002, with the following cast:

Scott .... Marc Morales
Angry Employee .... Jennifer Gawlik
Chris .... Chris Thompson
Melody/Ninja .... Marni Wandner/Christen Kreft
Manny .... Juliette Schaefer
Simon/Bathroom Man .... Christopher Frankie DiGennaro
Beth .... Aida Lembo
Erick/Michael .... Steven G. Holm
Barnaby Franklin/Jason .... Josh Mertz
Jerry .... John Fukuda
Russel .... Philippe Cu Leong
Marissa/Ninja .... Daisy Payero
Shelly/Freddie .... Roxane Policare
Jamielee/Shelby .... Jennifer Lieberman

1

A dark stage. Two male voices are heard. It's SCOTT and CHRIS, roommates who on every Friday night come to rent a movie at Galaxy Video. They're conversing outside the video store.

SCOTT: Are you clear?

CHRIS: Clear? On what?

SCOTT: On the plan.

CHRIS: What plan?

SCOTT: The plan.

CHRIS: Oh, the plan. *(Pause.)* Crystal. Can we go now?

SCOTT: Tell me then.

CHRIS: I know it.

SCOTT: Then tell me.

CHRIS: We don't have much time left.

SCOTT: Then tell me. Tell me. Tell me the plan.

CHRIS: Then can we do this?

SCOTT: Then we can do this.

CHRIS: Fine. We make our entrance through the front doors. We acknowledge the greet from the clerk and make our way down the third aisle, turn left at the sixth shelf avoiding the new release aisle…

SCOTT: And this will put us where?

CHRIS: In the horror section.

SCOTT: Where we will rent which film?

CHRIS: John Carpenter's *The Thing.*

SCOTT: And why are we renting this fine film?

CHRIS: Because we were supposed to rent it last week but we didn't.

SCOTT: And why was that?

CHRIS: Due to my obsession with a C. Thomas Howell film, I used my persuasive ways to manipulate you and force you to rent my movie, abandoning all hopes of renting *The Thing.*

SCOTT: You cried like a bitch.

CHRIS: Yes I did. Can we go now?

SCOTT: *The Thing.* We are renting *The Thing.*

CHRIS: Fine, *The Thing.* Can we go now?

SCOTT: Stick to the plan. Don't veer off the path.

CHRIS: Sticking and not veering. Can we go now?

SCOTT: *(Pause.)* Let's go.

2

Lights black out, and the song "99 Luftbaloons" is heard loudly. Lights flash and begin to reveal Galaxy Video. A Blockbuster-type video store. Two NINJAS appear and gracefully roll the front counter into place downstage center. There are two walls of videotapes positioned center stage, creating three aisles between the seemingly endless rows of videotapes. Videos and movie posters line the sides of the theatre as well. SCOTT and CHRIS walk past the front counter, where we see JERRY and RUSSEL, two Galaxy Video employees. JERRY greets them, but they ignore him and keep walking, exiting upstage.

JERRY: Welcome to Galaxy Video. *(He strikes the official Galaxy Video pose.)* How may we assist you? *(He looks at RUSSEL, another employee who is sitting in a chair pretending to do a crossword puzzle.)* How come you never salute?

RUSSEL: Because. I don't want to look like you.

JERRY: What's wrong with looking like me? I'd rather look like me than look like you. Do you know what I see when I look at me?

RUSSEL: Tell me.

JERRY: I see a person who is going somewhere because he cares. He cares about his job.

RUSSEL: So you are going on to become employee of the month?

JERRY: At least it's something.

RUSSEL: So what do you see when you look at me?

JERRY: Anger.

RUSSEL: Anger. That's good.

(A woman enters through a door stage left. It is BETH, a woman in search of a film.)

BETH: Excuse me.

JERRY: *(Jumps around.)* Welcome to Galaxy Video. *(Strikes the pose.)* How may we assist you?

BETH: You should give a girl a warning before you do that.

JERRY: Sorry. What may I help you with?

BETH: I am looking for…

RUSSEL: The chick flick section is that way, hon.

JERRY: *(Embarrassed.)* Sorry about him. He's a dork.

BETH: No. That's okay. *(To RUSSEL.)* What makes you think I am looking for a chick flick, Cowboy?

RUSSEL: You work here long enough you start to develop a vibe for what people want to rent. Darlin'.

BETH: Darlin'? Gina Gershon. *Showgirls.*

RUSSEL: *(Smiles.)* Could it be that I have been mistaken? Dare I ask her which film she seeks? If I am wrong I will apologize, and hang my head in shame. Which film do you seek?

BETH: *Midnight Cowboy*, Sailor. *Midnight Cowboy.*

RUSSEL: Business? Or pleasure?

BETH: Pleasure.

RUSSEL: I am sorry. *(Hangs his head in shame. Snaps back up.)* Twenty-seventh aisle. Fifth shelf.

BETH: Thanks, Dork. *(Exits into the store.)*

RUSSEL: *(Watches her leave.)* She is cool. Any woman who rents *Midnight Cowboy* for pleasure is cool. She is like that wave at the end of *Point Break*. She is beautiful, she is intriguing, she is dangerous.

JERRY: *(Does an impression of Jon Voigt. It's bad.)* "I'm a hustler. I'm a hustler."

RUSSEL: What the hell are you doing?

JERRY: My impression of Jon Voigt in *Midnight Cowboy.*

RUSSEL: Well, please don't do it anymore.

JERRY: Why not?

RUSSEL: Because it sucks. It sounds nothing like Jon Voigt.

JERRY: Listen, you! I never claimed to be an impressionist. I do one voice. Jon Voigt in *Midnight Cowboy.* I think I do it well, and so does my mom. If you don't like it you can just kiss my ass.

RUSSEL: *(Pause.)* Calm down there, Leif Garrett. You don't want me to get all Ralph Macchio in *The Outsiders* on your ass. Do you?

JERRY: I am sorry. It's just the only impression that I do...

RUSSEL: *(Hugs him.)* I know. I know.

(A man enters from the stage left door. It's BARNABY FRANKLIN.)

BARNABY FRANKLIN: Where am I? On the set of *Cruisin*?

RUSSEL: *(Turning around.)* Barnaby Franklin.

BARNABY FRANKLIN: Russel. Russel? You are not even worthy of two names. Hello, Jerry.

RUSSEL: I weep. So what are you doing here?

BARNABY FRANKLIN: What? Can't a former employee come back and visit his old stomping grounds? Besides. You guys have the greatest selection in the universe.

RUSSEL: The best in the galaxy. So. How's the Porsche?

BARNABY FRANKLIN: I don't have it anymore. I have a BMW. It's more grown up. How's the Malibu?

RUSSEL: I don't have it anymore. It broke down. I take the bus.

BARNABY FRANKLIN: That's too bad. *(Pulls out a card.)* Here's my card. Give me a call next time. I will drive you to the bus stop. See you on my way out. *(Exits.)*

JERRY: *(Concerned.)* Are you okay?

RUSSEL: Of course I am okay. Don't I look okay? *(Notices a customer behind JERRY.)* You have a customer.

(A NINJA enters the store.)

JERRY: *(Spins around.)* Welcome to Galaxy Video. *(Strikes the pose.)* How may we assist you?

3

Lights start to flicker different colors. "Turning Japanese" plays loudly. The NINJAS separate the front counter and roll the two pieces against the left and right walls; they then turn the video shelves inward, creating one long wall of videotapes. The music fades out as lights come up to reveal SIMON, a very odd employee. BETH appears from around a wall of videos.

BETH: Excuse me.

SIMON: *(Hurries up.)* Welcome to Galaxy Video. *(Tries to strike the pose but can't.)* How may we assist you? I can never get that. That crazy pose. I try. Jerry does it very well. Have you met Jerry? At the front counter?

BETH: Jerry? Oh, Jerry. *(Strikes the pose.)*

SIMON: That was good. *(Pause.)* Russel never poses.

BETH: Russel? Oh, Dork.

SIMON: *(Lost.)* Okay. Forgive my lackadaisical appearance. I was working. What may I get for you? *(He points at her.)*

BETH: *(Looks at him as if he is a little odd.)* I am looking for *Midnight Cowboy*. I think Russel sent me to the wrong aisle.

SIMON: That Russel is a kidder. *(He starts to go back to work.)*

BETH: *(Pause.)* Excuse me?

SIMON: Yes?

BETH: You were helping me?

SIMON: I was? So I was. What may I help you with?

BETH: *(Concerned.)* Are you okay?

SIMON: I am fine. How are you?

BETH: I am looking for *Midnight Cowboy.*

SIMON: Excellent film. Jon Voigt. Dustin Hoffman. Excellent film. *(Gets lost.)*

BETH: Can you tell me where it is?

SIMON: What?

BETH: *Midnight Cowboy?*

SIMON: Fourth aisle. Eighth shelf.

BETH: Thank you.

SIMON: You're welcome. That's English for you are welcome.

(BETH stares at him and walks away.)

4

BETH exits stage right around the wall of videotapes. As she walks away, lights start to fade and the theme song "Hold Me Now" begins to play. A red light slowly creeps up to reveal the NINJAS rolling the front counter back into place and turning the wall of videotapes back into aisles. Red lights fade, and a single white light comes up downstage left to reveal MANNY, a customer who believes that working in the video store is the cat's meow. Music fades out.

MANNY: *(He speaks with his profile to the audience.)* Do you realize how lucky you are? You have the greatest job in the world.

(A light slowly comes up on RUSSEL, who is sitting on the counter doing a crossword puzzle.)

RUSSEL: It's a video store, Manny.

(All lights fade up on Galaxy Video. People can be seen walking through the aisles.)

MANNY: I know it's a video store, I just think it's great!

RUSSEL: Thank you, Tony the Tiger.

MANNY: Think about it. You are in charge of priceless films.

RUSSEL: It's a video store, Manny.

JERRY: I can do an impression of Jon Voigt in *Midnight Cowboy.*

MANNY: Do it.

RUSSEL: Don't encourage him.

MANNY: You guys ever have a star come in and ask how their movie is doing?

RUSSEL: Manny? It's a video…

JERRY: Well. There was that one time when Fred Berry came in…

MANNY: *(Excited.)* Fred Berry? Rerun? From *What's Happening!!?*

JERRY: Yes.

MANNY: Which movie is he in?

JERRY: I believe he is in *Vice Squad.*

MANNY: Where?

(JERRY starts to tell him, but RUSSEL cuts him off.)

RUSSEL: Thirty-second aisle. Twelfth shelf.

MANNY: I'm off! *(Runs off into the aisle.)*

JERRY: Why do you do that?

RUSSEL: Do what?

JERRY: Send everyone to the wrong aisle.

RUSSEL: Keeps me amused. *(Pause.)* Taristata? Do you know if that's a word?

JERRY: What?

RUSSEL: Taristata? Me neither. I must go and find out. *(He starts to exit.)*

JERRY: Where are you going? We close soon.

RUSSEL: I am going in. Hold down the fort.

5

Lights start to fade as RUSSEL walks off into the aisles. In the dark, the two NINJAS move the front counter apart, placing the two pieces against the right and left walls downstage while a short bit from the movie The Outsiders *is heard. As it ends, SCOTT's voice is heard in the dark...*

SCOTT: Chris? Chris?

(A light slowly comes up in the aisle to reveal CHRIS. SCOTT enters the aisle from upstage center.)

SCOTT: Chris?

CHRIS: Hello, Scott.

SCOTT: What are you doing, Chris? We are supposed to be in the horror section. Not the new release section. Let's go.

CHRIS: Look what I found, Scott. *(Pulls out a video from behind his back.)*

SCOTT: What's that, Chris?

CHRIS: A movie.

SCOTT: We already have a movie. *The Thing*. Remember?

CHRIS: Yes. But this one has Ralph Macchio in it. You remember Ralph Macchio, don't you, Scott? *The Outsiders*, *Karate Kid* 1, 2, 3, but not 4. That one starred the girl from *Boys Don't Cry*.

SCOTT: Put the movie back, Chris. Slowly.

CHRIS: Don't turn your back on Ralph Macchio, Scott. Remember all the good times that he brought us?

(CHRIS is taunting SCOTT with the videotape; SCOTT knocks it out of CHRIS's hand.)

SCOTT: This is not happening again. This is not happening! We are renting *The Thing*! And nothing you do will change that. Not again. This is my night! My night.

(SCOTT exits upstage right. CHRIS crouches down and clutches the videotape.)

CHRIS: Go! And take your *Thing* with you. Don't worry, Ralph Macchio. I won't let him separate us.

(MARISSA and ERICK enter. MARISSA is talking on her cell phone while her boyfriend ERICK searches for a film.)

MARISSA: Brenda. Let me tell you. That girl was trippin. Asking me to be quiet during the movie. Shit. I paid my ten dollars like everyone else did. If I want to talk during a movie, like Bobby Brown said, "it's my prerogative."

ERICK: *(Looking for a film.)* We should rent this one. It's very good.

MARISSA: Hold on, Brenda. *Platoon*? Isn't Arnold Schwarzenegger in this? I don't think so baby. You know how I don't like those explosion movies.

(RUSSEL appears at the top of the aisle and watches.)

MARISSA: I have an idea. Why don't you go for a walk and let me rent the movie? You always like what I rent anyway. *(MARISSA continues to talk to Brenda on the phone and slowly exits.)*

ERICK: Okay. *(He places the film back on the shelf, walks up the aisle, and encounters RUSSEL.)*

RUSSEL: I heard what went down. Arnold Schwarzenegger in *Platoon*. Ouch. That's an Oliver Stone classic. Listen. I don't mean any disrespect, but she knows nothing about cinema.

ERICK: I know.

RUSSEL: But still you let her choose which film you will watch this evening. Why is that?

ERICK: You wouldn't understand.

RUSSEL: Fear? Fear of hurting her feelings? What about your feelings? I know, my friend. I know because I was once like you. I spent many a night watching bad cinema because I was afraid that if I spoke up I would hurt her feelings. But one sultry summer evening it all came to a head.

ERICK: What happened?

RUSSEL: I lost the girl. *(Pause.)* Small price to pay to be captain of your own cinema.

ERICK: What should I do?

RUSSEL: Like Luke Skywalker in *Star Wars*. You know your destiny. Only you can fulfill it.

ERICK: *(Upset.)* I have to go. *(Exits the aisle.)*

RUSSEL: There is another. There is another. *(Pause.)* Somewhere.

6

Lights start to flicker and Run DMC's "Tricky" starts to play. The front counter is moved into position by the two NINJAS. All lights come up on Galaxy Video as the music fades out. Three BREAKDANCERS enter.

BREAKER 1: Excuse me?

JERRY: *(Turns around.)* Welcome to Galaxy Video. *(Strikes the pose.)* How may we assist you?

BREAKER 1: We're looking for *Beat Street*. Do you have it?

JERRY: *Beat Street*? Excellent film. Ninth aisle fifth shelf. *(Tries to pop lock.)*

BREAKER 1: *(Laughing.)* Thanks man.

JERRY: Peace out!

7

The BREAKERS exit and walk off through the center aisle. The front counter is moved off the stage by the NINJAS as the lights fade out. SHELLY, a narcoleptic employee, enters wearing a walkman; as she puts her headphones on, "Karma Chameleon" is played and SHELLY dances to the music that only she can hear. MANNY enters from around the shelf, stage left.

MANNY: Miss, *miss*... Excuse me. You?

(SHELLY turns around and takes her headphones off; the music stops.)

SHELLY: Welcome to Galaxy Video. How may we assist you?

MANNY: Are you new?

SHELLY: Yes. Transferred in from the Crescent Avenue store about two weeks ago. Had a small problem with a shelf of videotapes. How may I help you?

MANNY: *Vice Squad*. I am looking for *Vice Squad*. Russel sent me to the wrong aisle.

SHELLY: That Russel. *Vice Squad*. I know exactly where that is. Let's see. Yes. F...

(She passes out in MANNY's arms.)

MANNY: *(Startled.)* Holy shit. Miss? Miss?

SHELLY: What? *(Hug.)* I am so sorry. *(Pause.)* I have narcolepsy.

MANNY: The disease River Phoenix suffered from in *My Own Private Idaho*?

SHELLY: Yes, that's it. So where were we?

MANNY: *Vice Squad*.

SHELLY: I know exactly where that is. Yes. *Vice Squad*. Fi... *(She passes out.)*

(MANNY looks at SHELLY and then runs off.)

8

Lights black out. SHELLY exits. The two NINJAS enter and move the shelves around to make a wall of videotapes. Lights come up to reveal SIMON working in the aisle. BETH enters from around the video shelf, stage right.

BETH: Hi.

SIMON: *(Getting up.)* Welcome to Galaxy Video. *(Tries to pose.)* How may we assist you? I can never get that right. Jerry does it very well. Have you met Jerry? At the front counter?

BETH: *(Confused.)* Do you remember me?

SIMON: Of course. You are the *Midnight Cowboy* girl. Ya hoo. Did you like it?

BETH: *(Pause.)* I haven't watched it yet.

SIMON: And why is that, young lady?

BETH: Because. You sent me to the wrong aisle.

SIMON: *(Surprised.)* I did?

BETH: Yes. You sent me to *Urban Cowboy.*

SIMON: Good movie. Debra Winger, John Travolta, the bull? *(He jumps around like he is riding a bull.)* Good movie.

BETH: Are you on drugs?

SIMON: No. Are you?

BETH: I don't think so. *Midnight Cowboy?*

SIMON: Twentieth aisle. Eleventh shelf.

BETH: *(Stares at him.)* Thank you. *(Exits stage right.)*

9

"Feel My Heat" from Boogie Nights *starts to play. Colored lights flash while the shelves are turned back into aisles by the two NINJAS and the front counters are put into place. Meanwhile, SIMON exits up the aisle as CHRIS passes him, walking down the same aisle. SCOTT can be seen walking down the opposite aisle. JERRY is now behind the front counter. As CHRIS reaches the front counter, all lights come up.*

SCOTT: Hello, Chris.

CHRIS: Scott.

SCOTT: Trying to rent a movie, Chris?

CHRIS: I am not trying. I am.

SCOTT: Well. Don't you need this to rent a movie? *(Holds up a membership card.)*

(JERRY nods his head.)

CHRIS: *(Trying to remain cool.)* Give me the card, Scott. I don't have time for games.

SCOTT: I do. I told you, Chris. The only movie that we are renting tonight is *The Thing.*

CHRIS: Scott, I don't have time for this!

SCOTT: You want it? Come and get it. It's my night tonight, Chris. *(Exits.)*

CHRIS: *(To audience.)* Usually I wouldn't play such childish games. I am too well refined for that. But I have to get home. I have some very important work to do for the government. Top-secret stuff. *(Pause.)* Basically, they want me to go up the Nung River in an Army patrol boat, find this crazed Army general, and kill him. Plus, I really love Ralph Macchio films. *(Exits.)*

(All lights fade out. Blackout is held for a beat while the front counter is moved off by the NINJAS. A pool of light comes up on MELODY, a customer who is facing the audience and looking at an imaginary wall of videotapes. She looks through the tapes until she finds one she likes. She then starts to sing the theme song from Karate Kid II, *"The*

Glory of Love." As she sings, SCOTT walks into her light.)

SCOTT: *(To CHRIS.)* It's my night. Tonight is my night. *(Holds up card.)* You are going to have to kill me for it, Chris.

(SCOTT walks out of MELODY's light, and CHRIS enters the light.)

CHRIS: Come on, Scott. I don't have time for this. *(A cell phone rings. CHRIS answers it.)* Hello? Yes. I know that I have work to do. I will be there as soon as I can. The boat will not leave without me. I have to go.

(CHRIS walks out of the light, and MELODY's voice fades out with the lights.)

10

Lights fade up, and we see RUSSEL standing in the center aisle. To his left, in the next aisle, we see four young TOKERS passing a joint. RUSSEL smells it and goes to investigate.

RUSSEL: Smells like a Cheech and Chong film exploded in here. *(To the kid with the joint.)* Give it.

FREDDIE: Russel? I thought you were cool.

JASON: Russel. Don't let the man get you down.

RUSSEL: I will try not to, Jason. I just don't want one of you little schmucks freaking out again and running down the children's aisle yelling, "Santa Claus is dead."

JASON: That only happened once.

MICHAEL: *(In denial.)* That is so not true.

(RUSSEL has since taken a hit.)

RUSSEL: *(Crouches down.)* So. What's the discussion for today?

JAMIELEE: Horror films. What has become of them? *Scream* was a success because it poked fun at horror films. But besides that? Movies like *Urban Legend*? Give me a break.

FREDDIE: What do you think, Russel?

RUSSEL: Well, Freddie, I think that horror films have lost their edge. They're a big joke. We laugh at them; they don't scare us anymore.

MICHAEL: Why is that, Russel?

RUSSEL: Because they don't have the right formula.

JAMIELEE: And what's the right formula, Russel?

RUSSEL: *(He is stoned.)* I will tell you, Jamielee. Family! Family.

JAMIELEE: Family? That doesn't sound like a formula.

MICHAEL: She is right. Sounds more like an ingredient.

RUSSEL: I am talking.

MICHAEL: Sorry.

RUSSEL: Family! What does every great horror film have in common? Family! In *Halloween*, Michael Myers was trying to kill his sister. In *Friday the 13th*, Ms. Voorhees was taking revenge for the death of her son Jason. In *A Nightmare on Elm Street*, Freddie's mother who was a nun was raped by a thousand maniacs.

JASON: So basically what you're saying is in order to make a good horror film, you just have to kill someone's mother?

RUSSEL: *(Confused.)* I am?

JASON: I've got a camera.

JAMIELEE: I've got a mom.

RUSSEL: *(Realizes that he is stoned.)* I got to go.

11

RUSSEL and the TOKERS exit. Downstage, lights fade up as the counter is moved into position by the NINJAS. JERRY is behind the counter. ANGRY EMPLOYEE enters through the door, stage left.

ANGRY EMPLOYEE: Jerry. I want my job back.

JERRY: Do I know you?

ANGRY EMPLOYEE: I met you for a short time five days ago when I came into work. It was my first day.

JERRY: Oh yeah. We didn't fire you.

ANGRY EMPLOYEE: I know. I quit.

JERRY: You quit. To whom did you quit to?

ANGRY EMPLOYEE: Myself. I was in the Folk Song Musical section fixing tapes when I noticed four tapes that were in the wrong place. *Fort Apache, the Bronx*, *Empire Records*, *War Games*, and *The Way We Were. Are any of these films folk song musicals!?* I don't think so. Then this woman comes over to me and asks if we had that movie that had that guy in it who was in that movie with the girl who was in that movie with that guy. *(Pause.)* At that moment I decided that I hated people. So I turned myself inward to search for an answer for what to do. I can do stuff like that: I take yoga. Quit. That was the answer. Quit. So I quit. To myself, and I walked out. I went to my therapist Doctor Kubrick, and I asked him why? Why do I hate people? He replied "Because you hate yourself." Wow. I do hate myself. But why? Why do I hate myself? I turned myself inward once again to find the answer. *(Pause.)* My art, I have been neglecting my art. I am an artist. I draw little stick people. I draw them well. But I've been neglecting them lately because of my yoga, and work. I love drawing my little stick people. You should always make time for those things that you love to do. *(Pause.)* I am better now. May I have my job back?

JERRY: Okay.

ANGRY EMPLOYEE: Thank you. *(She turns to walk away.)*

JERRY: Hold on! You can't walk into Galaxy Video without the official Galaxy Video launch.

ANGRY EMPLOYEE: No. I can. You gave me one five days ago when I was first hired.

JERRY: But today you were rehired. So today is your new first day. I am starting the countdown. Five, Four, Three, Two, One.

(ANGRY EMPLOYEE pauses.)

JERRY: One.

ANGRY EMPLOYEE: I am now part of Galaxy Video. How may I assist you.

12

ANGRY EMPLOYEE launches into the store. The front counter is moved offstage by the NINJAS. ANGRY EMPLOYEE bumps into SHELLY, who is listening to her walkman in the aisle and gives her the finger. ERICK enters the aisle and is looking at the videos. He picks one up.

SHELLY: Great film.

ERICK: *(Not paying attention.)* I am sorry?

SHELLY: *Buffalo 66*. Great film.

ERICK: *(Surprised.)* You've seen this?

SHELLY: Like ten times. I am a huge Vincent Gallo fan.

ERICK: "Don't move, don't touch me, don't do anything."

SHELLY: What?

ERICK: Nothing. It's just a line from the movie.

SHELLY: The photo booth scene.

ERICK: You have seen it.

SHELLY: Huge Vincent Gallo fan.

ERICK: You know he's in the movie *Basquiat*? For about two seconds.

SHELLY: The Chinese restaurant scene.

ERICK: You've seen it.

SHELLY: "You got a love bite on your neck. Your life is going down the toilet."

ERICK: "I lost my hand. I lost my woman. Johnny has his hand. Johnny has his woman."

BOTH: *Moonstruck.*

SHELLY: *(Pause.)* So. You going to rent it?

ERICK: No. I've seen it already. Besides, my girlfriend is picking the movie tonight.

SHELLY: That sounds like fun.

ERICK: *(Depressed.)* I got to go.

13

ERICK exits, and SHELLY goes back to her work. While working, she falls asleep again. Just then, RUSSEL walks past the aisle. He stops and debates whether or not he saw a body lying on the floor. He walks past the BREAKDANCERS in another aisle. They have found Beat Street. *Music comes up, and the BREAKERS start to breakdance. Each DANCER has a solo, then they all moonwalk past the front counter, pay for their movies, and moonwalk out the door, stage left. A MAN is walking in, passing them, making his way to the front counter.*

MAN: Excuse me.

JERRY: *(Turns.)* Welcome to Galaxy Video. *(Strikes the pose.)* How may we assist you?

MAN: Yeah, buddy. You got a bathroom here I can use?

JERRY: Yes. I do have a bathroom, and no, you can't use it. Customers only sir. Sorry.

MAN: You don't understand. I really got to go.

JERRY: I am sorry. Store rule, not mine. Customers only.

MAN: Man. Okay. How do I become a customer?

JERRY: Well, just rent one of our fine films. We have an infinite number of movies here at Galaxy Video.

MAN: I ain't a member.

JERRY: Well then, you can purchase one of our fine snacks from our concession area.

MAN: Okay. Give me these. *(Grabs a package of M&Ms with peanuts.)*

JERRY: Fine selection, sir. That will be nine dollars and ninety-nine cents.

MAN: For a pack of M&Ms?

JERRY: For a pack of M&Ms with peanuts.

MAN: Listen buddy. I really got to go. I am dying here.

JERRY: Okay. Seventeenth aisle. In the back, on the left… I think.

14

The MAN exits upstage. Lights cross fade, and the song "Harder" is played as the front counter is moved offstage by the NINJAS and the video shelves are turned forward, forming one long video shelf. Music fades, and SIMON is working in the aisle. BETH enters from around the video shelf, stage left. She lights a cigarette.

BETH: *(To SIMON.)* Excuse me.

SIMON: Welcome to Galaxy Video. *(Tries to pose.)* How may we assist you? I…

BETH: I know. You can never get the salute. But Jerry can.

SIMON: Yes he can. He can also do an impression of Jon Voigt in *Midnight Cowboy*. *(Yells to JERRY who is in darkness.)* Jerry, do your Jon Voigt in *Midnight Cowboy*.

JERRY: *(In the dark.)* "I'm a hustler, I'm a hustler."

SIMON: Wasn't that fantastic? He is going places.

BETH: *Midnight Run*.

SIMON: Good movie. Robert De Niro. "I want that Ness dead! I want his family dead!" Charles Grodin… *(Tries to think of a Charles Grodin line but can't.)*

BETH: I wanted *Midnight Cowboy*.

SIMON: So you did. I am sorry. I don't know where my head is today. Do you like cheese?

BETH: I just want my movie, *Midnight Cowboy*.

SIMON: First aisle fifth shelf.

BETH: *(Pause.)* Thank you.

15

BETH exits, and lights fade out. In the darkness, the video shelves are turned back into aisles. CHRIS is heard in the dark.

CHRIS: Scott? Scott?

(A scream is heard. Lights come up on SCOTT and ERICK. SCOTT has ERICK pinned and is about to hit him with a videotape. He notices his mistake.)

SCOTT: Sorry. My mistake. I thought you were my roommate.

ERICK: That's okay. *(Pause.)* Why do you want to beat your roommate with a videotape?

SCOTT: Because it's my night to rent and he is trying to deprive me of that honor. I won't let that happen.

ERICK: Couldn't you two just talk it out?

SCOTT: Chris is very tricky. He gets into your head and screws with you. Next thing you know he is renting the film. But not tonight.

ERICK: Which movie do you want to rent?

SCOTT: *The Thing*. I am renting *The Thing*.

ERICK: Fantastic film. I am in a similar situation. Right now my girlfriend Marissa is in another part of this store, and I know she is going to rent something that I am going to hate.

SCOTT: Then why don't you just tell her that you are renting the movie?

ERICK: It doesn't work that way.

SCOTT: *(Has an idea.)* Well my friend. It seems like we share a common interest. The interest in not watching bad cinema. *(Changes gears.)* Are you aware that one swift hit to the back of the head with a videotape will render anyone unconscious?

ERICK: Are you saying I should go hit Marissa in the back of the head with a videotape?

SCOTT: The thought did cross my mind. But no. I propose this. You take care of my problem, and I take care of your problem. That way, if the authorities get involved, there is no way they can link me to Marissa and no way they can link you to Chris. So what do you say? You are only one swift hit away from watching any fine film that you choose.

ERICK: That does sound great.

SCOTT: *(Goes in for the kill.)* What's your name?

ERICK: Erick.

SCOTT: I am Scott. So. Erick. Should we discuss our "problems"?

(Lights start to fade, a blue light fades up on SCOTT and ERICK as they talk. In the next aisle, a light slowly fades up on MELODY. She begins to sing the theme to The Godfather. *After a few moments, the two men shake hands and walk in separate directions in the aisle. When they get to the end of the aisle, they both light cigarettes and smoke them as the lights, and MELODY, slowly fade out.)*

16

The video shelves are turned forward by the NINJAS, and lights come up on SIMON. He is working. RUSSEL sticks his head from around the corner.

RUSSEL: Simon. *(He hides.)*

SIMON: Hello. *(Goes back to work.)*

RUSSEL: Simon. *(He hides.)*

SIMON: Who's that? Who's there?

RUSSEL: Simon. *(He hides.)*

SIMON: Who's that? Who's there? What do you want? Oh no. Not again. Mother? Make the voices stop. Make them go away. O God Mother blood! Blood!

RUSSEL: *(Freaked out.)* Simon! Simon! Calm down! Calm down! It's me!

SIMON: *(As if nothing happened.)* Hello, Russel. What brings you around these parts?

RUSSEL: *(Confused.)* Are you okay?

SIMON: Never better. How are you?

RUSSEL: Okay.

SIMON: That's good to hear, Russel. Because a year ago, you were in some pretty bad shape. With Barnaby stealing your screenplay idea and then Shelby leaving you. I thought you were going to lose it.

RUSSEL: *(Pause.)* Thank you, Simon.

SIMON: You're welcome, Russel. I know you see me as this odd employee. This fool. But I have eyes and I have ears. I see and listen. You walk these aisles every day, for what? There are no answers in these aisles, Russel. Just videotapes. Fiction, not reality. *(Pause.)* So, I will see you later? Perhaps over some tea and crumpets? That does sound yummy.

17

Lights fade out as RUSSEL exits stage right. The video shelves are turned into aisles by the NINJAS. A lighter is lit in the center aisle where we see the four young TOKERS.

MICHAEL: I got it. Let's make a horror film about a guy who sees his mother get hit by a car. Then he drives around hitting people with his car. We can call it "Road Rage."

JASON: And in the sequel, his brother from another mother does the killing.

FREDDIE: We'll call that one "Road Rage II."

(JAMIELEE gets up.)

JASON: Where are you going?

JAMIELEE: Can't a girl go to the bathroom? *(Exits upstage.)*

18

The lighter goes out and the theme song from A Nightmare on Elm Street *begins to play. The front counter is moved into position by the NINJAS. Music stops, and lights bump up. JERRY is at the front counter working. Enter SHELBY, RUSSEL's ex-girlfriend.*

SHELBY: Hi.

JERRY: *(Turning.)* Welcome to Galaxy Video… Shelby.

SHELBY: Jerry.

JERRY: What are you doing here?

SHELBY: I need to see Russel.

JERRY: Russel who?

SHELBY: Jerry.

JERRY: Oh, Shelby. This is not a good day. He's having a hard time. Barnaby Franklin is here.

SHELBY: What's that asshole doing here?

JERRY: Renting a movie. What do you want with him, Shelby?

SHELBY: I have something for him, *(Holds up a package.)* and I care. I still care.

JERRY: Then why did you leave him?

SHELBY: Because he was an asshole.

JERRY: That's true.

SHELBY: Where, Jerry?

JERRY: He's in there somewhere.

SHELBY: Spreading the Gospel of Russel. I miss that.

JERRY: They love him in there.

SHELBY: And out here. Thanks, Jerry.

19

SHELBY walks into the aisle as lights start to fade and music comes up. The front counter is moved offstage left and the video shelves are turned forward by the NINJAS. Lights fade up as the music fades out. SIMON is in the aisle working. BETH enters stage left from around the video shelf.

BETH: Excuse me.

SIMON: Welcome to Galaxy Video…

BETH: You sent me to the wrong aisle. Again. I am looking for *Midnight Cowboy*. Not *The Electric Horseman.*

(SIMON goes to speak.)

BETH: Don't speak. *Midnight Cowboy*?

SIMON: Thirty-ninth aisle first shelf.

BETH: I… Forget it. Listen. If you are wrong, I am going to come back and kick you. Hard!

20

BETH exits. Lights blink in time with the music. The video shelves are moved into aisles by the NINJAS. Lights come up on RUSSEL and MELODY.

RUSSEL: Melody, you ever notice how any moment in life can be set to music? It has its own soundtrack. Think about it. Any moment. Let's take my day for instance. With the way things have been going so far? It's definitely a Paul Simon's "Late in the Evening."

(As RUSSEL starts to read the back of a video box to himself, MELODY starts to sing Don Henley's "In a New York Minute.")

21

Lights start to fade out, and a recorded version of the song takes over as MELODY's voice fades out. The front counter is moved into position. Music fades out as lights fade up. MANNY is seen walking down the aisle, and JERRY is working at the front counter.

MANNY: Okay. Russel has sent me on a wild goose chase, and are you aware that one of your employees suffers from narcolepsy?

JERRY: Yes. Like River Phoenix.

(They bow their heads.)

MANNY: So where is it?

JERRY: What?

MANNY: *Vice Squad.*

JERRY: Oh, aisle fourteen ninth shelf.

MANNY: I am off.

22

As MANNY runs off into Galaxy Video, the front counter is moved by the NINJAS. As MANNY exits, he bumps into ANGRY EMPLOYEE. She is fixing videotapes in the aisle.

ANGRY EMPLOYEE: *(Noticing that a videotape is in the wrong place.) Night Shift? Night Shift?* What's wrong with this picture? *(Yells.)* THIS IS THE FUCKING HISTORY AISLE!!!! *(Catches herself.)* Little stick people. I must draw little stick people. They make me happy.

(ANGRY EMPLOYEE pulls out a pad and pencil and begins to draw. MARISSA enters the aisle and walks over to ANGRY EMPLOYEE who has her back turned.)

MARISSA: Excuse me. Do you have that movie with that guy in it that has that girl in it that was in that movie with that other guy?

ANGRY EMPLOYEE: *(The pencil breaks on the pad, and ANGRY EMPLOYEE slowly turns around.)* You.

MARISSA: Yeah, it's me. So what?

ANGRY EMPLOYEE: You.

MARISSA: Listen, you got a problem or something?

ANGRY EMPLOYEE: You.

MARISSA: Listen. I didn't come all up in here looking for no trouble. I am just looking for that movie with that guy who was in that movie with that girl...

ANGRY EMPLOYEE: SHUT UP!

MARISSA: *(Shocked.)* Excuse me? Who you think you talking to like that? Girl. You must be trippin. I will bust your ass.

ANGRY EMPLOYEE: NO! You won't. Because I am going to bust your ass.

MARISSA: *(Pause.)* You want to do this? You want to do this? We can do this. We can do this now. Right now.

(MARISSA starts to remove her earrings and then pulls a large jar of Vaseline from her purse to spread on her face. As the women argue, RUSSEL enters the aisle just in time to break it up.)

RUSSEL: LADIES! CALM DOWN! Calm down! You don't want me to get all Laurence Fishburne in *What's Love Got to Do With It* on your asses do you?

(They separate.)

RUSSEL: So what is going on here?

ANGRY EMPLOYEE: Russel. I hate that woman.

RUSSEL: Do I know you?

ANGRY EMPLOYEE: I met you five days ago when I first started. But then I quit. I looked inward and found the answer to my question. I can do stuff like that. I take yoga. I hate people. But I hate her more. How can you not know the name of one person in the film that you seek? She's the devil.

MARISSA: Who you calling the devil? No. I don't play that. I go to church every Sunday with my girls, and we sit up in the balcony and we praise Jesus. So don't be trying to wish up no bad spirits on me. I don't play that. *(Pause.)* You know what? You're sorry. You are not even worth my time. Bye. *(She exits.)*

ANGRY EMPLOYEE: You're sorry! I quit! *(She exits.)*

(RUSSEL stands in the aisle alone. Lights start to fade to black. RUSSEL walks upstage. The black light reveals an entire galaxy painted on the back wall. RUSSEL stands in the middle of all this. He is outlined by some colored light.)

RUSSEL: O my God. It's full of stars.

23

The video shelves are turned forward by the NINJAS. A light comes up on SIMON. SHELBY enters.

SIMON: "They took my thumb, Charlie..."

SHELBY: Hello, Simon.

SIMON: Shelby? How nice to see you.

SHELBY: It's nice to see you too.

SIMON: How may I assist you? Perhaps I may help you choose a film?

SHELBY: Russel?

SIMON: Russel? *(Thinks.)* Kurt Russell, *Escape from New York*, I have it right here.

SHELBY: Simon, where is he?

SIMON: Simon, where is he... no, I don't think we have that one. Thanks for coming. See you later.

SHELBY: Simon?

SIMON: *(Into Dennis Hopper.)* He's gone man. He's gone. He went off into the galaxy with his people. He feels safe with his people. He went off to find himself. What do you want me to say about him? You want me to say that he was a kind man? That he was a good man? That he was a knowledgeable man? That he was a movie man?

SHELBY: Simon! Where?

SIMON: He went that way.

24

Lights fade out. In the dark, the video shelves are moved into aisle formation by the NINJAS. CHRIS is heard in the dark. A light fades up on him.

CHRIS: *(Yelling.)* Scoooooooooott! Scott! This is not funny. I really have to get home. I have some important stuff to do. I am not leaving without Ralph Macchio. Call me a freak, call me what you want, but I like Ralph Macchio.

(A light bumps up in the aisle to reveal ERICK. He's holding a videotape. He's been listening to CHRIS.)

ERICK: *(Talking to himself.)* I like Ralph Macchio also. I can't do this. He likes Ralph Macchio, I like Ralph Macchio, how many Ralph Macchio fans are left in the world? Can we afford to take one out? I have no choice. I made a deal, and like Tina Turner said in *Mad Max: Beyond Thunder Dome*, "Break a deal, face the wheel."

(A chorus is heard in the darkness, repeating the line, "Break a deal, face the wheel." All lights fade out except for the one on ERICK and the one on CHRIS. The theme song from Halloween *starts to play as the light on ERICK starts to fade. At one point, CHRIS's light blacks out and a blue light comes up in the last aisle to reveal JAMIELEE. She is running away from Michael Meyers from* Halloween. *Right before he catches her, the light on them blacks out and a light bumps back up on CHRIS. This time, ERICK is standing behind him. Music stops. CHRIS is frozen in time.)*

ERICK: I can't do this. This is insane. If we took out everyone in the world who didn't agree with us, the world would be a pretty empty place. That was deep. Look at me. I was just about to hit this guy in the back of the head with a videotape because I am not happy with my relationship. But is that it? I am not happy in my relationship? I am not happy with the fact that she rents bad films, but does that mean I am not happy in my relationship? Everything else is okay. We talk, we laugh, we have sex, we have amazing sex! So what if she rents bad movies? Lots of people don't like the same types of films. A film does not make a relationship. Wow. I just had a John Cusak moment. *(Looks at CHRIS.)* Good luck with your Ralph Macchio movie. *(He remembers MARISSA.)* Oh man! Marissa!

(Blackout.)

(MARISSA's voice is heard in the dark. She is on the phone. As she speaks, a light fades up revealing MARISSA downstage in the aisle. SHELLY is upstage center, rearranging some tapes on the shelf to her left.)

MARISSA: Brenda. I'm telling you. This movie is dope. It has that guy in it from that movie with that girl. Yeah. And they have that car. Yeah.

(As MARISSA continues talking, Hitchcock-type music is heard. SCOTT enters from upstage in the aisle. He glares at MARISSA, holding a videotape. He starts to slowly approach MARISSA in time with the music. She doesn't see him because her back is turned. The music picks up as he gets closer. Then all of a sudden, SHELLY passes out, SCOTT trips over her, hitting his head on the floor, knocking himself out. As MARISSA slowly turns to see what happened behind her, ERICK appears downstage at the aisle's entrance. Music bumps out.)

ERICK: *(Seeing the mayhem behind her.)* Marissa!

(She looks at him.)

MARISSA: Hey baby, where you been? Look, okay, I got us a movie. It has that guy in it who was in that movie with that girl and they had that car.

ERICK: No

MARISSA: No. What?

ERICK: No. We are not going to rent that.

MARISSA: Why not?

ERICK: Because I know that I am not going to enjoy it, and I don't think that is fair. This is not just about you. It's about us and I feel that every time you rent a film, you don't think about us. You just think about you. But that happens in relationships; sometimes we don't think about one another, and that's why we need honest moments like this. So we can discuss, fix, and move on.

(She hauls off and slaps him in the face with the videotape. He falls, and she exits.)

ERICK: Well, that hurt. But was it worth it? *(Pause.)* In time I will look back at this day and laugh but for now I think I will just rent *Platoon*, go home, watch it and cry. Or maybe *Annie Hall*. It really doesn't matter. I'm the captain of my own cinema now. But what good is being a captain of an empty ship?

(ERICK exits. SHELLY slowly lifts up her head; she has been listening the entire time. MELODY provides some mood music, singing the theme to Casablanca. *A single colored light comes up on her in the next aisle. She sings a little bit, and SHELLY falls asleep again. MELODY stops singing. Lights cross fade, a single white special comes up on MELODY. Simultaneously, the whites on SHELLY and SCOTT slowly fade to red. MELODY starts to sing "The End" by the Doors. She sings it almost operatically and hauntingly. SCOTT lifts his head and stares out into the audience, almost in a trance. MELODY sings until the light fades out.)*

25

In the dark, the video shelves are placed forward by the NINJAS, one behind the other, facing the audience. Lights fade up on RUSSEL. He is sitting against the shelf looking at a videotape. Enter BETH from stage right.

BETH: How's the reading in this library?

RUSSEL: How goes the hunting?

BETH: Some dick sent me to the wrong aisle. Then another dick sent me all over the store.

RUSSEL: Yes. You have to watch out for those dicks. They can be pretty tricky. Care to have a seat?

BETH: Thanks, mind if I smoke?

RUSSEL: Yeah. It's a small rule, no smoking in public places.

BETH: But it's okay to smoke weed in here?

RUSSEL: Weed, what's that?

BETH: Get off of it, this whole place reeks like Willie Nelson.

RUSSEL: That's funny, that's very funny.

BETH: I'm a funny person.

RUSSEL: You want to go out?

BETH: No. *(Pause.)* Listen, don't take it personally. I think you're cute and if I was looking for a hot night, I'd go out with you. But I'm not looking for a hot night. I'm looking for a cold night. You know, one of those nights when you curl up on the sofa with someone you care about and watch a movie. I don't think that's you... just my opinion.

RUSSEL: So how does someone become a "cold night" person?

BETH: Make a decision.

RUSSEL: A decision about what?

BETH: What is it that you want to do with your life?

RUSSEL: And that will make me a cold night person? Explain.

BETH: Okay, it's just a theory. Ready? Once you make a decision, a true decision about what you want to do with your life, something happens. I believe it's a whole astrological thing, I don't know, but anyway, you just look at life in a whole new perspective. You start to feel like you have a purpose. Like you're actually doing something. And you start to feel that you're actually good enough for someone. No more doubts about it. You're hanging out for a while. That's a good thing for a girl to know.

RUSSEL: *(Thinks about it.)* A cold night person?

BETH: A cold night person.

(RUSSEL gets up to leave.)

BETH: Where are you going?

RUSSEL: I'm a little bit tripped out by what you said. I don't know you, but you made me think. Thank you.

BETH: You're welcome.

RUSSEL: By the way, you're in the wrong aisle.

BETH: Shit!

(RUSSEL walks around, reading the backs of video boxes as BETH exits. SHELBY enters.)

SHELBY: Hello, Russel.

RUSSEL: This day sucks.

SHELBY: Nice to see you too. Here. *(Throws him the package she has been holding.)*

RUSSEL: A gift? What is it?

SHELBY: When I moved out, some of your writings got mixed in with my stuff.

RUSSEL: And?

SHELBY: And I thought that someone else should read your work besides you. So I did some research and found someone who critiques people's work and sent it to him.

RUSSEL: Why does everyone steal my work!?

SHELBY: I didn't steal your work, you cocky shit. I took it by accident. I thought if someone else saw how good you are, you would see how good you are. Open your eyes and see what we see. Please?

RUSSEL: Do you miss me? 'Cause I miss you sometimes.

SHELBY: Yes. Sometimes.

(RUSSEL leans in to kiss SHELBY; she pushes him away.)

SHELBY: Don't be an asshole, Russel.

(SHELBY exits, and SHELLY enters.)

RUSSEL: Shelly. Let me ask you a question. How come movies like this get made? I will tell you why. Because people invest in them. They invest in shitty movies, and not the good ones. Why is that? Because the good ones are afraid. They are afraid that they too will be shitty. *(Realizes.)* Look at me getting all deep.

SHELLY: That's okay. Everyone has their moments. You just had yours. Russel? I just want to thank you for being so nice to me since I transferred here. After that incident in the Crescent Avenue store, I thought no one would ever speak to me again.

RUSSEL: Well, you did take out every aisle in the entire store. That was bad. Did anyone die?

SHELLY: No. Well. A frog.

RUSSEL: A frog?

SHELLY: A small child's pet.

RUSSEL: Oh. That's why they sent you here. The aisles are stronger.

SHELLY: I knew that. *(Pause.)* Russel? I am in love.

RUSSEL: I am flattered, Shelly, but I see myself more as a loner, a rebel.

SHELLY: *(Pause.)* Not with you.

RUSSEL: *(Pause.)* May I have a moment to be embarrassed? *(Takes two seconds.)* With whom?

SHELLY: Some guy in the store. I met him once, and the second time I met him he thought I was unconscious.

RUSSEL: Okay.

SHELLY: I am not really in love. I just feel that he is a real person. Not a fake person, and I like that. Do you know what I mean?

RUSSEL: Maybe.

SHELLY: It just seems that he is the type of person who cares about other people. And in my world that makes you real.

RUSSEL: So. Where do I stand in your world?

SHELLY: Real. Too real sometimes. There has to be a balance. Or else you lose yourself. *(Realizes.)* Wow. I just had a Meg Ryan moment.

RUSSEL: I am glad you did. *(Turns to put film back on shelf.)* So tell me…

(She passes out.)

RUSSEL: That had to hurt. Shelly? Shelly?

SHELLY: *(Waking up.)* I am sorry. It really sucks to be a narcoleptic. What were we talking about?

RUSSEL: I was asking you about him.

SHELLY: You know the story, Russel. Come in with your girlfriend to rent a movie. Walk out single.

RUSSEL: Yeah.

SHELLY: He talked about being the captain of your own cinema.

RUSSEL: Did he?

SHELLY: But how lonely it is if you have no one to share it with. I feel the same way, Russel. I can take home any movie I want. But what good is that if I have to watch it alone?

RUSSEL: I know. Does he…

(She passes out.)

RUSSEL: Great. Shelly? Shelly?

SHELLY: *(Waking up.)* I am sorry. Where were we?

RUSSEL: I was asking you if he knew how you felt.

SHELLY: What's the use?

RUSSEL: What do you mean?

SHELLY: I have narcolepsy, Russel. I leveled a video store and killed a frog. Who would want to be with me?

RUSSEL: We all have our problems. Granted yours is a little bit more extreme than others'. But that does not disguise the fact that you are a great and beautiful person.

SHELLY: You really think so?

RUSSEL: Yes I do.

SHELLY: You think he will think so too?

(ERICK enters the aisle.)

RUSSEL: I don't know. Why don't you ask him?

SHELLY: *(Sees ERICK.)* How's that for timing? Thanks, Russel. *(She goes over to him.)* Hi, my name is Shelly.

(She passes out in his arms.)

RUSSEL: Don't worry. She has narcolepsy. You two have fun.

26

RUSSEL exits. The video shelves are turned into aisles by the NINJAS, and we see MELODY standing in an aisle holding a tape. MANNY enters and notices that she is holding Vice Squad.

MANNY: *(Trying to play it cool.)* How you doing? *Vice Squad*? Have you seen it?

(MELODY shakes her head.)

MANNY: I have. It sucks. Yeah, worst movie I have ever seen. *(Scans the shelf.)* Here is a movie that you should rent. *Videodrome*. James Woods.

(She shakes her head no.)

MANNY: *(Getting angry.)* Listen lady. I have been up and down this store looking for that movie. I am all crazy! So if you think I am going to let you rent that movie, you are so mistaken. So give it up right now or else I am going to kick your ass. And trust me lady, I can do it. I have seen *The Matrix* one hundred and seven times. *(Strikes a goofy* Matrix *pose.)*

MELODY: *(Pause.)* I've seen it one hundred and eight. *(She removes her jacket to reveal* Matrix *gear. She then does three backflips.)* Bring it on.

MANNY: *(To audience.)* No good can come from this. *(Pause.)* Lady. Give me my movie!

*(*Matrix*-type music plays, and they battle. In the dark, lit only by strobe, we hear MANNY.)*

MANNY: Ouch!

27

Lights black out, and the front counter is moved into position by the NINJAS. Lights fade up on Galaxy Video. JERRY is at the front counter stacking videotapes.

JERRY: "I'm a hustler, I'm a hustler." That doesn't suck; maybe you suck, Russel. Yeah, that's it: you suck, Russel. He is so *Sweet Valley High*, and I am so *Babysitter's Club*. He is so *Webster*, and I am so *Diff'rent Strokes*. What you talking about, Russel?

(BATHROOM MAN enters from the aisle. He walks over to JERRY and punches him in the face. JERRY falls, sending videotapes everywhere. As the MAN exits, a large wet stain is seen on the front of his pants. The front counter is moved off by the NINJAS.)

28

BARNABY FRANKLIN is seen in the center aisle. RUSSEL enters from upstage center.

RUSSEL: Barnaby Franklin.

BARNABY FRANKLIN: *(Looking at a videotape.)* I do love this film. It's a Spielberg classic. I sense anger. Russel, are you still angry with me?

RUSSEL: Why shouldn't I be? You stole my idea.

BARNABY FRANKLIN: You can't copyright an idea, Russel. Besides, you asked me to come on as a second writer. I thought your idea was brilliant. I knew it would sell. But it was taking too long. That's why I suggested that we bring on two more writers. But you wouldn't have it. "It will ruin the integrity of the piece," you said. You want art, Russel, I want success. You want to paint the Sistine Chapel, I want to own it. I gave you an opportunity, Russel.

RUSSEL: An opportunity for what? To have my work sold to the highest bidder? Then butchered by someone who has no vision?

BARNABY FRANKLIN: It happened anyway, and you have nothing to show for it. I want success, Russel, and I will do anything to get it.

RUSSEL: Does that include screwing your friend over?

BARNABY FRANKLIN: You would be surprised how many new friends you can buy with a little bit of money. I must say though, Russel, those first couple of scenes that you wrote were brilliant.

RUSSEL: Why didn't you steal those too?

BARNABY FRANKLIN: I tried, but it wouldn't work. I wasn't you. I am a good writer, Russel, but you, you are a great writer. The three of us together couldn't come close to what you had written by yourself. It's funny. You're jealous of me for material reasons. I am jealous of you because of your talent. If you wanted, you could have everything that I have plus more. But I could never have what you have. You want art, Russel, but you know deep down in your heart there is no art without money.

(BARNABY FRANKLIN does a big musical number. The people in the store lend their voices as he performs. It reaches its climax with him climbing a small bunch of videotapes that lead up to the counter. He finishes and exits.)

JERRY: Hey! He didn't pay for that.

RUSSEL: *(Noticing the bruise on his face.)* What happened to you?

JERRY: *(Upset.)* What happened to me? You want to know what happened to me? *You* happened to me. I tried to be more like you, so I sent some guy who wanted to use the bathroom to the wrong aisle.

RUSSEL: That's bad. You never screw with someone who has to use the bathroom.

JERRY: I know that now. I can't believe I tried to be like you. Look at you. You're always late, you never dress properly, and when you do get here you spend the whole time walking through the aisles, giving people advice. Well, I have some advice for you, Russel. You better shape up because the ship of life is sailing without you.

RUSSEL: Shut up! Would you listen to yourself? You sound like a fucking fortune cookie. We work in a video store, Jerry. A video store! Of course I don't take it seriously. It's not what I want to do.

JERRY: So what are you doing here?

RUSSEL: Wasting time? *(Pause.)* I want to write movies so badly that I tricked myself into believing that working in a video store would help me get there. I feel like that kid in math class who thinks he understands the problem but when he is called upon to solve it, he can't because he doesn't understand. Maybe Barnaby's right. To hell with everyone else. Let's face it. After the smoke clears, who is going to be standing all alone? Me. *(He starts to leave.)*

JERRY: Where are you going?

RUSSEL: I don't know.

(RUSSEL exits as lights fade out. Lights come up on SIMON. BETH enters and kicks him.)

29

Lights black and come up on JAMIELEE. RUSSEL enters.

JAMIELEE: What's up, Russel?

RUSSEL: Jamielee? What are you doing in this aisle?

JAMIELEE: What, Russel? You think we just sit in the horror section all day and smoke pot? We move to other aisles. This one is my favorite. Eighties teen. John Hughes. He's like a god, Russel. *(She grabs a videotape.)* Look at this, Russel. *The Breakfast Club*. This is a work of art.

(RUSSEL begins to cry.)

JAMIELEE: *(Surprised.)* Russel? Are you crying?

RUSSEL: No.

JAMIELEE: Yes you are. Please stop.

RUSSEL: It's just that my life right now seems so screwed up.

JAMIELEE: Fine. You're screwed up. Please stop crying.

RUSSEL: It's just that I thought that I would be doing something different with my life at this point…

JAMIELEE: Russel? Please stop crying. You're freaking me out. Watching you cry is like watching Superman cry. Russel. You are like our superhero. We look up to you. We aspire to be like you.

RUSSEL: You want to work in a video store?

JAMIELEE: Sure. Not forever. That's why you are our hero. Because you do work in a video store, and you won't work here forever. You are going to move on to bigger and better things. That's why we like to talk to you. That's why we listen to you. You inspire us. That's why watching you cry brings me down. But I am young. In time I will learn how to deal with situations like this. Take care, Russel. *(Exits.)*

30

Lights fade out. A red light fades up to reveal SCOTT standing upstage center.

SCOTT: I have this dream that I am home alone with John Carpenter's *The Thing*. I place it inside my VCR and start to watch it. All of a sudden, the VCR turns into this giant mouth and it starts to chew up the tape. It's Chris's mouth. He then starts to spew videotape all over me like the pea soup scene in *The Exorcist*. When it's all over, I am completely covered from head to toe with videotape. I then start to be absorbed by the tape. It absorbs me until there is no more me to be absorbed. Tonight is my night. I will have my moment.

(CHRIS's voice is heard in the dark.)

CHRIS: Scott? Scott?

SCOTT: It is time…

(A chopper is heard in the distance. Strobe lights start to flash. SCOTT starts mock walking. As he does, the video shelves are moved on stage and give the illusion that SCOTT is walking through the video store. It reaches a climax when the front counter is moved into position and SCOTT heads for it. CHRIS intercepts SCOTT and knocks him into a video shelf, causing all the tapes to fall to the ground. There is a blackout, and fog is shot onto the stage. When the lights come back up, we see the whole video store destroyed. RUSSEL emerges from the wreckage, followed by BETH.)

RUSSEL: *(To BETH.)* Did you find what you were looking for?

BETH: Yes. *(Holds up a tape.)* How about you?

RUSSEL: I sure did.

(They exit separately. Music starts to play as the other cast members crawl from the wreckage. SHELLY emerges.)

SHELLY: Oh no, not again! *(She runs off.)*

(The end.)

THE LAST CARBURETOR

Leon Chase

LEON CHASE was born in 1973 in Phoenix but, since he only lived there a year, doesn't remember it at all. He grew up twenty miles south of Detroit in Riverview, Michigan, which was part of the larger sprawl of industrial suburbs known as "Downriver," notorious for a noxious concentration of steel mills, auto factories, chemical plants, refineries, sewage treatment plants, nuclear power plants, former Nike missile silos, abandoned salt mines, toxic waste dumps, and fishing. The *Last Carburetor* is Chase's first full-length play; he also wrote the book, music, and lyrics for *Temp!*, a musical comedy about office workers. A scene from this musical, which he directed, was produced by San Francisco's Popcorn Anti-Theater in January 2000. He holds a bachelor's degree in written communications from Eastern Michigan University, and his story "Acetylene" won second place in the *San Francisco Bay Guardian*'s 1997 Summer Fiction Contest. Chase lives in Brooklyn, New York, where in his daytime hours he poses as a carpenter to support his writing and music habits. He is a bass player in the New York garage rock band, The Ritchies, and often appears in Brooklyn dive bars as his country-singing alter ego, Uncle Leon. Chase is currently working on a new play which does not feature any motor vehicles. He does not own a car.

The Last Carburetor was first presented by Overlap Productions on November 30, 2001, at the Present Company Theatorium, New York City, with the following cast and credits:

Doug .... Wilbur Edwin Henry
Josh .... Paul Witte
Keith .... Jeremy Schwartz
Ayla .... Susan O'Connor
Karen .... Tara Gibson
Willie .... Rodney R. To

Directed by: Susanna L. Harris
Produced by: Tania I. Kirkman
Lighting Design: David Zeffren
Scenic Design: Charlie Calvert
Sound Design: Howard Harrison
Costume Design: Michelle Phillips
Stage Manager: Jeff Meyers

The Last Carburetor was remounted by Overlap Productions for an encore run on July 1, 2002, at Access Theatre, New York City, with the following cast and credits:

Doug .... Wilbur Edwin Henry
Josh .... Paul Witte
Keith .... Jeremy Schwartz
Ayla .... Susan O'Connor
Karen .... Lethia Nall
Willie .... Timothy Ford Murphy

Directed by: Susanna L. Harris
Produced by: Tania I. Kirkman
Lighting Design: David Zeffren
Scenic Design: Charlie Calvert
Sound Design: Howard Harrison
Costume Design: Michelle Phillips
Stage Manager: Jeff Meyers

Special thanks to Nancy Williams, Susanna L. Harris, Tania I. Kirkman, Alex Haddad, and—most of all—Erin Keating, without whom none of this would have happened.

Dedicated to the memory of Detroit Dragway, 1959–1998.

CHARACTERS

DOUG: 50. Ex-steel worker, former weekend drag racer. White.
KEITH: 31. Doug's oldest son.
JOSH: 28. Keith's younger brother.
AYLA: 21. Doug's daughter.
KAREN: 32. A waitress.
WILLIE: 22. Ayla's boyfriend. Vietnamese American.

SETTING

A rural area of Michigan, south of Detroit.

TIME

Late spring, 2000.

NOTES ON STAGING

The name "Ayla" is pronounced "**ā**-luh."

The word "Hemi" is pronounced "**hem**-ē." The term refers to a specific engine design, named for its unique hemispherical-shaped combustion chambers.

Although *The Last Carburetor* relies heavily on its setting and geographical references, actors should avoid the use of any obvious regional accents or affectations.

The car should never be seen by the audience.

ACT ONE
SCENE 1

Darkness. There is the deafening sound of a V-8 engine idling and revving, as if at the starting line of a drag race. It grows louder, then fades, replaced by the noise of a distant, passing jet plane.

DOUG, JOSH, KEITH, and AYLA are in various spots across downstage. A single light comes up on each of them as they speak.

DOUG: She wasn't mad, exactly. My wife. I guess it made about as much sense as anything I did in those days. The day I brought it home, she just came outside and walked around it. Put her hands on the hood. Asked me, "Why?" Hell, I didn't know. Because I could. Because I was crazy. Because the U.S. Army had just seen fit to put a cash value on certain, uh, *services* performed by me above Southeast Asia. Because I was twenty-one with a wife I hadn't seen in two years, a fresh hole in my side, and a son I'd never met. Because it was 1970 and the strips were still happening and gas was still cheap and for four thousand and thirty-five dollars cash you could walk into a car dealer and roll out in a fully loaded, race-ready street machine. The 1970 Plymouth Hemi Barracuda…

JOSH: *(Overlapping.)* The 1970 Plymouth Hemi Barracuda, one of the most perfect automobiles ever created. Plymouth Hemi V-8 engine. Four hundred and twenty-six cubic inches of unapologetic American muscle. Dual Carter five-fifty quad carbs with a Shaker cold-air induction, a Hurst pistol-grip four-speed and a Dana four-ten rear end. Four hundred twenty-five horsepower. In theory. It's been twenty-two years since it actually ran.

KEITH: I remember a backseat smell... A big red toolbox... Wrenches and pliers and chrome socket sets lined up in order... biggest to smallest... That smell, all the time... WD-40... Gasoline... Pot smoke... Mom on the bumper in a bikini top... Led Zeppelin... The Stones... Styrofoam coolers... Barbecue potato chips... Dad's hand with grease in the nails... letting me taste beer...

AYLA: Having been conceived much too late to enjoy the Great Golden Age of Dad's Muscle Car personally, I can only imagine the spectacular male love-fest that it surely must have been. Not that I'm actually, you know, enlightened enough or old enough or, let's face it, *man* enough to really understand. To hear Dad tell it, you'd think Jesus Christ himself used to show up at the strip every Sunday. Actually, judging from the pictures I've seen, that could totally be true. I guess I just missed out on all the fun. I've sure heard enough about it, though. And I did have the pleasure of witnessing the rusted, smashed leftovers that have occupied a hallowed space in the garage for, oh, my entire life. But we're not supposed to talk about that part, are we...

JOSH: Four hundred and ninety foot-pounds of torque. Compression ratio ten-point-two-five to one. It could do zero to sixty in five-point-eight seconds. They say, straight outta the showroom, no modification, it could take a quarter mile in eleven seconds and no change.

DOUG: Never took it quicker than the low thirteens myself. But then I never was much for the numbers. It was your mother who loved the speed, really, though she'll never admit it. Not now. She loved hanging out at the strip. Her and Keith both. Sundays at Detroit Dragway. It was pretty wild back then. Just different, you know. Big cars. No clean air laws. Nobody'd really heard of an oil crisis yet. We were all racing, or trying to race, or watching somebody else race. I mean, that was just what you did.

KEITH: At the strip there were hot dogs in little foil sleeves... Relish... A stream of laughing men... blue jeans... shaggy hair... sideburns... Thick veiny arms bulging out of T-shirts... reaching into engines... An announcer's voice, far away, with an echo... Like talking inside a garbage can.

JOSH: Weight: three thousand, four hundred pounds. One hundred and eighty-six-point-six inches long. Seventy-four-point-seven inches wide. One hundred and eight from wheel to wheel.

AYLA: I don't know what the hell Josh's story is. I mean he was what, like five years old when Dad crashed it? He always acted like it was his car, always reading the manual, rattling off his damn numbers. I used to catch him in the garage, sitting in the wreckage with his hands on the steering wheel. I think he had this idea that Dad was gonna let him fix it up when he was old enough. Which is a joke, even if Josh wasn't a total retard, which he is. Keith? Who knew what was going on in his head. All I know is he got his ass out of here in a hurry. He's living fat in California now. Rich and far away. You can't ask for anything better than that.

JOSH: The point is, there will never be cars like that again. Not with that kind of power and craftsmanship and simplicity. Hell, *people* don't even build half the stuff now. They got machines building other machines. You ever look under the hood of a new car? It's all plastic. You couldn't soup it up if you wanted to. I mean, what are you gonna do—*program* it to go faster?

KEITH: I always liked the noise... If Mom was around she'd make us cover our ears... Even then you could feel it, in your legs, rumbling up through the bleachers... Sometimes we'd stand right up against the barrier... Holding Josh's hand, like Mom said to, so he wouldn't wander and get run over... It was always summer... Josh's sweaty little fingers... gasoline... the legs of strangers... Cold orange pop in red paper cups.

DOUG: She didn't seem surprised when I wrecked it. Of course she wasn't real thrilled about keeping it around, either. By that time I had more to think about. Money. Kids. You know. You tell yourself you're gonna... One day it's years later. It doesn't matter, really, I guess.

AYLA: All I know is, three more weeks of classes and that's it. Gimme my handshake and my degree and I'm outta here. The first thing I'm gonna do is get far away from Michigan and all these loser people and my whole messed up family. The second thing I'm gonna do is score a cush job with some seriously fat bank, okay. And the third thing, after that—I'm gonna buy myself a sweet ride. I don't mean like horsepower and wrenches and all that white trash shit. I mean something slick. And so pimp, seriously. Like a Lexus or a Jag or like—

(Her cell phone rings. She answers.)

AYLA: Yeah? Hey, wassup, baby? Nothing, yo. Just bitching about my family, you know...

(Blackout.)

SCENE 2

DOUG's house. Late Friday night. At center stage is a fairly large kitchen, the right half of it occupied by a large dining table. The layout is prefab modern, but decorated in a forced "country" look—natural wood, pale blues, assorted baskets, and wooden ducks. There are three entrances. The first, an opening located at the down left edge of the set, leads to an unseen hallway and front door. The second, a solid door at up left center, goes straight to the garage. The third, a windowed door at right, past the table, opens onto a wide deck, which slants out and extends to the down right edge of the stage area. A coffeemaker and dirty dishes sit on the counter near the garage door. There are aluminum lawn chairs and a rickety charcoal grill on the deck.

The stage is in darkness. The sound of a jet passing overhead. Keys rattling. DOUG enters through the garage door and flips the light on. JOSH enters a moment after him.

JOSH: Where'd he go?

DOUG: I thought he was behind you. What, you let him just wander off out there? *(He goes back out the door and yells, out of sight.)* Keith? Keith! Over here. Through the garage. C'mon buddy. You're gonna kill yourself, walking around in the dark like that.

(He reemerges, followed by a very dazed KEITH, who is in filthy khakis and a windbreaker, unshaven, his hair wild. The garage door stays open.)

DOUG: He was standing around out front.

JOSH: In the dark?

KEITH: Lots of stars out there. *(He looks dazedly around the room.)* You got a new kitchen.

DOUG: Yep. New house, too.

KEITH: It's big. Clean. *(He wanders around the kitchen, inspecting random items. Lifts a glass from the counter.)* Did you always have these glasses? *(He looks back out the garage door.)*

DOUG: I don't know. I guess they're fairly—

KEITH: The car's the same. Different garage. Same busted car.

JOSH: He was hoping maybe it would fix itself if he moved it.

DOUG: *(Closing the garage door.)* You want something to eat, Keith? A beer?

JOSH: You didn't offer *me* one.

DOUG: You know where it is.

KEITH: Can I go to the bathroom?

DOUG: Sure. Sure you can. Just down this hall here, on your left.

(KEITH exits out hall doorway.)

JOSH: So nobody knows what happened to him?

DOUG: You heard the same thing I did. Cops got a trespassing call, found him asleep in some farmer's ditch. My address was in his coat pocket.

JOSH: That's it, huh?

DOUG: Nothing wrong with him. Medically, anyway. He didn't call you or anything, did he? Say he might be coming out this way?

JOSH: Nothing. Not in years.

DOUG: Well, he's here now... *(Awkwardly.)* Thanks for your help down there. You know, getting it cleared and all that.

JOSH: Sure.

DOUG: They seem like nice enough guys. For cops.

JOSH: Yeah, they're alright. They owe me a few favors. I do a lot of business down that way, close to the state line.

DOUG: Shit. I never thought I'd see the day when *you* got to come down and spring *his* ass out of jail.

JOSH: Yeah, well...

DOUG: Yeah...

JOSH: I guess I better hit the road.

DOUG: What, you're leaving? Now?

JOSH: I got a long drive back.

DOUG: Tonight? But your brother's here. How long's it been since you seen him? Six, seven years?

JOSH: I haven't been counting.

DOUG: You don't have to go back tonight.

JOSH: What, you want me to stay here?

DOUG: I don't know. I just thought... It's been a long time since we were all together like this. Us guys. It seems like if you haven't seen him in a while the least you could do—

JOSH: Cut the crap, Dad.

DOUG: What? Don't—

JOSH: You know damn well the only reason you called me is because I'm in good with the cops.

DOUG: That's not—

JOSH: Dad. It's cool. It's fine. Glad I could help.

DOUG: We don't even know why he's—

JOSH: I'm sorry. I got to go. *(He pauses, feeling in his pockets.)* Shit…

DOUG: What?

JOSH: I'm out of gas money.

DOUG: You asking *me*?

JOSH: I spent the last of my cash getting out here.

DOUG: The kidnapping business ain't paying you enough?

JOSH: Whatever. I haul my ass out here in the middle of the night—

DOUG: We don't even know what's wrong with him.

JOSH: Nothing's ever wrong with him.

KEITH: *(Returning from hallway.)* Everything's different.

DOUG: Here, you want to sit down, Keith?

KEITH: *(Sitting at the table.)* Different bathroom. Different hallway. I went the wrong way.

DOUG: You want something to eat? You got to be hungry after… whatever you been doing.

JOSH: The wrong way?

KEITH: Yeah. Down the hall. I ended up in the bedroom instead. Different bedroom.

JOSH: He told you—it's a new house.

KEITH: Sure is. Way out in the middle of nowhere.

DOUG: Yeah, beats the hell out of the old place in Detroit, don't it? Clean air. No streetlights. A little close to the airport, but you know… How 'bout a sandwich?

KEITH: Do you have any Popsicles?

DOUG: Popsicles? No, I don't think so.

KEITH: I could sure use a good Popsicle.

(JOSH breaks up laughing. DOUG throws him a look.)

DOUG: How 'bout a sandwich?

KEITH: Different house. Same bed. Where's Mom?

DOUG: *(Digging through refrigerator.)* Let's see what we got… I wasn't exactly expecting—

JOSH: *(To KEITH.)* She's not here?

DOUG: We got ham… and cheese… hot dogs… They're turkey dogs. I don't know if that's—

JOSH: Dad? Where's Mom at?

KEITH: She's not in the bedroom.

JOSH: Dad?

DOUG: I think there's a new thing of mustard in the—

JOSH: Dad!

DOUG: I thought you were leaving.

JOSH: I just wondered where Mom is.

DOUG: How the hell should I know?

JOSH: She *is* your wife. Usually at two in the morning a guy has some idea—

DOUG: Well I don't, alright? Keith, is wheat bread okay?

KEITH: My mouth is hot. I'd like a Popsicle.

JOSH: *(To DOUG.)* What are you talking about?

DOUG: She's gone, that's all.

JOSH: Where'd she go?

DOUG: She doesn't have any gas money for you if that's what you're—

JOSH: I'm serious. What does that mean, she's "gone"? Like on vacation?

DOUG: No, like she left.

JOSH: Like left *you*? Like split up?

DOUG: *(Making a sandwich.)* It looks that way, don't it?

JOSH: I don't know…

DOUG: Well it looks that way.

JOSH: She really left?

DOUG: What'd I just say?

JOSH: Bullshit.

DOUG: That's what *I* said.

JOSH: You're full of it.

DOUG: Fine, don't believe me…

JOSH: You're serious… When did… when…

DOUG: I don't want to get into it, with your brother so… the way he is…

JOSH: Did she say why?

DOUG: I guess she had her reasons.

JOSH: Well did she say anything about *us*?

DOUG: What are you trying to do, mess him up worse? I said I don't want to get into it. You want a beer?

JOSH: Yeah, alright. (*Gets a beer from refrigerator.)*

DOUG: *(Taking sandwich to KEITH.)* Here you go.

(KEITH grabs the sandwich and digs in. DOUG and JOSH move over and sit with him at the table. Awkward silence as they gulp beers and KEITH munches noisily.)

DOUG: That alright?

(KEITH nods.)

DOUG: Good. Good… Damn, Keith. It's been a long time. Hasn't it been a long time, Josh?

JOSH: Yeah.

DOUG: Yeah… (*To KEITH.)* You're, uh, looking good, though. Getting some sun, I imagine… I guess you got some pretty wild stories to tell us. You know, being in San Francisco all these years. Then showing up like… this…

KEITH: Mom left you, huh?

DOUG: No… yeah… We don't really need to get into that right—

KEITH: I don't blame her.

DOUG: No… I don't suppose you do. But that's not… We don't… I mean, I was thinking maybe you could, uh, tell us what you were doing out there in that ditch.

KEITH: In the ditch…

DOUG: You know. Where the cops found you.

KEITH: Sleeping, mostly.

DOUG: Sleeping.

KEITH: Yeah.

DOUG: And what about before that?

KEITH: Sitting.

JOSH: He means how did you end up there, you moron.

DOUG: *(To JOSH.)* You shut up. *(To KEITH.)* What I mean is—

KEITH: Did you guys see it?

DOUG: See what?

KEITH: The ditch where they picked me up.

DOUG: No. The cops told us—

KEITH: It was just road... Nothing but grass and weeds and trash and a little bit of trees. Just grass, mostly. Then there was this one spot, this one piece of land, with a fence around it. A chain link fence. There was nothing inside it. I mean, nothing different from all the miles of nothing all around it, all over the place. Nothing at all.

DOUG: And that's where you slept?

KEITH: I didn't mean to. I just kept looking at that fence and thinking about who could have put it there, like what kind of person would bother to put it up. Then I sat down there in the grass. Than I woke up, and there were the police.

DOUG: Okay. So what were you doing out there in the first place?

KEITH: I told you. I was walking—

JOSH: This is ridiculous.

DOUG: *(To JOSH.)* What'd I tell you?

JOSH: *(To KEITH.)* Last anybody heard you were off across the country making all kinds of money, doing whatever—

DOUG: Has it even occurred to your jarhead brain that maybe something bad has happened to him? Maybe he doesn't want to talk about it just yet.

JOSH: Well aren't you just mister compassion all the sudden!

DOUG: Nobody's making you stick around.

JOSH: What? Leave now? And miss another great fence story?

KEITH: I had a whole bunch of money. I'm not sure what happened to it.

JOSH: What the hell does *that* mean?

DOUG: It doesn't mean anything, you greedy bastard.

KEITH: Where's Ayla?

DOUG: She's at her place up in Ann Arbor. She finishes school this month. She said she e-mailed you about it.

KEITH: That's what I thought. I wasn't sure if I imagined it.

DOUG: I'll give her a call tomorrow, let her know you're here. She'll be happy to see you. Shit, she was still in high school last time you were around.

JOSH: You should see her now. Quite the pompous little bitch.

DOUG: Don't you ever have anything nice to say? *(To KEITH.)* I've got Sunday off. I'll tell her to come down for dinner. That'd be nice, huh, have all of you here together again.

JOSH: Yeah. Great.

DOUG: Why don't you make yourself useful and get some blankets for your brother. I got to get up for work soon.

(Blackout.)

SCENE 3

The exterior deck. Later Friday night. Cricket sounds. KEITH is in a lawn chair. JOSH joins him from the kitchen. Both speak slowly, as if struggling for the words.

JOSH: You're still up.

KEITH: So are you.

(JOSH unfolds another chair and sits down next to him. Not too close.)

JOSH: Nice night, anyway.

KEITH: It's awful loud.

JOSH: Loud? I thought you were the big city boy.

KEITH: City's different. It's louder here. All the bugs. And the airplanes. Not like the old house at all.

JOSH: What are you talking about? That place was way louder.

KEITH: No...

JOSH: We practically grew up in a factory. The overpass and the trains...

KEITH: Trains are different. They make a slow noise. Like animals. It used to put me to sleep.

JOSH: Gave me nightmares.

KEITH: Everything gave you nightmares.

JOSH: Not everything.

KEITH: Most things.

JOSH: Not everything, though.

(Long pause.)

KEITH: Is it better now?

JOSH: What?

KEITH: Do you still get them?

JOSH: Get what?

KEITH: Bad dreams.

JOSH: No.

KEITH: Never?

JOSH: No.

KEITH: It's okay if you do.

JOSH: Well I don't. I mean, I'm not saying that like it's a big deal. I'm just saying like, you know, I really don't...

KEITH: Okay.

JOSH: I mean, okay, maybe sometimes, you know...

KEITH: Yeah.

JOSH: But it's different when you're older. You understand what's real. You can keep it separate.

KEITH: Yeah.

JOSH: I mean, *I* can anyway...

(Long pause. Distant airplane sound. KEITH watches fearfully. Slaps his arm.)

KEITH: There sure are a lot of bugs out here.

JOSH: Keith.

KEITH: Yeah.

JOSH: What are you doing here?

KEITH: Just sitting.

JOSH: Fuck you, man. You know what I'm talking about. The ditch and the cops and all that. What were you doing there?

KEITH: Sitting.

JOSH: If you're in trouble or something, you can tell me. I can maybe help you out.

KEITH: I'm alright.

JOSH: I'm serious. I know a lot of people.

KEITH: You're still a bounty hunter?

JOSH: Skip tracing. It's called skip tracing.

KEITH: What's Dad say?

JOSH: We don't talk about it.

KEITH: Do you like it?

JOSH: Like what?

KEITH: What you do. Bounty hunting.

JOSH: Skip tracing. *(Pause.)* It's alright. I'm on my own. No bullshit. It's not as tough as it sounds, most of the time. A lot of just following people, catching them off guard. You do what you know how to do, you know.

KEITH: Yeah.

(Long pause.)

KEITH: Where do you think Mom went?

JOSH: Who the hell knows.

KEITH: Do you think she'll come back?

JOSH: What are you asking *me* for?

KEITH: Just wondering.

JOSH: He better figure something out. It's her job that's paying for this place.

KEITH: He seems a lot nicer to me than he used to be.

JOSH: I don't think he thought he'd ever see you again.

(Long pause.)

KEITH: PIN numbers.

JOSH: What?

KEITH: PIN. Personal Identification Numbers.

JOSH: I don't…

KEITH: At my company, where I worked, there was a number, a PIN number, to get into the building.

JOSH: Like on an alarm.

KEITH: Yeah. Exactly. You had to type a number in, next to the door. Then, in the elevator, there was this card you had to have to get to the right floor. And then there was another code you had to know to get into our offices, because, you know, there were a bunch of offices on the one floor…

JOSH: Yeah. Sure.

KEITH: Then, once you got inside the office, there was a password to log onto the computer. And another one to log onto the network.

JOSH: What's a network?

KEITH: It's like where a bunch of computers are connected… Not like *really* connected but like linked… like you all share… Do you ever think about all the stuff people use that they can't explain?

JOSH: I can't say I think much about it. You were always the electrical one.

KEITH: Yeah… This one morning I was outside the door to go into work. I was late, too. Laura was mad at me and—

JOSH: Laura? The girl you lived with?

KEITH: Yeah. I was late and thinking about that, I guess, and I was ready to go inside… except, I couldn't remember the code. You know how the more you try to remember something—

JOSH: The harder it gets, yeah.

KEITH: Yeah. I was trying to remember this number to get into the door, but I kept getting it mixed up with all the other numbers. The office code. My network password. My email password. The PIN number for my ATM card. The code for my voicemail. My home phone number. My cell phone number. Social Security. My credit card number. My account number at the bank.

JOSH: That's a lot of numbers.

KEITH: Yeah. They'd never been a problem before. Then, there I was, just standing there, all of it mixed up… so bad it made my head hurt…

JOSH: So how'd you get in?

KEITH: I didn't… I just left.

JOSH: Where'd you go?

KEITH: Here.

JOSH: What, you're saying you left work and just got on a plane and…

KEITH: No. I walked around for a long time, across the city… Have you ever been to San Francisco?

JOSH: Me? No.

KEITH: It really is a beautiful city… I had a burrito… Drank a beer… Threw my laptop in the bay. Took some buses. Got some rides. I met some cool people.

JOSH: You threw out a computer?

KEITH: All of it. Computer, phone, Palm Pilot…

JOSH: That's the stupidest thing I ever heard.

KEITH: …credit cards… bank cards… Discman…

JOSH: You're going back, right?

KEITH: I don't think so.

JOSH: But you got bills to pay. Rent and all that.

KEITH: I guess.

JOSH: What about the girlfriend?

KEITH: I don't know… I'm not sure she really liked me much anyway.

JOSH: What about your job and your bank account and—

KEITH: I don't care about that stuff.

JOSH: You better fucking care! What's wrong with you? You don't just leave money and computers and an apartment because you can't remember how to get into work one day.

KEITH: What do you do, then?

JOSH: I don't know… Jesus, Keith. That's not even like a real problem.

KEITH: Not anymore.

JOSH: Couldn't you just go to therapy or something? You're rich, right?

KEITH: Not anymore.

JOSH: Dad's gonna shit when he hears this one.

KEITH: Dad doesn't care what I do.

JOSH: Do you have any idea how much he talks about you? Do you know how many times I had to sit here and listen to him brag to everybody about his successful genius son?

KEITH: He never said that to me.

JOSH: And with Mom gone? Great timing, Keith. You're gonna break his stupid heart.

KEITH: Maybe. What do you care? You don't even like him.

JOSH: We don't get along so good. That doesn't mean I don't—

KEITH: Well he doesn't like you.

JOSH: What?

KEITH: He's hated you for a long time. You know that.

JOSH: Fuck you.

KEITH: It's not a secret. Ever since you were in the Marines.

JOSH: Alright, Mr. Know-it-all. We're not gonna go there.

KEITH: Alright.

JOSH: Damn, Keith. You really fucked up this time.

(Long pause.)

KEITH: He's still got the car.

JOSH: Can you believe it?

KEITH: I believe it.

JOSH: It's sad. Damn thing's rusting through. I told him, all those years. Fix it up, sell it, something. Christ, let *me* fix it. For years, I've told him that. He won't talk about it.

KEITH: The engine's probably still okay.

JOSH: That's what I tell him. I mean, he crashed it, but he didn't kill it. Front-end damage, mostly.

KEITH: But it's not trashed.

JOSH: No. But it will be, he lets it sit like that. Just wasting away. That thing's a classic.

KEITH: Yeah.

(Long pause.)

JOSH: He *said* that?

KEITH: What?

JOSH: About the Marine Corps.

KEITH: You remember how he was. Even when we were little. Especially then. Always going off on those scary stories about Vietnam. Making us promise not to be in the service.

JOSH: Yeah, I remember.

KEITH: Then you went off to the Persian Gulf.

JOSH: Ah yes...

KEITH: *That* broke his heart. Mom said he used to yell at the TV every night.

JOSH: He was pissed, alright.

KEITH: More sad than pissed. We *did* promise...

JOSH: What the hell does that mean, "promise"? We were little kids.

KEITH: It was still a promise.

JOSH: What the hell was I supposed to do? Bag groceries 'til I'm 40?

KEITH: Did you like it?

JOSH: What?

KEITH: The Marines.

JOSH: I don't think "like" is the word. It was good for me. Stopped me from stealing. Gave me some skills... You could *understand* it, you know? Everything was real simple... black and white. *(Pause.)* "Promises"... Since when does anybody in this family do what they say they're gonna do?

KEITH: Nice night, anyway...

JOSH: Yeah...

(Long pause.)

JOSH: He really said that?

KEITH: What?

JOSH: That he *hated* me?

KEITH: You know how he was then.

JOSH: But he actually *said* that? Like those were his exact words? That he *hated* me?

KEITH: I could be wrong.

JOSH: Yeah. You always were full of shit

(Blackout.)

SCENE 4

The kitchen. Saturday morning. DOUG is on the phone at left, with an orange Home Depot apron nearby. A half-empty pot of coffee is in the coffeemaker near the stove.

DOUG: *(Into phone.)* No, I'm serious… I wouldn't make that up… I'm serious, he's here… Yeah… What do you mean, "why?"

(As he speaks, JOSH enters from the hallway and struts past him, carrying a pump-action 12-gauge shotgun and a gun-cleaning kit. He lays it out on the table and carefully begins breaking it down and cleaning it.)

DOUG: Does he got to have a reason? He wanted to see us, that's all… Yeah… He's in the garage right now… No, she's gone. *(He notices JOSH and the gun.)* What the hell— *(Into phone.)* No, not you, Ayla. Hold on a second. *(To JOSH.)* What the hell do you think you're doing?

JOSH: I'm just cleaning it.

DOUG: Not in my house you're not!

JOSH: What? It's not like it's loaded.

DOUG: I don't care. You do that shit somewhere else! *(Into phone.)* I'm sorry. Your brother's being an asshole… No, Josh… Yeah, I know. So you coming for dinner tomorrow? Uh-huh… Well bring him along… No, I mean it. It'll be fun… Yeah… Alright. See you then. Bye. *(He hangs up. To JOSH.)* You know better than that. Get that shit out of here.

JOSH: I'm only—

DOUG: Get it out of here!

JOSH: Alright, jeez… *(He begins packing the gun up again.)* How's Ayla doing?

DOUG: Eleven o'clock and she's pissed that I woke her up.

JOSH: She coming down tomorrow?

DOUG: Yeah. She's bringing her new boyfriend.

JOSH: Another one?

DOUG: This one sounds serious. They been together a while. Willie. He's from Tennessee.

JOSH: *(In overblown Southern voice.)* Tennessee? Yee haw.

DOUG: Just be nice to them, alright?

JOSH: *(Going to refrigerator.)* Don't you worry, paw. I'll talk real slow for 'em. Damn. You got anything for breakfast besides hot dogs and beer?

DOUG: I thought maybe you and Keith could run up to Foodland's for me today. There's some money on the counter. I left you some extra for gas.

JOSH: At least there's coffee. *(He goes to coffee machine.)*

(KEITH enters from the garage in a slightly oversized, grease-smeared T-shirt and work pants, wiping his hands with a rag.)

JOSH: *(To KEITH.)* What have you been up to?

KEITH: You were right. The front end's trashed, but the motor's not so bad. Pretty gummed up. The front carburetor's shot but I think the other one might be worth saving…

JOSH: *(To DOUG.)* Do you know about this?

(DOUG ignores him.)

KEITH: *(To DOUG.)* Where are you going?

DOUG: Work. I got to be there in half an hour.

KEITH: On a Saturday?

DOUG: It's our busiest day.

KEITH: Making steel?

JOSH: Keith, Dad hasn't worked for a steel mill in fifteen years. You knew that.

DOUG: Yeah, well, we can't all be rich computer wizards. *(Glancing at JOSH.)* Or bums. You girls behave yourselves. *(He exits through the garage door.)*

KEITH: I could have sworn he made steel.

JOSH: Yeah, he did. *Fifteen* years ago. Before the plant closed. Don't you remember the infamous year of government cheese?

KEITH: I remember. It's just the order that gets all mixed up.

JOSH: You wanna tell me what you're doing out there?

KEITH: Just messing around.

JOSH: He let you just go out there in the garage and start messing around?

KEITH: Just for fun. I thought later maybe we could tear the heads down. See what the damage is.

JOSH: Oh yeah, just for fun... Do you have any idea how many times in my life I've asked him to let me work on that car? Do you? Do you remember?

KEITH: He always thought you'd screw it up.

JOSH: I know what he thought! "Screw it up." What the hell did he think I was gonna do to it? You can't screw up what's been wrecked!

KEITH: He doesn't seem to mind now.

JOSH: He doesn't mind because it's *you*! You know how I was about that car. I used to beg him! I used to check out mechanic manuals at the library. I had a subscription to *Hot Rod* magazine!

KEITH: I remember that. You were gonna save up and build your own, piece by piece, just to piss him off.

JOSH: All he had to do was just once say it was okay.

KEITH: It's just a car.

JOSH: It is not just a car! You know goddamn well that is not just a car! That is a 1970 Hemi fucking Barracuda. Do you know how many of those things were made? Do you?

KEITH: I never thought about it.

JOSH: Of course *you* didn't! Six hundred and fifty-two, Keith. Ever. In the entire whole complete history of the whole world, ever. And no amount of work or money or anything is going to make there ever be any more than that. There are people out there that would pay him a lot of money right now just for the privilege of towing that mess out of here.

KEITH: Really? How much?

JOSH: That's not the point! You can't get anything like that new! Not with that kind of engine, that much power that you can just, you know, put your hands in and mess around with.

KEITH: Why don't you just get your own?

JOSH: What?

KEITH: Why don't you just buy your own car? Something you can mess with?

JOSH: You really have been gone a while.

KEITH: What?

JOSH: This may come as a bit of a shock to you, but not everybody in the world has spent the last seven years getting rich off… whatever. Do you remember how it was around here, Keith? I mean, before this place and Mom's job and all that, when it was the five of us crammed in that shitty little house?

KEITH: I ate the same cheese you did.

JOSH: Yeah, you sure did.

KEITH: So?

JOSH: So I'm just saying that, for some of us, not a whole lot has changed. Some of us don't have some fancy life to walk away from. Some of us never had a nice cushy little scholarship to cover our ass…

KEITH: Some of us weren't out ripping off stereos in high school.

JOSH: You remember quite a bit when you want to. *(He takes money from counter.)* You want anything from the store?

KEITH: *(Going into hallway.)* Is that where you're going?

JOSH: Dad wants me to. Ayla's coming down with her white trash boyfriend tomorrow.

KEITH: *(From hallway.)* You could just leave with the money.

JOSH: No. He'd expect that. I figure I'll stick around a while and give you all a hard time.

(KEITH reemerges in a fresh T-shirt, with a jacket in his hand.)

JOSH: You going somewhere?

KEITH: Just out.

JOSH: Out where?

KEITH: Just taking a walk.

JOSH: Where you gonna walk to around here?

KEITH: Wherever.

JOSH: You gonna go sit in a ditch again?

KEITH: Maybe.

JOSH: Really, where you going?

KEITH: I don't know.

JOSH: You need a ride somewhere?

KEITH: *(Exiting through garage door.)* I'm fine. Your… your van scares me. I don't like riding with the gun.

JOSH: You're as bad as he is, you know that?

(Blackout.)

SCENE 5

Darkness. A table at extreme down left, with sugar and condiments, in a truck stop. KAREN, in a waitress uniform with a name tag, stands beside it. She is not wearing a wedding ring. DOUG is at extreme down center, in his Home Depot apron, with a broom. AYLA is standing down left. WILLIE is near her. Both are in trendy hip-hop clothes. As in Scene 1, the segments occur oblivious to each other, with separate lights coming up and down accordingly.

DOUG: *(Sweeping the floor.)* It's the grain that makes it. Not a lot of people know that, that steel has a grain. Like wood. Well, not exactly like wood. But it's a grain, you can see it. In a crankshaft, say. That's just an example. Crankshaft. Camshaft. Ball bearing. Anything solid like that. The way they pour it, if the mix is right, that makes it stronger. Real smooth grain. Most people don't think about it that way. Most people don't know shit. It's harder than you think. If the mix is wrong. Grain gets crossed. Weak. All that pressure. Crankshaft. Rail. Bridge. It don't matter. Grain's wrong, whole damn thing can just snap in half one day. Fucking useless.

(KAREN rushes past table with a handful of plates. KEITH enters from left.)

KEITH: Hey.

KAREN: Hold on. I'll be with you in—Holy shit! Keith?

KEITH: How you doing, Karen?

KAREN: What are you doing here?

KEITH: I came to see you. I had to hitch a ride. I didn't know if you'd still be here.

KAREN: Yeah. I'm still here.

KEITH: Yeah?

KAREN: Yeah… How are you?

KEITH: I'm good.

KAREN: That's good… This is so weird.

KEITH: Yeah…

KAREN: Yeah…

(Uncomfortable pause. He steps closer. He reaches up slightly. Awkwardly, then warmly, they embrace.)

(AYLA stands facing the audience, applying makeup, as if in a mirror. WILLIE is getting dressed.)

AYLA: You don't have to go if you don't want to.

WILLIE: Why wouldn't I want to?

AYLA: I'm just saying. It's not that big a deal.

WILLIE: You don't want me to go?

AYLA: Did I say that?

WILLIE: Have you told them anything yet?

AYLA: I'm just saying. If you're not into it, that's cool.

WILLIE: You just… You say it like…

AYLA: I'm not saying it like anything. I'm just saying.

WILLIE: Like you're embarrassed for them to meet me.

AYLA: Oh my god, not even! They're the ones I should be embarrassed about.

WILLIE: What, you met my parents when they were up here.

AYLA: Your parents are so nice. It's not even the same.

WILLIE: Your family's not nice?

AYLA: I don't know. They're just… trashy.

WILLIE: What? Like they live in a trailer?

AYLA: Oh god. Come on.

WILLIE: I got to meet them sometime.

AYLA: I guess.

WILLIE: So what have you told them?

AYLA: I mean, you're not "meeting" them, you know? I mean, it's not like I'm "bringing you home to meet them."

WILLIE: You haven't told them anything, have you?

AYLA: I mean, I am, but not like that.

WILLIE: About moving out? Chicago? Us living together?

AYLA: Jesus Christ! I'm gonna tell them! I'll tell them tomorrow, okay! Jesus Christ!

(KAREN and KEITH, still standing.)

KAREN: So how's California?

KEITH: Boring.

KAREN: Sure it is.

KEITH: It's like one big, slow movie with great scenery and awful characters.

KAREN: How long are you here?

KEITH: I don't know… How's school?

KAREN: Can't say I think much about it much anymore.

KEITH: Never?

KAREN: Not since I quit.

KEITH: So you did quit. You said you might. In the last letter.

KAREN: Yup.

KEITH: You think you'll ever go back?

KAREN: Wasn't there some kind of girlfriend? Someone you were living with?

KEITH: Yeah. Yeah.

KAREN: How's that?

KEITH: It's alright.

KAREN: Is she here with you?

KEITH: No.

KAREN: So what are you gonna do?

KEITH: I don't know. Eat lunch.

KAREN: I got a break coming. You want something?

DOUG: *(Still sweeping.)* It's not the power. Yeah, power's important. Horsepower. Air flow. It's all got to be there. Got to run right. Got to be timed right. All those parts, moving at the same time. Got to have the right gears. Know how to shift. That's what it is. Know how to drive. The human element, that's what wins the races. Clutch foot. Gas foot. Shifter. You got to know how to feel your way through it. All of it. You can't say what it is. You just got to know. You don't know that, you ain't shit. All the power in the world can't help you. Just spinning your goddamn wheels. *(He looks up quickly.)* What's that? Oh. Door frames, yeah. Aisle seven.

(KAREN and KEITH, seated at the table with a half-eaten plate of french fries between them.)

KAREN: So what is she like?

KEITH: She has a lot of black clothes. Expensive.

KAREN: But what is *she* like?

KEITH: Smart. Practical.

KAREN: You don't sound… satisfied.

KEITH: It's weird. Here's this person who used to be really interesting and… passionate. Then one day you realize you're in the middle of an argument about, like, venetian blinds or where to eat that night. Suddenly there's all this tension, this big unspoken weight over everything. And you think "I'm thirty-one years old. Why am I wasting my brain on this?"

KAREN: Wasting your brain…

KEITH: She's not a bad person. Just… different. She has that *way* about her. Not snotty, you know, but she had that… that way of walking into a room like she never doubted she should be there. That it should all be hers. Like…

KAREN: Like rich people.

KEITH: Yeah. *You* know.

(AYLA steps away from WILLIE, who remains unmoving behind her.)

AYLA: What I'd really like is a loft. Not huge, you know, but really classy and well laid out. And in a really good location, too, like you could just step outside and have really cool places nearby. Really cool things going on all the time. And cool furniture, you know, like arty shit. But not too arty, where it's just uncomfortable and annoying? Just really subtle and understated. That's how I want it all to be. Very subtle, and classy, and very comfortable, and spacious. And some really nice things. I mean, I'm not like one of those shallow people who needs a lot of stuff. But the stuff I do have is gonna be really fucking cool.

(KAREN and KEITH, still seated.)

KAREN: I just got sick of it. Professors. Departments. The egos. God, the egos. You'd think with grad school it would get better, right?

KEITH: Yeah, but the science part of it...

KAREN: *(Mockingly self-important.)* Science! Oh yes! The thrill of discovery! Jesus...

KEITH: You loved that stuff. I remember.

KAREN: What does that mean, I "loved" it? I understood it. I could crunch the numbers okay. Kiss the right ass when absolutely necessary.

KEITH: No. You used to be so... Don't you remember the airport? The summer we... you know...

KAREN: Yeah.

KEITH: Yeah. We used to park in that spot out by the runways. And we'd sit on the hood of the car—

KAREN: —and watch the planes. Yeah, I remember.

KEITH: Yeah... yeah. You would get so... passionate.

KAREN: That wasn't the science, Keith.

KEITH: No, it was. I mean, there was the other stuff too. But... don't you remember, you used to just go off about time-space and uncertainty principles and inflation theory...

KAREN: Jesus, you remember all that?

KEITH: Oh yeah, all of it... Let me see if I can get it right. You said the whole universe is expanding—

KAREN: Well *I* didn't say it.

KEITH: You know what I mean... Everything's expanding, flying out in every direction. And there's a formula for it. And at some point, the universe will hit this perfect size. This one weird, specific number...

KAREN: Critical density.

KEITH: Yeah... Critical density. And at that point, the universe will stop, and go the other way...

KAREN: Contract.

KEITH: Contract, yeah... And slowly, everything that had drifted apart will start getting closer again—

KAREN: I don't buy that theory anymore.

KEITH: Really? I loved that story. I loved all of them. Remember, you used to joke about those acceleration problems? "A car is traveling at—"

KAREN: That was a long time ago.

KEITH: I used to get so jealous of you.

KAREN: *You?* Jealous of *me*?

KEITH: Oh god yeah. I was good with computers. I never loved them. Guys like me took the easy route. Jobs. Money. The stuff I thought I was supposed to want.

KAREN: The stuff your dad wanted.

KEITH: Yeah... But you, you were the real thing. You went for the pure science of it. No compromise.

KAREN: Yeah right.

KEITH: I don't mean the people. I mean the science. The big picture.

KAREN: *(Snickering.)* You wanna talk about the big picture? One night, a couple winters ago. It was snowing. I was out getting coffee with a bunch of people from my department. Serious quantum mechanics geeks. And let's be honest, Keith, none of these people grew up on *our* side of town. You know what I mean. Expensive lattes and shit. So we're there, and we're all sitting by the window, going off about what we thought about this presentation on theoretical dark matter. Everybody's going out of their way to be real important, you know, all talking over each other. And I look outside, and right in front of us, on the other side of the big window, is this woman. Could be thirty, could be sixty. Obviously homeless. She's got on this pink coat, all dirty, and some kind of scarf on her head. Bags by her feet. She's just standing there in the snow. And she's screaming. I don't mean just like begging. I mean she's screaming, out loud. I realize that the people with me, inside, notice her too, but they're trying hard not to look. They're going along with this conversation, you know, staying really involved in this argument. Because nobody knows how to deal. There's no formula for how to deal with a nontheoretical, live screaming human. I tried to look away. I mean, I really tried to focus and make myself forget about it. But all I could think was how stupid we sounded. After that, I just couldn't buy it anymore. I can't explain it. I just couldn't… I couldn't believe in it.

KEITH: And she's better off now?

KAREN: What?

KEITH: You quitting school, waiting tables here… that's helping homeless people?

KAREN: I'm not an idiot, Keith.

KEITH: I *know* that. That's what I'm trying to—

KAREN: I just… when I'm here, I don't feel like I'm faking something. Like I'm trying to be…

KEITH: —one of *them*?

KAREN: I like it here. I talk to real people all day. It's nice.

KEITH: You're happy with that?

KAREN: I don't have anything to prove.

KEITH: But you had so much going for—

KAREN: Look at you. Everything's an argument. Even now.

KEITH: I just…

KAREN: What?

KEITH: I never forgot about any of this… About you.

KAREN: No. *(Calmly.)* You just left.

(AYLA, still separate.)

AYLA: When I was six years old Keith fixed my Speak 'n' Spell. I remember all the parts, laid out on the basement card table in neat little lines. He tried to explain it to me—six years old, right—and I pretended to understand just so he'd keep talking. It was all just wires and plastic to me. Still is. But when Keith opened it up and looked at it, he saw currents and paths. Possibilities.

The way I see it, okay, is like this. I'm gonna make it big because I want to, you know, because I try at it. Because I'm worth more than all this, and I swore to myself, ever since I was little, that I was never going to have to worry about money, ever. So I'll work hard, right, and it'll happen for me.

Keith, though, he had no choice. He's always been big. He sees how things fit together, the way everything works, at once. He can't help but see it that way. It's why he's brilliant, and it's why he got out and got rich, and it's why he will always, without trying, totally kick ass at everything he does.

(KAREN and KEITH, still seated.)

KEITH: I still have all your letters.

KAREN: Oh yeah? That seems like so long ago.

KEITH: Yeah. It isn't, really.

KAREN: Maybe not. Things were different then.

KEITH: Were they?

KAREN: For me. A lot has happened. I... I got married.

KEITH: Really?

KAREN: Really.

KEITH: I didn't know that.

KAREN: I didn't tell you.

KEITH: Well. Congratulations.

KAREN: Thanks.

KEITH: Anybody I'd know?

KAREN: No.

KEITH: But he's a nice guy, right? I mean, you're happy?

KAREN: Yeah. He's a good guy. Sweet. Reliable.

KEITH: That's good.

KAREN: Yeah. Yeah, it is. *(Pause.)* And look at you, you're not doing so shabby. You got your big job and your fancy girlfriend...

KEITH: Yeah...

KAREN: I mean, it's good, right?

KEITH: Oh yeah, definitely. It's just... Married. Wow.

KAREN: Yeah.

(AYLA and WILLIE, back in their original position.)

WILLIE: So you do want me to go with you?

AYLA: Oh my god! Have you ever, like, just made a fucking decision on your own, ever in your life?

WILLIE: I just... It's a pretty big deal.

AYLA: It is *not* a big fucking deal, alright?

WILLIE: Moving, Chicago... us...

AYLA: We're just going to hang out there.

WILLIE: I talked to my dad yesterday.

AYLA: Oh yeah?

WILLIE: He said he changed his mind. He's not going to help us out with any of it.

AYLA: *(Suddenly involved.)* Are you serious?

WILLIE: No. I just wanted to see what you'd say.

AYLA: Oh my god, you are such an ass!

WILLIE: So you want me to go or not?

AYLA: Whatever. You can figure it out.

WILLIE: He did say he's gonna help me buy those new turntables.

AYLA: Great.

WILLIE: Is this how it's going to be?

AYLA: What?

WILLIE: When we live together.

AYLA: Are you ready yet?

(DOUG is still sweeping, more frantically.)

DOUG: You keep your eyes on it. You watch the tach. Listen to the engine. You listen and you shift and you just drive… Maybe you're on the starting line of a drag strip. Maybe you're on a road somewhere. Maybe you been drinking. Maybe. Could be you're in a helicopter over the jungle. Could be you're on a road somewhere. You keep your eyes on things. Maybe you got kids. Maybe one's gone, far away. Took off before you could figure it out. Before you could realize that you never said one real, honest sentence to each other that wasn't mean. Maybe you crash the car. Maybe you figure out one day that your wife's gone. You think you remember her but she keeps getting mixed up with all the other things. The jobs. The cars. A medic screaming in your ear, his head low on the ground beside you. You watch and you listen. Try and figure out where things went to. Figure out one day your wife's gone. Keep driving. Figure out your wife's gone.

(KAREN is rushing back and forth. KEITH is gone. JOSH enters and sits at the cleared table.)

KAREN: Hi.

JOSH: How you doing?

KAREN: Alright. You need a menu?

JOSH: No, thanks, uh… *(He looks at her name tag.)* …Karen. Just coffee. *(He looks around.)* Busy day, huh?

KAREN: Not so bad.

JOSH: That your boyfriend?

KAREN: Who?

JOSH: That guy. That just left. That your boyfriend?

KAREN: Oh. No. Just somebody I used to know.

(Blackout. End of Act One.)

ACT TWO
SCENE 1

The kitchen. Late Sunday morning. DOUG, in a T-shirt and white briefs, stands at the counter, rooting through a soggy paper grocery bag. His wallet and keys sit nearby. JOSH enters from hallway.

JOSH: 'Morning.

DOUG: I guess you think this is pretty damn funny.

JOSH: What's that?

DOUG: *(Mockingly.)* What's that? *(He lifts out a wet, sticky Popsicle box.)* I ask for groceries, you bring back three boxes of melted Popsicles.

JOSH: Wasn't me. Must have been Wondergeek.

DOUG: Where's the stuff you bought?

JOSH: I forgot. Sorry.

DOUG: You forgot? You could fuck up a wet dream, you know that?

JOSH: I was busy.

DOUG: What, did the militia call you out?

(There is a sudden, harsh noise from behind the garage door—the sound of a starter cranking but never quite turning over. JOSH rushes to the garage door and opens it.)

JOSH: *(Yelling out the door.)* What the hell are you doing out there?

KEITH: *(Offstage.)* Messing around.

JOSH: Get in here!

(Starter noise again.)

DOUG: Is that the 'Cuda?

JOSH: Stop that!

DOUG: It sure sounds like it…

JOSH: Stop it!

(Starter sound stops.)

JOSH: Get in here!

DOUG: A little rough, but definitely—

(KEITH enters from the garage in greasy clothes.)

KEITH: I put a new battery in. The starter's fine. It's just the motor that—

JOSH: *(To DOUG.)* Are you hearing this?

DOUG: *(To KEITH, ignoring JOSH.)* Ayla's on her way here and your brother fucked up on the groceries. You mind taking the truck up to Foodland's real quick?

KEITH: I got us some Popsicles, but they all melted on the walk home.

DOUG: Yeah, I saw that. I was thinking maybe we could diversify a bit. Potato salad, hamburger meat... I think Ayla's a vegetarian again, so you better get some chicken too. *(To JOSH.)* I don't suppose you have my money from yesterday.

JOSH: I must have misplaced it.

DOUG: Imagine that. *(To KEITH.)* I guess you'll need some money, then... *(He reaches for his pocket, remembers he's not wearing pants, then gets his wallet from the counter. He hands KEITH money and his keys.)* Get some more beer, too.

KEITH: Alright.

(KEITH exits back out garage door. Distant sound of truck starting and leaving. This sound should be distinctly different from that of the Barracuda.)

JOSH: *(Mockingly high-pitched.)* Alright. Sure, paw. Anything you say.

DOUG: You got something you wanna say?

JOSH: Oh no. No. I'll just leave you and Opie here to play house with the ol' hot rod...

DOUG: I don't see why you have to be so damn negative all the time.

JOSH: Where'd he get a battery?

DOUG: *(Cheerfully.)* I don't know, but he better be careful. If he keeps it up, he's gonna have that damn thing running.

JOSH: Him? Oh, sure. As long as he doesn't run out of Popsicles.

(Sound of an approaching car, with techno bass booming.)

DOUG: That's not him again, is it?

JOSH: *(Listening.)* No, it's something flashy. A Mustang. *(He gets out and stares downstage, as if looking out a window, and grins.)*

DOUG: Shit. It's probably them already. I got to get some pants on.

JOSH: I thought those good ol' boys only drove Dodges.

DOUG: Let them in, alright?

JOSH: You bet, paw. Real Southern hospitality.

DOUG: Just try not to be an asshole. *(He pushes past JOSH and down the hallway.)*

(There is the sound of a doorbell.)

JOSH: *(Yelling down hall.)* Come on in! It's open!

DOUG: *(From hallway.) I* could have done *that*!

(AYLA and WILLIE enter from hallway. The fact that WILLIE is Asian visibly throws JOSH.)

AYLA: *(Keeping her distance.)* Hello, Josh.

JOSH: Hey, Ayla.

AYLA: This is Willie. Willie, this is my brother Josh.

WILLIE: How you doing, man.

JOSH: *(Making a big show of shaking his hand strongly.)* Hi there, Willie. How the hell are you?

AYLA: Where's Dad?

JOSH: He decided to change outfits at the last minute.

AYLA: How about my boy Keith?

JOSH: Dad sent him out to save the world.

AYLA: Oooh. Did I walk in on a little sibling rivalry?

JOSH: "Willie," huh? Is that short for something?

WILLIE: Yeah. William.

AYLA: Feel free to ignore him, Will. He's kind of a dick.

JOSH: Fuck you.

DOUG: *(Entering from hall, with his pants undone.)* Watch your language. *(To AYLA.)* And you—no analyzing your brother.

(He hugs her, then turns to WILLIE.)

DOUG: This must be Willie. How you doing?

(He shakes WILLIE's hand, politely.)

DOUG: You kids want a beer? It's all we got right now. I sent Keith out for groceries. You like hamburgers, Willie?

AYLA: *(Noticing DOUG's open fly.)* Dad!

DOUG: What? I can't ask what he likes to eat?

WILLIE: I like hamburgers.

AYLA: No you don't!

WILLIE: Sure I do. I just don't eat them much. But I don't mind...

DOUG: Why don't we sit outside. You too, Josh. I'll get the grill going. *(To AYLA.)* Don't worry, honey, Keith's picking up some chicken for you.

(They all follow DOUG out the door to the deck.)

AYLA: Dad, chicken is meat.

DOUG: It wasn't last time you ate with us.

AYLA: That was like a year ago.

JOSH: Six months.

AYLA: Shut up.

DOUG: *(To both of them.)* Hey! *(He wheels out the grill and goes about the process of cleaning the grate, dumping charcoal in, etc.)*

JOSH: *(Approaching WILLIE.)* That's a pretty fancy car you got out there, Willie. Is it new?

WILLIE: Yeah. It was my graduation present.

JOSH: Really? That's a hell of a present. That a four-point-six?

WILLIE: What?

JOSH: The engine. Four-point-six liter? Modular overhead cam?

WILLIE: Yeah, I guess.

JOSH: What's that mean? You "guess." It is or it isn't, right?

WILLIE: I don't know much about cars, really... I mean, that's what you pay a mechanic for, right?

(Awkward silence.)

AYLA: *(To DOUG.)* Willie's graduating this year too.

DOUG: Is that right? What's your degree in, Willie?

WILLIE: Business Information Systems.

DOUG: What's that, like computers?

WILLIE: Yeah, kind of. It's pretty boring stuff, actually.

AYLA: But it pays. Big time.

WILLIE: I figure it'll pay the bills, you know. You work a couple years, stash some money away. Then chill.

JOSH: Oh sure. Just like that.

DOUG: *(To JOSH.)* You just can't stand to see somebody do something with his life, can you?

JOSH: Why does everybody in this family insist that I don't have a job? I happen to do incredibly important and dangerous work.

AYLA: Josh is a professional redneck.

(DOUG laughs and goes inside.)

JOSH: You ever shoot a gun, Willie?

WILLIE: No…

JOSH: Really? Not even down in Tennessee?

WILLIE: There wasn't much call for it in Chattanooga.

JOSH: Yeah. I guess Chattanooga's more like a city, huh…

WILLIE: Yeah. With sidewalks and buildings and indoor plumbing…

JOSH: Well you ought to try shooting sometime. It really is an art.

AYLA: It's not *that* hard.

JOSH: What do *you* know?

AYLA: I shot a gun before. With you.

(WILLIE laughs.)

JOSH: That was a shotgun. It's not the same.

WILLIE: *You* shot a gun?

JOSH: It was just a shotgun.

AYLA: *(To WILLIE.)* Are you making fun of me?

WILLIE: No. It's just funny.

AYLA: It's not that funny.

WILLIE: Alright. Don't trip, yo.

(DOUG returns with a can of charcoal starter.)

DOUG: *(Doing a bad imitation of Moe from the Three Stooges.)* Alright, out of my way, ya ignoramuses…

WILLIE: Igno—what?

JOSH: Ignoramus. Didn't you ever see the Three Stooges?

WILLIE: Yeah! I used to love those guys!

AYLA: You did not!

WILLIE: Every Sunday morning, when I was a kid…

DOUG: You remember, Josh, you used to try and poke your brother in the eyes…

AYLA: Excuse me, we are *not* having a Three Stooges conversation.

WILLIE: What? You didn't like them?

JOSH: Keith liked Larry.

WILLIE: Who's Keith?

AYLA: I told you. My other brother. The smart one.

JOSH: Ha!

WILLIE: The one who lives in California?

JOSH: *Lived.* Past tense.

AYLA: *(To JOSH.)* What? Keith's moving?

JOSH: *(To DOUG.)* You didn't tell her anything, did you?

DOUG: Keith always wanted Larry to win.

AYLA: *(To JOSH.)* Tell me what?

JOSH: Our brilliant eldest brother decided to flip out.

DOUG: *(To JOSH.)* Now I wouldn't say *that...*

JOSH: *(To DOUG.)* Of course *you* wouldn't.

AYLA: What are you talking about?

JOSH: He showed up here all freaked out. He's been hitchhiking across the country. Pissed his life away. No job. No girlfriend. No money.

AYLA: I don't believe it. Dad, what's he talking about?

DOUG: Larry never won.

JOSH: You'll see.

AYLA: You're full of shit. You're just jealous or something.

JOSH: You should see him, he's like a goddamn mental patient.

AYLA: Yeah right.

DOUG: Curly won, sometimes. But never Larry.

WILLIE: I liked Shemp.

(Uncomfortable silence.)

DOUG: Nobody likes Shemp.

WILLIE: Well I did.

DOUG: Nobody likes Shemp.

JOSH: How can you like Shemp?

AYLA: Like it matters, okay?

WILLIE: What? He was funny...

JOSH: Shemp?

DOUG: That's alright. He can like whoever he wants. We don't need to talk about it.

(Blackout.)

SCENE 2

The truck stop. Early Sunday afternoon. KAREN is rushing back and forth, her hands full with plates. KEITH enters from down left.

KEITH: Hi.

KAREN: Oh. Hi.

KEITH: How's it going?

KAREN: Well, you know...

KEITH: Busy?

KAREN: Yeah. The Sunday church crowd.

KEITH: I guess you can't really talk right now, huh.

KAREN: No, not really.

KEITH: That's okay.

KAREN: Yeah. It's been crazy all day.

KEITH: Okay.

(KAREN goes out of sight, sets plates down, walks back by KEITH, who remains standing.)

KEITH: Do you work tomorrow?

KAREN: Tomorrow? Yeah. I got a double shift.

KEITH: How about after?

KAREN: After work?

KEITH: I guess you'll be pretty beat by then.

KAREN: Yeah.

KEITH: I probably shouldn't try and call you at home, huh.

KAREN: That might be a little weird.

KEITH: That's okay.

(Awkward pause.)

KEITH: I just want to…

KAREN: What?

KEITH: Nothing. Never mind…

KAREN: I uh… I got to… We're really busy…

KEITH: Sure. Okay.

KAREN: I'm sorry.

(Blackout.)

SCENE 3

The deck. Later Sunday afternoon. Empty beer bottles sit in various spots around the deck. DOUG and AYLA are by the grill. WILLIE is downstage, in a lawn chair beside JOSH. All have beer.

JOSH: *(To WILLIE.)* There we are. Just the two of us alone in the dark in this shithole motel. It's five in the morning, right. This scumbag's snoring away. No clue. I've got my .45 in my hand, just standing over him.

DOUG: *(Fanning the grill with a paper plate.)* I don't know what the hell the problem is. Maybe I got some bad charcoal.

WILLIE: What was the name of it?

AYLA: So, Dad…

DOUG: *(Studying grill.)* Yeah.

JOSH: The name of what?

WILLIE: The motel.

AYLA: Willie graduates this month.

DOUG: So you said…

JOSH: I don't know. It doesn't matter.

AYLA: And I graduate this month.

DOUG: Uh-huh.

JOSH: The important thing is, I got a gun in my hand. And I lean down and put it right up to this guy's temple.

AYLA: Willie wants to go to Chicago. He's going to get a job there.

DOUG: That's great.

JOSH: And I mean, we're talking a real lowlife here. Assault and battery on his ex-wife. Six years of unpaid child support. If I had my way, I'd just as soon put a bullet in his head right there.

AYLA: And I'm going with him.

(WILLIE sets his beer down and looks intently downward.)

JOSH: So I get right in this guy's face and I say—are you listening to me? I go "Good morning, sweetheart." And then I cock that goddamn gun, right next to his ear. Most distinct sound you ever heard in your life.

AYLA: Dad? Did you hear what I said?

JOSH: I tell you what, that fucker's eyes opened so goddamn fast. Scared the piss right out of him. Didn't even put up a fight.

AYLA: Dad?

JOSH: It's not all danger and adventure, though. Lots of hard work. You got to outsmart 'em, that's—

(WILLIE crouches down and lunges suddenly, then stands with his hands cupped and approaches JOSH.)

WILLIE: Check it out.

JOSH: What?

WILLIE: This grasshopper. It's huge.

JOSH: Man, don't come near me with that thing.

(Distant sound of truck approaching and shutting off.)

WILLIE: What, it's just—

JOSH: I'm serious. Get it away from me.

AYLA: Careful, Will. He might try and shoot it.

(KEITH enters the deck from the kitchen door. WILLIE drops the bug.)

AYLA: Keith!

(She rushes over and throws her arms around him.)

KEITH: I got hamburger. And potato salad. And chicken. And beer. And potato chips. It's all in the kitchen. You didn't say potato chips, but I thought, you know…

DOUG: That's fine, Keith. That's great.

KEITH: They're not the ruffled kind.

DOUG: That's fine.

KEITH: *(Going over to WILLIE, slightly away from the others.)* You must be the boyfriend… Do you know how many brands of potato chips there are? In one store?

JOSH: *(To AYLA.)* What did I tell you?

AYLA: He seems alright…

WILLIE: *(To KEITH.)* I never thought about it.

KEITH: Exactly.

JOSH: He's crazy.

AYLA: He's fine.

KEITH: *(To WILLIE.)* If you stop and think about it, you realize how stupid and pointless it all is.

WILLIE: It's just potato chips.

KEITH: That's what *I'm* saying…

AYLA: *(To JOSH.)* There's nothing wrong. You are *so* full of it.

JOSH: Go on, ask *him* then.

DOUG: Leave him alone. He's fine. He's been working on the car, you know.

AYLA: *The* car? I take it back. He is crazy.

WILLIE: *(Overhearing.)* What car?

DOUG: He almost got it started it this morning.

JOSH: He did *not*. He hooked up a battery. That's all he did.

DOUG: *(To JOSH.)* What the hell do you know?

JOSH: Well that's just the million dollar question, isn't it.

AYLA: Oh my god, can we please have just one family gathering that does not revolve around that piece of shit car?

WILLIE: What car?

KEITH: *(To WILLIE.)* A '70 Barracuda. In the garage.

AYLA: Oh no. I am not losing my boyfriend to this conversation.

JOSH: What's the matter, Ayla. Is it too *male* for you?

AYLA: No, just trashy.

JOSH: You hear that, Dad? We're *trashy*.

WILLIE: It's just car talk, right?

AYLA: It's never just car talk.

JOSH: Actually we aren't supposed to talk about it. Or weren't, anyway, until SuperKeith came along.

DOUG: Keith's doing alright in there. I believe if he stays at it, he'll have that thing running.

JOSH: Oh, you believe that, huh?

WILLIE: He should take care of it. That thing's a museum piece.

AYLA: Emphasis on "piece."

DOUG: It's not *that* old.

WILLIE: I'm serious. Another ten years, we won't even be driving cars.

JOSH: Maybe *you* won't.

WILLIE: Not gasoline ones, anyway.

DOUG: Now, I don't know about *that*...

KEITH: He's right.

JOSH: Shut up, Keith.

DOUG: *(To JOSH.) You* shut up.

KEITH: Electricity... Hydrogen cells...

WILLIE: Yeah, no shit, right?

KEITH: The death of internal combustion.

DOUG: *(To KEITH.)* Hey! That's enough of that talk.

AYLA: Can I just remind you that we are discussing a vehicle that has not actually been driven in, uh, *two decades*?

WILLIE: Nobody mentioned that part.

AYLA: They never do.

KEITH: *(To WILLIE.)* Cold fusion... genetic engineering... organic microtechnology...

WILLIE: Uh, you lost me.

KEITH: Computers the size of bacteria... Machines at the molecular level... They're working on it right now. They could burrow under your skin. You could breathe them up your nose and never know it...

AYLA: Keith?

KEITH: Electronic organisms that replicate. The complete codependence of human and machine. A total eradication of all the old rules. Do you understand what I'm saying?

WILLIE: No, not really.

JOSH: Don't mind him, Willie. Ayla says he's fine.

KEITH: *(To WILLIE, urgently.)* What do you go to school for?

WILLIE: Business Information Systems.

KEITH: Do you love business information systems?

WILLIE: Do I... I don't know if *love* is... I like it okay.

KEITH: *(Gravely.)* If you don't love it, it will kill you. Not your body, but deeper. Your brain. Your insides.

WILLIE: I don't think...

KEITH: You tell yourself a story to make it okay. It's just for a little while. It's for the money. The stability. Career. Status. Sex.

AYLA: Jesus, Keith.

WILLIE: I just came for the barbecue...

KEITH: *(Increasingly manic.)* You lie on your back in bed with fancy sheets above you, with the door double-locked, and little gray gadgets all around you, and the right car and the right clothes and the right woman in the bed beside you, and somewhere there's a string of zeros in the bank with your name on it, and still you can't sleep. Because when you try, you see everything that could have been. All the walks you didn't take, every book you didn't read, every nipple you never put your mouth on. You get so you hate to close your eyes, because when you do, you realize that, if you're lucky, there's one good thing out there, there's one thing that could have made you happy and you have gone and made yourself very, very far away from ever being near it again.

DOUG: Oh, that Keith. You never know what's gonna come out of his mouth, do you…

AYLA: Keith, you're just fooling around, right? Come on…

(KEITH is silent and dazed. JOSH laughs.)

AYLA: *(To WILLIE.)* He's not really like this. Not usually.

JOSH: He's fuckin' nuts.

AYLA: He is not. He can't be.

DOUG: No time at all, he'll have things fixed up and running.

JOSH: Yeah, tell him, Keith. Tell us all how you're gonna save the day.

AYLA: *(To JOSH.)* You are such an asshole.

JOSH: Who, me? Don't talk to me. Talk to your smart, successful big brother over there. Ask him how his life is going. Ask him where all his money is.

(KEITH is silent.)

AYLA: *(To DOUG.)* Are you going to let him be like this?

JOSH: What? I'm just asking a question. You know, shootin' the shit. *(To KEITH.)* You know how much your sister likes to hear about you. Tell her how great you're doing. Come on, Keith. Tell her the story. Tell her what you told me. Fences. PIN numbers. *(Pause. Relishing.)* Tell her about Karen.

KEITH: *(Suddenly fierce.)* What!

JOSH: Oooh! Did I hit a little nerve?

KEITH: What do you know about Karen?

JOSH: Gosh, Keith. What do you *want* to know?

KEITH: Don't mess around with me.

JOSH: Me? I'm shocked!

KEITH: What do you know?

JOSH: You tell me, Keith. You're the smart one, right? You're the one with all the goddamn answers…

(KEITH storms inside. Seconds later, the sound of the truck starting and leaving quickly.)

JOSH: How's that grill doing?

AYLA: What the hell was *that*?

JOSH: What?

AYLA: Oh come on…

DOUG: *(Poking at charcoal.)* I'd say it's just about ready.

AYLA: Where's he going?

DOUG: Keith? He'll be okay. He's just a little tired. Been working on the car all day.

AYLA: He didn't look okay.

JOSH: He hasn't been okay for a long time.

AYLA: *(To WILLIE.)* So, as you're starting to see, I'm not real torn up about leaving all this.

JOSH: Who's leaving?

DOUG: Nobody's leaving. I'm about to put the food on.

AYLA: We're moving to Chicago. Together.

JOSH: *(To WILLIE.)* Is that right?

WILLIE: Yeah. After we graduate.

DOUG: I just got to say, it's nice to have the whole family here together again.

JOSH: With a few glaring exceptions.

AYLA: When does Mom get back, anyway?

JOSH: What?

DOUG: Nice Sunday afternoon… Barbecue going… Gonna have the car running again…

JOSH: *(To AYLA.)* You don't know?

AYLA: Know what?

JOSH: Mom left him. Like for good.

AYLA: Yeah right.

JOSH: She's been gone all week.

AYLA: Yeah. In *Florida.*

JOSH: Florida…

AYLA: I talked to her last Saturday. She said she was going down to Aunt Beth's.

JOSH: Dad says she left him.

AYLA: Dad's crazy.

DOUG: Except for the rust and the radiator, it's not a bad car really. Nothing that can't be fixed…

JOSH: Dad, where's Mom?

DOUG: Bodywork, sure. Take a lot to make it look nice. The insides, though, if the motor's still good, well then…

JOSH: Dad, listen to—

DOUG: *(Suddenly.)* I think I know if my goddamn wife left me! I think maybe I know that much! *(He goes inside.)*

AYLA: Dad?

WILLIE: Maybe I should—

AYLA: No. I'm sorry. Just give me a minute. *(She goes inside.)*

JOSH: You need another beer, Willie?

WILLIE: No. I'm alright.

(Airplane sound overhead. WILLIE watches.)

JOSH: Well you just let me know. Wouldn't want you to feel uncomfortable or anything. *(He sits in lawn chair.)* I guess this must all look pretty weird to you.

WILLIE: That's families, man. They're always weird.

JOSH: Oh yeah? Is your family weird?

WILLIE: Sure.

JOSH: Yeah? They got problems?

WILLIE: Everybody's got problems.

JOSH: Is that right? How bad can it be, a bunch of rich folks buying Mustangs for sweet little kids like you.

WILLIE: Man, you got some issues.

JOSH: "Issues"? I like that. Is that a college word, or did you make it up yourself?

WILLIE: Ask your crazy family, you don't know what it means.

JOSH: *(Laughing.)* You're alright, Willie.

WILLIE: Whatever.

JOSH: No, I'm serious. You know I'm just messing with you.

WILLIE: Whatever, man.

JOSH: You know how it is. Things have been pretty strained around here lately. It's a tough thing, keeping a family together. Keeping anybody together. You know?

WILLIE: Yeah, sure.

JOSH: It can be rough, man… She likes you, though.

WILLIE: Huh?

JOSH: Ayla. She really likes you.

WILLIE: Yeah. I know.

JOSH: I mean she *really* likes you. I can see it.

WILLIE: That's good.

JOSH: You like her, right?

WILLIE: Yeah…

JOSH: Of course you like her. I mean, you two are gonna be moving out and living together, right?

WILLIE: Yeah.

JOSH: So you really *like* her. I mean, it must be pretty serious.

WILLIE: Serious?

JOSH: Yeah. I mean, like she must be the *one.*

WILLIE: I don't know about *that…*

JOSH: No, of course you don't. That's girl talk. But you like her, right?

WILLIE: Man, what *is* this—

JOSH: No, hey, I'm just asking. I'm sorry. It's just, you know. It can be weird.

WILLIE: Weird how?

JOSH: I don't know. She definitely likes you, though.

WILLIE: So?

JOSH: So, I'm just saying… I can see it. You know how she is.

WILLIE: Yeah… No.

JOSH: "No" what?

WILLIE: Like, how is she?

JOSH: What?

WILLIE: You said, "You know how she is."

JOSH: I did?

WILLIE: Just now.

JOSH: I said that? I don't know what I meant.

WILLIE: But you said it.

JOSH: No, man, it's not like a good or bad thing. She really likes you. Just be careful, that's all.

WILLIE: What does that mean?

JOSH: Nothing. I'm sorry. Don't listen to me.

WILLIE: No, you got something to say…

JOSH: No, really.

WILLIE: …just say it…

JOSH: Well, I mean, okay… she's my sister and your girlfriend and a good person and all. But come on, you know how women get.

WILLIE: What?

JOSH: How old are you? You've been around a few of them by now, right?

WILLIE: Yeah, sure.

JOSH: Well you know how they *get.* You know what I'm talking about.

WILLIE: No, I don't think—

JOSH: *Women.* They get these ideas, you know…

WILLIE: I'm not sure I—

JOSH: Okay. Like you and I. We know how things are, right? I mean, we *know how things are.* But women… They got… I don't know…

WILLIE: What?

JOSH: They got all these ideas about how shit's *supposed to be.* You know what I'm saying, right?

WILLIE: I don't know…

JOSH: Hey, it doesn't matter, man. I'm just talking, you know. The important thing is that you like her. You like her, right?

WILLIE: Yeah…

JOSH: And she's obviously serious about you.

WILLIE: Yeah…

JOSH: I mean, it's obvious that she's really into *you,* and not just, like, your car and your money and the sweet job you're gonna have…

WILLIE: What are you saying?

JOSH: I'm just saying, some girls are like that, you know.

WILLIE: Yeah…

JOSH: But she's not like that.

WILLIE: No…

JOSH: And you're serious about her. Right?

WILLIE: Right…

JOSH: Then shit, man. You got nothing to worry about.

(Blackout.)

SCENE 4

The truck stop. Later Sunday afternoon. KAREN is preparing to leave, with her apron and car keys in her hands. KEITH enters from left.

KEITH: Karen!

KAREN: You're back. Again. They're gonna give you a job here if you keep—

KEITH: Tell me how you know Josh.

KAREN: Who?

KEITH: Josh. My brother. Tell me how you know him.

KAREN: I never met your brother—

KEITH: Well he knows who *you* are.

KAREN: Keith, are you okay?

KEITH: No! This screws everything up. It can't be like this.

KAREN: You need to just—

KEITH: I need to find out how he knows about you!

KAREN: A lot of guys come in here, they know my name. I don't know who—

KEITH: Are you lying? Don't lie to me!

KAREN: Don't *you* fucking talk to me like that! I've been working all day and I don't need you coming in here all crazy and treating me like—

KEITH: I just want to know—

KAREN: Sit down, Keith!

(He sits, stunned.)

KAREN: Listen to me. I don't know what the hell you're talking about. I'm tired. And you are obviously messed up.

KEITH: Anything he gets his hands on… He breaks things. It's what he does. He can't know about this…

KAREN: About what?

KEITH: You… this place… how I feel…

KAREN: How you feel about…?

KEITH: You know.

KAREN: No. Say it.

(Long pause. KEITH is silent, not looking at her.)

KAREN: Keith, I'm leaving now. I'm going to walk out of here and get into my car and drive home. And I'm going to take a nap. And I'm going to be happy. And you, you're going to leave here and go back to California, to your nice apartment and your smart, practical girlfriend. And—

KEITH: No. It's gone.

KAREN: What's gone?

KEITH: All of it. The money. The house. Her.

KAREN: So all that stuff you told me about—

KEITH: It was all true. It's just gone now. I decided I didn't want it.

KAREN: Is that what you told *her?*

KEITH: No. I didn't tell her anything.

KAREN: What happened, then?

KEITH: I just walked away one day.

KAREN: How do you think *she* feels about that?

KEITH: I don't know.

KAREN: You didn't think of that?

KEITH: You don't know how it was there. It wasn't me. I tried. I just… I would read your letters…

KAREN: Forget about the letters.

KEITH: You're saying you didn't mean it? All that stuff you wrote?

KAREN: Maybe I thought I did, then…

KEITH: But now…

KAREN: It's getting late.

(She tries to leave. He stops her.)

KEITH: A car travels in a straight line for a quarter mile…

KAREN: What are you doing?

KEITH: …in… let's say twelve-point-five seconds. We'll give him some credit.

KAREN: Stop it.

KEITH: Assuming a speed of zero at the starting line, what's the rate of acceleration?

KAREN: Keith…

KEITH: It's easy enough, right?

KAREN: Why are you doing this?

KEITH: You don't know. Is that it? You don't remember how—

KAREN: What's there to remember?

KEITH: You forgot how. That's it. Your brain has deteriorated…

KAREN: *(Sarcastically.)* Yeah. That's it.

KEITH: You blocked it out, maybe. Everything you learned.

KAREN: *(Pushing past him, a little panicked.)* Whatever, Keith. I really have to—

KEITH: No. You got scared.

KAREN: *(Stopping.)* What?

KEITH: That's it, isn't it? Why you stopped. Why you quit.

KAREN: I didn't—

KEITH: Couldn't handle it.

KAREN: Didn't *want* to handle it.

KEITH: No, not the science. The science was fine. Even the people were okay, really. Lattes and all. *Success*, though—now, *that's* scary.

KAREN: You're crazy.

KEITH: Yeah. And you're a poor girl from a shitty place.

KAREN: What?

KEITH: *(Overblown voice.)* Who the hell does she think she is?

KAREN: Fuck you.

KEITH: We're working people! We don't take kindly to all this talk of *brains* and *ambition*...

KAREN: You can't talk—

KEITH: Too big for her britches. Too afraid of what she might be capable of. Miss Brainy Physics Lady. Ha! Can't even figure out a simple acceleration probl-

KAREN: *(Blowing up.)* It's not acceleration! Acceleration is based on velocity. You need a coordinate... a point of reference. *(Pause.)* Anybody could tell you that.

KEITH: No. I don't think most people could.

KAREN: Goodbye, Keith.

(She walks away. KEITH follows behind her.)

KEITH: Go on, then! Go back to your sweet little house, or whatever the hell you live in! And your stupid waitress job! Your real people and your naps and your stupid husband! Your—what did you call him—your reliable, sweet husband! Act like everything's just fine! Give him a kiss for me! Just go back to him and—

KAREN: *(Turning, yelling.)* That's not where I'm going!

(Silence.)

KAREN: I'm going home. Where I live, alone. There's no husband, Keith. There never was.

KEITH: You lied about that?

KAREN: I made it up.

KEITH: Why would you lie about that?

KAREN: Why did you lie about your girlfriend?

KEITH: That's different.

KAREN: Is it?

KEITH: I mean, marriage. To just make that up when you know... I mean, you can tell... Why would you—

KAREN: You make things crazy, Keith. You make everything a mess inside me. You always have. When you were three thousand miles away it was different, I could say things. Write things. It's just easier without you around.

KEITH: But the things you wrote...

KAREN: What the hell was I supposed to do, Keith? Sit here and wish for you? Hoping you'd get tired of whatever it is you've been doing and come back? You don't want me. You want to run off with some academic dream girl you got off of a bunch of old letters.

KEITH: You don't know how it's been for me.

KAREN: You're right. I don't. All I know is some poor woman's out there right now wondering where the hell her boyfriend went.

KEITH: That's different. That's all over. It's gone.

KAREN: It's not gone.

KEITH: What?

KAREN: It's all still out there, Keith. You just left.

(Blackout.)

SCENE 5

The kitchen. Sunday evening. JOSH is seated at one end of the table with AYLA and WILLIE adjacent on one side. The table is set haphazardly—a mix of paper plates and fancy dishes, styrofoam deli cups next to dinner candles, elaborate water glasses and beer in the bottle, half a loaf of wheat bread in a bag. There are two empty chairs as well—one at the table with a place setting, the other pushed against the wall. DOUG hovers around them, holding a glass serving plate piled with cooked hamburgers and chicken.

DOUG: I guess we can go ahead and eat before this gets cold. Just save some for your brother.

JOSH: He won't be back for a while.

AYLA: Like you'd know.

DOUG: *(Setting the dish down on the table and sitting, at the opposite end from JOSH.)* He better come back. He's got my truck.

(They all begin dishing food and eating.)

JOSH: You want me to make a plate for Mom, too?

DOUG: And he's still got work to do. *(To WILLIE.)* Did you get a chance to see the car, uh… I'm sorry. What's your name?

WILLIE: *(Biting into chicken.)* Willie.

AYLA: Dad, you knew that. What's your problem?

DOUG: You know Keith's been out there working on it. I think he'll have it running again.

JOSH: Where are the buns? Don't we have buns?

DOUG: Nothing's ever good enough for you, is it?

JOSH: I'm just asking—

DOUG: This is a relaxing family dinner and I'm not going to let any of your stupid talk ruin it. Use this bread.

AYLA: *(Poking distastefully at her chicken with a fork.)* Dad…

DOUG: *(To no one in particular.)* A lot of people don't realize it's the little stuff that throws you. Plug wires. Valve springs. Long as the block's okay, you can fix the rest. Just takes time.

AYLA: I don't think this chicken is done.

WILLIE: Mine's great.

AYLA: Well mine's not.

WILLIE: You just haven't eaten meat in a while.

AYLA: Well if I'm going to, it should at least be cooked all the way.

WILLIE: Why you got to complain?

AYLA: I am *not* complaining. I'm just saying—

WILLIE: You've been complaining the whole time we've been here.

JOSH: *(Loving it.)* Now, you two…

DOUG: There's plenty of chicken for everybody.

AYLA: All I'm saying is it's not cooked enough. What the hell's your problem?

JOSH: *(To WILLIE.)* So Willie, where are you from, originally? *(Mock embarrassment.)* I'm sorry, can I say that?

AYLA: Go ahead, Josh. You're gonna fucking say what you want anyway.

DOUG: Watch your language. This is a family dinner.

JOSH: I mean, I'm not racist or anything. Everybody came from somewhere, right?

WILLIE: I'm from Tennessee.

JOSH: Yeah, but I mean, you know... Where were you born?

WILLIE: Chattanooga. Born and raised.

JOSH: Is that right? Well how about your parents? I mean...

AYLA: I can't believe my own family...

JOSH: What? I'm just asking.

WILLIE: It's cool. *(To JOSH, tiredly.)* My mom and dad are Vietnamese.

JOSH: Is that right? Like from Vietnam?

AYLA: Hence the term "Vietnamese."

JOSH: Wow. That's something.

WILLIE: I guess.

JOSH: You know, Dad was in Vietnam for a while.

WILLIE: Oh yeah? Never been there, myself.

DOUG: Beautiful country, from what I hear. Can't say I really saw that side of it... can somebody pass me the mustard?

AYLA: Josh was in a war. Weren't you, Josh.

DOUG: We're not gonna talk about that.

JOSH: Willie already knew that. Didn't you, Willie?

WILLIE: I didn't know you were in a *war*.

JOSH: The Persian Gulf. Desert Storm.

WILLIE: I remember that. I had the T-shirt.

DOUG: *(To JOSH.)* What'd I tell you?

JOSH: You'll have to excuse us, Willie. Dad didn't have a very good time over there in your homeland...

AYLA: You are *so* tacky...

JOSH: ...so he has a lot of rules about what we're not supposed to talk about. Guns. The Marine Corps. Combat.

DOUG: *(Suddenly fierce.)* Playing cards on a goddamn ship is not combat!

JOSH: *(To WILLIE.)* You see what I mean?

DOUG: You and your goddamn G.I. Joe routine. I ought to kick your ass.

JOSH: Dad's real big on the nonviolence thing.

DOUG: You think I can't do it?

JOSH: What do *you* think, Willie?

WILLIE: What?

JOSH: Who do you think would win in a fight, right now?

AYLA: You both have got to be—

DOUG: *(To JOSH.)* You don't have your mother to hide behind now.

AYLA: I'm not gonna just—

JOSH: *(To AYLA.)* What the hell do you care? You're leaving forever anyway, right?

DOUG: Nobody's leaving forever. Nobody's going anywhere.

JOSH: Tell that to your wife.

AYLA: I told you! I talked to her. Nobody left anybody.

WILLIE: *(Moving to get up.)* I really think I—

JOSH: *(To WILLIE.)* What. Tell us what you think. You know so much…

AYLA: *(To JOSH.)* Don't talk to him like that!

WILLIE: *(To AYLA.)* You stay out of this.

AYLA: *Excuse* me?

WILLIE: I can stick up for myself.

JOSH: Yeah. He's a smart guy. Let him talk.

AYLA: Dad, are you gonna let him just—

JOSH: *(To WILLIE.)* Spoiled little smartass.

WILLIE: *(Getting up.)* You know what? I'm outta here…

AYLA: *(Getting up.)* No shit. Let's go.

JOSH: Aw, already?

(WILLIE walks off and exits through hall door.)

AYLA: Dad. We're leaving. I'm not coming back. Do you understand that?

DOUG: Nobody's leaving.

AYLA: No, Dad. I'm leaving. We're going back to my house. And in three weeks I'm going to finish school. And then we're going away, to Chicago, and I'm not going to talk to either one of you again. Dad, are you listening to me?

DOUG: Where's Keith?

AYLA: Dad?

(No response.)

AYLA: Alright, then. Fuck you guys. *(She turns away, calling down hall as she exits.)* Let's go, Willie. I got to get my bag.

DOUG: Keith's got the truck.

JOSH: He's gone, Dad.

DOUG: He's not done out there. We got to get that baby running.

(Distant sound of a car starting, peeling out, and driving away.)

JOSH: Forget about him.

DOUG: You don't know. You don't know anything. You never did know anything.

(AYLA screams offstage.)

AYLA: *(Entering from hallway, backpack in hand, frantic.)* I can't fucking believe this! He left! He fucking left without me!

JOSH: Who did?

AYLA: *(To JOSH.)* Don't give me that shit! *(She rifles through backpack, finds her phone, punches numbers, listens. Then yells into phone.)* You weak son of a bitch! I know you're there! I know you've got the phone right there with you! Answer me! Answer! Shit! *(She hurls the phone to the floor.)*

JOSH: I guess he didn't like us.

AYLA: *(Turning to JOSH.)* You! You did something. I don't know what, but you did something.

JOSH: You're crazy.

AYLA: Dad? You know Josh did something. You know how he is. Are you just gonna let him get away with—

JOSH: Now just calm down…

AYLA: Don't fuck with me Josh! It doesn't work on me. It never has.

JOSH: *(To DOUG.)* Listen to her. She's crazy.

AYLA: My boyfriend just drove off and left me stranded here!

DOUG: I could have told you he was no good.

AYLA: What?!

DOUG: He liked Shemp.

AYLA: You are unbelievable! Both of you!

DOUG: Nobody likes Shemp.

AYLA: I got to get out of here!

DOUG: I don't see what the hurry is. There's plenty of food.

AYLA: Dad? Are you listening to me?

DOUG: Get ourselves something to eat. Have another beer. Keith'll be back in a bit, get working on the car again...

AYLA: I'm serious...

DOUG: Can't be that hard, really. Long as the motor's okay. A few parts, sure. I'll talk to the guys down at the speed shop. Damn, it'll be nice to see that thing running again.

JOSH: *(Genuinely comforting.)* Yeah, Dad. Sure it will.

DOUG: Oh yeah. Get a new carburetor on there. Get the jets just right. Fuel and fire...

JOSH: We'll fix it up together. Just me and you.

AYLA: *(To JOSH, horrified.)* You're as insane as he is.

DOUG: Oh sure. Make it a family thing.

(Distant sound of the truck approaching and stopping.)

DOUG: Get it running. Get some paint on there. Oh man, you should see the heads turn when that baby pulls up.

AYLA: Dad...

DOUG: *(Oblivious to her.)* Your mother, she loves to ride in it. Take her out on a Saturday. Summertime. Nothing like it.

(KEITH enters from garage. Throughout the following, his words are slow and calm, his movements and expression frighteningly deliberate.)

AYLA: Keith! Oh my god. You've got to get me out of here.

(He looks past her, as if in a trance.)

JOSH: Back so soon, Keith?

DOUG: He came back to fix the car.

AYLA: Keith?

(KEITH ignores her. She turns and exits through the hallway.)

DOUG: You hungry, Keith? We saved you some food.

KEITH: Have you been outside? It's gorgeous. *(Walking out onto the deck.)* It smells like grass out here. Grass that's just been cut. Nothing but fresh-cut grass and clean air and road as far as you can see. I must have driven for miles. Just thinking. It's funny what you see when you slow down. When you're not looking. Power lines. Tanker trucks. All these machines. All this stuff waiting to go wrong.

DOUG: *(To KEITH.)* The way I see it, it's the radiator we got to think about. We got to fix the holes.

JOSH: Now wait a goddamn minute...

KEITH: You stop the truck. Pull over. Out in a field you see a billboard and you see the people in the picture. But you also see the paper that the picture's printed on. Huge sheets of it. Probably on a big machine, with thousands of moving parts made by machines run by other people.

JOSH: Yeah, people with jobs.

KEITH: It all came from somewhere. The ink on the paper. The glue. The wiring. The steel frame…

DOUG: Steel, now that's something else. A quantifiable quality. It's either good or it's not.

JOSH: Man, what is this bullshit? The fact is, you can't handle any kind of real—

KEITH: The fact is, there are things going on that you and I cannot possibly understand.

JOSH: I think I understand pretty well, actually.

KEITH: Before you can stop yourself, you see more. The objects all around you become raw materials, precise combinations of chemical compounds.

JOSH: I understand that you can't handle going to work in the morning, or paying your bills…

KEITH: But it goes deeper. You start to see atoms. Then the particles inside each atom. And the spaces between the particles.

JOSH: You don't see anything.

KEITH: Everything at its core is just a series of constant reactions between particles. They become a series of possible trajectories and past locations. By the time you see the path they've made, they're already somewhere else.

DOUG: Tracer bullets in the jungle. If you're looking at 'em, it's too late.

(There is the deafening sound of a shotgun from behind the garage door, followed by the sound of buckling metal. All are stunned, though only JOSH moves toward the door.)

JOSH: What the hell—

(Sound of a pump shotgun racking. The blast is repeated, this time followed by shattering glass. JOSH opens garage door and stops short. Sound of gun racking.)

JOSH: *(Yelling.)* What are you doing?

AYLA: *(Emerging from the garage, shotgun in hand.)* Don't you fucking move, Josh! Get back in there!

JOSH: She's shooting the car!

AYLA: Shut up!

(KEITH watches but doesn't move. DOUG is completely dazed.)

JOSH: She's shooting the car!

AYLA: Shut up!

JOSH: What do you think you're doing?

AYLA: *(Pointing his gun at him.)* I am shooting the car! I am shooting it and fucking it up and I am going to keep shooting it until it is completely shot and fucked up. And if you try to stop me, I am going to shoot you, Josh, and fuck you up!

JOSH: *(With forced calm.)* Ayla. That's a dangerous thing that you're doing. Now just… just put the gun down.

AYLA: What are you gonna do, Josh?

(AYLA goes back to the doorway, where she stands, partially visible, and shoots again, reeling from the recoil before she racks the gun again. Each time, the shots should be accompanied by the noise of metal or glass breaking. JOSH backs away, toward KEITH.)

KEITH: You see the empty space at the center of everything. Places and people continue in your absence.

DOUG: It's not supposed to happen this way. None of it.

(AYLA shoots.)

JOSH: No!

KEITH: All the things you thought were solid pieces of your life are cracking open and falling to the ground, and you are left standing in a field somewhere…

JOSH: Shut up, Keith!

KEITH: *(Suddenly direct, to JOSH.)* You do what you know how to do, Josh. But no one else is making you live this way. Not me. Not the Marine Corps. Not Dad. You can do anything.

JOSH: I said shut up!

(JOSH rushes at KEITH and punches him, knocking him to the floor. Then, with obvious military precision, JOSH grabs his knife from his belt and pins KEITH to the floor, holding the knife to his throat. There is a long moment as the severity of the act sinks in, particularly for DOUG.)

DOUG: This is not my family.

(JOSH, realizing its effect on his father, is stunned. As DOUG and KEITH speak, he will sink to his knees.)

KEITH: You can't hurt me Josh. There's nothing left to wreck.

DOUG: It's wrong. It's all mixed up.

KEITH: *(Slowly standing.)* It's gone. And it's everywhere. All the possible stories. Potential roles.

DOUG: This isn't real. None of it. I know where I am.

KEITH: *(Calmly going to the table and sitting.)* As uncontrollable as electrons. As family. Colliding, reacting off each other. Just missing.

(AYLA shoots.)

DOUG: I know where I am.

(The lights dim slightly, except directly on DOUG.)

DOUG: It's 1971. Summertime. I'm twenty-two years old. I have a wife. I have a son. I have a scar up my right side. I have a job, in a steel mill. It's shitty work but I'm glad for the money. I have a car. A beautiful car. A 1970 Plymouth Hemi Barracuda.

It's simple, really. I have a clutch. An accelerator. A shifter. One steering wheel. One dial. A quarter mile of flat pavement in front of me. Behind me… nothing.

(AYLA shoots.)

Outside, it's always sunset, the last warm light of Sunday. The sound of the crowd. Bright floodlights, like a carnival against pale blue. It's my last run of the day. In thirteen seconds—maybe sooner—it'll all be over.

(The engine sound from the beginning of Act One fades in faintly, growing louder as the speech ends.)

I got my foot on the brake. Hands on the wheel. I keep my eyes open. Watch the light. Listen. Hear the click of every cam on every pushrod on every valve on every cylinder. Perfect timing.

(Blackout as the sound fades out.)

(The end.)

OUT TO LUNCH

Joseph Langham

JOSEPH LANGHAM was born in 1969 in Gainesville, and grew up in the Texas cities of Odessa and Austin. He has a bachelor of fine arts degree in pre-professional acting from Southwest Texas State University and has studied acting and movement with John Jay Jennings, characterization with Larry Hovis, and directing with Richard Sodders. He wrote, directed, and performed in *Gilligan Stump! And Tha Perfesser...* and wrote and performed in *HAR HAR: An Evening With Harburg Harrisbrandt*; this latter received the Excellence Award for Solo Show at the New York International Fringe Festival. Langham is a multidisciplinary artist, and founder and artistic director of BrokenArmProductions, a company dedicated to all-original productions that stand firmly outside the norm. Currently, he is working on a nonverbal solo show and a romantic thriller written for two actors. He lives in Brooklyn, New York, with his wife, Monica Cortez-Langham, and their birds, Ralphy and Daisy Faye.

Out to Lunch was first presented by BrokenArmProductions as part of the New York International Fringe Festival (Elena K. Holy, Producing Artistic Director), on August 9, 2002, at the Kraine Theatre, New York City, with the following cast and credits:

Numba Won .... Jim Cherry
Numba Too .... Matthew David Barton
The Busboy .... Robert Zwaschka
The Waitress .... Monica Cortez
The JesterDishwasherFrenchChef .... Clint McCown
The Manager .... Mark McGriff
The Owner .... Richard Hinojosa
The Goils .... Jamie Chandler
The Goils .... Sara Najjar
The Owner's Wife .... Teresa Ryno
The Gunman .... Alvin Lotspeich

Direction and Sound Design: Joseph Langham
Stage Manager/Costumer/Running Crew: Katherine Decker
Lights and Sound Operator: Rik Sansone

Sound cues and song examples available on mini-disc or CD. Please contact BrokenArmProductions for more info (see p. iii). "Singin' in the Rain" was used with permission from EMI Music Publishing. Rights to produce this play include rights to perform all songs written by Joseph Langham only. "Singin' in the Rain" will require permission from EMI.

Special thanks: The production for this play was one of the most rewarding and fulfilling experiences I have ever had. Something unique occurred within this cast and crew, as there were no ego struggles or clique formations as so often permeate ye ol theatre scene. The cast showed up every day excited to see one another and to attack the project as a powerful ensemble. It was truly rare. I just wanted to take this opportunity to thank them, each and every one, for their brilliant contribution to this project, and their contribution to the offity, off, off theatre world as a whole. I would also like to thank Edward and Nancy Langham (Ma and Pa!) and my lovely wife Monica (who also played the waitress) for their continued support and unwavering understanding of the lofty dream. More thanks go out to Megan Riordan, Ed Lingan, and Maria Mason. In loving memory of Zane.

CHARACTERS

1: numba won. oh so very much like 2.

2: numba too. oh so very much like 1.

BUSBOY: the busboy. a giant, the biggest busboy in the world, and a fine dancer.

W: the waitress. if there were such a thing as a tri-polar disorder, man, would she have it.

JEST: jesterdishwasherfrenchef. the jester, oh yes, and he's also the dishwasher, oh and the french chef, what a talent.

MAN: the manager. a dancer at heart, yet another artist lost in the vast tumultuous sea that is the service industry.

OWN: the owner. he acts, dresses, and truly feels that he is king doody of doody mountain.

THE GOILS: the owner's entourage. two lovely buxom ladies scantily clad and all serving.

WIFE: the owner's wife. now we know who is truly king doody of doody mountain.

GUN: the lone gunman. timothy mcveigh meets the unibomber meets the IRA meets son-of-sam, pure ignorant violence personified.

PRODUCTION NOTE

all cast members, except the BUSBOY, must have some costume piece that is red for each time they are onstage. great care must be taken in regard to replaced foul language, so as not to give the new words any additional silly undertones.

as the audience arrives two men, 1 & 2, are eating and conversing inaudibly at a table. they are campers. the same eight-measure muzak loop is playing over and over in the background. there are a lot of dishes there arranged symmetrically.

to the side of the stage stands the biggest BUSBOY in the world. he is holding a bus tub and waiting. as the show progresses he gets more and more impatient with the campers. he doesn't make a peep. he only relays this through his facial expressions. he never leaves the stage.

when the audience is completely seated the campers push back their plates.

1: this is so relaxing.

2: yeah.

1: i like being this relaxed.

2: me too.

1: yeah.

2: yeah. *(pause.)* so, how's the job?

1: i quit.

2: yeah?

1: yeah.

2: wow.

1: yeah. i guess that's why i'm so dang relaxed.

2: you do look comfortable.

1: oh i am. i am.

2: that's good.

1: yeah man. real good.

2: i quit too.

1: your job?

2: yeah.

1: cool.

2: yeah.

1: this is a very positive, relaxing conversation.

2: yes, yes it is. very relaxing.

1: i'm so relaxed i bet i could just sit here all day.

2: do you mind if i join you?

1: not at all. not at all.

2: great.

1: sunday is one of the best days of the week.

2: it's the only day i leave the house.

1: me too. thanks to computers and delivery services, i don't have to leave. but sunday… sunday is voluntary.

2: here's to voluntary sunday.

(they toast coffee cups and sip. pause.)

1: oh yeah, i bought a scanner.

2: you did?

1: yeah.

2: cool.

1: very cool.

2: i agree. scanners are very cool.

1: yeah.

2: computers are the thing nowadays.

1: you know it. so is the net.

2: thank garsh for the net.

1: yes. thank garsh.

(they toast and sip. pause.)

2: have you scanned anything yet?

1: not yet.

2: not even to test it?

1: i need more privacy.

2: more privacy?

1: yeah.

2: why?

1: well… i plan on scanning my booty.

(pause.)

2: well… i guess you would need privacy to do something like that.

1: you know it my friend.

2: is it your wife in the way?

1: i'm not married.

2: i thought you were.

1: i was.

2: what happened?

1: i got fired.

2: i thought you said you quit.

1: well the end result is the same.

2: yeah. i guess so. so you got fired and she left you.

1: that's part of the reason.

2: there's more?

1: yeah. she got really jealous of my chat partner.

2: on the net?

1: yeah.

2: well, you don't need her. you need your chat partner. i couldn't live without my chat partner.

1: me neither.

2: why'd you get fired?

1: i got caught.

2: oh? doing what?

1: i was making copies of my booty.

2: i can see how that would upset your boss.

1: you should have seen him. he was furious.

2: i bet.

1: actually i was a little afraid for my life.

2: wow. that mad huh?

1: that mad.

2: how'd he catch you?

1: security camera.

2: there's just no privacy anymore.

1: yeah, you know ten years ago i coulda copied my booty and never got caught.

2: ah the good ol' days.

(they toast and sip.)

2: my boss threatened to kill me.

1: he did?

2: yeah. that's why i quit.

1: i would have quit too.

2: yeah but you got fired.

1: well, don't rub it in.

2: sorry. still friends?

1: absolutely.

(they toast and sip. enter WAITRESS.)

W: can i get you guys anything else today?

1: another job.

2: a new car.

W: you guys are very very funny.

1: thank you.

2: thank you.

W: so... are you ready for your check?

1: yes.

2: sure.

W: great i'll be right back.

1&2: we'll be right here!

(they toast and sip when they realize they spoke simultaneously.)

W: funny. very funny. *(exit WAITRESS.)*

1: i wonder if she means funny "ha ha" or funny "weirdos."

2: probably a combination of the two.

1: do you think she wants us to leave?

2: more than likely. we have been here having this extremely relaxing conversation for quite some time now.

1: yeah. i guess she's probably a little sick of us. garsh, you know, this really has been an extraordinarily relaxing afternoon. look, it's still early. i love brunch.

2: i love brunch too.

1: it's not quite breakfast...

2: it's not quite lunch...

1&2: brunch!

2: someone should open a 24 hour brunch place!

1: yeah!

2: oh yeah.

1: so what were you saying?

2: when?

1: before the waitress came.

2: i'm not sure.

1: something about how your boss threatened to kill you.

2: oh yes. his wife.

1: you were with his wife?

2: well...

(enter WAITRESS.)

W: here's your check.

1: thank you.

2: yes, thank you.

W: you guys come in here every sunday?

1: do we come in here every sunday?

2: i believe so.

W: i thought i recognized you.

1&2: and we recognize you.

(they toast and sip again.)

W: you guys are real good friends huh?

1: i'd say so. you?

2: yes. we meet here every sunday and sit here at the same table and have basically the same conversation and we have been doing this for years.

1: several years.

2: yes, several years.

W: you guys are amazing. you look alike, you sound alike...

1&2: we think alike.

(they toast and sip.)

W: amazing. do you have the same name?

(1 & 2 look at each other curiously. there is a great silence. it is apparent that 1 & 2 don't know each other's name. it is also apparent that they don't want to know.)

W: well?

1: there are certain things...

2: that we don't talk about.

W: oh, i see. well, uh... well, if you need anything else, my name is...

1&2: shhh!

(they both cover their ears.)

W: uh, okay. i see. no names.

1&2: it's safer that way.

1: that way no one really knows you.

2: no one can discover your secrets.

1: yes like your address.

2: or your credit card numbers.

1: or your dental records.

2: or your criminal history.

1: anonymity is the best.

2: even when it comes to good friends.

1: here here.

2: amen.

(they toast and sip.)

1: goodness, these seem to be bottomless cups.

2: yes. we have been sipping and toasting quite a bit.

W: that is an understatement.

(silence.)

W: well, okay. so, pay me when you're ready.

1: yes, yes. we know the rigmarole.

2: we have been here before you know.

W: oh i know. and i'm sure that you will be back.

1: what else is there to do?

(silence.)

W: i am unable to answer that question at this time.

1: here's my card.

W: thank you i'll be right back with your receipt.

1: no. thank you, miss.

2: yes, yes. thank you.

1: here's to great service.

2: the best.

(they toast and sip. WAITRESS begins to exit.)

1: oh miss?

W: yes?

2: could you bring us more coffee?

W: oh garsh. yes i suppose so. the customer is always right.

(lights follow WAITRESS to the BUSBOY who doesn't respond to her.)

W: garsh, will they ever leave? how long have they been here? is it still sunday? i'm not even sure it's sunday anymore. i think it could be monday or tuesday. who knows it may be next sunday for all i know. they have been here for so long, it could already be three sundays from now. it's always the same. don't they have food at their houses? don't they have coffee? i hate campers. do you know what a camper is? it's people who come in here and stay here until the friggin judgment day. they can see that we have a line of customers outside. they know that this is the busiest day of the week. they don't care. all they think of is their friggin selves. you know what i hate worse than campers? nothing. i really can't think of anything. i think i'd rather have red hot metal toothpicks shoved under my fingernails, then stick my hands in a bucket of lime juice and rinse with boiling salt water. do you see? do you see how much i hate campers? i would give up this miraculous manicure if they would just leave. see? see my nails? they are perfect. *(she looks at her own nails admiringly. then shock.)* holy frig! I BROKE A GALDANG NAIL! i bet i broke it on the coffee pot. or on the dessert stand. *(she begins to sob.)* it's them. it's all their fault. they broke my nail and they don't care. and, to top it all off, do you know what the worst part of them is? they don't tip. don't they know i only get paid $2 an hour? don't they know i have rent to pay? and manicures! how can i fix this nail if they don't tip? they take up your table for a friggin decade and then leave you doody! and now… and now… they want more coffee.

(silence as WAITRESS stares at BUSBOY. BUSBOY hasn't been paying attention to a word. he is still just intently staring at the campers' table.)

W: do you hear me? have you heard a word i said? are you deaf? can you speak english? hello? hello?

(she walks around the BUSBOY leeringly.)

W: my, my you are a big one. i bet you are the biggest busboy in the world. nice tush honey.

(she pats his tush. he doesn't react.)

W: i'll meet you back in the walk-in right now, big boy. i'm not wearing any panties. you can have your way with me on the butter buckets... hello? ah frig you!

(exit WAITRESS. beat. BUSBOY drops his bus tub. he picks it up. she almost made him lose his concentration. but he has it back. as lights back on campers we hear the sound of a random car pulling up outside. the motor dies, the door slams, the alarm goes tweep tweep and enter GUNMAN. he is dressed in camouflage pants, combat boots, and an inside-out coca cola t-shirt. he has a rather large handgun.)

GUN: excuse me, is this the federal building?

1&2: no.

GUN: abortion clinic?

1&2: no.

(GUNMAN blinks twice.)

GUN: doody.

(exit GUNMAN. we hear the alarm go tweep tweep, the door slam, and the random car tears away.)

1&2: funny...

(silence.)

1: what's taking so long with that coffee?

2: i don't know.

(they look about in search for the WAITRESS.)

1: i wish she would hurry.

2: me too.

(more looking about.)

1: what on earth could be wrong?

2: i don't know.

(looking about most intently.)

1: do you see her yet?

2: no.

(straining and looking about.)

1: do you think she went to guatemala?

2: to pick the beans?

(they laugh and toast but before they sip they realize they have no coffee. sudden anger.)

1: if that friggin waitress doesn't get here pretty friggin soon...

2: there'll be no friggin tip left on the friggin table.

(silence as they boil inside.)

1&2: *(standing.)* alright that's it. where's the friggin manager?!?

(trumpets flair and the JESTER comes onstage turning rather half-hearted cartwheels. 1 & 2 sit. he is wearing chef pants, a chef jacket, and a jester's hat.)

JEST: ah the manager. every customer's best friend. every waiter's worst enemy. you look like two healthy customers. the question is... are there any good managers? who knows? who cares? as long as the shirts are starched and the ties pulled tight. if the pants are pressed the world is impressed.

(JESTER notices the BUSBOY and sticks his tongue out at him. then, back to the audience.)

JEST: i'd like now to sing you all a song about the manager. guitar! i said guitar! boy! oh bother.

(JESTER exits and returns with guitar. he plays a country waltz in c.)

JEST: "oh manager, oh manager
you are so pressed and clean
you kiss the booty of customers
and to the servers you are mean."
thank you. thank you. stop. you are too much. please stop. oh i couldn't go on. thank you for this golden opportunity. my mother said i would never amount to anything, but you people are so kind. thank you. you there in the back, please sit down.

(trumpet flair.)

JEST: hark! what trumpet is this? oh yes i almost forgot. ladies and gentlemen. may i present to you, all the way from somewhere else... the manager.

(JESTER pulls confetti out of his pockets as MANAGER music swells. MANAGER enters amongst great hooplah. he is dressed extremely corporate. MANAGER music stops suddenly.)

MAN: what the heck are you doing out here? get back to the kitchen before i fire your worthless booty. and take off that stupid hat! and get a broom and sweep up this confetti.

JEST: you can beat me, chain me, torture me with little drips of water dripping endlessly on my forehead while i am roped to a board, drip drip drip, but you will never, i repeat never take away my hat!

(the JESTER pulls a large plastic knife and backs his way offstage.)

MAN: please forgive him for he knows not what he is. hello to you gentlemen. my name is...

1&2: stop!

MAN: what?

1&2: *(fingers in ears.)* no names. no names.

MAN: *(aside.)* take deep breaths. the customer is always right. *(to 1 & 2.)* okay then no names. how about giving me a nickname?

1: oo can i pick it?

2: no no let me.

MAN: you both can pick it.

1&2: yes!

1: that's a great idea.

2: that's why he's the manager.

(1 & 2 run to the side of the stage and huddle and discuss the nickname.)

MAN: *(to audience.)* i don't know how much longer i can take this. i told myself i would only manage for a year or so and now it has been ten years. all i ever wanted to do was dance the ballet.

(lights shift, ballet music begins. MANAGER begins to dance the ballet. 1 & 2 interrupt.)

1&2: we have it!

MAN: yes. yes. what is it?

1: go ahead.

2: oh no i couldn't. you.

1: alright then. we have nicknamed you...

1&2: the manager.

2: the sensible choice.

1: yes. we compiled all we knew about you...

2: and the choice was simple.

1: quite simple.

2: easy.

1: like stealing candy from a baby.

2: like stealing a baby from its mother.

1&2: the manager.

MAN: *(to audience.)* suddenly i am very afraid. i wonder if baryshnikov went through this. probably not. i wonder how you spell baryshnikov? b-o-r-... boriscnee... b-

1: hey you, "the manager."

2: yeah hey you.

MAN: yes? how may i help you?

1: well, we were concerned...

2: we were worried...

1: perhaps you can tell us...

1&2: WHERE'S OUR FRIGGIN COFFEE?!?

(enter WAITRESS. she is completely nude. 1 & 2 absolutely do not notice her.)

W: here's your galdang coffee. *(she pours coffee everywhere.)* look at these nails. perfect except for this one.

(she exits. BUSBOY drops his bus tub and picks it up again. 1 & 2 sit down in their respective seats. the MANAGER begins doing the ballet again in the background.)

1: well, it's about time.

2: yes.

1: her tip percentage was dropping.

2: 15%—14%—13%—

1: i say we leave it at 10.

2: ten percent?

1: no ten cents.

(they laugh and laugh and laugh.)

2: so. about your scanner.

1: oh i can't let you borrow it. i haven't even tried it yet.

2: oh no. i would never ask to borrow something you haven't even used. i was just curious about the privacy matter.

1: privacy matter?

2: yes, i asked earlier in our conversation if you had used your scanner yet, and you commented that you needed more privacy so you can scan your booty.

1: oh yes. and you asked if it was my wife in the way.

2: right.

(the MANAGER stops doing the ballet.)

MAN: i wonder if you two could excuse me. i really should have a talk with that waitress.

1: yes you should.

2: absolutely.

1: we prefer good service.

2: as opposed to bad.

1: amen.

2: hallelujah.

(they toast and sip. they both spit it out.)

1: cripe, this is hot coffee.

2: yes. perhaps we should sue.

1: perhaps you are right.

(pause.)

1: shall we switch seats?

2: let's.

(they switch seats and dishes. this is quite an ordeal. the MANAGER stares in disbelief. by the end of the bit the only things not switched are the salt and pepper shakers. the

MANAGER switches these for them. they do not like it. the MANAGER switches the shakers back the way they were. 1 & 2 are relieved.)

1: wow. your view is much better than mine.

2: oh i disagree. i say we keep this arrangement.

1: that's a great idea.

2: it was your idea to switch.

1: we are brilliant.

2: yes we are.

(they toast and sip carefully. MANAGER clears his throat.)

1: oh pardon us.

2: we forgot you were there.

MAN: most people do. may i be excused?

1: absolutely.

2: positively.

MAN: thank you.

1&2: no, thank you.

MAN: *(as he exits.)* the customer is always right. the customer is always right. the customer is al...

1: what a nice man.

2: not as nice as you.

1: nor you.

2: oh stop it.

(they toast and sip.)

1: curtains.

2: i'm sorry?

1: when she left she took the curtains.

2: oh i see. privacy.

1: right. how can i scan my booty when there are no curtains?

2: your neighbors might see...

1: that i have absolutely nothing...

2: better to do...

1: with my life.

2: than scan your booty.

1: and post it on the net.

2: for the whole world to see.

1: even my neighbors.

2: even your friends.

1: even my ex-wife.

2: and your ex-boss.

1: even the pope.

2: even garsh.

(long silence. they both look up.)

1: is the pope a name?

2: i think it's a title.

1: do you think garsh has a computer?

2: do you think the pope has one?

(long silence.)

1: if he did he could e-pray the big guy.

2: save on those pesky long distance charges.

1: could you imagine?

(they reflect.)

2: no.

(silence.)

1: so you got caught.

2: i'm sorry?

1: you said your boss threatened to kill you.

2: oh yes. his wife.

1: so you got caught with her.

2: yeah. but not doin it or nothing. i would never sleep with a married woman.

1: what were you doing then?

2: well i was holding her up over the copy machine so she could copy her booty.

1: the boss's wife?

2: yep.

1: wow. is she good lookin?

2: very.

1: you shoulda done her.

2: i don't think she likes me like that.

1: i see. so how did you get caught?

2: video camera.

1: there's just no privacy left in the world.

2: none at all.

1: did you see her booty?

2: just a copy.

1: did you keep a copy for yourself?

2: yeah. then i posted it on the net.

1: how?

2: how what?

1: how did you post it?

2: oh i scanned it in the computer.

1: you have a scanner?

2: yes.

1: why didn't you tell me?

2: you didn't ask.

1: to think of all the trouble you would have saved me.

2: sorry.

(silence.)

1: so did you see it?

2: what?

1: your posting.

2: yes.

1: did it look good?

2: very.

1: did you, you know.

2: yeah.

1: what's the address?

2: www.bossbooty.com.

1: oh my garsh, i've seen that one!

2: you have?

1: that is the greatest. what BLY did you use?

2: you know the standard CVG/RHH.

1: that's a good one. the 296 or 299 version?

2: much higher TTB in the 296.

1: yeah but you gotta admit that the CVM version of the BLY set at RHL is far better than either the 269 or the 299 CVG/RHH even with the ZZG plug in.

2: far better and far faster.

1: yes. yes. yes. ya know, my chat partner uses the same as you.

2: really? so does mine.

1: that's funny. i use the same as my chat partner.

2: it's a small world.

1: and getting smaller.

2: so what did you think?

1: your boss undoubtedly has the nicest bootied wife in all of history.

2: he does. so did you, you know?

1: galdang absolutely. thank garsh for computers.

2: thank garsh for the net.

1: thank garsh for chat partners.

2: yes thank garsh for chat partners.

1: thank garsh for towels.

2: and lubrication.

1: there's nothing better than looking at dirty pictures and chatting at the same time with a towel and some lubrication nearby.

2: except maybe sunday brunch.

1: except maybe sunday brunch.

(they toast and sip.)

2: is your chat buddy male or female?

1: i'm not sure. yours?

2: i don't know. i hope female. the way we talk.

1: me too. not for you, but for me.

2: i understand.

1: i knew you would. hey!

2: yeah?

1: shall we sing the song?

2: i think so, absolutely.

1: where is that jester?

2: i don't know. jester!

1: jester!

(enter JESTER. his chef jacket has been replaced by a stained tank top, stained towel, and rubber gloves. the hat is ever present.)

JEST: what the heck do you want? and make it snappy, i have dishes to wash.

1: you wash dishes?

JEST: you don't think i can make a living being a jester do you?

1: no probably not.

JEST: so then yes. i wash the friggin dishes in this friggin restaurant.

2: jeez. you are the most unhappy jester i have ever seen.

JEST: i'm a bitter dishwasher. but, i'm the happiest jester in the world. happy dance happy dance. too tee doo tee too. *(he does a little happy dance.)*

1: hey happy jester. my friend here and i want to sing the song.

2: yes please, would you accompany us?

JEST: delighted my friends. guitar! i said guitar! boy! oh bother. i'm going to have to find me a new boy. *(he exits and returns with guitar.)* my mother always said, "if you want something done, get your sister to do it." then i'd say, "but, mom, i don't have a sister." then she'd say, "then put your dress back on and get to work bootyhole." i miss mom. so, what key?

1&2: key of c!

JEST: a one, two, three, four.

*(all take turns with verse and harmonize on lines indicated with *. 4/4 country riff in c.)*

> i'd like to welcome all of you
> to the internet
> you can find what you want

but mostly you get
*naked ladies
*naked ladies
i hacked right past
my cyber nanny
so i could see
some real fine fanny
*naked ladies
*naked ladies
*i love naked ladies
*i look at them all the time
*when i see a naked lady
*push print and she is mine
i like titties
i like butts
i like to download
slimy sluts
*naked ladies
*naked ladies
every month
my bills are big
so i can see
some other guy frig
*naked ladies
*naked ladies
*if i was a naked lady
*i'd stay home all the time
*and look at myself in the mirror
*and touch it cause it is mine
so get yourself
on the internet
to heck with information
all you get are
*naked ladies
(big finish)
*naked ladies

(the JESTER bows like crazy as 1 & 2 applaud feverishly for his performance. this lasts for quite some time. probably too long, but then, this is one wacky play.)

1: oh garsh, thank you mister jester.

2: yes. thank you.

1: you are the best accompanist…

2: we have ever had.

JEST: my pleasure. well, i'd better get back to work.

1: okay.

2: okee dokee.

(they each hug the JESTER in turn. the JESTER doesn't hug back.)

1: thank you.

2: thank you.

JEST: you guys are funny. well, see you later in the show. *(JESTER exits.)*

1: i think that is the best we have ever performed that song.

2: i am forced to agree.

1: you are such a good friend.

2: and you.

(they hug. they part. they liked the hug just a little too much. they sit.)

1: do you think he meant funny "ha ha" or funny "weirdos"?

2: who can say?

(silence.)

1: what show do you think he was referring to?

2: who knows?

(the lights fade on them as MANAGER and WAITRESS enter from the kitchen in the middle of a conversation. lights up on MANAGER and WAITRESS. she is fully clothed except for one shoe missing. she is carrying a pot of coffee and two desserts.)

MAN: so do you understand what i mean by great service as opposed to good service as opposed to bad service as opposed to lazy service as opposed to overeager service as opposed to bitter service as opposed to condescending to speak to the customer service as opposed to sarcastic service as opposed to perky service as opposed to overly perky service as opposed to naked service as opposed to no service, little service, medium service, large service, plus size service? do you? do you understand?

W: yes sir.

MAN: and if you need help on the floor to give great service what do you do?

W: i ask for help sir.

MAN: right. now what do i always say about teamwork?

W: there is no "i" in teamwork.

MAN: very. very good. now what's our motto?

W: the customer is always right.

MAN: repeat!

W: the customer is always right!

MAN: the customer is always right, what?

W: the customer is always right sir!

MAN: i can't hear you!

W: the customer is always right sir!

MAN: good man! now get in there, apologize for the naked service, offer them dessert on the house, and fill that coffee!

W: yes sir!

MAN: will there be any more empty coffee cups in the house?

W: no sir!

MAN: i can't hear you!

W: no sir!

MAN: will there be empty tea glasses?

W: no sir!

MAN: water glasses?

W: no sir!

MAN: ketchup bottles left on the table after the meal is completed?

W: no sir!

MAN: will there be any overflowing ashtrays?

W: well, no sir. i thought smoking was illegal in restaurants in this city.

MAN: are you talking back?

W: no sir!

MAN: well, good then! i want you to repeat after me.

W: yes sir!

MAN: did i say "yes sir"?

W: no sir!

MAN: THEN DON'T REPEAT AFTER ME UNTIL I'VE SAID SOMETHING TO REPEAT!

W: yes sir!

MAN: now repeat after me.

(wait. wait.)

W: now repeat after me?

MAN: good man!

W: good man!

MAN: the government is a bunch of friggin idiots!

W: the government is a bunch of friggin idiots!

MAN: who the heck do they think they are?

W: who the heck do they think they are?

MAN: telling people what they can or can't put into their own bodies!

W: telling people what they can or can't put into their own bodies!

MAN: taking away our best customers!

W: taking away our best customers!

MAN: nonsmokers are uptight under tipping lousy bad mood customers...

W: nonsmokers are uptight under tipping lousy bad mood customers...

MAN: of course they too are always right...

W: of course they too are always right...

MAN: but, smokers rock!

W: but, smokers rock!

MAN: nonsmokers suck but we still have to kiss their ugly booties...

W: nonsmokers suck but we still have to kiss their ugly booties...

MAN: there is no big brother!

W: there is no big brother!

MAN: there is only big mother.

W: there is only big mother.

MAN: now stop repeating after me!

W: yes sir!

MAN: good man. now go. go. go.

W: yes sir! yes sir! yes sir!

(she does a one shoe walk over to the table. lights come up on 1 & 2. MANAGER exits most triumphantly.)

W: hello gentlemen. i am so sorry for the naked service that i have given you on this glorious day. the manager would like me to offer you dessert on the house.

1: naked service?

W: yes. when i came to refill your coffee earlier i was completely naked.

1: you were?

2: was she really?

1: i think so. why else would she be apologizing for being naked?

2: i don't think she should apologize at all.

1: shall we accept the dessert?

2: i don't know. what is it?

1: what kind of dessert have you brought for us?

W: mmmm chocolate cake.

1: *(hypnotized.)* chocolate.

2: *(hypnotized.)* chocolate.

W: mmmmmm.

1&2: mmmmmmm.

W: here you go.

(she sets it down. 1 & 2 just sit there staring.)

W: so do you forgive me?

1: yes. you can give us naked service any time you like.

2: oh please do. please do.

W: *(aside.)* it's amazing the power of chocolate cake. *(to 1 & 2.)* would you like more coffee?

1: what time is it?

2: later than before.

1: no thank you for coffee.

2: it is now time for us to begin drinking beer.

W: you want beer?

1: yes. what kinds do you have?

W: *(perturbed.)* light and dark.

1: i'll have lite.

2: i'll have dark.

1: you always have lite.

2: you always have dark.

1: something is different today.

2: yes it is.

1: odd.

2: very odd.

1: yet relaxing.

2: oddly relaxing.

1: yes.

W: i'll be right back.

(lights follow WAITRESS over to BUSBOY.)

W: did you hear that? now they want beer. i kissed booty. i apologized. i offered them dessert on the house. what does it take? what does it take to get them to leave? i tried the negative approach, ya know the naked service. that usually shocks the doody out of 'em and they run out screaming. not that i have a bad body. i have an immaculate body, but you know how badly the puritans' repressive influences have frigged over everyone's perception of nudity and sex. you get naked real close to people and, unless you are about to frig like wet dogs, they freak out, call it obscene, run away in terror, call the police. but not these two. they seem to have built up an immunity to naked ladies. there is only one thing on their mind. to sit in one spot for all of eternity. why? to make me insane. i am beginning to believe it's personal. i hate this job. i really really hate this job. i'm beginning to think that this isn't a job at all. it's punishment. punishment for something that i did in a former life. whatever it is i did it must have been real bad. i hope i enjoyed myself. garsh you are so stoic. i find that very sexy. very sexy indeed. i am about to do something very bad. here hold this.

(she hands BUSBOY coffee pot. he takes it with his hand that is not facing the audience. this causes him to let go his bus tub which causes the bus tub to fall to the side blocking the audience's view of the blowjob that the WAITRESS falls to her knees to give the BUSBOY. he reacts whimperingly but still doesn't utter a word nor let his gaze off of the campers' table. as she is doing her badness the lights fade up on 1 & 2 and down on WAITRESS and BUSBOY.)

1: what on earth could be taking that waitress so long?

2: she is so slow.

(silent search.)

1: this cake is just staring up at me.

2: mine too.

(silent search.)

1: i can't eat this cake without my beer.

2: me neither.

(silent search.)

1: did you notice that she was naked?

2: no. did you?

1: no. funny, i'll never miss a naked lady on the net.

2: but one in real life…

1: just passes me by.

2: do you mean funny "ha ha"…

1: or funny "weirdo"?

(silence.)

1: shall we switch seats?

2: let's.

(they switch seats and dishes again. another highly orchestrated and choreographed ordeal. as they are going through their ordeal, the lights fade on them and come up on WAITRESS and BUSBOY. she stands wiping her mouth.)

W: how'd you like that? hmm? you really are the biggest busboy in the world. i just love doing that to men. i guess i couldn't really do that to women now could i? well, there are other things i can do to women. someday i'll tell you about them. garsh i love being free to make my own decisions. frig the puritans! here give me that. you know what i'd like to do to you next? i'd like to get myself and one of my girlfriends…

(she takes the coffee pot back and whispers in his ear, then exits. he, of course, drops that dang bus tub again. he rapidly picks it back up and resumes anxiously waiting for 1 & 2 to leave. we hear the sound of random car pulling up again. the motor dies, the door slams, the alarm goes tweep tweep and enter GUNMAN as lights go back up on 1 & 2.)

GUN: excuse me, is this an elementary school?

1&2: no.

GUN: the olympics?

1&2: no.

GUN: subway station?

1&2: no.

(the GUNMAN blinks twice.)

GUN: frig me. i'm so friggin stupid. doodyhead. doodyhead.

(exit GUNMAN. we hear the alarm go tweep tweep, the door slam, and the random car tears away.)

1&2: funny…

(silence.)

1: wow.

2: what?

1: i had forgotten how great a view i had before.

2: come to think of it me too.

1: so where is that dang waitress? this cake is looking better and better.

2: and better. i think i saw her over by the biggest busboy in the world.

1: what was she doing?

2: i think she was helping him pick up his bus tub. poor fellow must be stupid. he keeps dropping that dang bus tub.

1: i noticed that as well.

2: i thought you might. you are very perceptive.

1: except when it comes to real life naked ladies.

(they toast and start to sip when they realize they have no coffee or water or tea, then…)

1&2: THE MANAGER! PLEASE COME KISS OUR BOOTY!!

(the JESTER comes rushing out and skips three circles around the table the whole while chanting…)

JEST: the customer is always right… the customer is always right…

(JESTER exits. MANAGER enters dressed in a black long-sleeved unitard with a scarf. he is smoking a fake "smoking" cigarette

[available at your local halloween shop].)

1: the strangest things happen in this place.

2: yes. i noticed.

MAN: whattaya want?

1: that is no way to speak to a customer!

2: don't you know that the customer is always right?

MAN: yeah, yeah. well i'm sick of it. i'm sick of all these rules. everywhere you go. no smoking, no parking, stop, go, the customer is always right, don't take candy from strangers, do this, do that, blah blah blah. well, i'm sick of it!! i want to be a ballerino, a ballet guy, what's the term for that? balleretta? balleronio? heck i dunno. but i'm for once in my short pathetic life going to follow my dream. and i'm going to break the rules. all of them. look mister mayor, i'm smoking in a restaurant, you nonsmoking republican nazi motherfrigger! stick your rules right up your tight little bootyhole, you son of a gun. and you know what? i'm talking to you you lousy friggin campers. DO YOU KNOW WHAT?

1&2: what?

MAN: *(starts skipping around the table chanting.)* the customer's always wrong... the customer's always wrong...

(enter the WAITRESS and the JESTER skipping and chanting...)

JEST&W: you're gonna get fired, you're gonna get fired...

(1 & 2 join the circle in opposite direction. they do-si-do with the staff chanting...)

1&2: where's our friggin beer... where's our friggin beer...

(this builds and builds until a huge trumpet flair and everyone stops.)

MAN: oh my garsh.

EVERYONE ELSE: what?

MAN: it's the owner.

W: it's the owner.

JEST: it's the owner.

1: it's the owner?

2: it's the owner?

MAN: you!! get back to the dishes. i thought i told you to sweep up this confetti. you!! get back there and brew some coffee or something. you!! sit down and act like you are enjoying yourself. you!! pick up that galdang bus tub!

(the BUSBOY is confused because he has already picked up the bus tub. he thinks it over and drops it.)

MAN: thank you. why can't all my employees be like you. quiet, diligent. ahh.

(the OWNER enters with his two GOILS. they are scantily clad and are carrying a throne made from a restaurant chair. he is short and heavy and dressed like a king.)

OWN: YOU!! what the heck do you mean the customer is always wrong?

MAN: i er uh...

OWN: shut up!! i'll have your head you lousy excuse for a leader. what the heck are you wearing? crispy cripe! i can see your little bitty balls. oh garsh, that is disgusting. goils, look away, the man has no penis. turn around for cripe's sake you are going to make my goils sick. ahh!! now i can see the crack of your booty. good garsh man, get back there and put on some clothes before you run off all my customers. you look like a friggin ballerina or something.

MAN: i'll have you know that i am a ballerino.

OWN: shutup! git!

(MANAGER exits rapidly.)

OWN: now where is that galdang jester he is supposed to give me an introduction?

(enter JESTER.)

JEST: i am soooo sorry sir. it completely slipped my brain. ya know the dishes are really piling up in there.

OWN: get on with it.

JEST: yes sir. ladies and gentlemen, all the way from a place far better than you, driving cars far nicer than you will ever drive, who was born with a silver spoon in his mouth, up his booty, and jabbed in both ears, able to fire an entire team in one breath without batting an eye, ladies and gentlemen may i please present to you the owner!

OWN: what about the song?

JEST: you would. you would. guitar! i said guitar! galdang you boy.

(exit JESTER. a huge fight is heard offstage. the JESTER gets thrown out onto the stage, where he brushes himself off and pulls up his sleeve and exits. more fighting is heard. enter JESTER with guitar. repeat country waltz.)

JESTER: "o owner o owner
you are so friggin rich
your children are living nightmares
and your wife is a bitch."
thank you all. you really love me. you there in the back sit down!

OWN: that is no way to introduce the owner! goils! show him how it's done.

(the OWNER's GOILS step in front of the JESTER and the lights change and disco music kicks in and the GOILS do an amazing musical disco dance number. the GOILS close their dance with...)

GOILS: the owner!

OWN: jesty baby. your job may be in jeopardy. now get back to the dishes.

JEST: *(to audience.)* my life is so glamorous. *(exit JESTER.)*

OWN: so how are you happy campers today?

1: fine.

2: okay.

1: except...

2: the manager was just sooo rude to us.

OWN: you really must forgive him. he is a little troubled. you see, many years ago he had a horrible accident. broke his leg and instead of being put in the medical hospital, he was accidentally switched with a mental patient and so was sent to a mental hospital where he spent ten long years. he tried to tell them that they had the wrong guy, but they just kept giving him the shock treatment and telling him he was crazy. his broke leg healed miraculously by itself (it must have been the padded cell) but the shock treatments really had a horrible effect. he started thinking that he could dance the ballet. he's never even been to the ballet. and that's when they let him go, right when he truly went crazy. funny isn't it? when i found him he was a homeless wreck. he told stories of living happily in a homeless camp until the mayor shut them all down. then he learned to sleep standing up, because he was afraid of the police. he had heard these horrible stories about how the police stuck things up people's booties just for being homeless or a foreigner. i felt so sorry for the poor son of a gun. don't get me wrong. i could care less for the homeless. in case you can't tell i am exorbitantly rich. we rich people don't give a frig about anything or anyone else. i think it generally happens after your annual passes six digits. when i was a five digit man i cared, yes i did. but that's all in the past now. i am now a seven digit man and personally, i could care less if the whole world shrivels up and dies. it doesn't matter to me because i am a scientologist and i know l.ron will save me from the depths of heck. i never really was afraid of the end of the world, ya know. i used to be a christian. that's why we use plastic to go containers. who cares about pollution as long as you have false hope to save you. no, i didn't help out the manager out of the goodness of my heart. there is no goodness there. i helped him out because i felt guilty. why did i feel guilty? i was never catholic. i was a strict protestant before i bought into scientology. i felt guilty because i'm the mental patient that he got switched with! ha ha ha ha ha ha ha ha ha ha ha. i spent one week in the medical hospital for a broke leg that healed faster than any doctor had ever seen before, and then i was set free. i was a homicidal maniac. i still am. i mean what better way to kill a whole buncha people than to start a restaurant? oh don't worry. i don't use poison. i just use waste. waste waste waste. paper towels, beer bottles, styrofoam coffee cups, freon for the air conditioners, freon for the walk-ins, i have twelve you know. me along with all the restaurants and big businesses and rich sons of guns in the world are going to kill off the entire population without anyone getting caught or blamed. and get this, due to organized religion, we, the rich and powerful, are all saved! of course you know poor people go to heck. they can't afford to be overly religious, especially when it comes to the true religion, scientology. so work hard gentlemen. take my advice. work very hard. will you work hard boys?

1&2: yes.

OWN: great. so please forgive the manager. it's not his fault. okay?

1&2: okay.

OWN: great! so how was brunch?

1: it was…

2: interesting.

OWN: great!

1: now we only have…

2: one question.

OWN: what's that?

1&2: WHERE'S OUR FRIGGIN BEER?

(OWNER walks slowly to his throne and sits. he bangs his scepter three times and shouts…)

Own: WAITRESS!!

(enter WAITRESS dressed as a ballerina with combat boots. she has the two beers.)

W: here's your galdang beer!

(she slams them down on the table. 1 & 2 slam their beers. after the slam…)

1: that was dark!

2: that was lite!

1: i ordered lite!

2: i ordered dark!

W: no you didn't. you ordered dark and you ordered lite.

1&2: no we didn't.

W: yes you did.

1&2: no we didn't.

W: yes you... wait a minute. did you switch seats?

1: um well...

2: well, you know...

W: you did! you miserable utterly useless motherfriggin customers. i can't take it! "can we have more coffee?," "can we have dessert?," "my food is cold," "my steak is underdone," "this potato's bad," moan whine moan. every galdang sunday it's the same thing. on the seventh day garsh rested but his waitress busted her friggin booty! i'm going to kill you sons of guns!!! with this butter knife!

(1 & 2 scream and run away around the table. the WAITRESS chases them.)

OWN: come on goils, let's stop that waitress from killing our bread and butter. there'll be no rapid killing in my restaurant! only slow death.

(OWNER sets down his scepter, and he and his GOILS join in the chase. the MANAGER enters.)

MAN: hey wait a minute! what the heck is going on here?

OWN: we've got to stop her she's going to kill the customers.

MAN: oh garsh.

(MANAGER joins in the chase. enter the JESTER. he takes up the scepter and bangs it three times.)

JEST: hear ye! hear ye! i have an announcement that is of great import!

(chase stops.)

JEST: now entering the parking lot in her brand-new convertible fancy car talking on the digital (or is it cellular?) phone... the most terrifying visage known to man... it's the owner's wife!!

(everyone screams and scrambles. the OWNER scrambles to his throne and pulls out conservative dresses for his GOILS, they put them on very quickly. 1 & 2 sit down and act like they are very comfortable and very happy. the WAITRESS and MANAGER fight over the broom to sweep up the confetti. the JESTER exits to the kitchen. the BUSBOY picks up his bus tub. after all this hubbub, the MANAGER and WAITRESS stand at attention beside the throne and the OWNER sits down. enter the WIFE. she is talking on the phone. she is dressed as a queen. she is such a witch.)

WIFE: yes darling i want another appointment today. so what if it's the third time in one day. i have a galdang hair out of place and i want it put back into place! i don't care if you have any customers, bump them! how dare you talk to me like that? don't you know who my father is? that's right. he's the mayor's best and richest friend. now don't frig with me or i will have you shut down for a health violation. who cares if you don't have any violations we'll make one up!!! that's better. yes. that time is fine. what's your name? what do you mean you'd rather not say? i see. well honey, you are a stupid friggin cunt!

(the entire cast gasps at her use of such a word. she hangs up and pulls a mirror from her bag.)

WIFE: what?

EVERYONE: nothing!

WIFE: hello everyone.

EVERYONE: hello!

WIFE: will you look at that hair. do you see? it's this one. it's completely out of place. everything looks nice in here. but, where's my throne?

(everyone rushes into the kitchen [except the BUSBOY] to get the witch her throne. she is left on the stage alone.)

WIFE: *(to audience.)* they are terrified of me. i don't know why. i assure you i'm nothing but a fair, level minded person.

(everyone busts out the kitchen door pushing a throne that is much larger than the OWNER's. they set it up directly beside the OWNER's. everyone back to places.)

WIFE: thank you all. you are so nice to me. what is this? is this dust on my throne? I SAID IS THIS DUST?

(the JESTER appears at the kitchen door with feather dusters. he passes them out to the rest of the cast. they all dust the doody out of that throne. they all pass the dusters back to the kitchen and go back to their places.)

WIFE: wonderful. i love my throne. how are you gentlemen doing today?

1: just wonderful.

2: just fine.

WIFE: and are you in need of anything?

1: no no not at all.

2: absolutely fine.

WIFE: why aren't you eating your cake?

1: um well… you see…

2: we like to have beer with our cake.

WIFE: WAITRESS!!!

(WAITRESS runs to kitchen.)

WIFE: beer with cake?

1&2: yes ma'am. it's good. it makes us happy.

WIFE: well, the customer is always right even when they are terribly terribly wrong.

(WAITRESS returns with beer.)

W: who had lite and who had dark?

1&2: i did.

W: right. *(she sets beers down gently and goes back to place.)*

WIFE: my darling?

OWN: yes sweetie pie.

WIFE: your secretaries are dressed very conservatively today. i like that.

OWN: thank you dear.

WIFE: isn't it wonderful to be rich?

OWN: yes dear.

WIFE: and republican?

OWN: yes dear.

WIFE: and a scientologist?

(the entire cast puts on its best goofy face and utters "ghhhhhhhhhhhhhhh." back to normal.)

OWN: yes dear.

WIFE: i just love it when they hook you up to that machine.

OWN: me too dear.

WIFE: so tell me why are the employees dressed as ballet dancers?

OWN: um, i'm not really sure, um…

MAN: er, uh, it's… ballet day.

WIFE: what?

W: um sure, um, that's right ma'am. it's ballet day here at the ol' restaurant. last week it was western week and um, we came dressed as cowboys.

WIFE: do the customers like that sort of thing?

1&2: um, yes, yes. we do. really we do.

WIFE: good. how's the cake?

1: we haven't exactly…

2: tried it yet.

WIFE: well, eat your galdang cake!!

1&2: yes ma'am.

(the cell phone rings its evil ring.)

WIFE: hold it!

(1 & 2 wait.)

WIFE: hello? yes? i see. okay. well what do you want me to do? they are your responsibility. this is why we have hired you. to walk them, feed them and clean up after them. i don't care. you can shoot her if she won't get down. yes fine. the gun is in the top drawer to the left. i said fine! *(she hangs up.)* it was the nanny. why did we have children?

OWN: because you said you wanted them.

WIFE: don't talk back to me!

OWN: sorry.

WIFE: sorry who?

OWN: sorry, dear.

WIFE: what the heck are you lookin at? eat yer friggin cake!

(they eat a bite and chew and chew and chew, then they rinse with beer.)

WIFE: so, how is it?

1: it's…

2: a…

1: little…

2: dry.

(the kitchen door flies open and out comes the JESTER with a ridiculous chef's hat and a fake mustache. he is carrying a cleaver. he speaks now with a french accent.)

JEST: what do you mean the cake is dry? you americans want everything moist, moist, moist. let me tell you something. the cake she is made with pudding and it is the most moist cake in all of the land. if my cake is too dry for you it is not the cake's fault but the fault of your wet, dripping, american tongues. your mouth is too wet. my cake, she is not dry. *(he lifts the cleaver and slams it down on the table. it sticks in the wood.)* this is what i think of your dry cake.

(he shoves their cakes into their faces, gets his cleaver, and exits.)

1: did you notice how much the cook looks like the jester?

2: i really can't see anything past all this chocolate.

WIFE: waitress!! get these men some napkins.

(she does so.)

WIFE: darling!

OWN: yes dear?

WIFE: fire that french cook. you know i hate the french.

OWN: and you know they hate you too.

WIFE: do i look like someone who gives a rat's booty what anyone thinks of them?

OWN: no dear.

WIFE: right! then fire that cook!

OWN: yes dear. *(he bangs scepter.)* cook!

WIFE: how does my makeup look?

1: you know this is the most relaxed i have been in years.

2: me too interestingly enough.

1: we should come here every sunday.

2: we do.

(enter JESTER.)

JEST: what the heck do you want?

OWN: you're fired.

JEST: you can't fire me. who'll do the dishes?

1: i knew it. you are the jester.

JEST: you didn't think i could make a living washing dishes did you?

1: apparently not.

(exit JESTER.)

W: *(to MANAGER.)* garsh you sure are sexy in that outfit.

MAN: i find myself drooling over you as well.

W: shall we dance?

MAN: let's.

(they begin dancing the ballet together. the BUSBOY is heartbroken. he drops his bus tub.)

WIFE: you know we really should take the convertible to the shop.

OWN: but why dear?

WIFE: i want the seats to smell like leather again.

OWN: yes dear.

(a blood-curdling scream comes from the kitchen. everyone but 1 & 2 and the BUSBOY...)

EVERYONE: what the heck was that?

OFFSTAGE: someone help me.

(everyone rushes to the kitchen but 1 & 2 and the BUSBOY. BUSBOY picks up his tub slowly and resumes staring at the campers. after a considerable silence.)

1: so when he caught you, that's when he threatened your life.

2: what?

1: you know, your boss, his wife, her booty.

2: oh yes. he threatened me, then his wife, then he fired me.

1: i thought you quit.

2: the end result is the same.

1: yes. don't you wish you could have done her right there on the copier?

2: oh yes i do.

1: i love ladies. wish i would have noticed when the waitress was naked.

2: me too to both. shall we go?

1: the waitress hasn't brought back my card yet.

2: you gave her your card?

1: well, i have to pay.

2: you are so honest.

1: you sound just like my chat partner.

2: and you sound like mine.

1: what is your partner's netname?

2: one.

1: oh my garsh. are you two?

1: you are one?

1: i am one.

2: i am two.

1: i thought sure you were a woman.

2: i thought sure you were a woman.

1: i'm not.

2: me neither.

1: i have been in love with you since the first day we chatted.

2: me too. not with me. but with you.

1: i always have felt a strange impulse to kiss you after brunch.

2: me too.

1: but i always dismissed it as a natural tendency...

2: not to be taken seriously.

1: i love you.

2: i love you too.

1: what do we do?

2: i don't know.

1: thank garsh it's the nineties.

2: actually it is the aughts.

1: aughts?

2: yes, you know those two little zeros at the end of the year.

1: I have once again learned something new from you my friend. So, thank garsh it's the aughts.

2: yeah, it's almost okay to feel this way.

1: frig me.

2: right here?

1: yes right here. let's frig like maniacs. right here. right now.

2: okay. i'm so glad i found you.

1: and i you.

(they both take off their clothes on opposite sides of the table. they are both wearing high school wrestling outfits. each pulls a pump out of his waistband. after each of the following lines, they pump three times and their crotches swell a little until at the end of this section they have huge erections.)

1: to think...

2: all this time..

1: looking at dirty pictures...

2: chatting...

1: masturbating...

2: i only wanted to be near you...

1: every sunday...

2: brunch...

1: who knew?

2: it was you...

1: i am number one.

2: i am number two.

(silence.)

1: now what?

2: i don't know.

(silence.)

1: let's embrace.

2: okay.

(they try to embrace without touching peni.)

1: shall i bend over?

2: shall i?

(silence.)

1: i'm really not sure...

2: what to do.

1: i can't bring myself...

2: to touch you...

(their erections fall with a hiss. they seem very depressed.)

1: i know!

2: what?

1: let's leave.

2: great idea.

1: it takes me five minutes to get home.

2: me too.

1: i'll see you on the net.

2: yes!

1: yes!

1&2: yes! i love you.

1: but thanks to computers...

2: and delivery services...

1: i never have to touch you.

2: joy! we will keep meeting here every sunday right?

1: of course. why change?

2: no reason. let's go. i'm horny as heck.

1: but wait!

2: what?

1: we still have beer.

2: let's finish the beer.

1: and wait for my card.

2: is the busboy growling?

1: i think he is.

(enter everyone else with the JESTER on a stretcher. he has a bloody rag over one hand.)

W: oh my garsh, the dishwasher cut his finger off.

WIFE: i thought he was the cook.

OWN: honey, please call an ambulance on your wireless.

MAN: i think i'm going to pass out. i hate blood.

JEST: i'll never play the guitar again!

W: oh my garsh!

EVERYONE: what?

W: the campers are wearing high school wrestling outfits!

(everyone screams and drops the JESTER.)

JEST: ow!

W: disgusting.

OWN: i never...

MAN: ugh.

OWN: let's get 'em.

W: who do they think they are?

MAN: campers think they rule the whole world. and they're nonsmokers. high school wrestling outfit wearing nonsmokers.

WIFE: KILL THE CAMPERS!

(all but BUSBOY and 1 & 2 chant: kill the campers, kill the campers, kill the campers...)

(we hear the sound of random car crashing through the walls and windows of an unseen area of the restaurant. a beat goes by. enter GUNMAN in a rage. he pauses briefly, leans outside the front door and we hear his car alarm go tweep tweep. he takes center stage.)

GUN: THIS IS FOR ALL RACES OTHER THAN MY OWN!!!

(blam! blam! blam! he kills the OWNER and his two "secretaries.")

GUN: THIS IS FOR ALL SEXUAL PERSUASIONS OTHER THAN MY OWN!! *(pause.)* IN THE MILITARY! *(pause.)* AND THE BOY SCOUTS! *(pause.)* AND ADOPTING BABIES!

(blam! blam! blam! he kills the WIFE, the JESTER, and the MANAGER.)

GUN: THIS IS FOR ALL POLITICAL SLASH RELIGIOUS VIEWS OTHER THAN MY OWN!!

(blam! blam! blam! he kills the WAITRESS and 1 & 2.)

GUN: pardon me? is this the post office?

(BUSBOY shakes head.)

GUN: dang. doodyhead, doodyhead, doodyhead. this antidepression drug really frigs with my sense of direction. will you look at all those innocent people. tsk tsk tsk. life is so random. are those two men wearing high school wrestling outfits?

(BUSBOY nods.)

GUN: funny. this world is just chock full of weirdos. what a shame. everyone is dead. except you. would you like me to shoot you too? join your friends?

(BUSBOY shakes his head.)

GUN: okay then. is this a tragedy?

(BUSBOY shrugs.)

GUN: let's call it a tragedy. this certainly isn't funny at all. well, have a nice day.

(GUNMAN sticks gun in his own mouth. blam! he kills himself. BUSBOY realizes that he is for once all alone. he looks at the audience and smiles broadly. he then begins singing "singin' in the rain" and joyfully cleans the dishes off the table while nimbly leaping to and fro over dead bodies in a highly choreographed song and dance. once the table is bussed and ready for the next customer, he begins humming the instrumental break in the song and doing an amazing soft shoe tap dance à la gene kelly. at the end of the song—the entire song—we hear sirens and see flashing lights.)

(the end.)

ASCENDING BODILY

Maggie Cino

MAGGIE CINO was born at 7:05 on a Friday morning in Philadelphia. Many years later, she attended Barnard College of Columbia University, and, later still, she found herself at the Dell'Arte International School of Physical Theatre. As an actor, Cino has appeared in *Die Like a Lady: Or What Barbara Got* by Carolyn Raship, *Molière's Monster* with the Wax Factory, and *No One* by Julia Lee Barclay. She co-created and acted in *Geek on Smack* (with Patty Litzen) and *Angry Little People* (with Carolyn Raship), which is soon to be filmed under the direction of Daniel Kleinfeld. Cino currently lives in Brooklyn, New York.

Ascending Bodily was first presented by Screaming Venus (Monica Sirignano, Artistic Director) as part of *Eve's Apple: A Festival of One Person Shows* on January 15, 2002, at the Kraine Theatre, New York City, with the following cast and credits:

Sadie .... Maggie Cino

Directed by: Dov Weinstein
Assistant Director: Sally McGuire
Lighting Designer: Miranda Hardy
Set Designer: Dan Maccarone
Production Manager: Barabbas Gould

Thanks go out to some very important people:

Ronlin Foreman and the Dell'Arte International School of Physical Theater, where Sadie was born.

Screaming Venus, especially Monica Sirignano and Alison Solomon, who took a leap of faith and agreed to produce this play before it had a title, let alone a script.

Rita Burns, my grandmother, to whom this play is dedicated.

Tony and Susan Cino.

Sally McGuire, Jessie McCracken, Daniel Kleinfeld, 399 Sackett Street, all the clowns in the boat, and all the venues at which this piece has been performed.

And thanks beyond thanks to Dov Weinstein, who sat through hours of rehearsal, listening, shaping, and creating a space for work to happen, and whose humor, phrasing, and storytelling gifts shine throughout the piece. Sadie wouldn't be half the woman she is without him.

AUTHOR'S NOTE

Ascending Bodily began its life not as an idea on the page but with the character. The original intention of the piece was to have it be primarily movement with some puppetry work involving the handbags. To that end, I had asked Dov Weinstein, whose work in this vein I had admired in the past, to help create the show.

But soon after they met, Dov and Sadie decided things should go a little differently. Sadie loves to talk, and she's had many wonderful things happen to her. Seeing this, Dov insisted she tell her stories as clearly as possible. By endlessly pointing out important phrases, suggesting structures, and creating improvs and scenarios, he gently teased this play into existence.

Now, my original thought was not entirely lost, and there is certainly movement and play with the bags in the production as it was eventually staged. After much thought, I have preserved the majority of the original stage directions as well as descriptions of the original character and bags. This is so the intent and mood of that production is clear to the general reader. However, in any productions of the play, the stage directions are of course only to be guidelines and the character should be created as the actor and director see fit.

It is a piece created for a particular character, but I am delighted at the possibility that others may see new and different opportunities for characterization and staging.

THE CHARACTER

SADIE. An old woman who happens to still be young. She is wearing a large picture hat, a tweed skirt, a pink camouflage top, a white mesh overshirt with feather boa sleeves, fishnet stockings, socks, and extremely high-heeled mules. She is many colors, but predominately pink.

THE BAGS

There are eleven bags. The bag Bob gave her (referred to in the stage directions as "Bob bag") is a beige leather clutch with two short handles. The moonstone bag (referred to in the stage directions as "the pink bag") is also a clutch, hot pink in color, with pearly buttons on it. The bag in which she spies the invisible gentleman in the Siberian Desert is black patent leather, and the bag given to her by the gentleman in the Serengeti Jungle is a large straw bag with flowers. The rest of the bags are a variety of shoulder bags and clutches placed specifically around her body.

THE SETTING

This very place. The stage is bare, with the exceptions of a hat rack upstage center and two small tables, one downstage left, one downstage right.

THE TIME

This very moment.

LIGHTING

Footlights. Because of the hat.

SADIE stands, wearing all of her bags. She is holding Bob bag in one raised hand and looking at it. Low, dreamy lights slowly rise.

SADIE: Have you ever found yourself suddenly alone?

I was standing on the plateau when I heard an enormous rumbling sound. Dozens of small, hairy creatures had begun to amass. The mating season of the teeny tiny llamas of the Himalayan Andes had begun.

Stampeding towards the cliff, the only thing that stood between the teeny tiny llamas and their destiny was our little woven house. Sensing the imminent peril, Bob stepped in front of the onslaught. But it was too late. The teeny tiny llamas had accumulated mass force, and they swept him up, shattering our little house.

One by one, the teeny tiny llamas tumbled over the cliff. Those that survived at the bottom would mate, producing the next generation of teeny tiny llamas.

Bouncing on their backs, Bob was hurled over the cliff, and began to rise. He rose up and up and up, until he was swallowed in all that blue.

(Her head bows. The lights change to a brighter, more ordinary daylight tone. When she lifts her head, she is in another mode, ready and excited to go out. As if there is a mirror there, she inspects her outfit, first holding Bob bag in front, and then holding the pink bag in front. But this only leads to upset and confusion.)

This is terrible!

(Stretches out arms so all eleven bags are inadvertently displayed.)

I have one too many bags!

(She takes off most of the bags she is wearing, and puts some of them on the stage left table and some of them on the stage right table. The pink bag and the black patent leather bag are put on the stage left table. The straw bag is on the stage right table. She keeps Bob bag in her hand.)

This won't do at all. I have a very special gentleman coming to see me, and I must be looking my very best.

I met him just the other day, while walking among the ancient stones. It was blue and gold in the twilight, and everything was very peaceful. When suddenly, a terrible wind surrounded me, and rain began to fall. I found shelter underneath a tree. But it was the most unusual tree I ever saw! And I looked up and up and up,

(Does so, and it becomes necessary to hold her hat on with one hand. This posture of arching up to the enormous gentleman is the one she uses to address him for the remainder of the piece.)

and it wasn't a tree at all, but an enormous gentleman, with a bald head like the moon, and he was crying. "Why are you crying?" I asked him.

(He does not respond.)

"Have you ever been to the Siberian Desert? I have!"

It was cold in the Siberian Desert. It was dark in the Siberian Desert. And I did not know where I was, or who I was going to meet, or what I was sent to do in the Siberian Desert.

(On each where/who/what, she takes a bag from the pile on stage left and puts it back into place on her person, leaving the pink bag where it is on the table. She does this as a cowboy might strap on guns for a shootout.)

And so I made my way to a dune and I cried and I cried and I cried. When suddenly (*Looks back, then forward.*) I heard a sound, but no one was there. And I cried and I cried and I cried. When suddenly (*Looks back, then forward.*) I heard the sound again. Luckily my motto, as I used to say to Bob, is "Always be prepared!"

(She raises the black patent leather bag to use as a mirror positioned to see what is behind her.)

To the naked eye he was invisible, but I could see him in the reflection of my bag.

He had black hair and broad cheekbones.

And he was crying as well!

"Why are you crying?" I asked him. But he just looked at me with sad, dark eyes and took my hand. And there, between his thumb and his forefinger, was the mark of the very people I had been sent to the Siberian Desert to find!

(Turns to the enormous gentleman and arches up to him.)

"So as you can see, crying made me a brand-new friend!"

The wind and rain had stopped, and my enormous gentleman was looking at me! And I knew, in that moment, that we must see each other again.

And I promised I would take that bag!

(Looks at pink bag still on stage left table.)

This is terrible! I can't take them both. Not only doesn't it look right, but it would be improper.

I am meeting my enormous gentleman friend very soon, and it's important to look your best when you meet a gentleman for the third time.

(During this, she picks up pink bag from stage left table, puts Bob bag on hat rack up center, comes back down left, poses with pink bag as if checking reflection in a mirror. Remembers Bob. Sinks, puts pink bag back on stage left table, moves back to hat rack and picks up Bob bag.)

When I was a young girl, I had a very special love of the sea.

(Holding Bob bag in front of her, moves it as if it were a boat going through gentle waves.)

As I grew, I would stand on the windy shore, watching the boats go by, moving into a world full of enticing possibilities. And then one day I saw my opportunity!

(Holding Bob bag the way one would ordinarily hold a clutch handbag.)

I was standing on the docks looking out at the boats when out of the corner of my eye I saw that

(Moves the bag up to the side of her face on an angle, and at the right moment one of the handles of the bag slides down.)

the gangplank had been left down! Oh, I felt it drawing me, that long slick expanse of wood, pulling me towards the dark hull and into the body of the ship.

I couldn't believe it!

(Holding the bag as one would ordinarily hold a clutch handbag.)

I was standing on the deck of the ship! Looking down at the blue sea below me and up at the blue sky above me! And I made my way to the prow of the ship.

(Holding bag up so it is ship again.)

And as I stood there, (*Raises one of the bag's handles.*) I felt a presence behind me. *(Raises the bag's other handle.)* I began to get very nervous. *(Shakes handle.)* Then I felt a motion beneath my feet, and the shore was moving further and further away!

(She begins to move the bag again; it is the ship on the water.)

We were off, and there was no turning back. I summoned up all of my courage, and I spun around

(Spins 360 degrees, and, on the other side, is holding the bag as one would ordinarily hold a clutch handbag.)

actually I spun around like this

(Spins 180 degrees.)

and when I spun around

(Spins 180 degrees again.)

I was face to face with the most beautiful gentleman I had ever seen. He had a small, wiry mustache and ruddy, weather-beaten cheeks. He looked at me and said,

"Hello."

and I said, "Hello."

and he said, "What are you doing here?"

and I said, "Standing."

and he said, "Really."

and I said, "Yes!"

and I said to him, "What is your name?"

and he said to me, "BOB!"

and we stood there, when suddenly the ship began to pitch and twist!

(Both she and the bag do.)

We had to cling to each other for support! And we were thrown overboard onto a rocky beach.

(Turns bag upside down, fingers holding it open from the bottom.)

And we looked up and up and up, and there was the biggest mountain we had ever seen.

But really, I must get dressed!

(Drops action with Bob bag, looks at pink bag.)

The second time I met my enormous gentleman I was walking among the ancient stones when I saw his great knees and his bald head like the moon. And I ran to them and looked up and up and up *(Does so.)* —and there was nothing above his knees, and his bald head was the moon. Then I heard laughter behind me and there was my gentleman friend! He reached across and broke off bits of the moon. They rained around me and he said,

"For you you you..." *(Does this in echo effect.)*

"This is so marvelous. This is the best present I've had since... have you ever been to the Serengeti Jungle? I have!"

It was dense and wet in the Serengeti Jungle,

(During this, she collects and puts on the bags from the stage right table, leaving the large straw bag where it is.)

and I was clearing my way through the underbrush. Ahead of me, I saw a light. And as I cleared away the last bit of underbrush, there in front of me was the most powerful gentleman I had ever seen. He was sitting at an enormous contraption. His great hands were moving nimbly over the wet palm fronds. His powerful leg was pumping the pedal. It took me a moment to catch my breath. But when I did I asked him,

"What are you doing?"

and he said to me, "Weaving."

"What are you weaving?"

"Baskets."

"What do you use them for?"

"Gifts."

So I watched him weave. And when he was done, there was the loveliest basket I had ever seen.

(Looks at straw bag still on stage right table, picks it up.)

He handed it to me and said, "For you."

(Turns bag around to reveal straw flowers on the other side, looks at audience.)

And so I went with him back to his tent, *(Looks at enormous gentleman, a bit too intently.)* to participate in ritual gift giving exchanges. *(Looks at audience with a wink.)* And that was how I became one with the people of the Serengeti Jungle.

(To enormous gentleman.) "These moonstones are so beautiful! I am going to make a bag with them, and I will have it with me when you see me next."

(Uses next line to walk to stage left table where the pink bag is.)

So, you see, I promised. And it is important to keep your promises because then people can trust you and if people can't trust you then you can't spend time with remarkable people.

(Picks up pink bag.)

Don't the moonstones gleam so beautifully?

(Holds up Bob bag.)

But this bag was my very first work of craftsmanship!

In the Himalayan Andes, Bob would hunt. One day he gave me the most beautiful skin. *(Looks at pink bag.)* I had just begun to explore my aptitude for craftsmanship *(Holds up Bob bag.)* and I made this bag! Bob laughed and said, "I will always think of you with that bag." The day I finished it,

(Return to opening tableau, light and mood shift accordingly.)

I was standing on the plateau when I heard an enormous rumbling sound. Dozens of small, hairy creatures had begun to amass. The mating season of the teeny tiny llamas of the Himalayan Andes had begun.

Stampeding towards the cliff, the only thing that stood between the teeny tiny llamas and their destiny was our little woven house. Sensing the imminent peril, Bob, my very first suitor, stepped in front of the onslaught. But it was too late. The teeny tiny llamas had accumulated mass force, and they swept him up, shattering our little house.

One by one, the teeny tiny llamas tumbled over the cliff. Those that survived at the bottom would mate, producing the next generation of teeny tiny llamas.

Bouncing on their backs, Bob was hurled over the cliff, and began to rise. He rose up and up, and his hands opened, and something dropped through the sky.

(Holding Bob bag in front, looking at it.)

My bag! He continued to rise up and up and up until he was swallowed in all that blue.

(Silence. Lights and mood return to ordinary.)

Well, I must be off. It's quite rude to keep a gentleman waiting.

(Hesitates, then notices audience. Speaks to a person in audience.)

Young man [young lady], let me see your hands. Oh, very nice! Those are very strong hands. They have very deep lines. Do you take care of them? Oh good.

(Hands the person Bob bag.)

Will you hold this a moment? Oh, very nice. Hold it up. And a little to the side. And grab it by the top. It looks very well on you! Would you hold it for me, for just a little while, while I'm out? And if you see a beautiful man with a wiry mustache and ruddy weather-beaten cheeks, tell him that I'll be back very soon, and that I think of him always.

I must be off.

(Goes to leave, then changes mind.)

Just one more thing.

(To person holding the bag.)

Do you think, if a person is taken bodily into the heavens, that they will ever return?

(Slow fade to black.)

(End of play.)

LAST CALL

Kelly McAllister

KELLY McALLISTER was born a Taurus in the year of the Fire Horse on May 6, 1966, in San Jose, California. He graduated from San Jose State University with a bachelor's in theatre arts with an emphasis on drama. McAllister has appeared as an actor at The Western Stage, in numerous productions of Expanded Arts Shakespeare in the Park(ing) Lot series, among many others. Also at Expanded Arts, he appeared in *Dracula 2000,* written by his brother, Jerry McAllister. Together, the three McAllister siblings—Jerry, Heather, and Kelly—formed the hope theatre, inc., of which Kelly McAllister is company manager. He also played the lead in the hope theatre, inc., production of the American professional premiere of Shakespeare's *Edward III.* McAllister wrote the libretto for an adaptation of Hans Christian Andersen's *The Snow Queen* for Children's Theatre Workshop. He won an award for Excellence in Playwriting for *Last Call* at the 2002 New York International Fringe Festival. He is a 2003 recipient of the GOLD (Graduate of the Last Decade) Award from San Jose State University. Currently, he is working on two one-act plays for *The Killer Bee's,* a short play festival being produced by the hope theatre, inc. He is also working on a new one-act play with the working title *Diary of a Teen-age Born-again* for the Brass Tacks Theater Company as part of its Rosetta Festival. McAllister lives in the Williamsburg section of Brooklyn, New York. He is left-handed, as is everyone in his family.

Last Call was first presented by hope theatre, inc. (Heather McAllister, Artistic Director), as part of the New York International Fringe Festival (Elena K. Holy, Producing Artistic Director), on August 10, 2002, at Theatre for the New City, with the following cast and credits:

David .... Brett Christensen
Sheila .... Christine Goodman
Jack .... Jack Halpin
Carlos .... R. Paul Hamilton
Karl .... John Patrick Nord
Vince .... Vinnie Penna
Jerry .... Matthew Rankin
Kristen .... Masha Sapron
Molly .... Sara Thigpen

Director: Jerry McAllister
Stage Manager: Michael Minn
Choreographer: Jessica Wallenfels
Assistant Director: Stacey Plaskett
Fight Director: Vinnie Penna
Assistant Stage Manager: Melissa Welburn
Lighting Design: Jerry McAllister
Sound Design: Kelly McAllister
Set Design: Heather McAllister
Costume Design: David Jordan
Production Photographer: Laurent Girard
Production Assistant: Eric "Speed" Smith
Technical Directors for the Fringe Festival: Peter Kyte and Julia Cole

Thanks to Nicole Bradin, Leona Pickering, Clayton Pax, Jay McAllister, Alison Norris, The Present Company, Turnip Theatre Co., Elizabeth Zambetti, Theatreworks-USA, Lexington Photo Labs, (t)here magazine, Marion Fuller, Mark Mendes, Friends of Lee Winston, Kim Brown, Anthony Di Maggio, Myles Reed, Willy Elder, Kisoo Kim, Mr. and Mrs. Kokkoris, Elizabeth Reynolds, Bart Lovins, and Jack Halpin.

AUTHOR'S NOTE

Last Call was first developed as part of a festival of new works at the Turnip Theatre Co. About thirty pages were written, and a staged reading was performed, directed by Elizabeth Zambetti. It then sat in my files for several years, until Jack Halpin suggested that I submit it to the New York International Fringe Festival, which I did, along with a note saying I would turn it into a full-length play. I then forgot all about it, until late April, when I got a letter from the Fringe Festival telling me that it was accepted and would be going up in August. I began work immediately. The play went from a quirky comedy with five male characters to a more serious, eleven-character drama/comedy, dealing with life, death, friendship, and other light subjects. The character Jack went from being a stupid, funny drunk guy to a damaged, sad man, haunted by his past and unable to control his circumstances very well. And all of a sudden, there were three women in the show. My one advice to other writers is this: when the voices in your head dictate the script to you, let them have their way.

This play uses a lot of music, in the form of songs played on the jukebox. The only song that I feel must be used is "Lights" by Journey. It captures a time and place, is both sentimental and sharp—a rarity in pop music. Almost all of the quotes in Jack's dream sequences are from poems by W.B. Yeats. The toast David makes is from Byron. Webelos is a scouting organization that covers the time between being a Cub Scout and being a Boy Scout. It is pronounced WE-buh-los.

CHARACTERS

SHEILA: Just turned 21. Art student, full of life, always looking for the next possible painting subject.

JACK: In his mid-30s, slightly brain damaged from a car accident he was involved in when he was 22.

DAVID: In his mid-30s, bright, energetic, and a manic existentialist since 9/11.

CARLOS: In his mid- to late 40s. The owner and bartender of Tom's, a bar in Salinas, California. Very patriotic. Vietnam vet.

KRISTEN: In her early 30s. Married to Karl. Sexy, and very bored with married life.

VINCE: In his mid-30s. Married to Molly.

JERRY: In his mid-30s. A dreamer, he works in a bookstore.

MOLLY: In her early 30s, married to Vince.

KARL: In his mid- to late 30s, owner of a chain of bookstores and a large split-level ranch house in Prunedale, a wealthy suburb of Salinas.

ACT ONE
SCENE ONE

A dark, empty bar in Salinas, California. There are a few empty tables and chairs, a jukebox, and one door to the outside. It is about ten minutes before dawn. SHEILA, a pretty young woman, twenty-one, is sitting at a booth. She is the only person in the bar. A noise is heard from the back area of the bar. SHEILA smiles. JACK cautiously walks in. JACK is in his early thirties. He has a somewhat frumpy appearance. JACK doesn't see SHEILA. A wolf is heard howling in the distance. JACK is scared by the howl at first, then smiles in recognition. He walks to the back of the bar and puts money in the jukebox. The song "Lights" by Journey starts to play. JACK begins to dance to the music, play air guitar, and sing along.

SHEILA: *(Loud enough for JACK to hear over the music.)* Nice butt!

JACK: *(Freezes. Slowly turns around.)* Hello?

SHEILA: *(Taking out a pencil and sketch pad.)* Don't move, I want to catch those buns.

JACK: Who's there?

SHEILA: I'll give you a hint. I'm a red hot, groovy sex kitten, and I love tomatoes and Chinese cooking.

JACK: Sheila?

SHEILA: In the flesh.

JACK: Sheila! Jesus, you scared me. *(Goes to light switch, turns on lights.)*

SHEILA: *(Rising.)* Wanna dance?

JACK: What are you doing here?

(She goes to JACK, puts her hands around his neck.)

SHEILA: You lead.

(They begin to slow dance.)

SHEILA: I've been waiting for you forever.

JACK: Huh?

SHEILA: I got the booze.

JACK: What booze?

SHEILA: Two four-packs of Bartles and Jaymes and a bottle of Jose. Do you think that's enough? Maybe I should have gotten some beer. Did you make the reservations?

JACK: Reservations?

SHEILA: For the room.

JACK: Room?

SHEILA: Tahoe. The lake. Where we're going tonight.

JACK: Tonight?

SHEILA: Stop fooling around.

JACK: Sheila—

SHEILA: If you didn't get us a room, I will kill you. Slowly, with great attention to pain.

JACK: Wait. Don't freak out. I think I remember now. We're going to Lake Tahoe, right? Yeah, Tahoe! We're finally gonna do it!

SHEILA: If you're a good boy.

JACK: Oh my God! The trip to Tahoe! I'm going to ask you to marry me!

SHEILA: *(Pause.)* You are?

JACK: Don't you remember?

SHEILA: Remember what?

JACK: *(He stops dancing.)* Sheila, what day is it?

SHEILA: Thursday.

JACK: No. I mean... how old are you?

SHEILA: Are you trying to piss me off?

JACK: No.

SHEILA: Remember how we had the party last night? The cake and presents and the card and all that? The Jagermeister? You threw up on Vince, and I had to drive you home. You puked all over the side of my car. Any of this ringing a bell?

JACK: Your birthday party at the beach.

SHEILA: My twenty-first birthday party, which officially begins tomorrow, which is what you are taking me to Tahoe for. You are such a moron sometimes. So, did you make the reservations or not?

JACK: Yeah, I did make a reservation. For two. Mr. and Mrs. Yeats.

SHEILA: I swear to God, you're such a freak. What is it about you and William Butler Yeats?

JACK: I don't know. I just liked him, I guess.

SHEILA: I did like the one you put in my card.

JACK: Card?

SHEILA: "Tread softly because you tread on my dreams." That's nice. I think I'm gonna paint that. In fact, I've just decided, I am definitely going to paint that poem, the essence of it. The title: "Dream Treading."

JACK: "He wishes for the cloths of Heaven!" *(Quoting from memory, as if he has said this many times before.)* "Had I the heavens' embroidered cloths,
Enwrought with golden and silver light,
The blue and the dim and the dark cloths
Of night and light and the half-light,
I would spread the cloths under your feet;
But I, being poor, have only my dreams;
I have spread my dreams under your feet;
Tread softly because you tread on my dreams." *(Amazed that he remembered the whole poem.)*

SHEILA: I'm gonna tread all over your ass this weekend.

JACK: I remember that. Didn't I make you a mix tape for the drive?

SHEILA: It's in the car right now. I can't believe you put Journey on it.

JACK: Journey rocks. They always makes me think of you.

SHEILA: Journey? Do the Dead Kennedys make you think of me too?

JACK: Sometimes. Hey, it's way past midnight. Happy birthday Sheila.

SHEILA: Jesus. I'm twenty-one. I can't believe it. I remember when twenty-one seemed so old. How can that be? How can I possibly be twenty-one? When did that happen? I'm old.

JACK: Yeah.

SHEILA: This is the last birthday where I get something worthwhile. Legal drinking. What do you get that's worth a turd after that?

JACK: I don't know.

SHEILA: I should make a painting about this. The title: "The Last Turd-worthy Birthday."

JACK: Sheila, what are you doing here?

SHEILA: We're going to Tahoe.

JACK: But you're... you know... why are you here?

SHEILA: This is where you said to meet. We'll have my first legal drink, and then it's off to Tahoe.

JACK: Yeah, but… we went to Tahoe… a long time ago. Didn't we?

SHEILA: What are you talking about?

JACK: Yeah. We got in a big wreck. Don't you remember?

SHEILA: *(She stares at JACK for a moment, beginning to remember, then violently shakes it off.)* I don't want to talk about that! It's July 3, 1988, and we are going to Tahoe. *(Goes to door, opens it.)* We are getting a room at Circus Circus under the name Mr. and Mrs. William Butler Yeats, we are going to win at twenty-one and lose at craps, we are going to have sex for the first time, and the second, you are going to get drunk and ask me to marry you, I am going to get even drunker and say yes, or actually "groovy," but I mean yes, and then… and then… we… *(She looks out the door for a moment, then lets it shut.)*

JACK: And then we decided to take a drive around the lake.

SHEILA: You just had to show me Cassiopeia and Scorpio and all that astronomy crap you learned in Boy Scouts.

JACK: Webelos.

SHEILA: Whatever. So we go driving around the lake. And we stop halfway around and go swimming. And the water is freezing. So we get out. And you hear a wolf howl.

JACK: I remember. *(Howls.)* And we warm each other up in the back of the car.

SHEILA: Yeah. Third time's the charm. And then we finish the Cuervo.

JACK: And you wanted to stay there. Sleep in the car. But I wanted to stay in the hotel.

SHEILA: Ah, fuck.

JACK: I don't remember what happened after that.

SHEILA: I remember. I woke up after the crash. I couldn't feel anything. The stars were really bright. I could make out Scorpio just above the trees, right where you said he'd be. I thought it would make a great painting. The title: "Star/Scorpion/Blood in the High Sierra." I could see you in the car, your head against the smashed windshield. Fucking seatbelts. One little click, and I could have still been in the car with you. Isn't that funny? One little click. God, I wish I had my paints! Then I just… went elsewhere. And now… now I guess I'm supposed to be wrapped up in the cloths of Heaven, Jack. But I don't want that. I want to stay here with you. You gave me your dreams, and I'm keeping them.

JACK: My dreams?

SHEILA: There are worse places to hang out. *(Looks out the door, hearing something in the distance.)* I gotta go now.

JACK: Not yet!

SHEILA: "Were you but lying cold and dead,
And lights were paling out of the West,
You would come hither, and bend your head,
And I would lay my head on your breast."
(Starts to leave.)

JACK: Wait. I don't remember that one!

SHEILA: Bye, Jack.

JACK: Sheila, wait!

(She stops.)

JACK: I wanted to tell you something. You… you look really nice tonight.

(She smiles, and leaves.)

JACK: Hey, was that last one Yeats too? *(He waits for a reply a moment. The music from the jukebox changes.)* Who did that? Sheila? You there?

(The lights change, pulsing with colors. JACK is having a waking dream. DAVID and CARLOS enter, doing the tango. DAVID is JACK's age, but a little more put together. He is in good shape, wearing a dirty T-shirt and blue jeans. CARLOS is in his mid- to late forties.)

JACK: David! What are you doing here?

DAVID: Only in his hometown, among his relatives and in his own house is a prophet without honor.

JACK: David? Is that Yeats too?

DAVID: Two plus two make four.

(DAVID spins off and out. CARLOS goes behind the bar, pulls out some whiskey, pours two shots, downs his, and offers the other to JACK.)

CARLOS: "When you are old and grey
and full of sleep,
And nodding by the fire, take down this
book,
And slowly read, and dream of the soft
look
Your eyes had once, and of their shadows
deep."

JACK: I've told you guys a million times, I don't remember those poems anymore.

KRISTEN: *(Popping up from behind the bar. She is roughly JACK's age, and quite fit, the result of working out at least once a day for the past ten years.)* What are you doing here?

(KRISTEN kisses CARLOS passionately. Turns to JACK.)

KRISTEN: Mind your own business!

(KRISTEN runs out the front door. CARLOS runs into back room.)

JACK: Kristen? What are you doing here? *(Pause. JACK covers his eyes, trying to get out of his fantasy.)* Ten nine eight seven six five four three two one… Not it! *(Music continues, softer. JACK is alone for a moment. He looks all about to see if anyone is still there. He goes to the bar, takes up the shot and downs it, winces, looks all around the bar.)* Olly-Olly-Oxen Free! *(Silence. A wolf howls in the distance. JACK howls in response, kneels.)* Sheila? Sheila, please come back. I think the world's playing hide-and-go-seek, and I'm it. I'm it and I don't know where anybody's hiding! *(Looks around for people hiding.)* And I didn't put this music on!

(VINCE enters from the front door. He is JACK's age. His bearing suggests both an attempt to appear like a teenager and a businessman. VINCE often quotes movies, and those quotes are marked with footnotes.)

VINCE: My name is Elmer J. Fudd, millionaire. I own a mansion and a yacht.[1] *(Sits at table. The music begins to grow louder.)*

JACK: Hey Vince, Sheila was just here!

JERRY: *(Entering. He is also JACK and VINCE's age. He is dressed in khaki pants, a blue oxford shirt with a name tag on it that says "Jerry," and Doc Martens.)* "…like
a laughing string
Whereon mad fingers play
Amid a place of stone,
Be secret and exult,
Because of all things known
That is most difficult."

(JERRY joins VINCE at the table.)

---

[1]Bugs Bunny, imitating Elmer Fudd, in a Warner Bros. cartoon whose name escapes me.

JACK: Hey Jerry! Sheila was here!

VINCE: Fatty and Skinny went to bed, Fatty rolled over, and Skinny was dead.

(JACK goes to bar, as CARLOS comes back from the back room and puts two beers on the bar. JACK picks them up and takes them to the table.)

CARLOS: "I would be ignorant as the dawn."

JACK: *(Returning to the bar.)* Where's Sheila? *(Puts out arm, as if to arm wrestle.)*

CARLOS: "I would be ignorant as the dawn
That has looked down
On that old queen measuring a town
With the pin of a brooch."

VINCE: *(Holds up his beer.)* Chipmunks are go!

JERRY: *(Holds up his beer.)* A whisper to a scream!

(They both down their beers.)

CARLOS: I'm a beautiful, red hot, groovy sex kitten, and I love tomatoes and Chinese cooking.

(JACK takes CARLOS's arm as if to arm wrestle. Begins to shout in an attempt to wake himself from what he perceives is a dream.)

JACK: Not it! Not it! Not it! Not it! Not it!

(Lights change back to normal. CARLOS easily wins the arm wrestling. JACK comes over to JERRY and VINCE, rubbing his arm. The song ends. There is a moment of silence.)

JACK: Did you guys notice anything… strange just now?

JERRY: Like what?

JACK: Oh, you know, people talking kind of funny, and dancing and stuff like that?

VINCE: What, did your phantom wolf pack run through town again?

JACK: I don't know. It was kind of like a dream.

VINCE: "And you were there, and so were you…"[2]

JERRY: I had a really weird dream last night.

VINCE: *(Searches his pockets for a pack of cigarettes.)* "Say bud, can you help a fellow American who's down on his luck?"[3]

JERRY: I was getting married.

JACK: You're getting married?

VINCE: Anybody got a cigarette?

JERRY: I'm not getting married.

VINCE: Who said you were?

JERRY: Jack.

VINCE: Jerry's getting married?

JACK: That's what he says.

JERRY: I said I dreamed last night I was getting married.

VINCE: "I dreamed last night I got on the boat to heaven."[4]

JACK: I dreamed about Sheila last night. The first night she came back.

VINCE: Shut the fuck up.

JACK: She said I had a nice butt. Then she went elsewhere. When is it?

JERRY: What?

---

[2]Judy Garland in *The Wizard of Oz.*

[3]Humphrey Bogart in *Treasure of the Sierra Madre.*

[4]Stubby Kaye in *Guys and Dolls.*

JACK: The wedding!

CARLOS: What wedding?

JACK: Jerry's getting married.

CARLOS: To who, Kristen?

JERRY: No.

VINCE: "It's a nice day for a white wedding."[5]

JACK: You should tell Karl before the wedding.

JERRY: Jack, there is no wedding.

VINCE: Who's got some ones for the jukebox?

JACK: I paid for the last set.

JERRY: Jack, I paid for the last set.

VINCE: I paid for the last set, moron. I pay for every set. Carlos, some change please?

JERRY: Let me tell you about my dream.

VINCE: Let me tell you about my dream. It's all about a wonderful world where I don't have to hear about your dreams.

JERRY: Jesus.

VINCE: "You don't fuck with the Jesus!"[6]

JACK: That's from that movie.

VINCE: Uh-huh. *(Heading to the jukebox.)* Any requests?

JERRY: How about the same ten songs you played last night?

VINCE: You don't like the music I pick? Fine. Why don't you pay for this set? And get your own fucking beer while you're at it.

JERRY: I'm just saying. It's not 1984 anymore.

VINCE: I'm not the one living with his parents.

CARLOS: You want the change?

JERRY: Fuck you.

CARLOS: Vince?

VINCE: *(Looking pointedly at JERRY.)* Any requests?

JERRY: *(Pause.)* You pick.

VINCE: *(Handing CARLOS a twenty.)* Here. And another round.

(JACK howls like a wolf, then listens for a reply.)

VINCE: Ah cut that shit out, Sheriff Lobo.

JERRY: You know, you can be a total dick sometimes. It's amazing Molly stays with you.

VINCE: Leave the old ball and chain out of this. I don't come here to talk about my wife.

JERRY: What do you come here for?

VINCE: What are you, my therapist? I come here for beer, music, and my so-called friends.

CARLOS: Here you go.

(VINCE takes the change and heads to the jukebox.)

JACK: *(Taking the beer from the bar.)* Thanks Carlos.

(Music begins to play. VINCE comes back to the table. Sits next to JERRY.)

VINCE: Fag.

JERRY: Asshole.

---

[5]Billy Idol from his song "White Wedding."

[6]John Turturro in *The Big Lebowski.*

VINCE: So you gonna tell me about your dream or what?

JERRY: I guess so.

VINCE: "The dream is always the same."[7]

JERRY: It started out with me making love to this beautiful woman on a desert island.

JACK: Was the water cold?

VINCE: Were you making love, or fucking?

JACK: Did you hear any wolves?

JERRY: Then, I'm at Strawberry Park Elementary, which somehow has become the place you go to when you want to get married. I go to the office, where Mrs. Speth hands me this form, and tells me to write down the name of the person I want to marry. I write Carol Brady.

VINCE: Mrs. Brady? From the Brady Bunch?

JERRY: I always liked her.

JACK: I like Alice.

VINCE: That's disgusting.

JACK: I always pictured her cleaning the house naked. And then Bobby would walk in unexpectedly and—

VINCE: Shut the fuck up.

JERRY: So, I hand the form back to Mrs. Speth, and she looks at me and smiles this knowing smile, and into the office walks Carol Brady, so I figure I gave the right answer. Carol says she has to go get ready. I walk down the hall to the multipurpose room, open the door, and it's full of women all dressed in blue satin dresses, with big blue fans. And they've all painted their faces blue.

JACK: Are any of them naked?

JERRY: No. Just creepy. And blue.

JACK: What kind of blue?

JERRY: Like the TV screen when the VCR is on pause.

JACK: I don't have a VCR.

VINCE: Shut the fuck up.

JACK: I just wanted to know what color blue they were.

VINCE: Dumb-ass.

JERRY: Anyway. Carol is at the altar. She's in blue too, face, fan, everything. Everyone's looking at me. The organ plays "Here Comes the Bride." I walk down the aisle. All of a sudden, in bursts the woman from the island. A riot breaks out. Dresses torn, makeup smeared. Finally, everyone is on the ground except the woman, Carol, and me. The woman screams, "Don't marry her! She won't suck your dick!"

JACK: Mary, Mother of God!

VINCE: Fuckin' A.

JERRY: So I say, "I'm not getting married to get my dick sucked. I'm getting married because I love her." The violins swell; Carol and I smile at each other, close to tears. We walk to each other and kiss. The woman sighs, defeated. Carol whispers something in my ear, and I laugh. "Besides," I say, "Carol says she'll suck my dick like there's no tomorrow." Everyone laughs. Carol Brady and I walk off into the sunset. And I'm blue now. Blue all over.

VINCE: That's it?

JERRY: That's it.

JACK: You married Carol Brady.

---

[7]Tom Cruise in *Risky Business.*

VINCE: And she promised helmet wash, for better or worse, till death do you part.

JERRY: Yeah. But I've become one of the blue people.

JACK: What the hell does that mean?

VINCE: You need to move out of your parents' house.

JERRY: Have you ever had a dream that you thought was supposed to be telling you something, but when you wake up you can't remember what it was you were supposed to be told?

VINCE: No. Dreams are just television for your brain while you sleep.

JACK: It was a wet dream.

JERRY: What?

JACK: You know, a wet dream, when you dream about women, naked, and you're naked too, and there's lots of food and music and nakedness, and you get all hot, and, you know, do your thing, and then you have to get up and wash the sheets before your mom finds them, 'cause she'll tell your dad to have that talk with you which he should have had a long time ago but isn't necessary because you already know all that stuff, but you don't want to go to your parents and say, "Mom, Dad, I know that if I put my penis in a vagina and... uh... ejaculate, it may end up in pregnancy, blah blah blah," so you wash the sheets and say you felt like cleaning, and you get a weird look, but that's all. You know, a wet dream.

VINCE: "You are a mental case."[8]

JACK: Didn't you have wet dreams?

VINCE: Do you know what my favorite phrase is?

JACK: Yes.

VINCE: Shut the fuck up. Isn't it beautiful? Shut the fuck up. Did you have wet dreams? Shut the fuck up. What color blue were they? Shut the fuck up. My name is Jack and I howl like a coyote.

JACK: Wolf.

VINCE: Shut the fuck up you fucking moron!

JACK: *(Covering his eyes.)* Ten, nine, eight, seven, six, five, four, three, two, one... NOT IT!

(Lights change to dreamland. VINCE and JERRY begin to howl like wolves. CARLOS joins in. JACK joins in. They howl a short, wordless song, prance about like wolves, and then resume their seats.)

VINCE: You know what my favorite phrase is?

JACK: Olly-Olly-Oxen Free!

VINCE: *(Pleasantly.)* Shut the fuck up you fucking moron.

(Lights change back to normal.)

JACK: I like lah-la-doody. You know, like when you see a pretty girl, you just go lah-la-doody.

VINCE: Just shut the fuck up.

(JACK howls at VINCE, who glares in reply.)

JACK: Why'd you stop? *(Howls again.)*

VINCE: Jack, what are you talking about? Come back to Earth.

JACK: But—

VINCE: Here, *(Hands him some cash.)* why don't you get us some more beer?

JERRY: Weird dream, huh?

---

[8]Bugs Bunny in *Hyde and Hare.*

VINCE: Well, yeah. But look at you. Over thirty, working in a bookstore, totally broke, and hopelessly in love with Kristen, who is married to Fievel, the village idiot who happens to own said bookstore.

JERRY: Maybe Kristen is who Carol Brady represented, and I've got to go find the chick from the island.

VINCE: You know what your problem is? You wish you were Sam. The problem with most guys is that they want to be Sam.

JACK: Sam?

VINCE: You know, on *Cheers*. Mayday Malone. Most guys wish they were Sammys. The leading man. The stud.

JACK: Like David?

VINCE: *(To JERRY.)* Hey, speaking of the prodigal son, any word from David lately?

JERRY: Not really. Just another postcard, signed like all the rest.

VINCE: What's it say again?

JERRY: "Having a great time, wish you were here. Mark 6:4-5."

VINCE: How many postcards has he sent?

JERRY: A lot.

VINCE: And what is that Mark 6 thing?

JERRY: It's in the Bible. Mark 6:4-5: "Only in his hometown, among his relatives and in his own house is a prophet without honor."

VINCE: What the fuck is that supposed to mean?

JERRY: That he won't be home for Christmas, I guess.

VINCE: Yeah. You know why? Because in his hometown, David can't be a Sammy. He has to be David Linington, local boy from the same boring suburb as the rest of us. See, in New York, he can be whoever he wants to be.

JACK: Who would Sheila be if she was in New York?

JERRY: Jack, shut the fuck up.

VINCE: *(Softer.)* I don't know who Sheila would be. But I think it's obvious that David is suffering from the syndrome.

JERRY: The syndrome?

VINCE: Look. Nobody wants to be anything less than good-looking and funny and successful, right? Perfect. They consider anything less a failure. Where are the Norms? Where are the Cliffies? Doesn't anyone want to be a buddy anymore? I think if we all stopped trying to be like Superman we'd be a lot happier.

JERRY: Superman? I thought you said we all wanted to be like Sam.

VINCE: Whatever.

JERRY: Are you saying I'm a Cliffie?

VINCE: No. I'm saying you're not a Sam.

JERRY: I never said I was.

VINCE: But you wish you were.

JERRY: Who wouldn't?

VINCE: That's all I'm saying.

JACK: Let's do shots.

JERRY: Good call. Jameson's?

VINCE: It's a must. Carlos, another round. And three Jameson's.

CARLOS: Want to wrestle for it?

VINCE: Look, you're not Lex Luthor, and I'm not Clark Kent, okay? I just want my drinks.

CARLOS: Jack?

JACK: No thank you.

CARLOS: Jerry?

JERRY: I'll just take my shot.

CARLOS: Your minds are weak.

JERRY: Here's to Kristen and Karl breaking up.

VINCE: "Here's to my brother George, the richest man in Bedford Falls."[9]

JACK: Here's to swimmin' with women.

VINCE: Huh?

JACK: Here's to swimmin' with women.

VINCE: Bowlegged women.

JACK: Huh?

VINCE: It's swimmin' with bowlegged women.

JACK: What are you talking about?

VINCE: "Here's to swimmin' with bowlegged women."[10]

(JACK stares, not understanding.)

VINCE: Just drink.

(JACK downs his shot. Covers his eyes, wincing. Lights change to dreamland. For a moment it looks like he might throw up. Everyone else runs off to hide.)

JACK: Ten, nine, eight, seven, six, five, four, three, two, one. Not it!

(Lights go back to normal. It is now the next day. CARLOS enters from the front door of the bar, closely followed by VINCE. They are in the middle of an argument.)

[9]Tod Karns in *It's a Wonderful Life*.

[10]Robert Shaw in *Jaws*.

CARLOS: I'm not taking it down. It's my bar, and I say what hangs in front of it. Period.

VINCE: It's stupid.

CARLOS: It's patriotic.

VINCE: I don't think so.

CARLOS: I don't care what you think.

JACK: Hi guys.

CARLOS: Hey Jack. Thanks for minding the bar. I just needed to get that put up out front.

JACK: What day is it?

VINCE: Jack, did you see what's hanging out front?

JACK: I don't know. It was yesterday just a moment ago.

VINCE: What am I asking the moron for?

CARLOS: Hey! You leave him alone.

JACK: It's okay. I am a moron.

(Enter MOLLY. She is about the same age as VINCE. She is pretty, but her clothes and hairdo are about five years out of date.)

MOLLY: Is that some kind of joke?

VINCE: Molly, what are you doing here?

MOLLY: I was just driving by when I saw that thing out front, and thought I'd pop in to find out what was going on. What's going on?

CARLOS: Nothing's going on, Molly. I just wanted to let people know where I stand.

MOLLY: I see. Well, it certainly is an eyecatcher. Carlos, may I have a glass of white wine, please?

JACK: Hi Molly.

MOLLY: Jack. Long time no see.

JACK: What?

MOLLY: I haven't seen your sweet face in months.

JACK: I just saw you this morning.

MOLLY: Not me, honey.

VINCE: What are you talking about, Jack?

MOLLY: He's just a little confused, as usual.

CARLOS: *(Handing MOLLY a glass of wine.)* Here you go.

JACK: But—

(Enter KARL. He is in his mid-thirties, and dresses in what is commonly referred to as business casual. His appearance is almost fastidious, but not quite well-kept. His hair is combed back, but he has a cowlick. His entire outfit seems to have been bought at the Gap: khaki pants, crew-neck T-shirt, and a pullover maroon sweater. He is wearing white, new sneakers, and, as he enters, he notices that he has recently stepped in some chewing gum.)

KARL: Ah, damn it anyway. *(Seeing the others.)* Oh. Excuse me. Hello Molly, Vince.

VINCE: Fievel.

KARL: *(To JACK.)* How are you, Jim?

VINCE: His name is Jack.

JACK: Are you talking to me?

KARL: *(Speaking louder and slower.)* Yes. Nice day, Jack, isn't it?

(JACK, confused, doesn't reply. KARL shakes his head as if to say, "how sad," and walks up to the bar.)

KARL: Hi Carlos. How are you today?

CARLOS: Okay, big guy. Cold one?

KARL: One Amstel light, please. Carlos, I hope you don't mind my asking, but what is that cross with Jesus on it wearing the American flag like a diaper doing hanging out front?

CARLOS: It's a loincloth.

KARL: What?

CARLOS: It's not a diaper, it's a loincloth.

KARL: Oh, I see.

CARLOS: That's my American crucifix out there.

KARL: I've never seen one like that before.

CARLOS: Me neither. But I think it's the least thing a patriotic, Christian American can do. Gotta show them where you stand.

KARL: Yes, I see.

CARLOS: You don't like it?

KARL: No, I do. It's just a little jarring at first. But I guess times like these are full of jarring sights. It's like that Chinese saying, "may you live in interesting times."

CARLOS: You got that right.

KARL: Right on, brother man. *(Just to CARLOS.)* So, have you tried the system yet?

CARLOS: Oh yeah! Worked like a charm. I laid a waitress down in Soledad just two days ago. Big blonde. From initial contact to punching her kitten took less than two hours. Of course, she was pretty drunk. How about you? Have you used the system yet?

KARL: Uh, not yet. I only want to try it on Kristen, you know, but haven't had the chance yet. She's been kind of busy lately, and, well, you know how women can be... but I'm sure it'll work once I try it. I mean, we're still very attracted to one another, it's just that we don't have a lot of time, what with the new store in Gilroy and all. *(To the room.)* Hey, has anybody seen Jerry?

MOLLY: Not me.

VINCE: What do you want Jerry for? Was he late again?

KARL: *(Tensing.)* No. Nothing like that. Although I do wish he were a little more punctual.

VINCE: So what do you want to see him about?

KARL: I'd rather not say.

VINCE: Oh, come on. What, is he embezzling from the bookstore?

KARL: *(Growing quite uncomfortable.)* No. I just need to speak with him.

VINCE: About what? Come on, Fievel, what's the big secret?

KARL: *(Suddenly yells out.)* It's none of your fucking business, Vince!

VINCE: *(Pause.)* Jesus Christ, what the fuck is your problem?

KARL: I'm sorry. *(To MOLLY.)* I'm sorry, Molly, I didn't mean to swear like that. It's just... I like Jerry. I do. I like all you people. You're a great group of folks.

VINCE: Gee, thanks.

KARL: I'm serious. I mean, Kristen used to be one of you. And I love her.

MOLLY: "One of you"? One of you what? Local folk?

KARL: No! Of course not. I mean, from your neighborhood is all.

MOLLY: Uh-huh.

KARL: Well, uh, look, I just need to talk with Jerry.

VINCE: About work?

KARL: No. *(Sighs.)* Carlos, a shot of whiskey please. It's not about work. Exactly. *(Takes shot, downs it, winces.)* He's always had a crush on Kristen. Did you know that? Of course you know that. Everyone in town knows that. It's true. Not that I can blame him, really. I mean, she's beautiful, and kind, and funny... Dear God, I love her.

VINCE: I don't think you have anything to worry about. I know Jerry's fond of Kristen, but—

KARL: It's okay. I'm not jealous or anything like that. Kristen and I have a great relationship. We do. I trust her with my life. But Jerry's... well.

VINCE: Hey, Karl, trust me, nothing is going on between Kristen and Jerry.

KARL: I know that. You think I wouldn't fire him if there was something going on? Because I would.

VINCE: So what's the problem?

KARL: *(Takes some crumpled papers out of his pocket.)* This is the problem. *(Reads.)*
"Somewhere in this world
A moonbeam is waiting
To light your face
As you take my hands
And open your mouth.
You say you don't know
What love is
I think I do
Love is your hair
The smile you force from me
Without even trying
It's knowing your voice
From across the room
My heart beating faster
As the sound
Touches my skin

Love is aching for that moonbeam
I can't look into your eyes
Without wanting to scream." *(Almost crying.)*

MOLLY: Can I see that? *(Takes poem from KARL.)*

KARL: Tell him to stop writing this bullshit. The fucking asshole! *(Takes a breath.)* I'm sorry. Listen, if you see Jerry, tell him I need to talk to him. I'm not angry. He just needs to get over it. And he needs to remember that she married me. Not him.

CARLOS: You got it, chief. Don't worry about it. Jerry's a good guy. He's just a little fucked up.

KARL: He's still in love with my wife.

MOLLY: I don't think that's true, Karl.

KARL: What would you know about it, Molly?

MOLLY: Like you said, she married you. How is Kristen? We never see her in the neighborhood these days. We miss her. After all, she used to be one of us.

KARL: She's fine. I got her managing the new store up in Gilroy, so she's pretty busy. But I think she likes that.

MOLLY: I'm sure she does.

KARL: Well, I have to go.

MOLLY: *(Folding up the poem, putting it in her purse.)* Tell Kristen I'm gonna call her for a girl's night out real soon.

KARL: She'd like that. How much do I owe you, Carlos?

CARLOS: It's on the house. And don't worry.

KARL: Thanks, pal.

CARLOS: Good luck using the system.

KARL: Right. Hey, do you want to ride with me to class tomorrow?

CARLOS: Sure.

KARL: Patterns. Roller coasters, excitement.

CARLOS: Excitement! Blood pumping! She'll be jumping into bed before you get the door closed!

KARL: *(Goes to door, looks outside where the crucifix is.)* God bless America!

CARLOS: Amen.

(KARL leaves.)

CARLOS: Poor guy.

MOLLY: Kristen is such a lucky woman.

VINCE: What an asshole.

MOLLY: Almost as lucky as me.

VINCE: Very funny.

MOLLY: Where is Jerry, anyway?

VINCE: He's at the library.

MOLLY: Why isn't he at work?

JACK: Jerry was at the Ramada this morning.

VINCE: *(Condescendingly.)* Sure he was, Jack.

JACK: I saw him in the Ramada parking lot this morning. Molly, don't you—

MOLLY: *(Interrupting.)* Jack, maybe you should go tell him that Karl is looking for him. He could be in trouble.

VINCE: Jerry's a big boy. He'll figure it out. *(To JACK.)* Stay and have a beer with me.

MOLLY: Some friend you are. Then I'll go. Oh, by the way.

VINCE: Yes?

MOLLY: I left my bank card on the dresser.

VINCE: Are you saying you need some cash?

MOLLY: Only if you want some groceries in the fridge when you get home.

(VINCE pulls out some cash, hands it to MOLLY.)

MOLLY: Jack, Carlos. Nice seeing you.

VINCE: When you see Jerry, tell him I'll be here tonight.

MOLLY: Sure. He might have gotten confused and thought you were at some other bar tonight. But don't you worry. I'll set him straight. *(Exits.)*

VINCE: Jack, where did you say you saw Molly this morning?

JACK: The Ramada.

VINCE: You sure?

JACK: No.

VINCE: Huh.

CARLOS: You want a beer?

VINCE: Just one. I'm closing the store tonight. Hey Carlos, what the hell were you and Fievel talking about? What's he mean about roller coasters?

CARLOS: Speed seduction. It's a course we're both taking. Speed seduction.

VINCE: Like Tom Cruise in *Magnolia*?

CARLOS: Sort of. It's all about using exciting words, and repeating them in certain patterns when you talk to a woman. Like you mention a roller coaster, how exciting it is, how it goes up and down, and while you do that you kind of point to yourself. See, that way, the woman thinks you're exciting too, like the roller coaster.

VINCE: And you're both in the class?

CARLOS: Yeah.

VINCE: That's great. Captain America and the village idiot taking classes on how to bag babes in a hurry. That's class. The fucker's married, and he's taking a speed seduction class.

CARLOS: Hey, Karl says he only plans to use it on Kristen.

VINCE: That's even worse. Using mind control on your wife. Fucking sick.

JACK: Why is Jerry at the library?

VINCE: Well, I'm not supposed to tell anyone, but he gave me this, *(Pulls out a large, overstuffed envelope.)* asked me to deliver it to Kristen up at the Gilroy store, and to tell her that he'd be at the library, waiting for her response. *(Opens envelope, takes out several pieces of paper, which he begins to read.)*

JACK: What's that?

VINCE: I think it's all one poem. *(Reads.)* "Kristen, or How I Stopped Worrying and Learned to Love from Afar." Catchy title. *(Continues to read.)* "You were born under a wandering star, I was born inside a black hole."

KRISTEN: *(Entering from the front door.)* Excuse me, boys, but was that my husband who just tore out of here?

VINCE: Kristen, we were just talking about you. Yes, that was Fievel who was just here. And on a related note, Jerry asked me to give you this and tell you he's at the library. But I wouldn't go there now if I were you. *(Hands the poem to KRISTEN.)* And if Fievel starts talking about roller coasters when you get home, punch him in the nose.

KRISTEN: His name is Karl, not Fievel.

VINCE: Whatever.

KRISTEN: And when was I supposed to meet Jerry?

VINCE: You're supposed to be there now.

KRISTEN: Carlos, a cosmo, please. Hi Jack.

JACK: Hi Kristen.

KRISTEN: How are the wolves today?

(JACK howls. KRISTEN howls in reply and takes drink from CARLOS.)

KRISTEN: Thank you. *(Howls again to JACK, gesturing toward the jukebox.)*

JACK: Okay. *(Checks pockets.)* I don't have any money on me.

KRISTEN: Of course you don't.

(KRISTEN opens purse, gives a dollar to JACK. JACK goes to the jukebox.)

KRISTEN: *(To VINCE.)* How's Molly been?

VINCE: Oh, fine. She's off warning Jerry that Karl found some poem he wrote to you.

KRISTEN: Oh, shit. Those stupid poems.

VINCE: You don't like them?

KRISTEN: *(A slow song begins.)* Have you read any of them?

VINCE: No.

KRISTEN: He's so tragic. It's almost funny. He writes me poem after poem about his love for me, his great, unrequited love, how the two weeks we dated in high school were the golden days of his life. How he thinks of no one but me, even when he's with someone else. That's not love. He doesn't love me. He doesn't even know me. Not really.

VINCE: Jerry's just a... a hopeless romantic.

KRISTEN: Keats was a romantic. Shelley was a romantic. Jerry is a prude. I'll tell you a little secret. I took him to this special beach I like to go to in Carmel one night about a year ago. Just for fun. I asked him, since he's such the poet, if he believed in free love; he was shocked. He said that it wouldn't be right. That I was a married woman. Which is just so much bullshit. He doesn't love me. He just mopes, and writes poem after poem about how sad his life is. One thing I'll say for Karl. He never writes poems. *(Takes her drink, sips it.)* He's stable. No surprises. Ever. *(Takes another sip.)* If I ever wrote a poem, I'd call it "Life Sucks—Get over It." *(Drains the rest of her drink.)* Actually, I write poems all the time. Dreary epics about staring into the abyss, lost princesses stranded in distant lands. *(Laughs.)* Of course, I can't stand any of them. Stupid, huh? Another cosmo. *(Music starts.)* Wanna dance?

VINCE: Yeah, sure.

JACK: *(Going to the bar.)* Diet coke.

KRISTEN: Where'd you say Molly was?

VINCE: Telling Jerry that Fievel—uh, Karl was looking for him.

KRISTEN: That's nice. *(Moving closer to VINCE.)* You ever write a poem for Molly?

VINCE: God no.

KRISTEN: Good.

(They dance for a bit, then she stops.)

KRISTEN: Did you ever write a poem for anyone? *(She is very close to him.)*

VINCE: No.

(He looks over to the bar. She grabs his face and turns it back to her.)

CARLOS: He didn't even mention roller coasters. *(Pulls out book from behind bar, consults it.)*

KRISTEN: I'm tired of poems. *(Their noses are almost touching.)* You know what I mean?

VINCE: I think so.

KRISTEN: Good.

(The lights shift back to a dreamlike quality. SHEILA enters and begins to dance with JACK. KRISTEN and VINCE kiss. JACK begins to howl. CARLOS howls. Actual wolves can be heard howling outside. VINCE and KRISTEN move to the floor. The lights go to black for a moment, and then come back up. Everything is as it was before the lights changed, except that SHEILA is now sitting at a booth in the back, watching the proceedings.)

KRISTEN: Well, I guess I better go find Karl and tell him to stop being such a worrywart. *(Exits.)*

VINCE: *(Going up to the bar.)* Shot of Jack please.

CARLOS: So now she's got her eyes set on you.

VINCE: No. It's not like that. She just likes to flirt.

JACK: She must like to flirt a lot.

CARLOS: Look, it's none of my business. Just don't do anything stupid here. *(Gives shot to VINCE.)*

VINCE: Hey, just 'cause she gets around doesn't mean anything is going on with her and me. Come on, I'm a married man. *(Downs shot, looks at his watch.)* Well, I should get going. *(Heads to the door.)* If Molly comes back, tell her I went looking for her.

CARLOS: Sure.

(VINCE exits. Lights fade.)

SCENE TWO

Later that night. Several empty soda glasses sit in front of JACK.

CARLOS: Another soda?

JACK: Sure.

(JACK looks over to SHEILA. She smiles, and waves.)

JACK: You better make it two. *(He looks at KRISTEN's last cosmo, which she never drank, picks it up, smells it, grimaces, puts it back down.)* Carlos, do you see anybody here besides me?

CARLOS: No.

JACK: Huh.

CARLOS: *(Handing JACK the sodas.)* Here you go. I gotta go do some inventory in back. Keep watch up here, okay?

JACK: Sure.

(CARLOS exits behind bar. JACK looks to make sure CARLOS is gone, then crosses over to SHEILA, handing her one of the sodas.)

JACK: Finally.

SHEILA: So. Vince and Kristen?

JACK: You think they're doing it?

SHEILA: Totally.

JACK: But Molly's so nice—

(Offstage, MOLLY screams, "You cocksucker.")

SHEILA: *(Hearing MOLLY.)* Shhh.

(The front door opens, JERRY enters, followed closely by MOLLY.)

MOLLY: What the fuck are you doing writing her poems?

JERRY: One poem.

MOLLY: I don't care how many poems it is, the point is, you're writing them to her, and unless you're fucking her, that makes no sense.

JERRY: It's none of your business.

MOLLY: Excuse me?

JERRY: I wrote that poem a long time ago.

MOLLY: How long ago?

JERRY: A long time.

MOLLY: Before us?

(He doesn't answer.)

MOLLY: You still love her, don't you?

JERRY: No!

MOLLY: You do! You're fucking me, but you love her. That's pathetic.

JERRY: You're the one that's married.

MOLLY: That didn't seem to bother you this morning.

JERRY: Can we just drop this?

MOLLY: I am such an idiot. Never again. Never fall for a loser. That's my new rule.

JERRY: Molly—

MOLLY: Look, Jerry, you're a sweetheart. Really. And I do care for you. But you are a totally fucked-up asshole, and the sooner you realize that, the better. *(Starts to leave.)*

JERRY: Will I see you later?

MOLLY: I don't know.

JERRY: Please?

(She exits.)

JERRY: Shit. Carlos? Carlos, you back there?

CARLOS: *(From within.)* One minute.

(JERRY sees JACK, who is hiding under the table. JERRY doesn't see SHEILA.)

JERRY: Jack? Jack, what are you doing down there?

JACK: I'm sleeping.

JERRY: How long have you been sleeping? Did you hear any of that?

JACK: Any of what?

JERRY: Nothing. Want a beer?

JACK: Sure.

(CARLOS returns from the back room.)

JERRY: Carlos, two Guinness.

CARLOS: Sure thing.

JERRY: Vince isn't around, is he?

CARLOS: Not yet. But it's only a little past ten. He's probably closing up shop.

JERRY: Good. *(Puts his head in his hands.)*

CARLOS: Rough day?

JERRY: I got fired today.

CARLOS: So that's why Karl was looking for you.

JERRY: He found me.

CARLOS: Ah.

JERRY: Yeah. Well, I guess it's back to substitute teaching for me.

CARLOS: But nothing's going on with you and Kristen. Everyone in town knows that.

JERRY: No kidding. You should tell Fievel that. Besides, he fired me for gross tardiness, not for his suspicions.

CARLOS: That, and the fact that you write love poems to his missus.

JERRY: It was one fucking poem!

CARLOS: Sure it was.

JERRY: What do you think she sees in him, anyway?

CARLOS: He's a nice enough guy.

JERRY: It's his fucking money, isn't it?

JACK: I like Karl.

JERRY: And when are you going to take that ridiculous thing down out front?

CARLOS: When the war is over.

JERRY: But we're not at war. We've made no declaration of war. We just blow shit up and call people evil. And the powers that be say it may go on for years and years.

CARLOS: Hey, those fuckers killed a lot of innocent people. American citizens. Now it's payback time.

JERRY: Eye for an eye, right?

CARLOS: Look, if someone fucks with you, you fuck with them. End of story.

JERRY: Jesus wearing the flag? How is that fucking with them?

CARLOS: We all gotta do our bit. I'll tell you this: you're never going to see a flag for Allah and all his terrorist buddies hanging out front. Not on my watch. *(Pulls out a dollar, smiling.)* Here, why don't you put some music on?

JERRY: Sure. *(Takes the dollar and goes to jukebox.)* What a day.

CARLOS: Don't worry about it.

(Music begins. It is "God Bless America.")

JERRY: What the hell? *(Coming back to the bar.)* Did you change the CDs in the jukebox?

CARLOS: You like it?

VINCE: *(Entering.)* Carlos, one Guinness— *(Notices the music.)* What the fuck is this?

JACK: Carlos changed the jukebox this afternoon after you left.

CARLOS: You got a problem with patriotism?

VINCE: This song sucks. It's boring, lame, retarded… it just sucks. This song in particular makes me feel less patriotic, like I live in the land of the geeks and the home of the lame.

CARLOS: That's your opinion.

VINCE: "I'm mad as hell, and I'm not gonna take it anymore."[11] I hate this song. I love my country, but I fucking hate this song. Three Jameson's.

CARLOS: You got it. But it's four, and you're buying.

(CARLOS pours four; they all raise their glasses, including CARLOS.)

CARLOS: Semper Fi.

(DAVID enters as they all down their shots.)

DAVID: "They dance and they samba—"

VINCE: *(Picking up the quote by instinct.)* "they sing ay caramba!"[12]

JACK: David!

---

[11]Peter Finch in *Network*.

DAVID: Three caballeros and Pancho Villa behind the bar.

JACK: What are you doing here?

DAVID: I came home.

VINCE: Where the fuck have you been?

DAVID: I was in Klamath Falls this morning. I was in Twin Falls, Idaho, day before. Out in the high desert. You should see it. And Niagara Falls. That was amazing. I had no idea how very large and beautiful and strange this country is.

JERRY: We got the postcards.

VINCE: What, are you taking time off from work to visit all the towns in the country with the word "Falls" in them?

DAVID: No, but that's not a bad idea. Who's up for a road trip, destination all towns with the word "Falls" in them?

CARLOS: Hey big guy.

(They shake hands, and squeeze each other's hand, waiting for the other to relent first.)

CARLOS: Your mind is weak. I will break you.

DAVID: Not tonight. Sir.

CARLOS: Don't call me sir.

DAVID: Sorry. Old man.

CARLOS: Don't apologize. It's a sign of weakness.

DAVID: Call it a draw?

CARLOS: No way, Jose.

DAVID: All right. I give.

CARLOS: You girls see that? He's become a man. What'll it be?

[12]Donald Duck and friends in *The Three Caballeros.*

DAVID: Just a big glass of water.

JACK: I can't believe it. David Linington, back home.

VINCE: How's corporate life?

DAVID: Fucked. I quit.

JERRY: You're kidding.

DAVID: I'm serious.

VINCE: You were pulling six figures.

JACK: And making a lot of money.

DAVID: Where's the profit of gaining the world if you lose your soul?

JACK: Huh?

VINCE: That's deep.

DAVID: I was either going to have to kill someone, or kill myself, or become an asshole. *(Raising his glass.)*
"Here's a sigh to those who love me,
And a smile to those who hate,
And whatever star's above me,
Here's a heart for every fate." *(Drinks.)*

JERRY: Sounds like a good move to me. I never could get used to you in a suit.

VINCE: You could never get used to any of us looking like anything other than the way we looked in college.

JERRY: You didn't go to college.

VINCE: No. But I went to the parties.

JERRY: We only invited you because you got free booze from your daddy's store.

VINCE: Fuck you.

JERRY: Fuck you.

DAVID: I see that everyone is pretty much the same.

JACK: I think I've gained a little weight.

JERRY: So, what's going on? Why did you quit?

(Subway noises begin. Sound of a station, late. Footsteps echoing. Only DAVID hears the noise. The lights change.)

JERRY: David?

DAVID: I just... I didn't want to end up being dead without ever having been alive.

JACK: Don't you have to be alive before you can be dead?

(JERRY and VINCE act like people at a station waiting for a train.)

DAVID: The world is full of misplaced corpses,

(VINCE looks down the track, at his watch, mutters "fuck it," walks off as if he is leaving the station.)

DAVID: broken people, desperately trying to mend themselves; buying Italian suits, smoking Cuban cigars, drinking overpriced vodka, wading through oceans of bullshit, never quite able to fix what's wrong with them, until, finally, they find themselves in their own tastefully decorated, empty, sad graves.

(Sound of a train approaching, grows to a crescendo. JERRY does a little dance, looking at DAVID the whole time. Lights go to black as train sound peaks. Lights come back up, and all is as before.)

JACK: So they're zombies?

DAVID: Sort of.

VINCE: Are you fucked up?

JACK: A little buzzed.

VINCE: Not you. David.

DAVID: I'm fine.

VINCE: Prozac?

DAVID: No.

JERRY: Mushrooms?

VINCE: Ecstasy?

JERRY: Acid?

VINCE: Ginseng?

DAVID: I'm fine.

JACK: Well, fucked up or not, it's great to see you.

JERRY: Yeah.

VINCE: Totally.

DAVID: How's the liquor store?

VINCE: Fine. I own it now that Dad's gone.

DAVID: Sorry I missed the funeral.

VINCE: Don't worry about it.

DAVID: No, really, I should have been there.

VINCE: Whatever. Just forget it, okay?

DAVID: How's your mom holding out?

VINCE: I said drop it.

DAVID: Okay. How have you been, Jack?

JACK: Groovy.

DAVID: I bought a book of Yeats in a secondhand store in Cheyenne, Wyoming, and thought of you.

JACK: I don't believe in zombies, but I believe in ghosts.

DAVID: Oh. Okay. Jerry.

(DAVID hugs JERRY.)

DAVID: So many times lately I wished you were there. I would see something interesting on the road, and wonder what you'd have to say about it. What's new?

What's something interesting you could tell me about?

JERRY: Well, not much. I finally moved out.

DAVID: You don't live with your mom and dad anymore?

JERRY: No. I live in the garage now. It's like my own place.

DAVID: I see. Kristen?

JERRY: Ah, you know. Same as it ever was.

DAVID: Do you still write her poems?

VINCE: Look, we're all still doing the same shit we were doing when you left. Okay?

JERRY: That's optimistic.

VINCE: It's true. Aside from the lines in our faces and a couple of deaths, what's changed in the last five, no, the last ten years? Nothing. David's gone nuts, but other than that—

DAVID: You just keep rolling the same rock up the same hill, day after day?

JACK: What rock? What the hell are you talking about?

VINCE: Nothing. He's talking about nothing. Right, Jerry?

JERRY: He does have a point.

VINCE: What, are you on his side?

JERRY: I'm not on anybody's side.

VINCE: Rolling the same rock up the same hill. What the fuck is that supposed to mean? I'm saying nothing's changed, and I mean it in a good way.

JERRY: Yeah, what's so bad about stability? Maybe I like living with my parents.

VINCE: I mean in a good way for me. For you, "This is Seti-Alpha-Five!"[13]

DAVID: Do you?

JERRY: What?

DAVID: Like where you are?

JERRY: Will everyone get off my fucking back?

DAVID: Hey, do you know what I told my boss when I quit?

VINCE: That he was a misplaced corpse, and that you were superior to him?

DAVID: I told him "Freedom is the freedom to say that two plus two make four. If that is granted, all else follows."

JERRY: What?

DAVID: Remember? *1984*?

JERRY: The year we graduated from high school?

DAVID: No. The book. You gave it to me when I first moved to New York. You put that quote in the front.

JERRY: I did?

DAVID: Yeah. And you said to look out for Big Brother. So I said that quote from *1984* to my boss, my equivalent of Big Brother.

JERRY: I gave you that book years ago.

DAVID: I know. But I didn't read it until this past fall. In fact, I just started reading all the books you've given me over the years, and they're fucking awesome. So thank you. Reading those books, I feel like I've gotten to know what you think like, what you would have wanted me to do.

JERRY: I didn't tell you to quit your job.

---

[13]Ricardo Montalban, in *Star Trek II, The Wrath of Khan.*

DAVID: Why else would you send me *The Bhagavad Gita*, or *One Flew over the Cuckoo's Nest*, or *A Moveable Feast*? Remember, "It is by being alive to difficulty that one can avoid it."

JERRY: *Bhagavad Gita*?

DAVID: *Tao Te Ching*. You understand?

JERRY: Jesus Christ. I sent you those books because I work in a bookstore and get them at a discount, not to inspire you to quit your job and become some kind of self-help guru.

VINCE: Tell him about the dream.

DAVID: What dream?

JACK: Jerry's getting married to Mrs. Brady. Only she's blue.

DAVID: Really?

JACK: Yeah. And she says she'll suck his dick.

VINCE: Shut the fuck up already.

JERRY: Everybody just shut up. What is wrong with you?

DAVID: Well, if you must know, I'm dying.

(There is a moment of stunned silence.)

JERRY: What are you talking about?

JACK: You're dying?

DAVID: Yeah. Probably not today. But soon.

VINCE: Ah, shit. I'm sorry.

DAVID: It's not your fault. We all gotta go.

VINCE: Yeah, but, hopefully not for a long time.

JERRY: Jesus Christ. Here I am, feeling sorry for myself, and... you're fucking dying! What the fuck is that? I mean, how did that happen? What, are you sick? You got... *(He can hardly say it.)* cancer?

DAVID: I don't mean I'm sick or anything like that. I just mean that I am going to die one day, and I wanted you all to know that.

VINCE: You're not sick?

DAVID: No. Just mortal.

VINCE: Oh, you are definitely high.

JERRY: Wait a minute. You're not dying of some disease?

DAVID: No. I'm dying in the same sense that we're all dying.

JERRY: What the fuck are you talking about?

DAVID: The scales have fallen from my eyes.

VINCE: "Nothing to see folks. He's doped up on goofballs."[14]

JERRY: You didn't find Jesus again, did you?

VINCE: "The power of Christ compels you!"[15]

DAVID: No. I just realized that I am going to die someday. I'm on a limited schedule.

VINCE: You just figured that out?

DAVID: Knowledge and belief are different things. I believe in death. I've seen it.

VINCE: Oh, you're just freaked out from 9/11. Everything's gonna be fine. Relax. This is a natural reaction.

DAVID: I'm not talking about 9/11. Not exactly. I mean, yeah, that freaked me out, and it sucked, and still sucks, but that wasn't the deciding factor.

JERRY: What the fuck are you talking about?

DAVID: I'm talking about blood and guts and life and death.

---

[14]Police Chief Wiggum in *The Simpsons*.

[15]Max Von Sydow in *The Exorcist*.

JACK: I don't understand.

DAVID: It's a long story.

JACK: What is?

DAVID: What happened to me.

JACK: What happened to you?

DAVID: Well, I guess it all started the night I tried to kill myself.

JERRY: You tried to kill yourself?

DAVID: I was going to.

VINCE: So first you're dying, and now you're trying to kill yourself?

JACK: What the hell are you talking about?

DAVID: It was about three months after 9/11. After everyone started acting like their normal, boring, creepy selves.

VINCE: Including you?

DAVID: Oh yeah. Especially me. Thousands of people dead. A war on terrorism that just gets curiouser and curiouser. Anthrax, some kid putting pipe bombs in mailboxes—things are totally fucked up. And there I am, buying this and selling that, closing deals like nothing ever happened. Keep going on like before. That's what everyone said to do to fight the terrorists. Keep going on like before. Even if you're an asshole, keep going on like before. It's all so fucked and weird. You ever feel like nothing makes sense, that time and space are all warped and you're just sort of floating through it, powerless?

JACK: All the time.

DAVID: So, one night, I go out drinking down on the Lower East Side, and I get into a fight with the bartender because he doesn't have the kind of vodka I like. I was screaming bloody murder at this guy because he didn't carry my brand. And in the middle of the argument, while I'm screaming, it hit me: I'm an asshole. And that was it. I had had enough. I walked to the nearest subway station, past beggars and drunks and dealers, past manholes puffing steam like smoke from Aladdin's lamp, down to the F train platform, and waited.

JACK: For what?

DAVID: People jump all the time. I'm surprised that more people don't do it. Just to see what happens. This other guy was there. Italian suit. Cuban cigar. A little rag doll in his hands. Talking to himself, laughing, dancing around. We both hear the train coming. He looks over at me, smiles, and tosses me the doll. I take this as a sign from God to keep on living. Then the guy jumps in front of the train.

JERRY: Jesus.

DAVID: So I got this doll, and parts of this dead guy on me.

JACK: He died?

DAVID: Yeah. He died. I took a long, long walk. Sometime after dawn I ended up in Central Park, sitting at Bethesda Fountain, crying like a baby.

JERRY: I'm sorry that happened to you, but—

DAVID: Do you remember when we went skinny-dippin' in the river that time?

JACK: Who went skinny-dippin'?

DAVID: I remember standing on the bridge, trying to figure out how high up I was, how cold the water would be… I was scared, you know? It's a pretty tall bridge… and up comes Jerry, buck naked. He turns to me, real peaceful, and just smiles. I've never forgotten that. Then he looks up to the sky and says "Oh Moon, grant us success in this, our endeavor," and pushes me off the bridge.

VINCE: What's so great about that?

DAVID: It was this perfect moment in time. It was like being a kid on the last day of school, with a whole summer ahead of me. Remember that, when it was June, and you knew July was coming, and that not one day of it had been spent yet? So I'm sitting there thinking about being a kid and Jerry on that bridge and that dead guy. And I took off my clothes and jumped into the fountain.

JACK: Buck naked?

DAVID: Yeah.

VINCE: You were not.

DAVID: Yes I was.

JERRY: You just took all your clothes off in the middle of Central Park?

DAVID: It was fun.

VINCE: Was all this before or after you quit your job?

DAVID: You should try it. *(Begins to take off shirt.)*

VINCE: I like my job.

DAVID: No. Getting naked in public. *(Continues to undress.)* When was the last time any of you were naked in public?

VINCE: Does the gym count?

DAVID: No. *(Starts to make chicken noises, "bock bock bock bock," etc.)*

JERRY: Carlos, will you tell him to keep his pants on?

CARLOS: I got nothing against nudists. If he wants to be naked, let him be naked.

VINCE: This is bullshit. What are you, fucking twelve?

DAVID: I wish. *(He is now totally naked.)*

JERRY: I don't believe this!

DAVID: Oh Moon, grant us success in this, our endeavor!

JERRY: Are we supposed to be impressed?

DAVID: Don't you think there might be a reason to exist other than the daily grind?

JERRY: Put your fucking clothes on!

DAVID: What in the hell has happened to you?

JERRY: Nothing has happened to me. For a long time now. I just keep rolling the same stone up the same hill.

DAVID: But you had it back then. You had a grip on something better than most of the shit that's out there.

JERRY: I was eighteen. I was drunk. I made up a little poem to the moon. Big deal.

DAVID: It was big to me.

JERRY: Just 'cause you quit your job and walk around naked doesn't mean you can come here and tell me how pathetic and useless and lonely I am.

VINCE: Right. He's got us for that.

JERRY: Fuck you Vince. And fuck you David. You're happy now. Great. I'm not. Sorry. And I don't think some idiot jumping in front of a train is going to change that.

DAVID: Carlos, maybe you can tell me: when exactly did Jerry lose his balls?

CARLOS: I don't think you should be talking about anyone's balls right now.

DAVID: Don't you ever wonder what the hell we're doing on this Earth?

CARLOS: I fought in a war. I don't have to think about shit like that. I just tend my bar, keep out of trouble, and put up with sorry assholes like you with too much time and money on their little college-educated hands. What am I doing on this Earth? Making a living, paying the rent, trying to get by.

DAVID: You're all insane. You know what I'm going to do? I'm going for a swim. And it's going to be cold, and I'm going to scream like a baby. I'm going to sing at the top of my lungs—

JACK: *(Starts to take off his shirt.)* What song?

VINCE: Well, Mary, I'm sure it'll be a lovely evening. Until the cops show up and take you back to whatever loony bin it is you escaped from.

DAVID: Jerry, you coming?

JERRY: Me? No. I'm just a geek who lives at home.

DAVID: Come on.

JERRY: Go preach your sermon somewhere else.

VINCE: You better be careful when they put you in the big house.

DAVID: Right outside that door is an entire world. Come with me! Can't you feel it out there?

VINCE: What?

DAVID: Life! You know how sometimes after driving for a while you can't remember any of the drive? Like you've been sleep-driving or something? What if the end of your life was like that? You can't remember any of it, but somehow, you've gone from point a to point b. And then you die. Fuck that. Let's pull over and walk.

JACK: I'll go. *(He is now naked.)* I don't know what the hell you're talking about with the car and all, but the swimming and singing sounds pretty cool.

JERRY: You know what you're like? A Hare Krishna.

VINCE: Or a Moonie.

DAVID: Fine. Sit there and do nothing. Jack and I are gonna go live a little.

JERRY: Hey David, how do you pay for all this living you're doing?

DAVID: How do you pay for what you're doing?

JERRY: Have fun with the freak show, Jack. You dumb-ass.

JACK: Okay. See you guys later on?

VINCE: Carlos, another round?

JACK: O Moon… O Moon… what was it you said?

(JACK opens the door, to reveal MOLLY and KRISTEN. There is a moment of awkward silence. JACK covers his privates with his hands.)

JACK: Hi girls.

DAVID: Molly! Kristen! I was hoping I'd see you two. You both look great!

(He goes to hug MOLLY, who gestures that a hug is not a good idea. He turns to KRISTEN, and she also gestures that a hug at the moment is not a good idea.)

DAVID: *(To MOLLY.)* I don't think I've seen you since before your wedding. How are you?

MOLLY: David? What the hell are you doing here? *(Walks into the bar. She has had a few drinks too many. She begins to laugh, and turns to KRISTEN.)* And you said that nothing, that uh, that nothing ever happens in this town worth mentioning. Ha!

KRISTEN: *(She too is a bit tipsy.)* The last thing I expected to see tonight was David

Linington and his magic penis. What is this? A nudists' club?

MOLLY: Put that thing away! It could be loaded!

VINCE: Honey, why don't you go home, and I'll explain everything tomorrow.

MOLLY: *(To VINCE.)* Why aren't you naked? Scared to show them your little pecker?

KRISTEN: *(To DAVID.)* What are you doing here?

DAVID: We were just going swimming down at the bridge. Care to join us?

KRISTEN: I see you forgot your suit.

JACK: We didn't forget anything! Not this time!

(JACK howls in glee, holds door for SHEILA; both exit.)

DAVID: *(Looking out at JACK.)* I gotta go.

(DAVID looks back to JERRY, takes a ragged doll spattered with blood out of his bag, hands it to JERRY.)

DAVID: Jerry? Last call.

JERRY: I hope you drown.

DAVID: Don't make me do anything drastic.

(JACK is heard howling in the distance.)

DAVID: Ladies, it was great to see you both. Molly, Kristen, nice to see you both as well. *(DAVID runs off.)*

KRISTEN: He looks healthy.

MOLLY: Should we join them?

VINCE: Very funny. What are you doing here?

MOLLY: Girls' night out. Just wanted to tell you I'll be home late.

KRISTEN: Mind if we join you?

VINCE and MOLLY: Yes!

MOLLY: Girls' night out means no boys.

VINCE: *(Overlapping MOLLY.)* We're bonding here. Man talk. You know. *(Going to bar.)* Carlos, another round.

KRISTEN: Fine. *(Ambling up to JERRY.)* I was just being polite, anyway.

MOLLY: I'll get the car. *(Exits.)*

KRISTEN: How are you doing?

JERRY: Oh, I'm just having a fantastic day. You look nice.

KRISTEN: So do you.

JERRY: How's Karl?

KRISTEN: Pissed.

JERRY: Sorry about the poem thing.

KRISTEN: I should have burned them.

JERRY: Yeah.

KRISTEN: Why don't you meet some nice girl, and fall in love with her?

JERRY: Because I love you, Kristen. I've loved you since the day I met you. And I don't care who knows about the poems I wrote you. *(Stands up, yells out.)* I LOVE KRISTEN! I'VE ALWAYS LOVED HER!

KRISTEN: Jerry, stop that right now! *(Pulls him down to his seat.)* Listen to me. You're very sweet, but you need to calm down. Right now. I know you love me, and think I'm fabulous, and all that. And I am. I just don't need anyone to love me. Anyone. I'm married, for Chrissakes. I just want a little excitement now and then. Not poems about moonbeams and wet paint and boo hoo hoo. Excitement. Not love. I'm not leaving Karl. You understand, don't you?

(MOLLY yells offstage, "Kristen!")

KRISTEN: Gotta go. Molly and I are getting reacquainted. I forgot how fun she was. *(Goes to door.)* Hey Vincent, my little buddy—after several drinks with your neglected wife, who deserves far better than you, I have decided that you need to fuck off. Nothing personal. Kiss, kiss. 'night Jerry. 'night Carlos. *(Exits.)*

JERRY: What was that all about?

VINCE: Dames. Who knows? "Of all the gin joints, in all the world, she walks into mine."[16] I'm putting some music on. Any requests?

JERRY: How is any of this like *Casablanca*?

VINCE: I don't know. *(Brings a drink to JERRY.)* Nice reunion.

JERRY: What a crock of shit.

VINCE: Here's to Moon-Boy and Jack getting busted for indecent exposure to fish.

JERRY: Here's to… nothing. Absolutely nothing at all.

SCENE THREE

Later that night. JERRY and VINCE sit at the table, which is covered with several empty bottles and shotglasses. A very full ashtray sits in front of them. CARLOS is behind the bar.

VINCE: "You stupid humans, with your stupid minds! Stupid, stupid, stupid!"

JERRY: *Plan Nine from Outer Space.* "I think I ate a bug."

VINCE: *Hearts of Darkness.* "You fuck my wife?"

JERRY: *Raging Bull.* "Fuck you, Dave."

VINCE: *Glengarry Glen Ross.* "Bring me a dead baby boy."

JERRY: *Man Bites Dog.* "Can I borrow your underpants for ten minutes?"

VINCE: *Sixteen Candles.* "You fuck my wife?"

JERRY: You just did that one. *Raging Bull.*

VINCE: *(In a serious voice.)* Did you fuck my wife?

JERRY: Now you don't even sound like him.

VINCE: Did you fuck my wife?

JERRY: *(Pause. He looks away from VINCE.)* I don't know what the fuck you're talking about.

VINCE: *(Stares at JERRY for a moment, then smiles.)* I'm just fucking with ya. Just for shits and giggles. Hey, wanna hear a good one? You'll love this. *(Starts to laugh.)* I fucked Kristen. How do you like that? Fucked her blue!

JERRY: What?

VINCE: *(Laughing.)* Oh, yeah. Many times. So, if you fucked Molly, it's okay. We all have little indiscretions. So fuck it.

JERRY: What are you talking about?

VINCE: Nothing. I'm just fucking with you. *(Pause.)* Did you?

JERRY: What?

VINCE: Fuck Molly?

JERRY: No. I wouldn't do that to you. Jesus. *(Gets up, heads to the bar.)* Carlos, another Bud. Fucking Christ. Want one?

(VINCE nods.)

JERRY: Make it two. *(JERRY takes the two beers, returns to the table. Pause.)* So, did you?

[16]Humphrey Bogart in *Casablanca.*

VINCE: What?

JERRY: Fuck Kristen?

VINCE: No. I wouldn't do that to you.

(They sit for a moment in silence.)

VINCE: "I have seen things you people wouldn't believe. Attack ships on fire off the shoulder of Orion."

JERRY: *Blade Runner*. "Fuck this fucking game."

(The door opens, and DAVID walks in, wearing nothing but the American flag wrapped around him like a diaper.)

DAVID: Jack has asked me to retrieve his clothes.

(JACK, from outside, yells "Yeah!")

CARLOS: What the fuck do you think you're doing wearing the flag like that?

DAVID: It got cold.

CARLOS: You got exactly one minute to put that back where you found it.

DAVID: You don't like my new outfit?

CARLOS: I'm serious. That's a sacrilege.

DAVID: Oh, I see. I suppose wrapping it around a crucifix and hanging it in front of your bar is patriotic.

CARLOS: Damn right.

DAVID: Tell you what. You name me all ten amendments to the Constitution that make up the Bill of Rights, and I'll take it off.

JACK: *(From outside.)* Can I please have my clothes back please?

DAVID: Sorry. Where are Jack's clothes?

(CARLOS points to the booth, where they are sitting on one of the benches, next to DAVID's clothes.)

DAVID: Thanks. *(He picks up the pile of clothes and exits. Offstage.)* Jack? Where are you?

JACK: *(Off.)* Behind the Volvo.

JERRY: What are the ten amendments?

VINCE: Who gives a shit?

(MOLLY enters, walks straight to VINCE, stands in front of him for a moment, and slaps him in the face, then fiercely turns to JERRY.)

MOLLY: He's fucking her! Why don't you write a poem about that?

(Blackout.)

ACT TWO
SCENE ONE

Same as before. JERRY and VINCE sit at table. CARLOS is upstage. MOLLY enters, walks straight to VINCE, stands in front of him for a moment, and slaps him in the face, then fiercely turns to JERRY.)

MOLLY: He's fucking her! Why don't you write a poem about that? *(She goes to the door, turns back.)* Fuck the both of you, you little fucking assholes.

(She exits through the door, passing DAVID, who has put some of his clothes back on.)

DAVID: What'd I miss?

JERRY: I knew it. You fucking asshole.

VINCE: Ah, shit. *(Runs to door, stops, turns back.) Bull Durham.*

(VINCE exits. JACK enters, with his clothes on, walks to table, sits.)

JERRY: I gotta get out of here.

DAVID: Wait. I thought of something I wanted to tell you. It'll just take a minute.

(KRISTEN appears in the doorway. JERRY freezes at the sight of her. DAVID takes out A Moveable Feast, *and reads.)*

DAVID: "His talent was as natural as the pattern that was made by the dust on a butterfly's wings. At one time he understood it no more than the butterfly did and he did not know when it was brushed or marred. Later he became conscious of his damaged wings and of their construction and he learned to think and could not fly any more because the love of flight was gone and he could only remember when it had been effortless."

JERRY: David, I appreciate that you want me to get up and out there, to improve my life and live in the moment and all that bullshit. I do. But at this point in time, I need you to fuck off and die. I don't know if you realize this, but most people don't like it when other people tell them how to live. It's considered rude.

(DAVID starts to say something, but JERRY cuts him off.)

JERRY: Just don't even look at me. *(He turns to KRISTEN.)* How's Vince? You know, Vince? Your fuck buddy?

(KRISTEN steps toward JERRY.)

JERRY: You're right. I don't need someone like you. You fucking slut! *(Exits.)*

DAVID: Is everyone here crazy?

KRISTEN: I think you may be right on that one. Oh God, I have to get out of this place. *(She begins to cry.)* I just want to run and run and keep on running, until I drop dead on the pavement. You know? I hate my fucking life. The town floozy, married to Fievel, the village idiot. What a joke. I've become everything I used to hate. Isn't that funny? Why aren't you laughing at my joke?

DAVID: Because it isn't funny.

KRISTEN: Oh, that would explain it. *(Cries even more.)*

DAVID: I know how you feel. I was a total asshole just a few months ago. I think I still am.

KRISTEN: Really?

DAVID: Ask Carlos.

(She looks to CARLOS, who nods his head positively.)

DAVID: I'm a total asshole.

KRISTEN: You know what I want to do?

DAVID: What?

KRISTEN: Go bodysurfing. Right now. I know a little beach near Carmel. We could get there in forty minutes.

DAVID: I don't know.

KRISTEN: Please? I'm drunk and pissed and upset, and I need a friend. What a fucking night. I try and do the right thing, tell Molly about my little tryst with Vince, I mean, at the time it seemed like the right thing to do, but fuck if it didn't go over quite as well as I had hoped. I mean, what are you supposed to do? Keep quiet and feel like shit, or tell the truth and feel like shit.

DAVID: Maybe you should try not fucking her husband.

KRISTEN: Spare me your judgmental bullshit, alright?

DAVID: I'm sorry.

KRISTEN: Now what am I supposed to do? Go home to Karl and our beautiful split-level ranch house up in Prunedale? You knew me in high school. Did I ever strike you as the type to end up living in Prunedale?

DAVID: No.

KRISTEN: I wanted to move to Watsonville! But no, Karl was adamant about Prunedale. You know, that's about the only thing he ever had any balls about. Prunedale.

DAVID: Why'd you marry him?

KRISTEN: Oh, what the fuck do you know? I was young, he was rich and cute. So I did. Big fucking deal. I kept thinking it would get better, okay? It just didn't happen. And the next thing I know, I'm over thirty, never went to college, and have nothing to call my own. I don't even have any children. *(Laughs.)* I'm barren. How's that for ironic? I got a sex drive that won't quit, but I can't produce the goods. At first, I thought it was Karl, but, according to the doctors... well, never mind.

DAVID: I'm sorry.

KRISTEN: Ah, it's okay. It's actually pretty nice. Our house. I just can't go there tonight. I need to do something different. You know? Something that makes me feel alive. Like going to Carmel with an old friend for a little night swimming.

DAVID: Carmel?

KRISTEN: You have a car, right?

DAVID: Yeah, I still have a car. I haven't been able to give that up just yet. Of course, once my savings run out—

KRISTEN: *(Heading to the door.)* I'll navigate. *(Exits.)*

DAVID: *(Heading to the door. Grabs his clothes off the bench.)* Carlos, Jack, don't tell anyone about this. If Jerry found out, it would only hurt him.

CARLOS: If I told all the people who come here what their friends do here behind their backs, I wouldn't have any customers left. They'd all kill each other.

JACK: *(Howls.)* "I would be ignorant as the dawn
That merely stood, rocking the glittering coach
Above the cloudy shoulders of the horses;
I would be—for no knowledge is worth a straw—
Ignorant and wanton as the dawn."

DAVID: Great. *(Exits. A moment after leaving, comes back in, hands the flag to CARLOS, salutes him, exits.)*

JACK: I guess I should get going.

CARLOS: Yeah, it's past closing time.

JACK: Did Sheila come by while I was out with David?

CARLOS: Not tonight, Jack, not tonight.

(CARLOS takes bus tub from behind bar, begins to pick up empty bottles, ashtrays, etc. JACK exits. A lone wolf is heard, howling. Lights fade.)

SCENE TWO

It is early evening, the following day. Patriotic music is playing on the jukebox. CARLOS is behind the bar. VINCE is sitting at the booth. JACK is standing.

VINCE: You played what in a graveyard?

JACK: Hide-and-go-seek. It was really fun. And David was it!

CARLOS: You're lucky you weren't arrested.

JACK: We weren't doing anything wrong. Just playing.

VINCE: In a graveyard. Naked.

JACK: Yeah. It was great.

VINCE: Any wolves?

JACK: No. Maybe they were sleeping.

CARLOS: You keep away from David. He's not right.

JACK: He's my friend.

VINCE: Jack, you fucking idiot, I'm your friend. Carlos is your friend. David is nobody's friend but David's.

(A wolf howls in the distance.)

JACK: You shut up. I like David. He told me that—

VINCE: Shut the fuck up. Carlos, while I pee, could you pour me a cold one? *(Exits to back room.)*

CARLOS: You got it, big guy.

(SHEILA enters, sits at booth opposite JACK.)

JACK: *(To SHEILA.)* You missed it last night!

SHEILA: Did you get the room?

JACK: What?

SHEILA: The room. Lake Tahoe. Where we're going this weekend?

JACK: I told you, that was a long time ago.

SHEILA: Not to me.

(JERRY enters.)

JERRY: Hey Jack. Carlos.

CARLOS: Hey big guy. Cold one?

JERRY: Sure.

(VINCE returns from the back area.)

JERRY: Vince, I gotta talk to you.

VINCE: Yeah. I know. Look, about Kristen—

JERRY: Just let me talk for a minute. I got a lot to say. First, you were right. I have been having an affair with Molly. I know it was wrong, and I don't expect you to forgive me right away, but I am sorry, and I wanted to tell you the truth.

VINCE: You fucked my wife?

JERRY: And you fucked Kristen. But it doesn't matter. That's all over. I'm leaving here. David was right. We gotta live now, right now. I'm thirty-six years old and have lived in this town my whole life. That isn't what I wanted. I want to see... everything. The Atlantic Ocean. Paris. Other horizons, you know?

VINCE: Ah, Jesus. Et tu, Brutus?

JERRY: I just wanted to tell you that before I left. About me and Molly. You're my buddy, and I love you. Carlos, thanks for all the good times. I think your politics are fucked up and wrong, but that you're a good man, and I consider you a friend. Jack, one time when you got really drunk, we took pictures of you naked with a dog, and put them on the net. I'm sorry. I love you, buddy. So, I guess that's all I wanted to say. Now I gotta convince Kristen to come with me.

VINCE: So where is she?

JERRY: Who, Molly?

VINCE: No, Kristen. She's not with you?

JERRY: No. I thought you might know where she is.

JACK: I know where she is.

JERRY: Where?

JACK: I can't say.

VINCE: Why not?

JACK: I can't say. *(Howls like a wolf.)*

VINCE: Where the fuck is she?

(DAVID enters. He is rather disheveled.)

DAVID: Hey guys. Carlos, you got any coffee?

CARLOS: Yeah, but it's pretty old.

DAVID: That's okay. Just give me a big cup, black.

JERRY: David! I need to talk to you. I've been thinking a lot about what you said last night, about living and dying and all that, and I think you're right.

DAVID: Jerry—

JERRY: You were right. I'm not that kid who stood on the bridge anymore. I can barely remember him.

DAVID: Jerry, listen—

JERRY: It's okay. You were right. I've spent the last ten years of my life working at a soul-sucking job I hate, going to the same bar every night, telling the same jokes, listening to the same songs. Well, no more. From now on, I'm living for the moment.

VINCE: Oh, Jesus. The madness is spreading.

JERRY: You only say that because you're scared that I'm right. That you've been wasting your life memorizing movie quotes and song lyrics while the world passed you by. And that's okay, if that makes you happy. It just doesn't do the trick for me anymore. So tomorrow, I'm taking off for points unknown. Just me and Kristen and the open road.

VINCE: You and Kristen?

JERRY: Hopefully. I think she's been waiting for me to do something like this.

DAVID: Jerry—

JERRY: You can come with us too! It'll be great!

DAVID: Jerry, will you just shut up already!

JERRY: What?

KARL: *(Entering.)* Has anyone seen Kristen? Anyone? I've called the store in Gilroy. I've called the cops. I don't know what to do. She went out with Molly last night and never came home. Did Molly say anything to you about her, Vince? I can't reach Molly at your number. What if—

CARLOS: Calm down, big guy. Kristen is fine. I promise you.

KARL: She is?

CARLOS: Yeah, she is.

KARL: Where is she? Why hasn't she answered her cell phone?

CARLOS: I can't tell you.

KARL: Why not?

DAVID: Karl, hi. David Linington. I don't think we've met.

KARL: Who are you?

DAVID: Nobody. A friend of Kristen's.

KARL: Do you know where she is?

DAVID: The Ramada.

KARL: What's she doing there?

DAVID: Sleeping.

KARL: *(Stares at DAVID for a moment, then looks away.)* Oh. I see. Yes. Well, that accounts for where she is. Yes.

JERRY: Wait a minute. How do you know where she is?

KARL: Jerry, where she is is none of your business.

DAVID: It's not what you think.

JERRY: First Vince, now you. That's just great.

KARL: Excuse me, Jerry, but I don't see how you can… it's not your place… she's my wife!

VINCE: Oh shut the fuck up, Fievel.

KARL: You know something, Vince? I don't like you. You're a mean, petty little man. Carlos, I won't be going to class tonight. You'll have to find another ride. I'm sorry. *(Exits.)*

JERRY: You fucking asshole!

DAVID: Nothing happened. I swear. She's a beautiful, sweet, fucked-up woman. All we did last night was go swimming, and talk.

VINCE: All night at the Ramada? Right.

DAVID: Jerry, listen to me. Nothing happened between me and Kristen. Nothing like what you're thinking. But I have to tell you. There is nothing happening between you and her either. Let her go.

JERRY: I gotta get out of here. *(Exits.)*

DAVID: Got any good movie quotes for the situation, Vince?

VINCE: Fuck you, asshole. *(Exits.)*

DAVID: How are you, Jack?

JACK: Fine. That was fun in the graveyard last night.

DAVID: Yeah. Carlos, can I get a big glass of water?

CARLOS: Fucked up enough people's lives yet?

DAVID: What?

CARLOS: You're a real shit disturber, you know that?

DAVID: I'm just trying to find some kind of truth.

CARLOS: Nobody wants your truth.

DAVID: I do.

CARLOS: Then keep it to yourself. Stop trying to change the world.

DAVID: I'm not trying to change the world. I'm trying to save my friend.

CARLOS: Same thing. People may say they want things to change, but they won't buy that change from the guy whose fucking their women. It doesn't work that way.

DAVID: What am I supposed to do?

CARLOS: I don't care.

JACK: Let's go play hide-and-seek again. Maybe I can get Sheila to come.

DAVID: Sheila's dead, Jack.

JACK: I know that. Whose grave do you think I was hiding behind last night when you couldn't find me?

DAVID: You ever been to Mexico?

JACK: No.

DAVID: Me either. Want to go?

(JACK smiles, looks to SHEILA, as if for permission to say yes. SHEILA fervently shakes her head negatively.)

JACK: I can't. I got a date with Sheila tonight. I'm sorry.

DAVID: Oh. I see.

(Enter MOLLY.)

MOLLY: Carlos, got any coffee?

CARLOS: It's cold. I'll brew you a fresh pot.

MOLLY: Thanks. Hello Jack. David.

JACK: Hi Molly. Hey, what do you think about Mexico?

MOLLY: What?

JACK: David wants us to go. But I can't. Not today.

MOLLY: *(To DAVID.)* What, are you just making your way through everybody, fucking up all our lives one by one?

DAVID: I think so.

MOLLY: I note you haven't fucked with any of the womenfolk yet.

DAVID: Oh, you just haven't been around this morning. I think I managed to screw up Kristen's life a little last night, too.

MOLLY: Does every guy in this town have to fuck her?

DAVID: Oh, we didn't fool around. We just talked about life, and she read me some of her poems, and went swimming. She's a nice girl.

MOLLY: Aside from the fact that she uses Karl for his money.

DAVID: Yeah. There is the whole marriage thing.

MOLLY: Ah yes, the marriage thing.

DAVID: Doesn't anyone get divorced anymore?

MOLLY: Oh, yes.

DAVID: This whole trip is going very differently from how I envisioned it.

MOLLY: What did you think would happen?

DAVID: I don't know. That I would show up, collect Jerry, and take off on a big road trip.

MOLLY: Jerry has a way of disappointing people.

DAVID: You know what the worst part of happiness is? Not being able to give it to people who need it.

MOLLY: I wouldn't know about that.

DAVID: What?

MOLLY: Happiness.

DAVID: Really?

MOLLY: Well, I shouldn't say that. There've been times when I've been happy. Plenty of times. I went camping up on Mt. Toro once, with Jerry and Vince, back in that other world that was my life. About a year before I got married. I had this cute little camping outfit. I even had a pith helmet. Jerry and Vince called me Jane Goodall, and I called them my chimps. We slept under the stars, cooked over an open fire. We laughed the entire weekend. I don't think I've been up there since that weekend. One minute ago, I swear it wasn't any longer, I was standing on that mountain with Jerry and Vince, laughing and young and ready for the world. Then I blinked my eyes, had a few glasses of wine, and presto… here I am.

DAVID: Have you ever been to Mexico?

MOLLY: Does Tijuana count?

DAVID: Not really.

MOLLY: Then no.

DAVID: Want to go?

MOLLY: What?

DAVID: I can't stay here. I thought coming home would be… clarifying. But everything here is just as fucked up as I am, maybe even more so. These past few months on the road, I was happy for the first time in I don't know how long. I went where my heart told me to go. For the first time since I was in that other world that was my life, I followed my dreams. I'd wake up so happy that sometimes I'd cry, just seeing the sunrise. But I didn't have anyone to share it with, to tell me it was real.

MOLLY: So you want me to go with you to Mexico to tell you it's real?

DAVID: Yeah. Look, you and Jack are the only people around here who seem to have any clue about life, and Jack can't come, so that leaves you.

MOLLY: Gee, when you put it like that—

DAVID: I'm going to Mexico. I got room in my car for one more. I would enjoy your company. A lot.

MOLLY: Why aren't you asking Kristen?

DAVID: Because she's crazy. I have a strict rule. No traveling companions who are nuts.

MOLLY: I don't know.

DAVID: Molly, time is flying by. I swear to God, one minute ago, I was twenty-one. Then I blinked my eyes, had a few glasses of wine, and presto—I'm thirty-five. At this rate, I'll be dead tomorrow. And I am going to see Mexico before I die. If you want to stay here, I understand. But I'm leaving.

MOLLY: When?

DAVID: Now. Today. Right now.

MOLLY: Give me two hours.

DAVID: Really?

MOLLY: Make it one hour.

DAVID: Okay.

(MOLLY goes to the door.)

MOLLY: And David? I'm not going as your paramour.

DAVID: I didn't ask you to come to be my new fuck buddy.

MOLLY: As long as we're clear. *(Exits.)*

CARLOS: Yep, a real shit disturber.

DAVID: I understand you're taking a class in speed seduction. That's nice.

CARLOS: David, listen to me. I know you're having fun, being alive and all that. But in a month or two, maybe a year, all that is going to fade away, and all you're going to be is dead broke and stuck. You want that?

DAVID: If it's going to fade away, shouldn't I grab it while I can?

CARLOS: I don't really care what you do. But Molly is a nice girl.

DAVID: What do you want her to do? Stay here, married to a husband she doesn't love? Keep having an affair with a guy who doesn't love her?

CARLOS: Just leave her alone.

JACK: Don't listen to him, David.

DAVID: What?

JACK: You ride down to Mexico with Molly. Road trips are the best. I took a road trip with Sheila to Tahoe one time. We saw Scorpio. She said groovy.

CARLOS: Jack, stay out of this.

JACK: I'd go with you, but I got a date tonight.

CARLOS: Jack—

(JERRY enters. Walks up to DAVID.)

JERRY: Did you fuck her, yes or no?

DAVID: What?

JERRY: Kristen. Did you fuck her, yes or no?

DAVID: Are you out of your mind?

JERRY: Apparently so. You tell me I'm some fucking bug with dust on his wings, that I'm a spineless, boring dweeb, and then turn around and spend the night at the Ramada Inn, fucking the girl I've loved since I was fifteen. I must be crazy.

DAVID: Jerry… ah, what's the use? I give up. I don't know you anymore.

(Enter KARL.)

CARLOS: I'll tell you one thing that isn't in the Bill of Rights: fucking over your buddies.

KARL: *(To DAVID.)* Do you love her?

DAVID: Huh?

KARL: Do you love her? I understand if you do. And I don't blame you.

DAVID: Karl—

KARL: Let me finish, please. As long as you love her, I can stand it. But if you're just some fly-by-night, meaningless fling, then I have to ask you to stop. She doesn't need that kind of attention. She's a good woman, and deserves better.

DAVID: Karl, I promise you, there is nothing going on between Kristen and I. We spoke last night, and I read some of her poetry—

KARL: Her what?

DAVID: You know she writes, don't you?

KARL: Oh, yes. Her poetry. Of course.

JERRY: She doesn't write poetry, you lying son of a bitch.

DAVID: Well, she read me about ten poems last night.

KARL: How were they, the poems?

DAVID: Sad.

JACK: I know a sad poem.

JERRY: Not now Jack.

JACK: Sheila wrote it.

KARL: Who's Sheila?

JACK: My girlfriend.

JERRY: Jack, shut up already.

JACK: "I dreamed that one had died in a strange place
Near no accustomed hand;
And they had nailed boards above her face,
The peasants of that land."

JERRY: Look, the real question is, did he fuck her or not?

JACK: "Wondering to lay her in that solitude,
And raised above her mound
A cross they had made out of two bits of wood,
And planted Cypress round;"

JERRY: Did you fuck her or not?

DAVID: I didn't sleep with her! And it wouldn't matter if I did!

KARL: You didn't?

DAVID: What is wrong with you people? You're more obsessed with fucking than you are with living!

JACK: "And left her to the indifferent stars above
Until I carved these words:"

KARL: I just need to know what happened.

JACK: "She was more beautiful than thy
first love,
But now lies under boards."

JERRY: Jack, will you shut up? Shut your fucking stupid mouth. He fucked Kristen, and you're babbling some fucking poem? Shut the fuck up!

CARLOS: That's it! Everybody, take it outside. Jerry, apologize to Jack. Karl, go home. Nothing happened last night. David, go away.

JERRY: I'm not apologizing to anybody. Fuck you, Carlos!

CARLOS: *(Pause.)* What did you say?

JERRY: *(Goes to door.)* That's right. Fuck you. Fuck all of you. *(Exits.)*

KARL: Well, that was... unpleasant. Carlos, I'm going home now. Pick you up for class later?

CARLOS: You got it, big guy.

KARL: *(To DAVID.)* I believe you. *(To JACK.)* Jim, see you around. *(Exits.)*

CARLOS: What are you waiting for?

DAVID: Carlos, I am leaving. Soon. After today, you will never see me again, if I can help it.

CARLOS: Good, 'cause you are one ugly son of a bitch.

(DAVID exits to the restroom.)

JACK: Did you like the poem?

CARLOS: It was nice, Jack.

(Lights change to dreamland. Offstage, we here DAVID say, "ten, nine, eight, seven, six, five, four, three, two, one... ready or not, here I come!" JACK takes a chair from one of the tables and sets it downstage, and hides. SHEILA, who has been in the booth upstage the whole scene, creeps up to JACK and startles him.)

SHEILA: Boo!

JACK: Hey, I thought you'd be here.

SHEILA: What's going on?

JACK: Sshh. *(Whispers.)* David's it.

SHEILA: Why didn't you call me last night?

JACK: I was busy.

SHEILA: Is there someone else? Just tell me.

JACK: I gotta finish the game.

SHEILA: There's someone else, isn't there?

JACK: Sheila, how can you say that?

DAVID: *(Offstage.)* Come out, come out, wherever you are.

SHEILA: Promise me that we'll always be together, Jack.

(DAVID enters from the door, looking for JACK. He spots him, and pounces.)

DAVID: Gotcha!

JACK: You win. David, you remember Sheila, don't you?

DAVID: Of course I do. You miss her?

JACK: What are you talking about? She's right here.

SHEILA: *(Standing up to leave.)* Don't forget, party tomorrow night, and the next night, you will boldly go where no man has gone before. *(Exits.)*

JACK: No!

DAVID: Jack, what's going on?

JACK: She always does that.

DAVID: Who?

JACK: Sheila! We hang out for a little bit, and then she leaves.

DAVID: Where do you think she goes?

JACK: Elsewhere.

DAVID: Where's that?

JACK: I don't know. Tahoe, maybe. She liked it there. *(Points up.)* Do you see those stars that look sort of like a big letter E?

DAVID: I think so.

JACK: *(Reverently.)* That's Cassiopeia, Duchess of Tahoe. Queen of Elsewhere.

DAVID: Jack?

JACK: Yeah?

DAVID: What happened to our lives?

JACK: What do you mean?

DAVID: What happened to the people we used to be?

JACK: I think they went elsewhere.

DAVID: *(Sighs, looks up at the sky.)* Pretty night, isn't it?

JACK: Yeah.

(DAVID tags JACK on the arm.)

DAVID: You're it! *(Runs off.)*

JACK: *(Brushing off the chair he has been hiding behind, as if it is a gravestone, and reads.)* "She was more beautiful than thy first love,
But now lies under boards."
(Lights back to normal.)

CARLOS: *(Continuing as if in the middle of a story he has been telling.)* And so I said, "Have you ever done something really exciting, like go on a roller coaster and sat in the front car?" While I'm doing this, I sort of motion to myself, like this *(Motions to himself.)*—Jack, are you paying attention?

JACK: *(Getting up.)* I'm sorry Carlos, what were you saying?

CARLOS: I sort of motion to myself, like this. *(Does so.)*

VINCE: *(Entering.)* Carlos, double shot of Jack, pint of Guinness, and no mention of women.

CARLOS: You got it, big guy.

JACK: Hey Vince. Where's Molly?

VINCE: Jack, not today. Please. This is one of those don't-fuck-with-me-or-I-will-rip-your-head-off-days, so back off.

CARLOS: Here you go.

VINCE: Thanks. *(Downs shot.)*

CARLOS: Want to talk about it?

VINCE: Can you explain this to me? I fuck someone else, and I'm an asshole. She fucks someone else, and she's a lonely woman doing what she has to do. Where's the logic in that?

CARLOS: What are you doing looking for logic in a woman?

JACK: That's not very nice.

VINCE: Ah, shut the fuck up.

KRISTEN: *(Enters, walks up to bar.)* Carlos, do you have any hot tea?

CARLOS: I don't know. Maybe. I'll have to check. Give me two minutes. *(Exits to back.)*

KRISTEN: Hello.

VINCE: Are you speaking to me? To what do I owe the honor?

KRISTEN: Stop acting like such a child.

VINCE: Oh, I'm sorry. Should I thank you for dumping me?

KRISTEN: Probably.

VINCE: And thanks so much for telling Molly. That was special.

KRISTEN: I don't have time for you, Vince. I'm looking for David.

VINCE: Of course you are.

JACK: Hi, Kristen.

KRISTEN: Hello, Jack. How are you?

JACK: Tired.

KRISTEN: Me too. Do you know where David is?

JACK: I'm not sure. I think he's meeting Molly here in a little bit. What day is it?

KRISTEN: What's he meeting Molly for?

VINCE: Yeah. What is David the nudist meeting my wife for?

JACK: They're going to Mexico.

VINCE: Oh. I see. Are the wolves taking them there? Or is Sheila giving them a ride? They better be careful if she is, Sheila has been known to drink and drive.

KRISTEN: Jesus, Vince, you are a fucking little asshole, you know that? A petty, mean, shitty little asshole.

VINCE: So says the slut.

JACK: Leave her alone, Vince.

VINCE: Shut the fuck up, Jack.

DAVID: *(Entering.)* Vince, I don't believe in violence anymore, but if I hear you tell Jack to shut the fuck up one more time, I will beat the living shit out of you. No shit. Hello, Kristen.

KRISTEN: David. What's this about Mexico?

DAVID: How did you know about that? Well, it doesn't matter, I suppose. I'm going to Mexico. Leaving tonight.

KRISTEN: Can I go with you?

DAVID: I don't think so.

KRISTEN: I won't get in the way. I'll just go for the ride for a week or so. Then I'll catch a bus back home.

DAVID: To Prunedale.

KRISTEN: Yeah.

DAVID: I thought you hated it.

KRISTEN: I do.

DAVID: Kristen, you have to get out of there.

KRISTEN: And do what?

DAVID: I don't know.

KRISTEN: Why don't you take me with you?

DAVID: I can't.

KRISTEN: Is Molly going with you?

DAVID: Yes.

KRISTEN: I see. Well, I like her. Have fun.

DAVID: Why don't you leave anyway? Why do you need me to take you away?

KRISTEN: You know, for such a smart guy, you're an idiot.

CARLOS: *(Reentering.)* I don't have any tea.

KRISTEN: That's okay. One cosmo, please.

DAVID: I'm sorry.

KRISTEN: Don't worry about me. *(Takes out cell phone, speaks into it.)* Home. *(Holds phone to her ear.)* Karl? It's me. I'll be home later tonight. Much later.

DAVID: How can you write such lovely poems, and stay in that stifling atmosphere?

KRISTEN: *(Into phone.)* No, I just needed to get some space.

DAVID: Jesus.

KRISTEN: *(Into phone.)* What? What roller coaster?

VINCE: "I am in a world of shit."[17]

KRISTEN: *(Into phone.)* Okay. Gotta go. Yeah. *(Puts cell phone away.)*

DAVID: You know, Karl loves you.

KRISTEN: I know. *(Takes a big swig of her drink.)* He loves me. Treats me like a goddess. Like I'm special. *(Takes another swig.)* You know what he calls me? Athena. Goddess of Wisdom. Isn't that sweet?

DAVID: I think so.

KRISTEN: Oh, what do you know about anything? You think you know anything about life?

MOLLY: *(Entering with a small bag.)* Vince. Kristen. Nice to see you both. Carlos, how are you? Good old, secret-keeping Carlos. Hi Jack. David, I'm ready to go.

KRISTEN: Oh, that is good. She's ready to go. Don't keep her waiting, David. Go on. Do us all a favor, and get in your car and drive away. Forever. *(Finishes her drink.)*

VINCE: Finally, a voice of reason.

KRISTEN: Vince, shut the fuck up. *(Goes to MOLLY.)* You want to know what's worse than cheating on your husband? Listening to someone's poetry all night, and then giving her the cold shoulder. That's hurtful. *(Exits.)*

[17]Vincent D'Onofrio in *Full Metal Jacket.*

VINCE: Molly, what are you doing?

MOLLY: I'm leaving you, Vince. I'm sure you've seen something like this in one of the millions of movies you've watched in the past ten years.

VINCE: Molly—

MOLLY: Vince, please. It's been over for a long time. Let it go.

VINCE: Well, fuck you, too!

MOLLY: David, I'll be waiting out front. *(Exits.)*

DAVID: Well, I gotta go.

VINCE: Thank God.

DAVID: Carlos, Vince, good luck.

CARLOS: Do us a favor, and don't come back. Ever.

DAVID: I think that won't be a problem.

JACK: Really?

DAVID: Jack, come with us. There's nothing for you here.

JACK: I can't. I told you, I got a date tonight.

DAVID: Well, then this is goodbye.

JACK: Forever?

DAVID: I don't know. Maybe. Maybe not.

(Goes to door. JERRY enters as DAVID is leaving. They look at each other for a moment. DAVID leaves, and JERRY walks to the bar.)

JERRY: Carlos, shot of Jameson's, and a Guinness.

CARLOS: Coming right up, big guy.

JERRY: Hey Jack. Vince.

VINCE: Hey, buddy. Hell of a night, huh?

JERRY: Hell of a day too.

CARLOS: *(Handing JERRY his drinks.)* Here you go.

JERRY: Thank you.

(JERRY goes to table where VINCE is sitting, sits. JACK joins them.)

VINCE: "What do you want to do tonight? I don't know, what do you want to do?"

JERRY: *(Pause.) Marty*. Chicks, man.

VINCE: *(Thinks for a moment.)* What the hell is that from?

JERRY: Life. Women. Fucking whores.

JACK: Sheila's not like that.

JERRY: What?

JACK: What you said. And Molly and Kristen aren't like that, either.

VINCE: Jack, fuck you and your fucking bullshit ghost stories and howling wolves and fucking date with miss dead-for-a-long-time.

JACK: Sheila—

JERRY: Sheila's dead, Jack. She's gone. Forever.

JACK: No. I saw her last night.

VINCE: She's fucking dead. She got drunk with you and crashed the car, and now she's dead and you're an idiot.

JACK: But she still comes by—

JERRY: Jack! Shut the fuck up! Vince is right. There is no Sheila anymore! That's all in your head!

JACK: Ten, nine, eight, seven, six, five, four, three, two, one… NOT IT!

VINCE: Cut the crap. She's gone and you know it.

(JACK howls.)

JERRY: Wake up Jack.

JACK: No. You're both lying!

VINCE: So where is she now? Why doesn't she come and prove us wrong? Why doesn't anyone else ever see her?

JACK: I don't know.

VINCE: I'll tell you why. Because all that's left of Sheila is some rotting bones.

JACK: *(Howls.)* Not it! Not it! Not it!

JERRY: Jack, listen to us. She's gone. High school, happiness, Sheila, it's all gone.

CARLOS: That's it! You two leave him alone.

JERRY: Carlos, we're just telling him the truth.

VINCE: Come on, look at the guy. He needs to get back to reality.

CARLOS: And you two need to get the fuck out of my bar. Now.

JERRY: But—

CARLOS: Now!

(JERRY and VINCE begin to exit.)

CARLOS: And don't come back.

(VINCE turns to appeal to CARLOS.)

CARLOS: Ever!

(CARLOS follows them to the door. They exit. CARLOS looks after them for a moment, then looks back to JACK, who is on the floor, in extreme confusion and sorrow.)

CARLOS: Jack? You okay?

(JACK does not respond.)

CARLOS: Jack?

JACK: *(Hides between the chairs.)* Not it!

CARLOS: Take it easy.

JACK: *(Snaps back to reality. Looks around.)* What did Vince mean about rotting bones?

CARLOS: Nothing.

JACK: *(Stands, walks to CARLOS.)* She's really dead, isn't she?

CARLOS: Yeah.

JACK: I loved her.

CARLOS: I know.

JACK: Was David here?

CARLOS: Yeah.

JACK: Is he dead?

CARLOS: No. *(Pause.)* Hey, you want a burger? A big cheeseburger from In-N-Out Burger?

(JACK doesn't reply.)

CARLOS: You stay here, and I'll get us a couple of burgers. Keep an eye on the place, okay Jack? Okay?

JACK: Okay.

(CARLOS exits. JACK sits for a moment, goes to jukebox, puts a dollar in, selects a song, goes back to table. "Lights" by Journey starts to play. JACK lays his head in his hands and weeps. SHEILA enters, walks to JACK, hugs him.)

SHEILA: You ready?

JACK: Sheila!

(Hugs her tightly. They dance for a bit.)

JACK: I knew they were lying.

SHEILA: Let's go.

JACK: Where?

SHEILA: Tahoe.

JACK: What about my hamburger?

SHEILA: We'll get you one once we get to the lake.

JACK: "And bending down beside the glowing bars,
Murmur, a little sadly, how Love fled
And paced upon the mountains overhead
And hid his face amid a crowd of stars."

(They exit together. Curtain.)

PLAYS AND PLAYWRIGHTS 2001

Edited by Martin Denton

Nine outstanding new plays from off- and off-off-Broadway's 1999–2000 season.

Washington Square Dreams **by Gorilla Repertory Theatre** — eight ten-minute plays set during an outdoor performance of *A Midsummer Night's Dream.*

Fate **by Elizabeth Horsburgh** — romantic flights of fancy in a compact comedy about a pair of passionate strangers.

Velvet Ropes **by Joshua Scher** — two innocents trapped in an art museum contemplate the nature of humor, performance, and art.

The Language of Kisses **by Edmund De Santis** — an estranged mother and daughter come to terms with the past and themselves in this moving drama by the author of *Making Peter Pope.*

Word to Your Mama **by Julia Lee Barclay** — channel surfing through a turn of the millennium mind.

Cuban Operator Please... **by Adrian Rodriguez** — short play about the effects of exile and death on the relationship between a father and son.

The Elephant Man—The Musical **by Jeff Hylton & Tim Werenko** — John Merrick gets to sing and dance on Broadway.

House of Trash **by Trav S.D.** — a raucous populist musical farce about a garbageman moonlighting as a Baptist preacher.

Straight-Jacket **by Richard Day** — brilliantly funny and incisive satire of Hollywood and hypocrisy.

ISBN 0967023424

Retail: $15.00

Additional information can be found on the web at http://www.nytheatre.com/nytheatre/books.htm

Available in bookstores and on line or order directly from the publisher

Send a check or money for $15 (plus $4 shipping) to:

The New York Theatre Experience, Inc.
P.O. Box 744, Bowling Green Station
New York, NY 10274-0744

PLAYS AND PLAYWRIGHTS 2002

Edited by Martin Denton

Ten plays heralding new voices for a renewed theatre.

***The Death of King Arthur* by Matthew Freeman** — the classic legend brought to the stage in an epic verse drama with a contemporary sensibility.

***Match* by Marc Chun** — one-act play of random chance bringing together five ordinary people with extraordinary results.

***Woman Killer* by Chiori Miyagawa** — two Brooklyn families are torn apart in this startling drama about the nature and origin of evil.

***Halo* by Ken Urban** — tales of life and love squandered in late twentieth century New Jersey.

***Shyness Is Nice* by Marc Spitz** — hilarious and profane farce about two thirty-year-old virgins.

***Reality* by Curtiss I' Cook** — comedy/murder mystery set in a world where not even the playwright can be sure of getting out alive.

***The Resurrectionist* by Kate Chell** — drama set in seventeenth century England about a young woman caught up in a web of graverobbing and murder.

***Bunny's Last Night In Limbo* by Peter S. Petralia** — a boy discovers his sexuality in this quirky and innovative one act.

***Summerland* by Brian Thorstenson** — a lonely young man and his mother search for happiness in an America where everything still seems possible.

ISBN 0967023432

Retail: $15.00

Additional information can be found on the web at http://www.nytheatre.com/nytheatre/books.htm

Available in bookstores and on line or order directly from the publisher

Send a check or money for $15 (plus $4 shipping) to:

The New York Theatre Experience, Inc.
P.O. Box 744, Bowling Green Station
New York, NY 10274-0744

ABOUT THE AUTHOR

MARTIN DENTON is executive director of The New York Theatre Experience, Inc. He is the founder, reviewer, and editor of nytheatre.com, one of the premier sources for theatre reviews and information on the Internet since 1996. Denton is a member of the American Theatre Critics Association and The Drama Desk. He is the author of *The New York Theatre Experience Book of the Year 1998* and the editor of *Plays and Playwrights for the New Millennium, Plays and Playwrights 2001,* and *Plays and Playwrights 2002.* He is passionately committed to discovering and fostering interesting new American drama wherever it can be found. He lives in New York City with two Siamese cats, Logan and Briscoe.

THE NEW YORK THEATRE EXPERIENCE

The New York Theatre Experience, Inc., is a nonprofit New York State corporation. Its mission is to use traditional and new media to foster interest, engagement, and participation in theatre and drama and to provide tangible support to theatre artists and dramatists, especially emerging artists and artists in the nonprofit sector. The principal activity of The New York Theatre Experience is the operation of a free website (http://www.nytheatre.com) that comprehensively covers the New York theatre scene—on, off, and off off Broadway. The New York Theatre Experience also publishes yearly anthologies of new plays by emerging playwrights.

If you would like to contact Martin Denton or would like to know more about the current and future plans of The New York Theatre Experience, Inc., please send an email to martin@nytheatre.com.